NOV 2004
WATERLOO REGIONAL LIBRARY
3 6501 00340 9393

iPhoto 4

THE MISSING MANUAL

*The book that
should have been
in the box*

D1299828

iPhoto 4

THE MISSING MANUAL

David Pogue and Derrick Story

POGUE PRESS™
O'REILLY®

Beijing • Cambridge • Farnham • Köln • Paris • Sebastopol • Taipei • Tokyo

iPhoto 4: The Missing Manual

by David Pogue and Derrick Story

Copyright © 2004 Pogue Press, LLC. All rights reserved.
Printed in the United States of America.

Published by Pogue Press/O'Reilly & Associates, Inc.,
1005 Gravenstein Highway North, Sebastopol, CA 95472.

May 2004:   First Edition.

Missing Manual, the Missing Manual logo, and "The book that should have been in
the box" are registered trademarks of Pogue Press, LLC.

Many of the designations used by manufacturers and sellers to distinguish their
products are claimed as trademarks. Where those designations appear in this book,
and Pogue Press was aware of a trademark claim, the designations have been capi-
talized.

While every precaution has been taken in the preparation of this book, the pub-
lisher assumes no responsibility for errors or omissions, or for damages resulting
from the use of the information contained herein.

RepKover.™
This book uses RepKover™, a durable and flexible lay-flat binding.

ISBN: 0-596-00692-6

Table of Contents

Part Two: iPhoto Basics

Part Three: Meet Your Public

Part Five: Appendixes

The Missing Credits

About the Authors

David Pogue is the weekly computer columnist for the *New York Times* and the creator of the Missing Manual series. He's the author or co-author of 30 books, including ten in this series and six in the "For Dummies" line (including *The Flat-Screen iMac, Magic, Opera,* and *Classical Music*). In his other life, David is a former Broadway show conductor, a magician, and an incorrigible pianist (photos await at *www.davidpogue.com*).

He welcomes feedback about Missing Manual titles by email at *david@pogueman. com*. (If you're seeking technical help, however, please refer to the help sources listed in Appendix C.)

Derrick Story is the managing editor of O'Reilly Network (*www.oreilly net.com*) and Mac DevCenter (*www.macdevcenter.com*), which he created in December, 2000 for O'Reilly & Associates. His other books include *Digital Photography Pocket Guide, 2nd Edition; Digital Video Pocket Guide;* and *Digital Photography Hacks*. Derrick continues to hone his shooting skills through his photo business, Story Photography (*www.storyphoto.com*), which specializes in digital imaging and special events. His photographs are featured throughout this book.

About the Creative Team

Joseph Schorr (co-author, first two editions), a former *Macworld* contributing editor, began collaborating with David Pogue in 1982—on musical comedies at Yale. Years later, they co-authored six editions of *Macworld Mac Secrets*. Joseph made his first foray into the world of photography long before the digital era—at age eight, when he built his own pinhole camera (from a cardboard box) for a school science project.

Now that Joe is a product manager at Apple, he's not technically supposed to work on books like this. Still, many chapters of this book are based on his original prose.

Nan Barber (editor) co-authored *Office X for the Macintosh: The Missing Manual* and *Office 2001 for Macintosh: The Missing Manual*. She's the principal copy editor for the Missing Manual series, having edited the Missing Manual titles on Mac OS X, Mac OS 9, AppleWorks 6, iMovie, Dreamweaver, Windows XP, and Mac OS X Hints. Email: *nanbarber@mac.com*.

Rose Cassano (cover illustration) has worked as an independent designer and illustrator for 20 years. Assignments have spanned everything from the nonprofit sector to corporate clientele. She lives in beautiful Southern Oregon, grateful for the miracles of modern technology that make living and working there a reality. Email: *cassano@cdsnet.net.* Web: *www.rosecassano.com.*

Dennis Cohen (technical reviewer) has served as the technical reviewer for many bestselling Mac books, including several editions of *Macworld Mac Secrets* and most Missing Manual titles. He is the author or co-author of *FileMaker Pro 7 Bible, Mac Digital Photography, iLife Bible,* and numerous other books. Email: *drcohen@mac.com.*

Phil Simpson (design and layout) works out of his office in Stamford, Connecticut, where he has had his graphic design business since 1982. He is experienced in many facets of graphic design, including corporate identity, publication design, and corporate and medical communications. Email: *pmsimpson@earthlink.net.*

Acknowledgements

Every photograph I publish reflects the help and generosity of these people: The late Don Swanson, who gave me my first camera (an Argus C3) and inspired my vision; Al McCombs, who published my first photo in the *Chino Champion* when I was eleven years old; Jerry Saba, who showed me the magic of a print coming to life in a tray of developer; Dennis Tannen, who freely shared everything he learned at Brooks Institute of Photography and never asked for anything in return; and Jan Blanchard, who has helped me through countless wedding assignments.

—Derrick Story

The Missing Manual series is a joint venture between Pogue Press (the dream team introduced on these pages) and O'Reilly & Associates (a dream publishing partner). I'm indebted, as always, to Tim O'Reilly, Mark Brokering, Glenn Bisignani, and the rest of the gang.

I'm also grateful to proofreaders Kate Briggs, John Cacciatore, Stephanie English, Danny Marcus, and Sada Preisch; to Glenn Reid, the genius; to Apple's Fred Johnson and Greg Scanlon; and to David Rogelberg. Above all, thanks to Jennifer, Kelly, and Tia, who make these books—and everything else—possible.

—David Pogue

The Missing Manual Series

Missing Manuals are witty, superbly written guides to computer products that don't come with printed manuals (which is just about all of them). Each book features a handcrafted index; cross-references to specific page numbers (not just "see Chapter 14"); and RepKover, a detached-spine binding that lets the book lie perfectly flat without the assistance of weights or cinder blocks.

Recent and upcoming titles include:

- *Mac OS X: The Missing Manual* (Panther Edition) by David Pogue

- *FileMaker Pro 7: The Missing Manual* by Geoff Coffey

- *iMovie 4 and iDVD: The Missing Manual* by David Pogue

- *GarageBand: The Missing Manual* by David Pogue

- *iPod & iTunes: The Missing Manual, 2nd Edition* by J.D. Biersdorfer

- *iLife '04: The Missing Manual* by David Pogue et al.

- *Switching to the Mac: The Missing Manual* by David Pogue

- *Mac OS X Hints: Panther Edition* by Rob Griffiths

- *Dreamweaver MX 2004: The Missing Manual* by David Sawyer McFarland

- *Mac OS 9: The Missing Manual* by David Pogue

- *Office X for Macintosh: The Missing Manual* by Nan Barber, Tonya Engst, and David Reynolds

- *AppleWorks 6: The Missing Manual* by Jim Elferdink and David Reynolds

- *Windows XP Home Edition: The Missing Manual* by David Pogue

- *Windows XP Pro: The Missing Manual* by David Pogue, Craig Zacker, and Linda Zacker

Introduction

In case you haven't heard, the digital camera market is exploding. In 2003, sales of digital cameras—close to *24 million* of them—finally overtook the sale of traditional film cameras. Within the next three or four years, companies like Nikon, Kodak, Canon, Minolta, and Olympus will be selling far more digital cameras than film-based models.

It's taken a few decades; the underlying technology used in most digital cameras was invented in 1969. But film is finally on the decline.

And why not? The appeal of digital photography is huge. When you shoot digitally, you never have to pay a cent for film or photo processing. You get instant results, viewing your photos just moments after shooting them, making even Polaroids seem painfully slow by comparison. As a digital photographer, you can even be your own darkroom technician—without the darkroom. You can retouch and enhance photos, make enlargements, and print out greeting cards using your home computer. Sharing your pictures with others is far easier, too, since you can burn them to CD, email them to friends, or post them on the Web. As one fan puts it: "There are no 'negatives' in digital photography."

But there is one problem: When most people try to *do* all this cool stuff, they find themselves drowning in a sea of technical details: JPEG compression, EXIF tags, file format compatibility, image resolutions, FTP clients, and so on. It isn't pretty.

The cold reality is that while digital photography is full of promise, it's also been full of headaches. During the early years of digital cameras, just making the camera-to-computer connection was a nightmare. You had to mess with serial or USB cables;

install device drivers; and use proprietary software to transfer, open, and convert camera images into a standard file format. If you handled all these tasks perfectly—and sacrificed a young male goat during the spring equinox—you ended up with good digital pictures.

iPhoto Arrives

Apple recognized this mess and finally decided to do something about it. When Steve Jobs gave his keynote address at Macworld Expo in January 2002, he referred to the "chain of pain" ordinary people experienced when attempting to download, store, edit, and share their digital photos.

He also focused on another growing problem among digital camera users: once you start shooting free, filmless photos, they pile up quickly. Before you know it, you have 6,000 pictures of your kid playing soccer. Just organizing and keeping track of all these photos is enough to drive you insane.

Apple's answer to all these problems was iPhoto, a simple and uncluttered program designed to organize, edit, and distribute digital photos without the nightmarish hassles. iPhoto 2, released in January 2003, and iPhoto 4, released a year after that, carried on the tradition with added features and better speed. (There was no iPhoto 3. Keep that in mind if someone tries to sell you a copy on eBay.)

To be sure, iPhoto isn't the most powerful image management software in the world. Like Apple's other iProducts (iMovie, iTunes, iDVD, and so on), its design subscribes to its own little 80/20 rule: 80 percent of us really don't need more than about 20 percent of the features you'd find in a full-blown, $650 digital-asset management program.

Today, millions of Mac fans use iPhoto. Evidently, there were a lot of digital camera fans out there, feeling the pain and hoping that iPhoto would provide some much-needed relief.

What's New in iPhoto 4

You'll find welcome nips and tucks everywhere in iPhoto 4, but here are the big-ticket items:

- **Speed.** Despite the brilliance of iPhoto 1 and 2, however, one criticism dogged it year after year: it was just too gosh-darned slow. By the time you filled it with, say, 2,000 pictures, iPhoto had all the pep of a pet rock. Web sites and books described ugly workarounds, like breaking up your Photo Library into smaller chunks.

  iPhoto 4 ends the tyranny of sluggishness. Even on an average-speed Mac, keeping 15,000 or 25,000 photos in a single iPhoto library is no big deal. Switching between modes, changing slideshows, zooming out and back, opening the program to begin with—Apple has goosed the speed of just about everything.

- **The control bar.** What's the first thing you want to do after dumping fresh photos off the camera into iPhoto?

Look at them, of course. View them at full-size for the first time. Rotate the pictures that you took with the camera turned 90 degrees. Delete the stinkers.

The obvious iPhoto tool for this purpose has always been the slideshow. Unfortunately, every time you spotted a photo that needed help (or needed trashing), you had to cancel the slideshow, make the change, and then start the show again.

In iPhoto 4, once a slideshow begins, wiggle your mouse to summon the new slideshow control bar. As the slideshow progresses, the control bar's buttons can pause the show, go backward, rotate a photo, delete a bad shot, or apply your star rating to a picture. Details on page 92.

- **More slideshow goodies.** The control bar isn't the only newsworthy slideshow enhancement of iPhoto 4. If you click the Slideshow button at the bottom of the window, you'll find a few other treats in the resulting dialog box. You can now specify what kind of crossfade you want between the slides in your show, like Wipe or the immortal Cube effect.

The Display checkboxes superimpose titles, star ratings, or slideshow controls onto the bottom of the screen during the show.

And if you click the Music tab of the dialog box and study it hard, you'll find one of the most eagerly awaited new features of iPhoto: the ability to specify an entire iTunes playlist of songs to accompany the show. No longer must you listen to the same two-minute pop song, looping over and over again throughout your eight-minute slideshow.

- **Star ratings.** You can rate your photos now, from one to five. Later, you can exploit your ratings in several ways: by making them appear, in gray, stamped beneath the thumbnails of the photos you've rated; by sorting your collection so that the best ones appear at the top; by collecting them all into a smart album (read on); and so on.

- **Smart Albums.** *Albums* are subsets of photos, and a key organizational tool in iPhoto. iPhoto 4, though, can create albums for you, thanks to *smart albums.* These are self-updating folders that display pictures matching certain criteria that you set up—all pictures that you took in 2003, for example, or all photos that you've rated four stars or higher. (If you've ever used smart playlists in iTunes, you'll recognize the idea immediately.)

- **Recent Rolls.** In previous iPhoto versions, the top of the Source list included one icon called Photo Library (every single picture in your collection), and another called Last Import (the most recently imported batch).

That structure wasn't always the most convenient, however. If you dumped your pictures onto the Mac at the end of each day of a Disney World trip, the Last Import feature wasn't much help. What really wanted to see was the last several digital dumps in one group.

iPhoto 4 makes all of this much easier. iPhoto can also present your photos broken down by year or by recent month. A new icon called Last Rolls reveals your last batch of imported pictures—or two, or three, or whatever you've specified in iPhoto's Preferences.

There's even a new "Show photo count for albums" option that places a number in parentheses after each album name, representing how many pictures are inside.

• **Batch Processing.** iPhoto 4 now offers a "batch processing" feature that manipulates text labels for a selected group of photos. You can change all the selected photos' names (to Ski Trip 1, Ski Trip 2, and so on); change the dates they were taken, in effect rewriting history; or change their Comments boxes to a certain matching blurb.

• **Photo sharing on the network.** One of the coolest features of iTunes is the way you can "publish" certain playlists on your home or office network, so that other people in the same building can listen to your tunes. The only question was: Why couldn't iPhoto do the same thing with pictures?

Now it can. When you turn on "Share my photos," other people on your network see your albums show up in their Source lists, above the list of their own albums. They can freely drag them into their own iPhoto albums, and then edit them, print them, and otherwise treat them like their very own photos.

• **More designs.** When you publish photos to a .Mac Web page, you have more canned layout designs to choose from—namely, the 17 of them that are available to .Mac members who create Web pages online. There's also a new photo-book layout called Collage that lets you specify captions for some pages but not for others. (Ordering these gorgeous photo books is no longer limited to U.S. shutterbugs, either.)

• **More effects.** In Edit mode, the Black and White button is now joined by a Sepia button, which makes the selected photo look old and brownish, for that old-time daguerreotype look.

• **More commands.** The new File→New Film Roll From Selection command creates a new film roll from a batch of highlighted photos, thus splitting them up from their original roll.

Similarly, the File→New Album From Selection command saves you a few steps when you want to file away a particular clump of pictures into a new album.

About This Book

Don't let the rumors fool you. iPhoto may be simple, but it isn't simplistic. It offers a wide range of tools, shortcuts, and database-like features; a complete arsenal of photo-presentation features; and sophisticated multimedia and Internet hooks. Unfortunately, many of the best techniques aren't covered in the only "manual" you get with iPhoto—its sparse electronic help screens.

This book was born to address two needs. First, it's designed to serve as the iPhoto manual—the book that should have been in the box. It explores each iPhoto feature in depth, offers shortcuts and workarounds, and unearths features that the online help doesn't even mention.

Second, this book is designed to give you a grounding in professional photography. Together, the digital camera and iPhoto can produce presentations of stunning visual quality. They give you the *technical* tools to produce amazing photos, but nothing more. Most people don't have much experience with the *artistic* side of shooting—like lighting, manual shutter control, and composition—or even how to use the dozens of features packed into the modern digital camera. This book will tell you all you need to know.

About the Outline

This book is divided into four parts, each containing several chapters:

- Part 1, **Digital Cameras: The Missing Manual,** is the course in photography and digital cameras promised above. These three chapters cover buying, using, and exploiting your digital camera, choosing the proper image resolution settings, and getting the most out of batteries and memory cards. This section of the book creates a bridge between everyday snapshots and the kinds of emotionally powerful shots you see in magazines and newspapers.

- Part 2, **iPhoto Basics,** covers the fundamentals of getting your photos into iPhoto, organizing and filing them, searching and finding them, and editing them to compensate for weak lighting (or weak photography).

- Part 3, **Meet Your Public,** is all about the payoff, the moment you've presumably been waiting for ever since you snapped the shots—showing them off. It covers the many ways iPhoto can present those photos to other people: as a slideshow, as prints you order from the Internet or make yourself, as a handsome hardbound gift book, as a Web page, by email, or as a QuickTime-movie slideshow that you post on the Web or distribute on CD or even DVD. It also covers sharing your iPhoto collection across an office network with other Macs, and even how to share it with other account holders on the same Mac.

- Part 4, **iPhoto Stunts,** takes you way beyond the basics. It covers a miscellaneous potpourri of additional iPhoto features, including turning photos into screen savers or desktop pictures on your Mac, exporting the photos in various formats, using iPhoto plug-ins and accessory programs, managing (or even switching) Photo Libraries, and backing up your photos using iPhoto's Burn to CD command.

At the end of the book, Appendix A offers troubleshooting guidance, Appendix B goes through iPhoto's menus one by one to make sure that every last feature has been covered, and Appendix C lists some Web sites that will help fuel your growing addiction to digital photography.

About→These→Arrows

Throughout this book, and throughout the Missing Manual series, you'll find sentences like this one: "Open the System folder→Libraries→Fonts folder." That's shorthand for a much longer instruction that directs you to open three nested folders in sequence. That instruction might read: "On your hard drive, you'll find a folder called System. Open it. Inside the System folder window is a folder called Libraries. Open that. Inside *that* folder is yet another one called Fonts. Double-click to open it, too."

Similarly, this kind of arrow shorthand helps to simplify the business of choosing commands in menus, as shown in Figure I-1.

Figure I-1:
In this book, arrow notations help to simplify folder and menu instructions. For example, "Choose ⌘→Dock→Position on Left" is a more compact way of saying, "From the ⌘ menu, choose Dock; from the submenu that than appears, choose Position on Left," as shown here.

About MissingManuals.com

At *www.missingmanuals.com,* you'll find news, articles, and updates to the books in this series.

But if you click the name of this book and then the Errata link, you'll find a unique resource: a list of corrections and updates that have been made in successive printings of this book. You can mark important corrections right into your own copy of the book, if you like.

In fact, the same page offers an invitation for you to submit such corrections and updates yourself. In an effort to keep the book as up-to-date and accurate as possible, each time we print more copies of this book, we'll make any confirmed corrections you've suggested. Thanks in advance for reporting any glitches you find!

In the meantime, we'd love to hear your suggestions for new books in the Missing Manual line. There's a place for that on the Web site, too, as well as a place to sign up for free email notification of new titles in the series.

The Very Basics

You'll find very little jargon or nerd terminology in this book. You will, however, encounter a few terms and concepts that you'll see frequently in your Macintosh life. They include:

- **Clicking.** This book offers three kinds of instructions that require you to use the mouse or trackpad attached to your Mac. To *click* means to point the arrow cursor at something onscreen and then—without moving the cursor at all—press and release the clicker button on the mouse (or laptop trackpad). To *double-click,* of course, means to click twice in rapid succession, again without moving the cursor at all. And to *drag* means to move the cursor while keeping the button continuously pressed.

  When you're told to ⌘-*click* something, you click while pressing the ⌘ key (next to the Space bar). Such related procedures as *Shift-clicking, Option-clicking,* and *Control-clicking* work the same way—just click while pressing the corresponding key on the bottom row of your keyboard.

- **Menus.** The *menus* are the words in the lightly striped bar at the top of your screen. You can either click one of these words to open a pull-down menu of commands (and then click again on a command), or click and *hold* the button as you drag down the menu to the desired command (and release the button to activate the command). Either method works fine.

Note: Apple has officially changed it calls the little menu that pops up when you Control-click something on the screen. It's still a *contextual menu,* in that the menu choices depend on the context of what you click—but it's now *called* a shortcut menu. That term not only matches what it's called in Windows, but it's slightly more descriptive about its function. *Shortcut menu* is the term you'll find in this book.

- **Keyboard shortcuts.** Every time you take your hand off the keyboard to move the mouse, you lose time and potentially disrupt your creative flow. That's why many experienced Mac fans use keystroke combinations instead of menu commands wherever possible. ⌘-P opens the Print dialog box, for example, and ⌘-M minimizes the current window to the Dock.

  When you see a shortcut like ⌘-Q (which closes the current program), it's telling you to hold down the ⌘ key, and, while it's down, type the letter Q, and then release both keys.

If you've mastered this much information, you have all the technical background you need to enjoy *iPhoto 4: The Missing Manual.*

Part One:
Digital Cameras:
The Missing Manual

1

Welcome to Digital Photography

Apple's marketing team came up with a cute slogan for iPhoto 2: "Shoot like Ansel; organize like Martha." Today, of course, that slogan would never fly—and the reference to Martha Stewart is only half the problem.

The truth is, iPhoto doesn't help you shoot like Ansel Adams, either. In fact, it does absolutely nothing for your photography skills.

But this book will. The first three chapters cover both the basics and the secrets that the pros use to take consistently good photographs. After all, if you're going to the trouble of mastering a new program, then you should be rewarded with stunning results. Or, put another way: Beautiful pictures in, beautiful pictures out.

Meet Digital Photography

When you use a film camera, your pictures are "memorized" by billions of silver halide crystals suspended on celluloid. Most digital cameras, on the other hand, store your pictures on a memory card.

It's a special kind of memory: *flash* memory. Unlike the RAM in your Macintosh, the contents of flash memory survive even when the machine is turned off. You can erase and reuse a digital camera's memory card over and over again—a key to the great economy of digital photography.

At this millisecond of technology time, most digital cameras are slightly slower than film cameras in almost every regard. Generally speaking, they're slower to turn on, slower to autofocus, and slower to recover from one shot before they're ready to take another.

Once you've captured a picture, however, digital cameras provide almost nothing but advantages over film.

Instant Feedback

You can view a miniature version of the photo on the camera's built-in screen. If there's something about the picture that bothers you—like the telephone pole growing out of your best friend's head—you can simply delete it and try again. Once the shooting session is over, you leave knowing that nothing but good photos are on your camera. By contrast, with traditional film photography, you have no real idea how your pictures turned out until you open that sealed drugstore envelope and flip through the prints. More often than not, there are one or two pictures that you really like, and the rest are wasted money.

Instant feedback becomes a real benefit when you're under pressure to deliver excellent photographs. Imagine the hapless photographer who, having offered to shoot candid photos during a friend's wedding reception, later opens the envelope of prints and discovers that the flash had malfunctioned all evening, resulting in three rolls of shadowy figures in a darkened hotel ballroom. A digital camera would have alerted the photographer to the problem immediately.

In short, digital photographers sleep much better at night. They never worry about how the day's pictures will turn out—they already know!

Cheap Pix

Digital cameras also save you a great deal of money. Needless to say, you don't spend anything on developing. Printing out pictures on a photo printer at home costs money, but few people print every single shot they take. And where are most of your prints now? In a shoebox somewhere?

Printing out 4 x 6 prints at home, using an inkjet photo printer, costs about the same amount as you'd pay at the drugstore. But when you want enlargements, printing your own is vastly less expensive. Even on the glossy $1-per-sheet inkjet photo paper, an 8 x 10 costs about $1.50 or so (ink cartridges are expensive), compared with $8 from the drugstore. A poster-sized print from a wide-format photo printer (13 x 10) will cost you about $3.50 at home, compared with $20 from a photo lab.

Take More Risks

Because you have nothing to lose by taking a shot—and everything to gain—digital photography allows your creative juices to flow. If you don't like that shot of randomly piled shoes on the front porch, then, what the heck, erase it.

With the expense of developing taken out of the equation, you're free to shoot everything that catches your eye and decide later whether to keep it or not. This is how a digital camera can make you a better photographer—by freeing up your creativity. Your risk-taking will lead to more exciting images than you ever dreamed you'd take.

More Fun

Add it all up, and digital photography is more fun than traditional shooting. No more disappointing prints and wasted money. Instead, you enjoy the advantages of instant feedback, flexibility, and creativity.

But that's just the beginning, since now there's iPhoto. Suddenly photography isn't just about producing a stack of 4 x 6 pieces of paper. Thanks to iPhoto, now your photos are infinitely more flexible. At the end of the day, you get to sit down with your Mac and create instant slideshows, screen savers, desktop pictures, professional Web pages, and email attachments. Shoot the most adorable shot ever taken of your daughter, and minutes later it's on its way to Grandma.

Photography doesn't get any better than this.

Buying a Digital Camera

Citizens of the world bought nearly 50 million digital cameras in 2003, and that was just the beginning. In 2003, in fact, analysts reported that digital cameras were outselling film cameras for the first time.

The major players in this market are Sony, Olympus, Nikon, HP, Kodak, and Canon. They're not alone, however. Every company ever associated with electronics or cameras—Panasonic, Casio, Leica, Kyocera, Minolta, Konica, and so on—also has a finger in the pie. Each company offers a variety of models and a wide range of prices, which compete fiercely for your dollars. Some of these companies release new models *every six to twelve months*. And, exactly as in other high-tech industries, each generation offers better features, improved resolution, and lower prices.

If you're in the market for a new digital camera, the rest of this chapter is for you. It's dedicated to helping you find that diamond in the rough: the camera with the features you need at a price you can afford.

Don't worry about the different marketing categories for cameras: entry level, consumer, prosumer, pro, whatever. Just read about the features available in the following pages—presented here roughly in order of importance—and consider how much they're worth to you.

Image Resolution

The first number you probably see in the description of a digital camera is the number of *megapixels* it offers.

A pixel (short for *picture element*) is one tiny colored dot, one of the thousands or millions that compose a single digital photograph. You can't escape learning this term, since pixels are everything in computer graphics.

You need at least one million pixels—that is, one megapixel—for something as simple as a 4 x 6 inch print. Thus the shorthand: Instead of saying that your camera has 3,300,000 pixels, you'd say that it's a 3.3-megapixel camera.

What you're describing is its *resolution*. For instance, a 5-megapixel camera has better resolution than a 3-megapixel camera. (It also costs more.)

So how many pixels do you need?

Pictures on the screen

Many digital photos are destined to be shown solely on a computer screen: to be sent by email, posted on a Web page, pasted into a FileMaker database, turned into a screen saver, or used as a desktop picture.

If this is what you have in mind when you think about digital photography, congratulations. You're about to save a lot of money on a camera, because you can get by with one that has very few megapixels. Even a $150 2-megapixel camera produces graphics files that measure 1600 by 1200 pixels—which is already too big to fit on, for example, the 1024 x 768–pixel screen of an iBook laptop without zooming or scrolling.

Printing out pictures

If you intend to print out your photos, however, it's a very different story.

The typical computer screen is actually a fairly low-resolution device; most pack in somewhere between 72 and 96 pixels per inch. But for the photo to look as smooth as a real photograph, a *printer* must cram the color dots much closer together on the paper—150 pixels per inch or more.

Remember the 2-megapixel photo that would spill off the edges of the iBook screen? Its resolution (measured in dots per inch) is adequate only for a 5 x 7 print; any larger, and the dots become distractingly visible and speckled. Everybody in your circle of friends will look like they have some kind of skin disorder.

If you intend to make prints of your photos—and you'll be in very good company—shop for your camera with this table in mind:

Camera Resolution	Max Print Size
0.3 megapixels (most camera phones)	2.25 x 3 inches
1.3 megapixels	4 x 6 inches
2 megapixels	5 x 7 inches
3.3 megapixels	8 x 10 inches
4 megapixels	11 x 14 inches
5 megapixels	12 x 16 inches

These are extremely crude guidelines, by the way. Many factors contribute to the quality of an 8 x 10 print—lens quality, file compression, exposure, camera shake, paper quality, the number of different color cartridges your printer has, and so on. You may be perfectly happy with larger prints than the sizes listed here. But these figures provide a rough guide to getting the highest quality from your prints.

Memory Capacity

The memory card that came with your camera is a joke. It probably holds only about six or eight best-quality pictures. It's nothing more than a cost-saving placeholder, foisted on you by a camera company that knew full well that you'd have to go buy a bigger one.

When you're shopping for a camera, then, it's imperative that you also factor in the cost of a bigger card.

It's impossible to overstate how glorious it is to have a huge memory card in your camera (or several smaller ones in your camera bag). You quit worrying that you're about to run out of storage, so you shoot more freely, increasing the odds that you'll get great pictures. You can go on longer trips without dragging a laptop along, too, because you don't feel the urge to run back to your hotel room every three hours to offload your latest pictures.

You'll have enough worries when it comes to your camera's *battery* life. The last thing you need is another chronic headache in the form of your memory card. Bite the bullet and buy a bigger one.

Here's a table that helps you calculate how much storage you'll need. Find the column that represents the resolution of your camera, in megapixels (MP), and then read down to see how many best-quality photos each size card will hold.

Camera Resolution	2 MP (1600 x 1200)	3.3 MP (2048 x 1536)	4.1 MP (2272 x 1704)	5 MP (2560 x 1920)
Card Capacity	How many pictures	How many pictures	How many pictures	How many pictures
8 MB	7	3	2	0
16 MB	14	8	7	0
32 MB	30	17	14	8
64 MB	61	35	30	17
128 MB	123	71	61	35
256 MB	246	142	122	70

Memory Cards

The *kind* of memory card your camera uses isn't nearly as important as the factors listed earlier in this discussion. But once you've narrowed down your potential purchase to a short list of candidates, it's worth weighing the pros and cons of the cards they use.

- **CompactFlash.** CompactFlash cards are rugged, inexpensive, and easy to handle, which makes them very popular. You can buy them in capacities all the way up to

8 GB. That's a *lot* of pictures—hundreds and hundreds. *Pros:* Readily available; inexpensive; wide selection. *Con:* They're the largest of any memory card format, which dictates a bigger camera. A 128 MB CompactFlash card costs about $30.

- **SmartMedia.** These cards are wafer-thin and reasonably priced. Unfortunately, their capacity is limited. *Pro:* Affordable. *Con:* Storage capacity limited to 128 MB. These cards are quickly disappearing, in favor of more compact formats like xD-Picture Card and Secure Digital (SD). A 128 MB card costs about $35.

- **Memory Stick.** Sony created this format as an interchangeable memory card for its cameras, camcorders, and laptops. Memory Sticks are great if you're already knee-deep in Sony equipment, but few other companies use them. *Pro:* Works with most Sony digital gadgets. *Cons:* Works primarily with Sony gear; maximum size is 256 MB. A 128 MB Memory Stick starts at about $35, depending on the brand (Sony's own are the most expensive).

- **Memory Stick Pro.** Sony's latest memory card is the same size as the traditional Memory Stick, but can hold much more. Sony's latest digital cameras accept both the Pro type and the older Memory Stick format, but the Pro cards don't work in older cameras. At this writing, you can buy Pro sticks in capacities like 256 MB ($60), 512 MB ($85), and 1 GB ($380).

- **Secure Digital (SD).** These extremely tiny cards are no bigger than postage stamps, which is why you also find them in Palm organizers and MP3 players. In fact, you can pull this card from your camera and insert it into many palmtops for enhanced viewing. *Pros:* Very small, perfect for subcompact cameras. *Cons:* Maximum size is 512 MB. Relatively expensive; a 128 MB SD card costs about $50.

- **xD-Picture Card.** The latest Fuji camera and Olympus cameras require a new, proprietary format called xD (see Figure 1-1). Its dimensions are so inconveniently small that the manual warns that "they can be accidentally swallowed by small children." *Pro:* Some cool cameras accept them. *Cons:* Relatively expensive compared to other memory cards ($50 for a 128 MB card). Limited capacity (512 MB max, at this writing). Incompatible with cameras from other companies. Also

Figure 1-1:
The tiny Secure Digital card (left) is gaining popularity because you can use it in both your digicam and PDA. The even tinier xD-Picture Card (middle) works only with Fuji and Olympus cameras. The larger CompactFlash card is still the most common (especially in larger cameras).

incompatible with the memory card slots in most printers, card readers, television front panels, and so on.

- **Microdrive.** Some CompactFlash cameras can also accommodate the IBM Microdrive—a miniature hard drive that looks like a thick CompactFlash card. For a while, the 1 GB model was very popular with pro shooters, but it's slipping in the polls now that you can get CompactFlash cards of up to 8 GB.

If you already own some memory cards from a previous camera (or even an MP3 player), you have a good incentive to buy a new camera that uses the same format. Otherwise, compare price per megabyte, availability, and what works with your other digital gear.

If all other factors are equal, however, choose a camera that takes CompactFlash cards. They're plentiful, inexpensive, and have huge capacity.

Tip: When buying memory cards, shop for price: there's little quality difference, if any, between big-name brands and lesser-known companies. Furthermore, in general, premium cards labeled "high performance" don't actually speed anything up. (The exception: Certain high-end cameras whose specs indicate that they can store photos at 7 MB per second or faster—mostly professional digital SLR cameras).

Battery Life

In many ways, digital cameras have arrived. They're not like cell phones, which still drop calls, or wireless palmtops, which are excruciatingly slow connecting to the Internet. Digital cameras are reliable, high quality, and generally extremely rewarding.

Except for battery life.

Thanks to that LCD screen on the back, digital cameras go through batteries like Kleenex. The battery, as it turns out, will probably be the one limiting factor to your photo shoots. When the juice is gone, your session is over.

Here's what you'll find as you shop for various cameras:

- **Proprietary, built-in rechargeable.** Many smaller cameras come with a "brick" battery: a dark gray, lithium-ion rechargeable battery. (These subcompact cameras are simply too small to accommodate AA-style batteries, as described next.)

The problem with proprietary batteries is that you can't replace them when you're on the road. If you're only three hours into your day at Disney World when the battery dies, that's just tough—your shooting session is over. You can't exactly duck into a drugstore to buy a new one.

Some cameras come with a separate, external charger for this battery. The advantage here is that you can buy a second battery (usually for $50 or so). You can keep one battery in the charger at all times. That way, when the main battery gives up the ghost, you can swap it with the one in the charger, and your day goes on. (Or, in Disney World situations, you can take both batteries with you for the day.)

All of this is something of a pain, and not nearly as handy as the rechargeable AAs described next.

But it sure beats any system in which the camera *is* the battery charger. When the battery dies, so does your creative muse. You have no choice but to return home and plug in the camera itself, taking it out of commission for several hours as it recharges the battery.

• **Two or four AA-size batteries**—Some cameras accept AA batteries, and may even come with a set of alkalines to get you started.

If you learn nothing else from this chapter, however, learn this: *Don't use standard alkaline AAs.* You'll get a better return on your investment by tossing $5 bills out your car window on the highway.

Alkalines may be fine for flashlights and radios, but they're no match for the massive power drain of the modern digital camera—not even "premium" alkalines. A set of four AAs might last 20 minutes in the digital camera, if you're lucky.

So what are you supposed to put in there? Something you may have never even heard of: *rechargeable nickel-metal-hydride (NiMH)* AAs. They last *much* longer than alkalines, and because you can use them over and over again, they're far less expensive.

Figure 1-2:
You'll probably want to buy twice as many NiMH rechargeable AAs as your camera requires. That way, you can keep one set in the camera, and the other in the charger, so that you'll never have downtime.

You generally won't find NiMHs in department stores, but they're available in national drugstore chains and they're easy to find online (for example, *www.buy. com*). A charger and a set of four NiMH AAs cost about $30 (see Figure 1-2).

The beauty of digital cameras that accept AAs is that they accommodate so many different kinds of batteries. In addition to rechargeable NiMH batteries, most cameras can also accept something called AA *photo lithium* batteries. They're a lot like alkalines, in that they're disposable and can't be recharged. However, because they last many times longer than regular AAs, they're much more expensive. They're also ideal to carry in the camera case for emergency backup.

The final advantage of this kind of camera is that, in a pinch—yes, in the middle of your Disney World day—you can even hit up a drugstore for a set of standard alkaline AAs. Sure enough, you'll be tossing them in the trash after only about 20 minutes of use in the camera—but in an emergency, 20 minutes is a lot better than nothing.

Tip: Some cameras offer the best of all worlds. Certain Nikon CoolPix cameras, for example, come with a proprietary lithium-ion "brick" and a matching charger—but they *also* accept all kinds of AAs, including alkalines, rechargeables, and the Duracell CRV3 battery (a disposable lithium battery that looks like two AAs fused together at the seam). You should always be able to get juice on the road with *these* babies.

Size and Shape

You could have the best digital camera on the planet, but if it's bulkier than a Volvo, you'll wind up leaving it home and missing lots of good shots.

The trick is to balance the features you need with the package you want; unfortunately, the smaller the camera, the fewer the features you usually get. For example, you'll rarely see a connector for an external flash (a *hotshoe*) or a rotating flip screen on a camera that fits in your shirt pocket.

Once you've balanced features against size, do whatever you can to get your hands on your leading candidate. Is it too small to hold comfortably? Does your index finger naturally align with the shutter release? Are you constantly smudging the lens with your other fingers?

Your camera should become a natural extension of your vision. If you're not bonding with it, your pictures will reflect that—or, rather, your *lack* of pictures.

Lens Quality

In the early days of digital photography, cameras had interesting electronics, but only so-so lenses. And if you've ever tried reading fine print through a cheesy magnifying glass, then you have some idea of how the world looks though bad optics: lousy.

Fortunately, the scene is much sharper now. Sony, Olympus, Canon, Leica, and Nikon all take pride in the lenses for their digital cameras, and they have solid reputations for great glass as a result. (The camera makers not listed here sometimes buy their lenses *from* Olympus, Canon, and Nikon.)

This particular criterion, important though it may be, isn't something you'll have much control over. There's no measurement for the quality of a lens, and no way for you to tell how good it is simply by looking. The closest you can come is to read the reviews in photo magazines or the Web sites listed in Appendix C.

Zoom

When you read the specs for a camera—or read the logos painted on its body—you frequently encounter numbers like this: "3X/10X ZOOM!" The number before the slash tells you how many times the camera can magnify a distant image, much like a telescope. That number measures the *optical* zoom, which is the actual amount that the lenses can zoom in (to magnify a subject that's far away).

Note: If you're used to traditional photography, you may need some help converting consumer-cam zoom units (3X, 4X, and so on) into standard focal ranges. It breaks down like this: A typical 3X zoom goes from 6.5mm (wide angle) to 19.5mm (telephoto). That would be about the same as a 38mm to 105mm zoom lens on a 35mm film camera.

Then there's *digital* zoom, the number after the slash. Much as computer owners mistakenly jockey for superiority by comparing the megahertz rating of their computers—little suspecting that higher megahertz ratings don't necessarily make faster computers—camera makers seem to think that what consumers want most in a digital camera is a powerful digital zoom. "7X!" your camera's box may scream. "10X! 20X!"

When a camera uses its *digital* zoom, it simply reinterprets the individual pixels, in effect enlarging them. The image gets bigger, but the image quality deteriorates. In most cases, you're best off avoiding digital zoom altogether.

Base your camera-buying decision on the *optical* zoom range—that's the zoom that counts.

Flip Screen

Every digital camera has a little LCD screen, but on some specially endowed models, you can flip and swivel the screen around to allow multiple viewing angles (Figure 1-3). These cameras let you hold it any way you want—at your waist, above your

Figure 1-3:
Flip screens first appeared on camcorders and were soon adapted to digital cameras. Left: The best ones flip all the way out from the camera, providing multiple viewing angles.

Right: Others allow tilting upward and downward, but remain attached to the camera back.

head, even at your ankles—and still frame the shot without contorting yourself into a pretzel.

If you're stuck in the middle of a crowd, but want a shot of the parade, then tilt the screen, raise the camera over your head, frame the shot, and shoot. Want to create that low-angle Orson Welles shot for added drama, or snap a terrific baby's-eye-view photo without having to crawl around in the dirt? It's easy with a flip screen.

Manual Controls

Cheapo digital cameras are often called *point-and-shoot* models with good reason: You point, you shoot. The camera is stuck in perennial *program mode,* which means it does all the thinking.

More expensive cameras, on the other hand, let you take your camera off autopilot.

Don't assume that all you'll ever need is a point-and-shoot. Read Chapter 3 first. There you'll learn all the amazing, special-situation photos—sports photos, night-time shots, fireworks, indoor portraits, and so on—you can take *only* if your camera offers manual controls.

If you opt for a camera with manual controls, shop for these features:

- *Aperture-priority mode* lets you specify how wide the camera's shutter opens when you take the shot. It's probably the most popular manual control mode, because it's easy to use but offers lots of control. Chapter 3 describes how to use aperture priority to create backgrounds with softly out-of-focus backgrounds, among other great effects.

- *Shutter-priority mode* is particularly handy for freezing or blurring shots. It lets you tell the camera how *fast* the shutter should open and close: fast to freeze sports shots; slow for nighttime shots, or to turn a babbling brook into an abstract, fuzzy blur.

- *Manual mode* allows you to set the aperture and the shutter speed independently. When you hit the right combination, the camera lets you know that you've set the right exposure and can take the picture.

If you're looking for a camera that you can grow with as your photo skills increase, then manual controls are features worth paying for.

Autofocus Assist Light

Even though autofocus technology has been around for years, it's still not a perfect science. There are plenty of lighting conditions, like dark interiors, where your camera will struggle to focus correctly. Autofocus works by looking for patches of *contrast* between light and dark—and if there's no light, there's no focusing.

An autofocus assist light (or *AF assist*) neatly solves the problem (Figure 1-4). In dim light, the camera briefly beams a pattern of light onto the subject, so the camera has enough visual information on which to focus.

Variable "Film" Speeds

Back in the old days, when photographers had to walk through ten-foot snow drifts just to get to school (uphill both ways), they also had to carry around different film types for different lighting situations. They would use *400-speed* film in dim lighting, *100-speed* film in bright outdoor light, and so on. You might have heard these film speeds referred to as the *ISO settings*.

Autofocus assist lamp

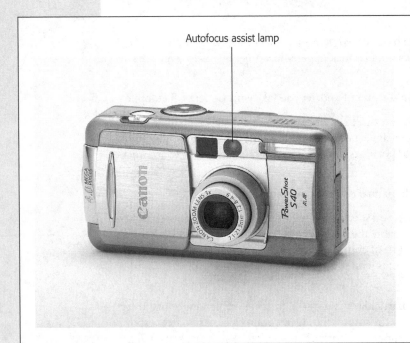

Figure 1-4:
An AF assist light, like the one on the Canon Power-Shot S series, will greatly improve your percentage of properly focused shots. You might want to put this item near the top of your desirable-features list. (Ditto for the sliding, built-in lens cover, which makes the camera self-contained and handy.)

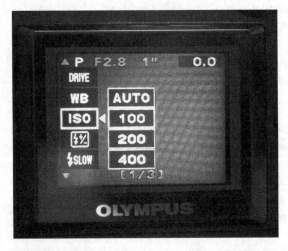

Figure 1-5:
Some cameras provide a menu of film speed options, often under the label "ISO," which is a measurement of light sensitivity familiar to film photographers.

Even though digital cameras don't need different kinds of film, most still let you "bump up" the speed by pushing a button (Figure 1-5).

You'll find out more about speeds in Chapters 2 and 3. For now, it's enough to note that a choice of film speeds gives you greater flexibility when shooting indoors or outside at night.

Built-In Sliding Lens Cover

Let's face it: Detachable lens covers are a pain. If you tie it to the camera with that little loop of black thread, it bangs against your hand, or the lens, when it's windy. If it's loose, it's destined to fall behind the couch cushions, pop off in your camera bag, or get mixed in with the change in your pocket.

Some cameras, especially compact models, eliminate this madness. They have sliding lens covers that protect the optics, as shown in Figure 1-4. Just sliding the cover open both turns the camera on and makes its zoom lens extend, ready for action. When you're done shooting, the lens retracts and the cover slides back in place.

The drawback of built-in lens protectors is that they generally prevent you from adding filters, telephoto lenses, and other attachments. If you're looking for a portable travel mate to take on vacation, the sliding lens cover should be high on your list. On the other hand, if a serious picture-making tool is your focus, then make sure it accepts attachments.

Attachments

Digital camera owners never even consider attaching filters, telephoto lenses, and external flashes. But if you're coming from a traditional film-camera background, and you're a fairly serious photographer, this may be one of the first features you think about.

Figure 1-6:
Some consumer digital cameras can accommodate accessory lenses and filters using an optional adapter. You can extend the power of this Olympus, for example, by adding telephoto, wide angle, and macro lenses.

In general, most of the big, heavy, traditional-design digital cameras can accept such attachments. Most tiny, capsule-shaped, subcompact pocket cameras can't.

The trick to a happy accessory life is calculating how hard they are to attach. The process often entails fitting the camera with tubular lens adapters (attachable via tiny threads). Nothing is more frustrating than stripping the threads on your camera body because you couldn't get the adapter ring to screw in properly (Figure 1-6).

So after you find a camera that accepts the attachments you want to use, pay attention to *how* they attach. Usually the smaller the adapter and the finer the threads, the more patience you'll need. Your sanity may be at stake here.

Shutter Lag

Shutter lag is the time it takes for the camera to calculate the correct focus and exposure before it actually captures the scene. In most camera models under $1,000, this interval amounts to an infuriating one-second delay between the time you press the shutter button and the instant the picture is actually recorded. Unfortunately, that's more than enough time for you to miss the precise moment your daughter blows out the candles on her birthday cake, your son's first step, and that adorable expression on your cat's face. Fractions of a second are a lifetime in photography (Figure 1-7).

Figure 1-7:
"Did you get me jumping backward over the coffee table? Did you get it? Tell me you got that shot! Tell me you got it…" Every digital photographer has a collection of these missed shots, thanks to shutter lag.

You can reduce or minimize shutter lag in either of two ways. First, you can set the camera's focus and exposure manually, as described in the next two chapters. That way, there's no thinking left for the camera to do when you actually squeeze the shutter button.

Most people, though, eventually learn instead to *prefocus*. This trick involves squeezing the shutter button halfway, ahead of time, forcing the camera to do its calculations. Keep your finger halfway down until the moment of truth. Now, when you finally squeeze it down all the way, you get the shot you wanted with very little delay.

Unfortunately, neither of these techniques works in all situations. Manually focusing and prefocusing both take time and eliminate spontaneity.

Until the electronics of digital cameras improves, the best you can hope for is to buy a model with the smallest shutter lag possible. You won't find this spec in brochures, though; your best bet is to visit one of the camera-review Web sites listed in Appendix C. Many of them list the shutter-lag timings for popular cameras.

Burst Mode (RAM Buffer)

When you press the shutter button on a digital camera, the image begins a long tour through the camera's guts. First, the lens projects the image onto an electronic sensor—a *CCD* (Charge-Coupled Device) or *CMOS* (Complementary Metal Oxide Semiconductor). Second, the sensor dumps the image temporarily into the camera's built-in memory (a memory *buffer*). Finally, the camera's circuitry feeds the image from its memory buffer onto the memory card.

You might be wondering about that second step. Why don't digital cameras record the image directly to the memory card?

The answer is simple: Unless your camera has state-of-the-art-electronics, it would take forever. You'd only be able to take a new picture every few seconds or so. By stashing shots into a memory buffer as a temporary holding tank (a very fast process) before recording the image on the memory card (a much slower process), the camera frees up its attention so that you can take another photo quickly. The camera catches up later, when you've released the shutter button. (All of this is one reason why digital cameras aren't as responsive as film cameras, which transfer your images directly from lens to film.)

The size of this memory buffer in your digital camera affects your life in a couple of different ways. First, it permits certain cameras to have a *burst mode,* which lets you fire off several shots per second. That's a great feature when you're trying to capture an extremely fleeting scene, such as a great soccer goal, a three-year-old's smile, or Microsoft being humble.

A big memory buffer also permits *movie mode,* described later. It can even help fight shutter lag, because the ability to fire off a burst of five or six frames improves your odds of capturing that perfect moment.

As you shop, you probably won't see the amount of memory in a certain camera advertised. But keeping your eye out for cameras with burst mode (and checking out *how many* frames per second it can capture) is good advice.

Figure 1-8:
This image is actually four pictures stitched together using the Panorama Mode.

Panorama Mode

How many times have you showed a travel picture to a friend and remarked, "It looked a lot bigger in real life"? That's because it *was* bigger, and your camera couldn't capture it all. Capturing a vast landscape with a digital camera is like looking at the Grand Canyon through a paper-towel tube.

Digital camera makers have created an ingenious solution to widen this narrow view of life: panorama mode (Figure 1-8). With it, you can stitch together a series of individual images to create a single, beautiful vista, similar to what you saw when you were standing there in real life. The camera's onscreen display helps align the edge of the last shot with the beginning of the next one.

Software Bundle

When reviewing the software bundle included with a camera you're considering, look for Mac OS X compatibility—not for importing and organizing the pictures (you've got iPhoto for that), but for editing them and stitching together panoramas, if your camera offers that feature.

Don't rule out a good camera if the software isn't perfect; for most purposes, iPhoto may be all the software you ever need. But if you're torn between two cameras, favor the one with Mac OS X software in the box.

Tip: You can keep track of all the latest imaging programs for Mac OS X by checking Apple's Web site: *www.apple.com/downloads/macosx/imaging_3d/.*

Noise Reduction

The longer the exposure to record a scene, the more important *noise reduction* becomes. When you shoot nighttime shots, what should be a jet-black sky may exhibit tiny colored specks—*artifacts*—that put a considerable damper on your photo's impact. (The longer the shutter stays open, the more artifacts you'll get, as the camera's sensor gradually heats up.)

A noise reduction feature usually works like this: When you press the shutter, the camera takes *two* shots—the one that you think you're getting, and a second shot with the shutter completely closed. Since the camera's electronics produce the visual noise, both shots theoretically should contain the same colored speckles in the same spots. The camera compares the two shots, concludes that all of the colored specks it finds in the *closed*-shutter shot must be unwanted, and deletes them from the real shot.

Chances are you'll have to dig through the literature or the specs on the manufacturer's Web site to find out whether the camera you're considering has this feature. But if you're a nighttime shooter, it's worth investigating.

Tripod Mount

Nobody *likes* to use a tripod with a digital camera. But there are moments when a tripod is necessary for a beautiful artistic shot, such as streaking car lights across a bridge, or almost anything at night.

So take a moment to turn your camera candidate upside down and inspect the socket. Is it plastic or metal? Metal is better. Where is it positioned? Near the center of the base is better than way off on one side or another.

The location and composition of the tripod mount isn't going to be a deal breaker, but it's certainly worth the short time it takes to examine while the sales clerk is writing up your order.

Movie Mode

Almost every digital camera claims to capture video; some do it better than others.

Cheaper cameras produce movies that are tiny, low-resolution QuickTime flicks. These mini-movies have their novelty value, and are better than nothing when your intention is to email your newborn baby's first cry to eager relatives across the globe.

But more expensive cameras these days can capture QuickTime flicks at a decent size (320 x 240 pixels, or even full-frame 640 x 480 pixels) and smoothness (15 or 30 frames per second), usually complete with soundtrack. Better cameras place no limit on the length of your captured movies (except when you run out of memory card space). More on this topic in Chapter 3.

Price

The P word is a painful subject in the world of electronic photography. Feature for feature, digital cameras simply cost more than traditional film cameras. Yet whereas a 35mm film camera will probably remain current and serviceable for at least five years, whatever digital camera you buy will probably be discontinued by its manufacturer *in under a year*.

Figure 1-9:
At www.shopping.com (a price-comparison site), start by searching for the brand, price range, or resolution you want. Then sort the results by the store's customer rating. Buy your camera from a store that has been rated with four stars or more; watch out for low prices that come with ridiculously inflated "shipping" charges.

The pace of obsolescence will slow down as the technology levels off. But for now, when you evaluate how much you're willing to spend, keep in mind that this might be a one-year purchase at worst, and a two-year investment at best.

At this writing, a good 3-megapixel camera costs about $200; you'll pay $275 to $500 for "prosumer" cameras in the 4- to 5-megapixel range. (Of course, you can also find extremely professional models that cost $1,000 and up.)

Whatever you do, price-compare before you buy. You'll be astonished at the differences in prices you'll find from store to store. Begin your search at, for example, *www. shopping.com* (Figure 1-9).

Composing Brilliant Photos

If your eyes are bleeding from the technical underbrush of Chapter 1—bells, whistles, megabytes—switch on your right brain. This chapter has little to do with electronics and everything to do with the more artful side of photography: composition.

What follows are four tips that photographers have been using for years to create good pictures regardless of the camera type. These time-honored secrets can be applied to digital imaging too. Good composition is just as important with a $199 digicam as it is with a $3,000 pro digital SLR—and just as enjoyable.

This chapter offers suggestions that will immediately improve your pictures. But first, a few words about composition itself.

Composition

Composition is the arrangement of your picture, the interplay between foreground and background, the way the subject fills the frame, the way the parts of the picture relate to each other, and so on.

Will the shot be clearer, better, or more interesting if you move closer? What about walking around to the other side of the action, or zooming in slightly, or letting tall grass fill the foreground? Would the picture be more interesting if it were framed by horizontal, vertical, or diagonal structures (such as branches, pillars, or a road stretching away)? All of this floats through a veteran photographer's head before the shutter button clicks.

It's easy to think, "Hey, it's a picture, not a painting—I have to shoot what's there." However, the fact is that photography is every bit as creative as painting. You have more control over the composition than you realize.

Note: If the primary thrust of your photographic ambition is to take casual vacation pictures, some of the following suggestions for professional composition may strike you as overkill.

But read them anyway. If you let some of these tips rub off on you, you'll be able to apply them even in everyday snapshot situations. There's no law against casual vacation pictures being *good* casual vacation pictures.

The Rule of Thirds

Most people assume that the center of the frame should contain the most important element of your shot. In fact, 98 percent of all amateur photos feature the subject of the shot in dead center.

Figure 2-1:
Top: When shooting a head and shoulder portrait, frame the shot so that her eyes fall on the upper imaginary line, a third of the way down the frame.

Bottom: When shooting a landscape, put the horizon on the bottom-third line if you want to emphasize the sky or tall objects like mountains, trees, and buildings. Put the horizon on the upper third line to emphasize what's on the ground, such as the people in the shot.

For the most visually interesting shots, however, dead center is actually the *least* compelling location for the subject. Artists and psychologists have found, instead, that following the so-called Rule of Thirds ensures better photos.

Imagine that the photo frame is divided into thirds, both horizontally and vertically, as shown in Figure 2-1. The Rule of Thirds contends that the intersections of these lines are the strongest parts of the frame. Putting the most interesting parts of the image at these four points, in other words, makes better composition.

Save the center square of the frame for tight close-ups—and even then, aim for having the subject's eyes on the upper-third line.

Get Closer

Step one to better pictures: Get closer. Step two: Get closer still.

Move your feet toward the subject, and don't stop moving them until the subject fills the frame (Figure 2-2). Of course, the zoom lens on your camera can help with this process quite a bit.

Figure 2-2:
Top: This otter shot seemed like a great photo at the time it was taken. Once it was uploaded to iPhoto, however, it became something of a disappointment. It looks bland, because the otters were too far away and at an uninteresting angle.

Bottom: By getting (or zooming) closer, however, you get far more interesting results. In this case, the photographer had to apply the time-honored skill of patience, waiting for the sea otters to drift within better range. Sometimes getting closer means waiting for the action to come to you.

Try it with your dog. Take the first picture standing where you normally would stand—probably about five feet away and above Rover's head.

Now prepare to take a second picture—but first crouch down so that you see the world at dog level. Come close enough to the dog so that he can almost lick your camera lens. (But don't let him *do* it; dog slobber is very bad for optics.)

Take the second picture. Load both photos into iPhoto and study them. The first shot probably looks pretty boring compared to the second one.

Clearly, you weren't thinking about *composition* the first time. You were thinking about *taking a picture* of your dog.

The point is, *taking a picture* is usually a mindless act that doesn't result in the most memorable photos. Getting closer to create an interesting *composition* makes for compelling photography.

Tip: Filling the frame with your subject also means that you'll have less uninteresting background to crop out before making prints. As a result, you'll get higher resolution (more pixels) in the printout, which enhances the photo's quality.

Eliminate Busy Backgrounds

Busy backgrounds destroy photographs (Figure 2-3, top). Unless the intent of your image is to confuse and irritate the viewer's eye (headbanger music CD album cover, anyone?), do what you can to eliminate distracting elements from your picture. Remember, you want to make it easy for the viewer to find the key elements of your composition, and enjoy them once they're there.

In other words, don't become so enamored with your subject that you don't notice the telephone wires that seem to run through her skull. Train your eye to examine the subject first, and then survey the surrounding scene.

Here are some problems to look out for—and avoid—in the backgrounds of your shots:

- **All forms of poles.** Telephone poles, fence posts, street signs, and malnourished trees can creep into your photos and ruin them.

- **Linear patterns.** Avoid busy background elements, such as bricks, paneling, fences, and zebra skins.

- **Parts of things.** When people see a "part of a thing" in your picture—for example, the front of a tractor, the leg of a ladder, the rear end of a camel—they can't help but wonder what the rest of it looks like, instead of focusing on your subject.

Tip: Get in the habit of scanning all four corners of your frame before clicking the shutter. That way, you'll catch those telephone poles and street signs that you wouldn't normally see until it's too late.

Look for backgrounds that have subtle tones, soft edges, and nondescript elements. Moving your subject forward, away from the background, can help soften the backdrop even more.

Figure 2-3:
Top: Egads! What's this picture about? The people? The boats? Linear elements in the background usually spell doom for people shots.

Bottom: Avoid the clutter and opt for a more soothing background, such as water, sky, or any other subtle element. Your subjects—and audience—will thank you.

Go Low, Go High

Change your camera angle often. This is where a flip screen comes in handy, as described in Chapter 1.

Put the camera on the ground and study the composition. Raise it over your head and see how the world looks from that angle (Figure 2-4). If possible, walk around the subject and examine it from left to right.

Or adopt this technique: When you first approach an interesting subject, take the picture, just to get a safe one in the camera. Then change your angle and take another shot. If you have time, get closer and take a few more. Work the subject for as long as the opportunity presents itself.

More often than not, the "safe" shot will be your least favorite of the series. You'll probably find the latter frames far more compelling.

Figure 2-4:
Top: To really capture the "feel" of this breakfast nook, raise the angle of the camera, even if it means standing on a chair to do so.

Bottom: Try going low, too. "Getting to the bottom of things" provides you with dramatic angles and impressive images. And in this case, it's the only way to capture the whole thing; without stooping down and shooting up, you would have brought home only a photo of a black-painted panel.

The Right Way to Compose

Finally, one last suggestion: Consider the pointers in this chapter as guidelines only. There is no one right way in photography; when you come down to it, the best photos are the ones you *like*.

Beyond the
Simple Snapshot

There you sit, surveying your boxes of old photos. Snapshots of your family. Snapshots on vacation. Snapshots of tourist attractions. But they're all *snapshots.*

Then the professional photos in some magazine or newspaper hit you. There's the brilliant close-up of a ladybug on a leaf, with the bushes in the background gently out of focus. There's the amazing shot of the soccer player butting the ball with his head, frozen in action so completely that you can see individual flecks of sweat flying from his hair. There's the incredible shot of the city lights at night, with car taillights drawing colorful firefly tracks across the frame.

You can't help but wonder: "How do they *do* that? And why can't I do it too?"

Actually, you probably can. Some of these special shots require special gear, but most of them involve nothing more than good technique—and knowing when to invoke which of your camera's special features. With a little practice, you can take pictures just as compelling, colorful, and intimate as the shots you see in the magazines.

This chapter is dedicated to laying bare the secrets of professional photographers. May you never take another dull snapshot.

Sports Photography

Everybody's seen those incredible high-speed action photos of athletes frozen in mid-leap. Without these shots (and the swimsuit photos), *Sports Illustrated* would be no thicker than a pamphlet.

Through a combination of careful positioning, focusing, lighting, and shutter-speed adjustments, this kind of photo is within your reach. As a handy bonus, mastering the frozen-action sports picture also means you've mastered frozen-action water splashes, frozen-action bird-in-flight shots, and frozen-action kid moments.

Tip: Don't get frustrated if, despite learning all of the following techniques, many of your pictures don't come out well. Sports photography produces lots of waste. Pros shoot dozens, sometimes hundreds, of frames just to get one good picture.

In short, a very low good-to-bad ratio is par for the course in this kind of shooting. But what the heck? It isn't costing you anything, and one great shot can make the entire effort worthwhile.

Getting Close to the Action

If your digital camera has a zoom lens, it's probably a 3X zoom, meaning that it can magnify the scene three times. Unfortunately, if you're in the stands at the football game, hoping for action shots of an individual player, 3X is not powerful enough. What you really need is one of those enormous, bazooka-like telephoto lenses that protrudes three feet in front of the camera.

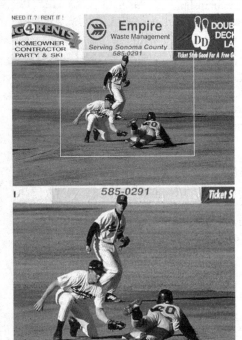

Figure 3-1:
You might not be able to afford a digital SLR with a $10,000 super telephoto lens attachment. But if you have a 3-megapixel camera or an even better one, here's a way to "zoom in" on the action.

Shoot at your camera's highest resolution—zoomed in as much as you can (top). Once the picture is in iPhoto, you can "zoom in" even further by cropping the portion of the picture you want to keep (page 140). Thanks to the high resolution of the original photo, you'll still have enough pixels to make a nice print or slide show, and the photo is much more effective this way (bottom).

But that doesn't mean you can't still capture good shots. Find a position on the sidelines that puts you as close to the action as possible. Zoom in with your camera and then use the trick shown in Figure 3-1.

If it's a bright, sunny day, the standard "automatic everything" setting of the camera might work just fine. Take a few sample shots, trying to get the action as it's coming at you.

Tip: If you still can't fill the frame with the action you want, consider turning on the camera's *digital zoom*. As noted in Chapter 1, you should avoid using the digital zoom most of the time, because it compromises image quality.

Still, at low levels (2X or 3X, for example), the deterioration in image quality might be tolerable. Experimenting with this feature might be worthwhile when covering a spectator sport, for instance.

Fast Shutter Speeds

If the results are blurry because the motion is too fast, you'll have to instruct the camera to use a faster shutter speed.

Unfortunately, the cheapest, point-and-shoot-only cameras don't offer any such setting—you get what you pay for. But even cameras a slight cut above those basic ones offer a solution to this problem.

Shutter-priority mode

As noted in Chapter 1, certain cameras offer manual controls that pay off in just such special occasions as this.

In this case, what you want is the feature called *shutter priority*. In this mode—a time-honored feature of traditional film cameras—you tell the camera that the *speed* of the shot is what matters. You want the "film" exposed for only 1/500th of a second, for example.

Understanding what this mode does is slightly technical, but extremely important.

Whenever you take a picture, the amount of light that enters the camera is determined by two things: the *speed* of the shutter opening and closing, and the *size* of the opening of the diaphragm in the lens (the *aperture*).

If you want to freeze the action, you'll want the shutter to open and close very quickly. As a result, you're admitting less light into the camera. To prevent the picture from being too dark, the camera will have to compensate by opening its "eye" wider for that fraction of a second—that is, you want it to use a larger aperture.

In shutter-priority mode, that's exactly what happens. You say, "I don't care about the aperture—you worry about that, little camera buddy. I just want this picture *fast*." The camera nods in its little digital way and agrees to open up its aperture wide enough to compensate for your fast shutter speed.

Exactly how you turn on shutter-priority mode differs radically by camera. On some cameras, you have to fiddle around with the menu system (see Figure 3-2); on others, you simply turn the little control knob on the top to a position marked *S* or *Tv* (old-time photography lingo for *time value*), as shown in Figure 3-3.

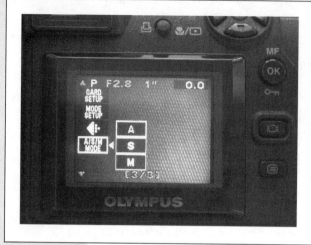

Figure 3-2:
Camera makers often position advanced controls where they're difficult to find—like buried in the onscreen menus, as shown here. On this Olympus, you have three alternative exposure modes: "A" for aperture priority, "S" for shutter priority, and "M" for manual mode. To freeze action, choose "S" for shutter priority. Then set your camera's shutter speed to 1/500th of a second or faster (such as 1/1000th) to freeze the action.

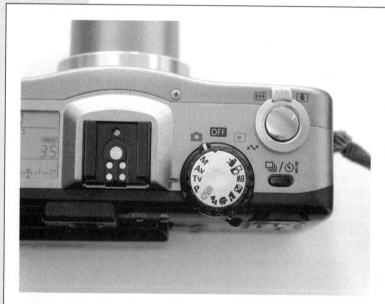

Figure 3-3:
Your camera may have shutter priority and you don't even know it. That's because the Tv designation (as shown on the mode dial here) is also used for this setting. No, it's not television mode; Tv stands for timed value, another name for shutter priority.

In any case, once you're in this mode, you must use some kind of dial or slider to indicate how *fast* you want the shutter to snap. You might start with 1/500th or 1/1000th of a second and take another series of shots. (The screen may show only

"500" or "1000," but you'll know what it means.) If the result is too dark, slow down the shutter speed to the next notch; the camera is opening the aperture as wide as it can.

Focusing and Shutter Lag

Whenever you try to photograph something fast, you may run headfirst into a chronic problem of digital cameras called *shutter lag*. That's the time the camera takes to calculate the focus and exposure from the instant you squeeze the shutter button to the instant the shutter actually snaps. It's usually at least one second long. Unfortunately, a delay that long means death to perfect sports photography. You'll miss the critical instant every time.

The circuitry in cameras, like the $1,000 digital SLR models from Canon and Nikon, is fast enough to make shutter lag a non-issue. In other cameras, you should adopt one of these solutions:

- **Prefocus.** Suppose you're trying to get a shot of the goalie in a soccer game. Take advantage of the time when he's just standing there doing nothing. Frame the shot on your camera screen.

  Then, as the opposing team comes barreling down the field toward him, press the shutter button just halfway. Half-pressing the shutter makes the camera calculate the exposure and focus *in advance*. (Making those calculations is what constitutes most of the camera's shutter lag.) Keep the button half-pressed until the moment of truth, when the goalie dives for the ball. *Now* squeeze the shutter the rest of the way. This technique nearly eliminates shutter lag, freezing the action closer to the critical moment.

  This is only one example of how *anticipating* the critical moment pays big dividends in sports photography. With a little practice, you can learn to press the shutter button *right before* the big moment, rewarding you with the perfect shot.

- **Use burst mode.** Most recent digicams offer something called *burst mode,* in which the camera snaps a series of shots in rapid succession, for as long as you hold down the shutter button. It's something like the motor drive on a traditional film camera, so often featured in movies in which the main character is a photographer.

  Most cameras can capture only about two frames per second, but that's still enough to improve the odds that one of your shots will be good. With a little practice, using the burst mode can help you compensate for shutter lag—especially if you anticipate the action.

Light Metering

Ordinarily, a digital camera calculates the amount of light in a scene by averaging all light from all areas of the frame. And ordinarily, that system works perfectly well.

In sports photography, however, the surrounding scene is usually substantially brighter or darker than the athletes, leading to improper exposure of the one thing you really want: the action.

Fortunately, many cameras offer *spot metering*. In this mode, you see little bracket markers (or a square or circle) in the center of your viewing frame (Figure 3-4). You can use these brackets to tell the camera which portion of the scene to pay attention to in calculating the exposure. By turning on this feature for sports shooting, you'll make sure that the athlete is correctly lit, background notwithstanding.

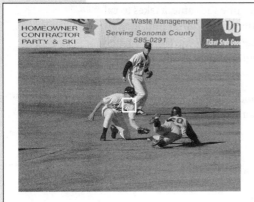

Figure 3-4:
In this picture, the athletes are brighter than the baseball field. If you were to use your camera's normal "averaging" or "evaluative" mode, there's a good chance that the players would be too bright, or overexposed. By using spot metering, you can tell your camera to set the exposure for the smaller area in the center of the frame. Now the subjects of the photo will be correctly exposed!

Portraits

You may have noticed that in most professional photo portraits, the background is softly out of focus. Unless you have the cheapest camera on the planet, you can create a similar great-looking effect yourself.

In photographic terms, a shot with a soft-focus background is said to have a *shallow depth of field*. The term "depth of field" refers to how much of the picture is in focus. When you're photographing your family in front of the Great Wall of China, you'll probably want a *deep* depth of field, so that both the people and the background remain in focus. But in typical headshot-type portraits, you'll want a *shallow* depth of field—and a blurry background. Figure 3-5 should make this more clear.

So how do you control the depth of field? Here are a few ways.

Trick 1: Zoom In

It might not seem logical that you'd want to use your camera's zoom lens (if it has one) for a portrait. After all, you can get as close as you want to the subject just by walking.

But thanks to a quirk of optics, zooming in helps create a shallow depth of field, which is just what you want for portraits. (Back up if zooming puts the camera's vision too close to the subject.)

Trick 2: Move the Background Back

The farther away your model is from the background, the softer the background will appear. If you choose an ivy-covered wall as your backdrop, for example, position your subject 10, 20, or 30 feet away from the wall—the farther, the better.

Figure 3-5:
Top: The trick to creating a soft background is to use a large aperture opening, such as f-2.8 or f-4. (Quirkily enough, low f-numbers indicate larger aperture settings; see the table on page 43.)

If your camera has an aperture-priority mode, then you can lock in this setting; the camera will set the correct shutter speed for you. Also, note that the farther away the subject is from the background, the softer the background will appear. Set your focus on the subject's eyes and take the picture.

Bottom: When you want your entire scene in focus, from front to back, then you want a deep depth of field. You can do this by setting your aperture to f-8, f-11, or f-16 (in aperture-priority mode). If you focus on an object about one third of the way into the scene, everything should be rendered sharply.

Unfortunately, using an aperture like f-11 in low light might force your camera to use a slow shutter speed. You might have to steady it with a tripod to avoid "camera shake," which means blurriness.

Trick 3: Choose a Wide Aperture Setting

You may remember from page 37 that two factors determine how much light fills a shot: how long the shutter remains open (the shutter speed) and how wide it opens (the aperture).

In sports photography, what you care about most is usually the shutter speed. In portrait photography, what you care about most is the aperture setting—because the size of the aperture controls the depth of field. Low-numbered aperture settings like f-2.8 or f-4 are referred to as *wide aperture settings* by photographers because they let lots of light through the lens. These wide settings also help create soft backgrounds for portraits.

The portrait setting (program)

Many cameras offer a *portrait* mode, often designated on the control dial by the silhouette of a human head (Figure 3-6). Setting the camera to this mode automatically creates a short depth of field, blurring the background.

Figure 3-6:
If you don't want to mess with aperture settings, you can use the portrait mode on your camera, if it has one—indicated on this camera and many others by a silhouette of a human head.

Aperture-priority mode

More-expensive cameras offer more control over depth of field in the form of an *aperture-priority mode.* It lets you tell the camera: "I want to control how much of this shot is in focus; that is, I want to set the aperture. You, the camera, should worry about the other half of the equation—the shutter speed."

Entering aperture-priority mode (if your camera has it) may be as simple as turning a dial to the A or AV position, or as complicated as having to pull up the camera's onscreen menu system.

(See Figures 3-2 and 3-3 for examples of how you can turn on shutter-priority mode. Aperture-priority mode is very similar, and is usually located right next to shutter priority.)

In any case, once you've turned on this mode, you adjust the aperture by turning a knob or pressing the up/down buttons. On the screen, you'll see the changing *f-stop* numbers, which represent different size apertures.

This table should offer some indication of what you're in for:

f-stop	diameter of aperture	depth of field	background looks
f-2	very large	very shallow	very soft
f-2.8	large	shallow	soft
f-4	medium	moderate	a little out of focus
f-5.6	medium	moderate	a little out of focus
f-8	small	moderately deep	mostly in focus
f-11	small	deep	sharp
f-16	very small	very deep	very sharp

Making the Shot

Position your model so the backdrop is in the distance. Check for telephone poles or anything else that may appear to pierce the model's head. If you can, shoot on a cloudy day, first thing in the morning or late in the afternoon; these are the best situations for outdoor portraits, when the light is softer and more flattering. Otherwise, try to place the model in open shade, like under a tree.

Adjust the flash settings so the flash is forced to go off, which will provide a nice supplemental burst of light. Don't stand more than ten feet away from your subject or your fill flash won't reach.

Finally, zoom in and start shooting. You'll notice that if you're standing within ten feet (so the flash will reach) and zooming in as much as your lens allows (to help soften the background), your model's upper body will fill the frame. That's what you want. Unwittingly, most snap shooters stand too far away from their subjects.

After a few frames, review your work and adjust as necessary. The soft background effect probably won't be as strong as it would be if you were using a pro camera with a telephoto lens, but you will definitely notice a pleasant difference.

Existing-Light Portraits

Cameras love light, that's for sure. And in general, you need the flash for indoor shots.

But not always. Some of the best interior photos use nothing more than light streaming in from a window. Images that use only ambient light without adding flash are called *existing light* or *natural light* photos.

This technique isn't right for every situation. But when it's appropriate, existing-light photos have these advantages over flash photography:

- **More depth.** The problem with the flash is that it illuminates only about the first ten feet of the scene. Everything beyond that fades to black.

In existing-light photography, on the other hand, your camera reads the lighting for the entire room. Not only is your primary subject exposed properly, but the surrounding setting is too, giving the picture more depth.

- **Less harsh.** The light in an existing-light photo generally comes from a variety of sources: overhead lights, windows, lamps, and reflections off walls and ceilings. All of this adds up to softer, more balanced light than what you get from the laser beam generated by your built-in flash.

- **More expressive.** Too often, flash pictures produce the "deer in the headlights" look from your subjects—if indeed the close-range flash doesn't whitewash them completely. Existing-light pictures tend to be more natural and expressive, and the people you're shooting are more relaxed when they're not being pelted by bursts of light.

An existing-light indoor portrait has a classic feel, because it's reminiscent of those timeless paintings by great artists like Rembrandt.

Keep It Steady

In a natural-light portrait, keep the flash turned off (that's why it's called *natural* light). The camera's shutter will have to remain open for a relatively long interval to admit enough light for a good picture. As a result, you'll need to keep the camera very steady—which often means you'll need a tripod.

Pocket tripods are great for this type of shooting. They weigh only a few ounces, steady the camera well, and can be used on all kinds of surfaces like tables, countertops, and so on.

Once the tripod is steady, you face another challenge: taking the picture without jiggling the camera when you push the shutter button. Even a little camera shake will blur your entire image, creating an out-of-focus appearance.

If a remote control came with the camera, use it. If not, use the camera's self-timer feature, which counts off, say, ten seconds before snapping the picture automatically.

Tip: If your camera has a burst mode, here's a great chance to use it. Your finger pressing the shutter button is likely to ruin your first shot by introducing camera shake—but because it will thereafter remain down without moving, the second or third shot of the burst will look much steadier.

In either case, do what you can to persuade the subject to keep still; during a long exposure like this, fidgety people mean blurry portraits. (Of course, you can use this effect to your advantage, too, if you want to create a moody interior picture with ghostlike subjects.)

The Camera Setup

If you have adjustable "film speed" settings (page 22), then you might want to use the 200 or 400 setting to make your camera more light-sensitive. (On the other hand, if you do have enough light for a decent exposure, then don't increase the film speed, because it'll slightly degrade the image quality.)

How can you tell if you don't have enough light and need to increase the film speed? Review your test shot. (Zoom in to the LCD screen, magnifying the photo, to inspect it more closely.) If it's too dark or has motion blur, increase the film speed from 100 to 200. Take another test shot. If things are still looking dark, try one more time at 400 speed. And open the drapes all the way.

Also consider turning on spot metering (page 40). It permits the camera to make exposure decisions based only on the subject, without being affected by the lighting in the surrounding background.

The Model Setup

You'll need a window, tripod, trusty digital camera, and willing model for this project (Figure 3-7).

Turn your model three-quarters toward the light coming in the window. You may want to put the camera on a tripod (page 54) to avoid camera shake.

Tip: Great painters of the past preferred the light coming through a *north* window for their portraits, especially in the early hours of the day. Try this setting for your existing-light portraits.

Figure 3-7:
When "on the go," you can get great results with a tabletop tripod, or by resting your elbows on a table and slowly squeezing the shutter. Make sure the flash is turned off. If you have a spot meter, you might want to direct it to the subject's face to achieve that perfect exposure.

Now look at the lighting the way the camera would see the scene, not the way you would normally view it (see the box on page 47). If there's a noticeable difference between the brightest area of the model's face and the darkest area, then you may want to add a little of what's called *fill light*.

If you were a serious photographer with actual photographic gear lying around—and maybe you are—you could use a low-power flash as a fill light. Of course, then it would no longer be an *existing*-light portrait.

It's a better idea to find a reflector and position it so that light bounces off it onto the dark side of the model's face. A reflector is a common piece of photographic gear; it's essentially a big white shiny surface on its own pole. If you don't have lighting equipment sitting around the house, but you really want this portrait to look good, just rig a big piece of white cardboard or white foam board to serve as a reflecting surface.

When you think you've balanced the tones, take a picture and review your results. Chances are that the shadow areas look darker to the camera than they do to your eyes. In that case, move the reflector closer to brighten the shadows.

White Balance (Color Balance)

Here's a mind-bending example of the way your eyes and your camera see things completely differently. It turns out that different kinds of lights—regular incandescent lightbulbs, fluorescent office lighting, the sun—cast subtle tinges of color on everything they illuminate. When you shoot non-flash photos indoors or in open shade outside, you'll get a bluish or "cool" cast. If you shoot without a flash under incandescent lighting, then the shots will have a "warmer" tint, mostly yellow and red.

So why haven't you ever noticed these different lighting artifacts? Because your brain compensates almost instantly for these different *color temperatures,* as they're called. (Your brain does a lot of compensating for light. Ever noticed how your eyes adjust to a dark room after a couple of minutes?)

But to a camera, tints are tints—and you'll see them onscreen and in your printouts. Unfortunately, they can detract from your photos. For example, portraits with warmer casts are generally more pleasing to the eye. But natural light from the window imparts a bluish cast, which isn't good for skin tones.

In the "old" days of traditional film photography, you would have corrected the color temperature by placing a screw-on filter over the lens. On a digital camera, you can change the color temperature by adjusting something called the camera's *white balance* (or *color balance*). Almost every digital camera has this function.

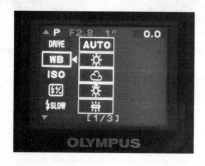

Figure 3-8:
Most digital cameras let you adjust color balance. Sometimes the setting is labeled "WB" (white balance, which is essentially the same thing as color balance). Most of the time, you can leave this setting on Auto. But if the tones start looking too cool or too warm, you might want to override auto and make the adjustment yourself.

Most cameras have a little knob or menu offering these icons (see Figure 3-8):

- The sun icon represents normal daylight conditions in direct light.

- The cloud icon is for overcast days, open shade, and window-illuminated interiors.

- The lightbulb icon is for incandescent lighting.

- The bar icon is for fluorescent lighting.

(If you're used to working with traditional camera filters, the sun is your "Sky 1A" filter, the cloud is your "81B warming" filter, the lightbulb is your "80A cooling" filter, and the tube is the "FLD fluorescent correction" filter.)

Tip: When you're using the flash, change your camera's color balance from *auto* to *cloudy*. Electronic flashes tend to produce images that have a *cool cast*. Switching to the cloudy setting on your digital camera warms them up nicely.

Taking the Picture

With time and practice, you'll be able to "calibrate" your eyes so that they see shadows the same way your camera does. You'll spend less and less time testing before the shoot, and more time creating your classic image.

UP TO SPEED

The Tale of Two Perceptions

The reason photographic lighting is such a challenge is that you have two different systems operating at once: your eyes and your camera.

Your pupils are super-advanced apertures that constantly adjust to ambient light. Even in extreme conditions, such as when you go from a completely dark theater to the bright lobby, it only takes seconds for your optical system to adjust.

Furthermore, you can look at a scene that contains both deep shadows and super-bright highlights—and see detail in both areas simultaneously. Your eyes, optical nerves, and brain are constantly adjusting to interpret the ever-changing landscape around you.

Too bad your camera can't do the same.

Whereas your eyes can pick up the entire *tonal range* of a scene (the shades from brightest white to darkest black), a camera can pick up detail in only a slice of it. For example, if you're shooting a bright sky filled with clouds and trees casting deep shadows on meadow grass, you have a decision to make. What parts of this scene are most important to you? The bright sky, the trees, or the deep shadows? On a good day, your camera will be able to record detail in two out of the three.

With practice, you can learn to see the world the way your camera does, to the great benefit of your photos. For example, try setting up a natural-light scene, such as a still life with fruit. Put the camera on a tripod. Study the scene with your eyes, and then photograph it. Compare what the lens records with the image in your head.

Are they the same? Probably not. How are the two images different? Make a few notes about your perceptions as compared to what the camera captured, and then repeat the exercise with a different scene.

When the image in your head begins to match the one on the camera's LCD screen, then you've truly begun to see the world with a photographic eye.

As you've figured out by now, creating a great natural-like portrait means learning to work with light as though it's a paintbrush. It takes time and practice to become proficient at this, but even your first efforts will probably surprise you with their expressiveness.

Tip: Don't be too quick to delete shots from the camera before viewing them on the computer screen. Existing-light shots sometimes contain subtleties that don't appear on tiny LCD screens. You'll be pleasantly surprised by many of the images that may have looked uninteresting when viewed on your camera's two-inch display.

Self-Portraits

Sometimes it's easier to take your own picture than to hand the camera to someone else—especially when you're practicing with your camera.

The preceding discussion about blurring the background applies to pictures you take of yourself, too, of course. But there are a few other considerations.

If you're on vacation, the natural scenery might be all the backdrop you need. If you're shooting a picture to use on a résumé or to post on your Web page, however, find a well-lit room with some open wall space. The blank wall (preferably light-colored) will serve as your backdrop. Natural light coming in from windows is best for this setup.

Find a stool or a low-back chair without arms, and position it about five feet in front of your backdrop. If possible, it should face the brightest window in the room.

Next, you'll need a way to position your camera. A standard tripod is best, but you can use a pocket tripod (page 54) on top of a table if necessary. Either way, position the camera about five feet from your stool.

Tip: In a pinch, you can use a standard hotel-room lamp as a tripod. The threads that are designed to secure the lampshade to its support bracket are exactly the right diameter for your camera's tripod socket!

Turn on the flash. The ambient room lighting is often be bright enough to provide overall even illumination, but the flash will provide a little burst of front light to smooth out facial blemishes and put a twinkle in your eyes.

The best cameras for self-portraits have a flip screen and a remote control. The flip screen lets you preview how you look in the frame before you shoot the shot, and the remote control lets you actually take the shot while sitting comfortably on your stool.

If you don't have these options, put your camera in self-timer mode. To help you frame the shot while you're not actually on the stool, use a table lamp as a stand-in.

Check your hair and clothing in a mirror, press the shutter button to trigger the self-timer countdown, and then sit on the stool (preferably *after* removing the table lamp).

Once the camera fires, play back the photo on the screen. Did you zoom in close enough? Are you in focus and centered in the frame? How does the lighting look?

If you need to add a little light to one side of your face or the other because it's appearing too shadowy, you can construct a homemade reflector out of white cardboard or similar material. Position your reflector as close to you as possible (although not in the photo itself) and angle it so it "bounces" light off the brightest light source onto the area requiring illumination. This will help lighten up the dark areas.

Shoot another round. Once you get the basic setup looking good, experiment with different angles and facial expressions. One advantage of taking your own portraits is that you can be more creative (Figure 3-9). Remember, you can always erase the embarrassing frames—or all of them. Remember, too, that self-portraits don't have to be dull headshots; they can be every bit as interesting as any other photo.

Figure 3-9:
Left: Here's a traditional head shot—a staple of unemployed actors, corporate annual reports, and Most Wanted lists. Note the solid background. The camera was on a tripod and the self-timer tripped the shutter.

Right: To shoot an informal self-portrait, hold the camera at arm's length with the lens pointed back at you.

Kid Photography

Children are challenging for all photographers. They're like flash floods: fast, low to the ground, and unpredictable. But with a little patience and perseverance, you can keep up with them and get the shot (Figure 3-10). Here are some tips:

- **Be prepared.** Rule one for capturing great kid pictures is to have your camera handy at all times, charged and with memory-card space to spare. Great kid shots come and go in the blink of an eye. Parents don't have the luxury of keeping their equipment snugly stowed away in a camera bag in the closet.

- **Get down there.** The best kid shots are generally photographed at kid level, and that means getting low. (Flip screens are particularly useful for kid shots, because they let you position the camera down low without you actually having to lie on the ground.)

- **Get close.** Your shots will have much more impact if the subject fills the frame, plus you won't have to do as much cropping later in iPhoto.

- **Prefocus.** Shutter lag will make you miss the shot every time. In many cases, you can defeat it by prefocusing—that is, half-pressing the shutter button when the kid's not doing anything special. Keep your finger on the button until the magical smile appears, then press fully to snap the shot.

- **Burst away.** Use your camera's burst mode to fire off several shots in quick succession. Given the fleeting nature of many kids' grins, this trick improves your odds for catching just the right moment.

Figure 3-10:
If you want great-looking kid shots, you've got to play on their turf. That means getting down on your hands and knees, or even your tummy.

- **Force the flash.** Indoors or out, you'll want the flash to fire, since it provides even illumination and helps freeze the action. Switch your camera's flash setting so that it's always on.

- **Make it bright.** See page 62 for a discussion of red-eye, but don't bother using the *red-eye reduction* flash mode on your camera. By the time your camera has finished strobing and stuttering, your kid will be in the next zip code.

  If red-eye is a problem in your flash photos of kids, make the room as bright as possible, shoot from an angle that isn't dead-on into your kids' eyes, and touch up the red-eye later in iPhoto, if necessary.

- **Fire at will.** Child photography is like shooting a sports event—you'll take lots of bad shots in order to get a few gems. Again, who cares? The duds don't cost you anything. And once you've captured the image of a lifetime, you'll forget about all the outtakes you deleted previously.

Theater Performances

Capturing stage performances is difficult even for professional photographers. What makes theater lighting tricky is that the bright main light on the actors is often right in the same frame with a subdued or even darkened background. If you photograph this composition "as is" in automatic mode, then the camera calibrates the exposure, brightening up the image enough to display the dominant dim background. As a result, the spotlighted actors turn into white-hot, irradiated ghosts.

Your built-in flash is useless under these conditions (unless you climb right up onto the stage beside the actors, which is generally frowned upon by the management). The

Figure 3-11:
Top: Brightly lit actors and dark backgrounds are a recipe for photographic disaster. The actors' faces have bleached out completely.

Bottom: To overcome this challenge, use your camera's spot meter (if it has one) and direct it toward the actors, not the background. Your odds for an acceptable exposure will increase dramatically.

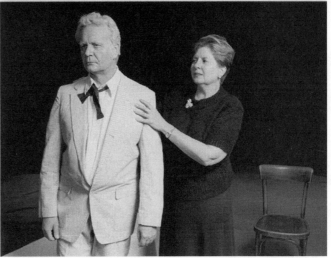

typical range for the camera's flash is about ten feet, after which it's about as useful as a snow-cone machine in Alaska. *Turn your flash off* at theater performances—because it's annoying to the rest of the audience, because it's worthless, and because it's usually forbidden.

To overcome this challenge, use the other tools built into your camera. If you have a *spot meter mode,* you have a fighting chance. As noted previously, your camera generally gauges the brightness of the scene by averaging the light across the entire frame—a recipe for disaster when you're shooting the stage.

Spot metering, however, lets you designate a particular spot in the scene whose brightness you want the camera to measure. (You indicate what spot that is by positioning a frame marker that appears in the center of the frame.) Point the spot-metering area at the brightly lit actors. The camera then sets the exposure on them instead of on the vast expanse of the dimly lit set (Figure 3-11).

Not all cameras have a spot-metering mode. But even basic cameras generally offer some kind of *exposure compensation,* an overall brightness control. For theater situations, try lowering the exposure to –1 or –1.5, for example. The objective is to darken the entire scene. The background will be *too* dark, of course, but at least the actors won't be "blown out."

Finally, if you know ahead of time that you want pictures from a particular performance, do what you can to secure a ticket in the first few rows. When it comes to theater shooting, the closer you get, the better.

Tip: Depending on the kind of performance you're trying to photograph, getting the right lighting may be just the tip of the iceberg. Getting *permission* to photograph might be the greater obstacle.

In these cases, consider taking your pictures at the dress rehearsal. (This means you, parents of kids in school plays.) Not only is the management likely to be more permissive, but you'll be able to sit right there in the front row, to the immense benefit of your photos.

Underwater Photography

Water is the mortal enemy of digital cameras. Still, you can buy waterproof enclosures for many camera models, which opens up a whole new world of photographic possibilities.

Sometimes these enclosures are made by the camera manufacturer. Canon, for example, makes clear plastic cases for a number of its digital cameras. For other models, you can often find enclosures for sale at Web sites like *www.ikelite.com* or *www.uwimaging.com.*

The good news is that these enclosures protect the camera at depths down to 100 feet, for example, and provide access to the camera's controls. The bad news is that the underwater housing can cost as much as the camera!

When shooting underwater, force the flash to turn on; it's dark down there. You might also want to play with the color balance adjustment to help offset the bluish tint of the water. If your camera has a dial that lets you call up different lighting presets, try the Cloudy setting to warm up the tones.

Oh, and don't try to change the batteries while you're down there.

Travel Photography

Digital cameras are perfect vacation companions. Memory cards are easy to pack, there's no film for airport X-rays to wash out, and when the day is done, you can review all of your images on the camera's LCD screen, on your laptop, or on the hotel room TV.

Shooting on the road presents unique photo opportunities that simply aren't available at home—like museums, fjords, and Cinderella's Castle. Here's how to master those moments and add a little spice to your vacation slide show.

Packing up

Digital cameras may be small and compact, but they're often accompanied by just as much accessory junk as film cameras. Here's a pre-trip checklist:

• **Batteries.** The laws of photography dictate that you'll run out of juice at the precise moment the perfect shot appears.

If your camera comes with its own proprietary, rechargeable battery, consider buying a second one. Charge both batteries every night, and take them both with you during the day. (Pack the charger, too.)

If your camera accepts AA-type batteries instead, you have much more flexibility. Bring your set of NiMH rechargeables, as described as page 17, and their charger. Also pack an emergency set of disposables, like alkaline AAs or Duracell CRV3 lithium disposables, if your camera accepts them.

• **Memory cards.** Nobody ever said, "Oh, I wish I'd bought a smaller memory card." You'll be grateful for every last megabyte.

As a rough rule of thumb, figure that you'll wind up keeping 36 shots a day (not including the ones that you delete right off the camera). If you have a 3-megapixel camera, a 64 MB card might be enough for one day of shooting. If you brought a laptop on the trip, you can rush back to the hotel room each night and offload the pictures into iPhoto, freeing up the card for the next day's shooting.

If you don't plan to take the laptop along, buy a much bigger memory card (or several). If you're on the road for a week with that hypothetical 3-megapixel camera, you'll need at least 448 megabytes to hold those 36 pictures a day. It's generally cheaper to buy two 256 MB cards than one 512 MB card, but shop around to get the best deal possible (*www.shopper.com,* for example).

• **Camera bag.** If your camera didn't come with a case, get one for it. Not only will it protect your camera (even if it's a compact model with a self-closing lens cover), but it will keep all of your batteries, cards, and cables together.

Tip: If you can find a camera bag that doesn't *look* like a camera bag, it's less likely to be ripped off. An insulated beverage bag does nicely, for example.

• **Tripod.** Nobody likes to lug a tripod across Europe—or across town, for that matter. But if you're a serious photographer, or aspire to be one, you'll occasionally need a way to steady your camera.

A miniature tabletop tripod like the UltraPod 2 is an ideal compromise. It weighs only four ounces, costs $22, and provides solid support for your camera in a variety of situations. A quick search at *www.google.com* should help you find a mail-order company that carries it.

• **Weatherproofing.** Keep a couple of plastic bags tucked in your carrying case for use in bad weather. Digital cameras hate water, but some of nature's most dramatic shows occur at the beginning and end of storms.

• **Lens cloth.** Microfiber lens cloths are light, inexpensive (about $5), and easy to pack—and they're the best way to keep your optics sparkling clean. They look like a regular soft cloth, but they actually have thousands of microfibers that "grab" smudges off your lens and whisk them away.

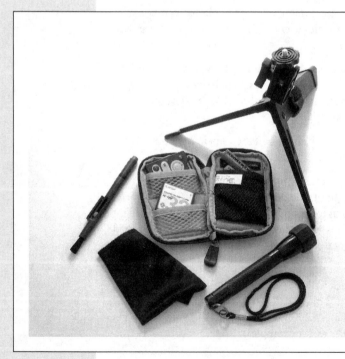

Figure 3-12:
The semi-serious travel photographer's toolkit includes, from left to right: Lens brush to whisk away dust; microfiber cloth for smudges on lens; Lowepro pouch containing remote control, spare memory card, and extra batteries; portable tripod; and flashlight.

- **Small flashlight.** Don't risk losing a great night shot just because you can't read your camera's controls. Pack a small flashlight to help you work in dim lighting situations.

The Museum Challenge

Many museums permit photography, provided you keep the flash off and don't use a full-size tripod. Digital cameras are particularly well suited to these assignments.

Once you're in, here are some techniques to consider:

- You might want to increase the "film speed" setting to 200 or 400 to better handle the dimmer interior lighting. (See page 22.)

- Museums often use halogen lightbulbs to illuminate the artwork, which could lend a red or yellow cast to your photos.

  If your particular camera automatically adjusts its color balance nicely, then no problem. But if your sample shots look too "warm" (reddish or yellowish), consider switching the camera's white-balance control to the incandescent setting (usually denoted by a lightbulb icon on the control dial).

  If that doesn't improve the pictures, adjust the camera's white balance as described on page 46 (if your camera offers this feature).

- How do you take a picture of what's in a glass display case without getting nasty reflections?

  The trick is to put the front of your lens barrel right against the glass. You'll probably have to zoom out all the way to frame the shot properly.

- Finally, hold the camera steady when shooting in museums. Because of the low lighting, your camera will probably choose a slow shutter speed, which introduces the possibility that the camera will shake, introducing blur. The steadier you hold your camera, the sharper your shots will be.

Portraits on the Road

In standard headshots, you generally want to frame the subject as tightly as possible. But when you're traveling, you want to include the background so it might suggest your location.

Unfortunately, many travelers include *too much* information about the location (see Figure 3-13). In reality, sometimes you need two shots to convey one message.

Get Creative

Picture taking should be fun while on vacation. You won't be graded on your shots; it's not a term paper to be turned in at the end of the week. So enjoy the process of shooting as much as the trip itself.

Digital cameras encourage playfulness. You can try something silly, look at it on the LCD screen, and—if it's too incriminating—erase it before anyone else discovers just *how* amateur an amateur photographer you really are. The bottom line: taking pictures should be part of your vacation.

So here are a few ideas for you to try the next time you're exploring the world:

- **Get in the picture.** Almost every digicam comes with a self-timer. Position the camera so that you have an interesting background, trip the timer, and get in the shot. It's really fun if you're with a group, too.

- **Try the close-up mode.** Almost every digital camera offers a *macro* (super-close-up) mode that lets you get within inches of your subject. The world is a very different place at this magnification. Let your imagination run wild. Everything is a potential shot, from local currency to flower petals.

- **Vary the shots.** The standard shot of your travel companions standing posed in front of the Grand Canyon is fine, but that's only the beginning. The so-called "little shots," such as your son staring out the train window, or your friend buying flowers from a street vendor, are often more compelling than the typical "stand in front of a building and smile" photo.

- **The city lights from your balcony at sunset.** There's a magic moment every day at twilight when the city lights come on right before the sun sets. Grab your camera, park it on a wall or windowsill for stability, and take a few shots.

- **Shoot from the passenger-side window.** Ask your travel companion to take the wheel as you drive along. Sitting on the passenger side of the car, roll down the window and look for interesting pictures. Don't worry about the background blurring and other little glitches, because they're often what make the pictures compelling.

- **Signs and placards instead of notes.** Museums, monuments, and national parks are all loaded with informative signs and placards. Instead of taking notes and

Figure 3-13:
Left: If you take a portrait when your subject is standing in front of the entire tower, your travel companion appears to be the size of a microbe. Instead, start by taking an establishing shot of the monument—the "postcard picture" that shows the entire structure.

Right: Then move closer to the tower and shoot the portrait of your partner in front of an element of the structure. When you show your pictures to people at home, first show the establishing shot, then show the portrait with an element of the location. It's a very effective technique.

lugging brochures, take pictures of these tidbits of information. When you put together your trip slide show in iPhoto, these will make great introductory shots for each segment.

- **Shooting through shop windows.** Storefront displays say so much about the local culture. But taking pictures through glass can be tricky, thanks to unwanted reflections. As when shooting glass display cases in museums, the trick is to zoom out, and then get the front of the lens barrel as close to the window as possible. The closer you are, the fewer reflections you'll have in your picture.

Now that you're armed with lots of ideas and techniques, you're probably getting the itch to take a vacation. When you go, don't forget your camera, a few memory cards, and plenty of battery power.

Outdoor Portraits

Everybody knows what the camera's built-in flash is for, right? It goes off automatically when there's not enough light.

Unfortunately, everybody also knows how ornery and feeble these flashes are. If you're too close to the subject, the flash blows out the picture, turning your best friend into a ghost face that looks like it was photographed during a nuclear test. If you're farther than about eight feet away, the flash is too weak to do anything useful at all.

No matter what kind of camera you have, however, you'll take your best pictures when *you* decide to use the flash, not when the camera decides. Believe it or not, the camera's automatic mode is wrong about half the time.

UP TO SPEED

Cautions on the Road

Camera-toting tourists are prime targets for thieves—and digital cameras make delicious loot. When you're on the road, keep in mind the following tips, which are designed to help you bring home more than just memories:

- Consider packing your camera gear in a backpack or a fanny pack instead of a traditional camera bag. That way, you're not walking through the streets of India with a bag that screams, "I'm an expensive camera—steal me!"

- Carry your camera bag onto the plane instead of checking it with the luggage.

- Secure the camera strap to your body when touring.

- Be wary when handing your camera to strangers for group shots. They may run away with it. Use the camera's self-timer to take pictures of yourselves—or at least use your best judgment in summing up passersby.

- Keep an eye on your equipment as you go through airport security. The best plan is to have your travel mate go through security first, then send through your collective equipment, then you go through. That way you always have someone close to your stuff.

- Don't leave your camera lying around your hotel room. If you leave it behind, put it in the room's safe.

Outdoor portraits represent a perfect example. If you leave the flash setting on "auto" when you shoot outdoors, you can guess what will happen: The camera will conclude that there's plenty of light and won't bother to fire the flash.

The camera has correctly concluded that there's enough light *in the entire frame*. But it's not smart enough to recognize that the person you're photographing is, in fact, in shadow (Figure 3-14).

Figure 3-14:
Left: The camera is reading the background, the lawn, the reflections...everything except what you really care about: the person in the foreground. As a result, your subject is underexposed and too dark.

Right: Forcing the flash solves the problem nicely.

The solution in this situation is to *force* the flash on—a very common trick. Provided you're close enough to the subject, the flash will provide enough *fill light* to balance the subject's exposure with that of the surrounding background. (If you're using your on-camera flash, stand within about eight feet of the subject so you can get enough flash for a proper exposure.)

This kind of fill flash will dramatically improve your outdoor portraits. Not only will it eliminate the silhouette effect when your subject is standing in front of a bright background, but frontal light is very flattering. It softens smile lines and wrinkles, and it puts a nice twinkle in the subject's eyes.

How do you take your flash off auto mode? Most cameras offer a couple different flash settings. Look for the icon that represents a lightning bolt with an arrow tip on the end—the universal icon for electronic flash. Generally, if you push the button next to this icon, it cycles through the flash modes on your camera. These usually include *auto flash* (no icon), *red-eye reduction* (eyeball icon), *no flash* (universal "circle with a diagonal line through it" icon) and *flash on*, and *forced flash* (stand-alone lightning bolt icon). For your outdoor portraits, cycle through the icons until you get to the forced-flash mode.

(In full automatic mode, by the way, you may not be allowed to change the flash mode. Try switching into the portrait mode first.)

Tip: If you're that rare digital photographer who owns an external flash attachment, use *it* in situations where you need a fill flash. The more powerful strobe illuminates the subject better and provides a more flexible working distance.

It's also the only way to go if your subject wears glasses. If the flash is on a dedicated cord, you can raise it a couple feet above the camera to minimize the reflection of the flash in the glasses.

Rim Lighting

Once you've experimented with fill flash, try this variation that pros use to create striking portraits: *rim lighting*.

Position the subject with her back to the sun (preferably when it's high in the sky and not shining directly into your camera lens). Now set your camera to fire the flash (the lightning bolt, not the automatic setting). If the sun is shining into the lens, block it using your hand or a lens shade.

The first thing you'll notice is that the sun creates a *rim light* around the subject's hair (Figure 3-15). You'll also notice that her eyes are more relaxed and open. In one swift move, you've made your subject more comfortable and improved your chances for a dramatic portrait.

Figure 3-15:
Remember how you were always told to have the sun at your back when taking a picture. That's not the best advice for portraits. In fact, you want the sun on the model's back to create a rim-light effect. Notice how her hair and her shoulder are highlighted? Remember to turn on your fill flash so the model's face isn't underexposed. If your camera accepts filters, try a softening filter on rim light shots; the effect can be quite pleasing.

If you were to shoot the picture right now, without the fill flash, the result would be the classic *backlit photo*. In other words, the background would be nicely exposed—but the subject would be shadowy or even silhouetted. You would join the throngs who, on a daily basis, ruin golden opportunities for great photographs.

Once again, the solution is to force the flash, creating a nice fill light.

Now take a few pictures and review your work onscreen. If your model is too bright, move back a few steps and try again. If she's too dark, move a little closer.

When it works, rim lighting creates portraits that you'll be very proud of. It's not the right technique for every situation, but sometimes it produces jaw-dropping results.

Tip: If your camera accepts filters, try a *softening filter* for your rim-lighting shots. It can reduce facial wrinkles and create a nice glow around the subject's head.

Open Shade

Working in open shade, like the shadow of a tree, produces less dramatic portraits than rim lighting, but very pleasing ones nonetheless.

The open shade eliminates harsh shadows around the face and keeps the subject from squinting. Here again, forcing the flash on your digital camera is a great idea. Look for a subtle background without distracting elements.

The beauty of this technique is that you capture an evenly lit, relaxed subject with a perfectly exposed background. You won't even notice that it was shot in the shade.

Indoor Flash

Over the years, you've probably seen plenty of indoor flash pictures that have a pitch-black background and an overexposed, practically nuked subject.

Many factors conspire to produce these stark, unflattering shots, but one of the major contributors is, once again, your camera thinking on its own. You're letting *it* decide when to turn on the flash and which shutter speed to use.

First of all, you don't always need the flash. Indoor photography offers many opportunities for stunning "existing light" portraits and moody interior shots, as described earlier. And when you do have to turn on the flash, you can make certain adjustments to preserve the ambiance of the room so that your background doesn't fall into a black hole.

Slow-Synchro Interiors

There are two reasons why your flash shots often have a pitch-black background. The first problem is that the light from a typical digital camera's flash reaches only about eight to ten feet. Anything beyond this range, and you've got yourself an inadvertent existing-light photo.

If your camera has a *manual mode* that allows you to dictate both the aperture (f-stop) and shutter speed, you can easily overcome these problems. Once in manual mode, try this combination as a starting point for flash photography indoors:

- Set your film speed to 100 (page 22).

- Set the aperture (f-stop) to f-5.6.

- Set the shutter speed to 1/15th of a second.

- Use the forced-flash mode. (*Don't* use the red-eye reduction feature.)

Now hold the camera as steady as possible. At these slow shutter speeds, your shots are more vulnerable to camera shake, and therefore to blurriness. Your flash will help freeze everything in its range—but the background, not illuminated by the flash, may blur if the camera isn't steady.

Take a shot. As you review the picture, you'll see that it looks much different than what you're accustomed to. Specifically, it has more room ambiance and background detail.

If your camera doesn't have a manual mode, all is not lost. Almost every consumer model has a setting called *nighttime* or *slow-synchro* mode. This setting is often indicated by a "stars over a mountain" icon. The intention of this mode is to shoot portraits at twilight, as described in the next section. But you can also use nighttime mode indoors to "open up" the background (Figure 3-16). Granted, you don't have as much control with this setting as you do with manual mode, but you might be pleasantly surprised with the results.

Figure 3-16:
Tired of having your flash subjects lost in a black hole of darkness? Try using what photographers call "slow-synchro flash." Set your camera's shutter speed and aperture manually to control the exposure of the background. The camera's flash will ensure the subjects are exposed properly.

Twilight Portraits

Twilight is a magic time for photographers. The setting sun bathes the landscape in a warm glow, providing a beautiful backdrop for portraits. This is an ideal time to shoot any type of shot.

First, you'll need a tripod or some other means to steady the camera. There's far less light during this time of day, and therefore the shutter slows down considerably.

Now inspect your camera's flash options. Look for an option called either *slow-synchro* or *nighttime*—a setting that synchronizes your flash with the very slow shutter. Look for a "stars and mountain" or "stars and person" icon.

Now position your model in front of the most beautiful part of the landscape and take the picture.

When you push the button, the camera opens the shutter long enough to compensate for the dim twilight lighting, capturing all of the rich, saturated colors. The flash, meanwhile, throttles down, emitting just enough light to illuminate the subject from the front.

The result can be an incredibly striking image that will make your travel pictures the talk of the office. It's a great technique when shooting somebody standing in front of illuminated monuments and buildings at night, sunsets over the ocean, and festive nighttime lighting.

Tip: If your subject is rendered too bright (overexposed by the flash), move back a few feet, zoom in, and try again. Conversely, if your subject is too dark (underexposed by the flash), move in a couple of feet.

UP TO SPEED

How to Really Get Rid of Red-Eye

For years now, camera manufacturers have been inflicting *red-eye reduction mode* on their customers. It's a series of bright, strobing flashes that's not only annoying to the people you're photographing, but it doesn't even work.

What causes red-eye? In a dimly lit room, the subject's pupil dilates, revealing more of the retina. On cameras where the flash is close to the camera lens (as it almost always is), the light from the flash shines through the dilated pupil, bounces off the retina, and reflects as a red circle directly back into the lens. (The same thing happens to animals, too, except that the color is sometimes green instead of red.)

The solution is to move the flash away from the camera lens. That way, the reflection from the retina doesn't bounce directly back at the camera. But on a camera that fits in your pocket, it's a little tough to achieve much separation of flash and lens.

Since camera makers couldn't move the flash away, they went to Plan B: firing the flash just *before* the shutter snaps, in theory contracting the subjects' pupils, thereby revealing less retina. Alas, it doesn't work very well, and you may wind up with red-eye anyway.

You have three ways out of red-eye. If you can turn up the lights, do it. If you have that rare camera that accepts an external, detachable flash, use it. And if none of that works, remember that iPhoto has its own red-eye-removal tool (page 147).

Landscape and Nature

Unlike portraiture, where *you* have to arrange the lights and the models, landscape photography demands a different discipline: patience. Nature calls the shots here. Your job is to be prepared and in position.

Shoot with Sweet Light

Photographers generally covet the first and last two hours of the day for shooting (which half explains why they're always getting up at five in the morning). The lower angle of the sun and the slightly denser atmosphere create rich, saturated tones, as well as what photographers call "sweet light."

It's a far cry from the midday sun, which creates much harsher shadows and much more severe highlights. Landscape shooting is more difficult when the sun is high overhead on a bright, cloudless day.

Layer Your Lights and Darks

Ansel Adams, the most famous American landscape photographer, looked for scenes in sweet light that had alternating light and dark areas. As you view one of these pictures from the bottom of the frame to the top, you might see light falling on the foreground, then a shadow cast by a tree, then a pool of light behind the tree, followed by more shadows from a hill, and finally an illuminated sky at the top of the composition.

A lighting situation like this creates more depth in your pictures (and, yes, lets you "shoot like Ansel").

Highlight a Foreground Object with Flash

Sometimes you can lend nature a helping hand by turning on your flash to illuminate an object in the immediate foreground. Remember, just because your eyes can see detail in the dark area at the bottom of the frame doesn't mean that your camera can. Look for an interesting object—a bush, perhaps. Move the camera close to it and zoom out. Then turn on the flash and shoot. The effect can be stunning.

Sunsets

Your camera usually does a good job of exposing the sky during sunset, even in automatic mode. Keep the flash turned off and shoot at will.

Tip: Keep an eye on your shutter speed (if your camera shows it). If it goes below 1/30th of a second, you may need a tripod or some other steady surface to prevent camera shake. Activate the self-timer or remote control to avoid jiggling the camera when you press the shutter.

The biggest mistake people make when shooting sunsets has nothing to do with the sky—it's the *ground* that ruins the shots. Your eyes can make out much more detail in the shadowy ground than your camera will. Therefore, it's not worth trying to split the frame in half, composing it with the sky above and the ground below. The bottom half of your photo will just be a murky black blob in the final image.

Instead, fill your composition with 90 percent sky and 10 percent ground or water. This arrangement may feel funny—at least until you look at your prints and see how much more dynamic they are with this composition.

Tip: Many photographers make the mistake of leaving the scene right after the sun dips below the horizon. Hang around for another 10 minutes or so; sometimes there's a truly amazing after-burst of light.

Weddings

Weddings dominate special event photography, not to mention being the primary income source for a huge percentage of professional photographers.

If you can shoot an entire wedding, then you're prepared for any other event that comes your way. For example, graduations are just weddings without the reception. Birthday parties are just weddings without the ceremony.

If you're a guest, one critical element of successful photography at a wedding is not interfering with the *hired* photographer's posed shots. Introduce yourself to the photographer and ask if it's OK to take a couple of shots right after the pro has finished each setup. You'll generally receive permission—and the opportunity to capture the highlights of the day.

Tip: As a digital photographer, you can bring a new dimension to the celebration that most pros don't even offer: immediacy. If you like, you can hook up your camera to a TV to play the pictures back while the reception is still going on. Or, thanks to iPhoto, you can have shots on the Web before the pro even gets his film to the lab. Put your favorites together and add a little music; suddenly you have a QuickTime movie for downloading.

Shots to Look For

In part, your success at shooting a wedding depends on your ability to anticipate the action. If you've been to any weddings recently, you probably know that you can expect classic photo ops like these:

- **Before the wedding.** Bride making final dress adjustments, alone in dress, with mother, with maid of honor, with bridesmaids, and so on. The groom with his best man, with his ushers, with his family.

- **During the ceremony.** The groom waiting at the altar, his parents being seated, the bride's mother being seated, the processional, the bride coming down the aisle, the vows, the ring ceremony, the kiss, the bride and groom coming back down the aisle. Oh, and of course the obligatory adorable shots of the flower girl and ring-bearer boy walking down the aisle looking dazed.

- **Directly after the ceremony.** The wedding party at the altar, the bride and groom with family, the bride and groom with officiate, close-up of the bride's and groom's hands on the ring pillow.

- **During the reception.** Guests signing the guest book, the bride dancing with groom/father/father-in-law, the groom dancing with mother/mother-in-law, the cake table, the cake cutting, the cake feeding, the toasts, the bouquet tossing, the decorated getaway car.

Tip: One of the advantages you might have over the hired photographer is that you'll *know* people at the wedding. You'll therefore have the opportunity, in theory at least, to take candid, relaxed pictures of the guests—a sure bride-and-groom pleaser.

POWER USERS' CLINIC

Built-In Flash vs. External Flash

More expensive digital cameras offer serious photographers a wonderful feature: a place to plug in an external flash attachment.

An external flash moves the light source away from the lens, which reduces red-eye, especially if the flash is on its own separate bracket rather than a hot shoe right on the camera. The external flash makes your camera's battery last longer, too, because it has its own batteries. You'll be grateful during long events like weddings.

The most versatile way to attach an external flash is with a standard hot shoe right on top of the camera, as shown here. You can either connect the flash directly, or you can use a "dedicated" flash cord that allows you to move the flash away from the camera, but still retain "communication" between the two.

Some cameras just aren't big enough to accommodate a hot shoe. To circumvent this problem, some camera makers have engineered a system that uses a tiny socket on the camera that connects to the flash via a proprietary cord

and bracket. This system isn't the height of versatility, but it does allow you the flexibility of an external flash on a very compact camera.

A wedding is one key example of a situation where you'll find this useful. When you're not the primary photographer, you won't get the prime shooting locations during big events (like the cake cutting). Therefore, you'll need all the flash power possible to get the shots even when you're out of position—another advantage of an external flash unit.

Finally, a detached flash attachment gives you more flexibility, because you can use it to bounce light off the wall or ceiling to provide fill lighting for certain shots.

A good external flash with a dedicated cord costs at least $200, and, of course, only the fancier digital cameras can accommodate them. But as you become more serious with your photographic pastime, you'll find that external flashes help you capture shots that on-camera flashes just can't get.

That's the checklist for a professional photographer, of course. If you're one of the guests, use that list only for inspiration. Wedding days provide dozens of opportunities for memorable pictures. If you get only a fraction of them, you'll still have plenty to share at the end of the day.

Photographing Objects

Most people usually photograph people and places. Every now and then, however, you'll need to photograph *things:* stuff you plan to sell on eBay, illustrations for a report, your personal belongings (for insurance purposes), and so on.

The *macro* (close-up) mode of your digital camera makes it easy to shoot objects. All you need to do is set up and light your shot; the camera does the rest.

The Home Studio

The trick to lighting any object professionally, whether it's a painting or a teapot, is to position *two* lights, each at a 45-degree angle to the plane of the subject.

At a hardware store, buy a couple of lamps. Sometimes called shop lights, they have clamps and ball joints to lock the lamp at a certain angle.

Note: Buy lamps that accommodate regular lightbulbs, not the high-powered halogen models that melt everything within 50 yards.

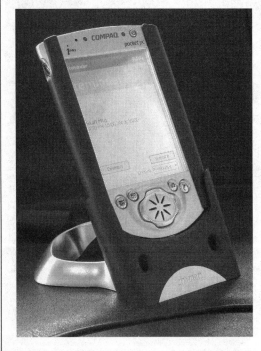

Figure 3-17:
You don't need to build a home studio to produce great product shots. This picture was created by setting a table next to a north-facing window. A piece of white cardboard was used as a reflector to "bounce" some light back into the shadow side of the object. The background: a legal-sized, leather notepad cover angled in an "L" shape to give the shot an "executive" look.

Regular 100-watt "soft light" bulbs work fine. While you're at the hardware store, look for some white *butcher paper* or some other paper that will give you a seamless background at least six feet long and four feet wide. (Camera stores also sell paper backdrops for about $30 a roll.)

Now you're ready to set up your temporary photo studio. Slide a table against the wall, then hang your butcher paper about three feet above the table. Tape it to the top surface of the table, making sure that it has a gentle curve as it goes from vertical to horizontal. Place the item that you want to photograph in the center of the table, about a foot in front of the paper curve.

Next, it's time to set up your lights. You can use chair backs to clamp your lights, which should be pointing directly at your subject at a 45-degree angle, about three feet away from the subject, pointing slightly downward.

Note: Some photographers eschew the two-light setup, preferring a bit of shadow on one side of the object. For this effect, use only one light; on the opposite side, create a reflective surface like a white piece of cardboard, aluminum foil, or white foam board. Make sure that the reflector bounces the light toward the object's non-illuminated side.

Now your subject is evenly lit, with a minimum of glare and harsh shadows. Even though this homemade product rig might not look beautiful, the shots you create with it can be very appealing (Figure 3-17).

Some other tips:

- Adjust your camera's white balance for the type of light you're using (page 46). Uncorrected incandescent lights produce an overly warm (reddish) cast; flash tends to produce images a bit on the cool (bluish) side.

- A tripod helps keep the camera in precise position.

- If your camera has a manual-focus mode, use it to lock in the focus on the object's area that's most important to you.

- Once your camera is positioned and focused, you may find its remote control or self-timer mode convenient, so you won't have to constantly bend over during the course of a long shot.

You're ready to shoot.

Natural Lighting for Objects

Of course, you won't always be at home with a bunch of lights and roll paper at your disposal. Many of your object shots will be more spontaneous, impromptu affairs, or you may decide that a home studio isn't your cup of tea. In these cases, let nature provide the lighting.

In taking natural-light shots like this, the trick is to keep your subject out of direct sunlight, which would create harsh contrast and "hot spots" on the object's surface. Instead, work in open shade, preferably in the morning or late afternoon hours when the light is the "sweetest." A north-facing window is perfect for this type of shooting.

Once again, pay close attention to the background. You might have to get creative in setting up the shot so that it has a continuous background without any distracting edges.

Finally, set the white balance controls (page 46) to the "cloudy" setting to offset the blue cast created by open shade.

Nighttime Photography

Because photography is the art and science of capturing light, you wouldn't think that nighttime would present many photo opportunities. But in fact, nighttime pictures can be the most spectacular ones in your portfolio. City lights, river lights, sky lights, and even car lights can stand out like bright colors on a black canvas.

Unfortunately, you won't get far in this kind of photography without a tripod. You can practice the following techniques by bracing the camera against a wall—but you'll find the job infinitely easier with a true tripod.

Trailing Car Lights

You've seen this shot on postcards and in magazines: neon bands of light streaking across the frame, with a nicely lit bridge or building in the background. The trick to these shots is to keep the shutter open long enough for the cars to pass all the way from one side of the frame to the other (Figure 3-18).

When using film cameras, photographers rely on something called the camera's "B" setting, in combination with a *cable release* (a shutter button on the end of a cord). The "B" setting (short for *bulb*) keeps the shutter open for as long as you hold down

---

BUYERS' GUIDE

How to Buy a Tripod

A tripod has two parts: the legs and the *pan head*. The camera attaches to the pan head, and the legs support the head.

You can buy a tripod with any of three pan head types. *Friction heads* are the simplest, least expensive, and most popular with still photographers. *Fluid heads* are desirable if you'll also be using your tripod for a camcorder, as they smooth out panning and tilting. (This means you, iMovie fans.) They're more expensive than friction heads, but are well worth the money if you're after a professional look to your footage. Finally, *geared heads* are big, heavy, expensive, and difficult to use.

The tripod's legs may be made of metal, wood, or composite. Metal is light and inexpensive, but easier to damage by accident (thin metal is easily bent). Wood and composite legs are much more expensive; they're designed for heavier professional broadcast and film equipment. The bottoms of the legs have rubber feet, which is great for use indoors and on solid floors.

Good tripods also have *spreaders* that prevent the legs from spreading apart and causing the entire apparatus to crash to the ground. If your tripod doesn't have spreaders, put the tripod on a piece of carpet, which prevents the legs from slipping apart.

the release. Many a photographer has stood out in the cold, thumbs pressing down on icy cable releases, softly counting: "One thousand one, one thousand two, one thousand three…"

Your digital camera probably doesn't have a "B" setting (although a few do have bulb modes). But you can capture these dramatic shots if your camera offers a shutter-priority mode (see Figures 3-2 and 3-3). In this mode, you can tell the camera to keep the shutter open for a long time indeed—for car-taillight photos, four seconds or more.

Tip: When preparing for nighttime shooting, pack a pocket flashlight so you can see the camera's controls in the dark.

Try to find a vantage point high enough to provide a good overview of the scene. A nicely lit building, bridge, or monument in the background provides a nice contrast to erratic lights created by the cars passing through the scene.

Put your camera on a tripod or some other steady surface, and set it in shutter-priority mode. After you've composed your shot, set the shutter for four seconds. The camera

Figure 3-18:
Don't wait until complete darkness for this type of shot, or your sky will go pitch black. Twilight is the best time to shoot streaming car lights.

will control the aperture automatically. Use your remote control, if you have one, or your camera's self-timer mode.

When you see cars coming into the scene, trip the shutter. Review the results on the LCD screen. If the streaks aren't long enough, then add a couple seconds to the shutter setting; if the streaks are too long, subtract a second or two.

With a little trial and error, you can capture beautiful, dramatic taillight shots just like the postcards you've seen for years.

Nighttime Portraits

Nighttime portraits can be extremely interesting, especially when your subject is in front of a lit monument or building.

Put your camera on a tripod or steady surface as you compose the background. The key to this shot will be opening the aperture very wide, to admit as much light as possible. You can do this in one of two ways.

Aperture-priority mode

If you can put your camera into *aperture-priority mode*, as described on page 41, set the aperture to f-2.8 or f-4.

Take a shot of just the background and review it onscreen. If it looks good, turn on your flash (fill-flash mode) and position your subject within ten feet of the camera. Ask your subject to stand still until you give the OK to move. When you take the picture, the flash will fire very briefly, but the shutter will stay open for another second or two to soak in enough light to pick up the background.

Review the results on the camera. If your subject is too bright, move the camera farther away. Move closer if the subject is too dark.

Nighttime-flash mode

If your camera doesn't have an aperture-priority mode, it might have a *nighttime-flash* mode. It's pretty much the same idea—it opens the aperture very wide—except that you can't control precisely *how* wide. The camera will attempt to properly expose the background while providing just enough additional flash for your model.

Try it. If your model is too bright or too dark, move closer or farther.

Time-Lapse Photography

Time-lapse photography is an effective way to depict a subject changing from one state of being to another: a butterfly emerging from a cocoon, the unfurling of a rose bud, and so on. Obviously, the result you want is a movie, not a still picture—but that's just fine with you. You've got a Mac, and the Mac has QuickTime.

The idea is that you'll take a picture at regular intervals—once an hour, for example. At the end of eighteen hours, you'll have eighteen images that you can upload to iPhoto for processing. (You'll also be very tired, but that's another story.)

You'll then be able to use iPhoto's Export to QuickTime command, which turns your still frames into a live-action movie at the frame rate you specify. Chapter 11 details this process.

When setting up for a time-lapse shoot, keep these things in mind:

- Use a tripod. You want every shot to have precisely the same angle, distance, and composition.

- You don't want a lot of changing background activity in your sequence of shots, since it will distract from the main subject.

- Keep the camera plugged into a wall jack (an AC adapter is an extra purchase with most camera models). Changing the batteries once the time-lapse process has begun is sure to alter the camera's original positioning.

- Focus manually (if your camera allows it) to ensure sharpness in every frame.

- Avoid the flash. Close-range flash shooting generally blows your subject into blinding white.

POWER USERS' CLINIC

Star Trails

If you *really* want to impress your friends with your budding photographic skills, try capturing *star trails*. Surely you've seen these dramatic shots: one star, located in the center of the frame, remains a point of light, but all the other stars in the universe seem to carve concentric circle segments around it, as though the galaxy were spinning dizzily.

That one fixed star, in case you were wondering, is the North Star. It remains steady as all the other stars seem to travel in a circular path around it, thanks to the rotation of the earth.

Find some place dark with a clean horizon line. If you want the ground in the shot at all, compose the frame so that the sky fills 90 percent of it, and the ground occupies the bottom 10 percent.

The setup for this shot is the same as with the taillight trails, except that you have to keep the shutter open much longer—at least fifteen seconds for very short trails as in the example here, or (if your camera can handle it) up to fifteen *minutes* for dramatic star trails. (The photo here, showing the Pleiades constellation [sometimes referred to as the Seven Sisters], was captured with a shutter speed of just a few seconds. The stars are already beginning to "trail.")

The longer the exposure, the longer the star trails, so push your camera to the limit. If the trails aren't bright enough, then increase your camera's light sensitivity by changing the film speed (page 22) to 200 or 400.

• Experiment with exposure intervals. Try one shot every fifteen minutes for one project, and then repeat the project again using 30-minute intervals. With a little trial and error, you'll find the perfect setting for your subject.

Once you've captured your sequence of shots, upload them to iPhoto. Chapter 11 has the full details about creating QuickTime movies of your slide shows. For time-lapse movies, the process is just as described there, with a few additional suggestions. They include:

• Don't crop individual photos. You want them to line up with each other in the finished movie.

POWER USERS' CLINIC

Infrared Black-and-White Photography

Black-and-white photography no longer dominates the print world as it did during the heyday of *Life* magazine, but it's still popular. Black-and-white shots impart a special artistic feeling that's often lacking in color shots.

Unfortunately, many of the tricks used by expert black-and-white artists aren't readily available to casual photographers employing digital means without a visit to high-end image editors like Photoshop. There is, however, a powerful black-and-white alternative that doesn't require an advanced degree in photo editing: *infrared* photography.

Infrared photography deals with the spectrum of light that you can't see but your digital camera can. It's an option only if your camera accepts filters—and if you're willing to buy an *infrared* filter, which eliminates the visible spectrum and captures only the infrared rays.

The first thing you'll notice in infrared photography is that the blue sky goes dark and that most trees turn very light. Glare is minimized, as you can see by the road in the before-and-after examples shown here.

The most popular filter for digicam infrared photography is the Hoya R72. If your camera accepts filters, then go to the camera store, attach the R72, and look at a brightly lit scene on the LCD screen. You'll know right away if your camera is suitable for this kind of photography.

Cameras that work well with infrared include the Nikon CoolPix 800 and 950, Canon G1 and S10, Olympus C-3000 series, and Kodak DC 260. Many others will also work. In an attempt to improve overall picture quality, some camera makers add internal filtering—but unfortunately this only disables their infrared capability. The Canon G2 and the Nikon CoolPix 990 exhibit this problem, for example, even though both their predecessors worked well for infrared black and white.

If you're lucky enough to have a camera that can capture infrared images and accept filters, then get your hands on a Hoya R72 and go have some fun. You can create some astonishing pictures that will attract lots of attention.

• Put all of the pictures into a new album.

• In iPhoto's Export to QuickTime dialog box, choose a duration for each frame along the lines of .25, .50, or 1.0 seconds.

Digital Movies

Movie making probably wasn't what you had in mind when you bought a digital *still* camera. Even so, most cameras offer this feature, and it can come in handy now and then.

Movie mode lets you capture QuickTime video, often with sound, and save it to your memory card right alongside your still pictures. Some cameras permit only 30 seconds of video per attempt; others let you keep recording until the memory card is full.

Once you've transferred the movie to your Mac, you can play it, email it to people, or post it on a Web page.

Note: iPhoto doesn't do movies. In other words, you must transfer the movie file to your Mac using whatever transfer software came with the camera. Most recent models simplify this process: When you plug their USB cable into the Mac, the camera's memory card appears on the Mac OS X desktop as though it's an external disk drive. You can just double-click it to open it. Inside, you'll find two folders: one that contains your still photos, and another that contains the movies.

If your camera doesn't appear on the desktop as a disk, you'll have to buy a USB memory-card reader, as described on page 87.

These movies have modest dimensions (typically 320 x 240 pixels), so it's best to keep your expectations low. Even so, life is filled with situations when a few frames of QuickTime are better than no movies at all.

Just keep these pointers in mind:

• **Remember your memory.** Digital movies, even these low-quality ones, fill up your memory card in seconds. Remember, you're shooting twelve or fifteen little pictures *per second.* This is 512 MB or 1 GB card territory.

• **Steady the camera.** If you don't have a tripod, put the camera strap around your neck, pull the camera outward so the strap is taut, and only then begin filming. The strap steadies the camera.

• **Don't try it in the dark.** The flash doesn't work for movies, so look for the best lighting possible before composing your shot.

Tip: If you've upgraded your copy of QuickTime to QuickTime Pro (by paying $30 and visiting the Apple Web site), you can combine several short movies into one longer one. Open movie B; choose Edit→Select All; choose Edit→Copy.

Now open movie A. Scroll to the very end, and then choose Edit→Paste.

Cameraphone Photography

There's an old photographer's saying: the best camera is the one you have with you. The day you're faced with a photo op and your multi-megapixel wonder machine is stashed in your sock drawer at home, you'll be thankful if there's a *cameraphone* in your pocket—a cellphone with a tiny, built-in lens that takes tiny, built-in pictures.

Of course, cameraphones don't have all of the whiz-bang settings that you've come to adore on your digicam, but you can still take perfectly good shots (see Figure 3-19). Here's a look at the most common cameraphone settings and how they can help you take better pictures.

- **Picture size.** This option gives you the choice between two resolution settings: large and small. (They would be more accurately labeled *small* and *smaller*, but that wouldn't fly with the marketing department.) Choose large, which is usually about 640 x 480 pixels. You can't make a very big print with these images, but they're handy for emailing.

- **Night mode.** Since most cameraphones don't have flashes, manufacturers had to figure out a way to let you take pictures indoors. What they came up with is *night mode*. Ironically, this setting doesn't work very well in darkness. But in typical indoor light, night mode is pretty good. Turn it on for all indoor photography or whenever the light is less than full sunshine.

- **Effects.** You may get a menu of oddball settings called *effects*. Here you can change from normal color photography to things like sepia, black and white, or even negative, which is perfect for that X-ray look you've been yearning for. Generally

Figure 3-19:
Cameraphones are designed for moderately close portraits. Head-and-shoulders compositions usually turn out well. But beware of super close-ups of friends and family! Those wide-angle lenses built into phones (shown at right on a Treo 600) can distort your subject, potentially resulting in estrangement from loved ones. Compose your portraits as shown at left; you'll get the shot and keep your friends.

When all looks well, hold steady and squeeze the shutter button (often the phone's Enter button, shown here on a Sony Ericsson cameraphone).

speaking, don't bother with the options in this menu; shoot your pictures in living color. You can always add an effect later in iPhoto—with much greater control.

- **Default name.** This setting, if you have it, is actually pretty handy. Instead of catchy file names like IMG_3091.jpg, you can instruct your camera to use something more friendly, such as Greece Vac 001. Just remember to change the setting once you return home, or your friends might wonder why the shot of the Golden Gate Bridge is called Greece Vac 765.

- **Self-timer.** Often considered the best way to include the photographer in family group shots, the self-timer is also a great tool for getting sharp pictures in less-than-perfect lighting. Rest the camera on any steady surface, compose the image, activate the self-timer, and press the shutter button. The camera counts for about 10 seconds and then shoots the shot. (As usual, the steadier the camera, the sharper the shot will be.)

Often, you'll want to use these settings in combination, like using night mode and a self-timer to take crisp indoor photos.

Tip: One problem with cameraphones is that there's no tripod socket. How the heck do you compose your self-timer shots without a tripod? Figure 3-20 shows one option.

You're probably not going to win any photo contests taking pictures this way. But in a pinch, at least now you know how to squeeze every drop of quality from the one camera you'll always have with you.

All that's left is figuring out how to get the pictures into iPhoto; see page 301 for that.

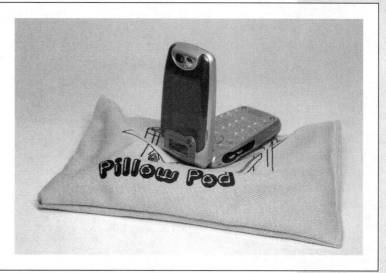

Figure 3-20:
How do you steady a camera that doesn't have a tripod socket? This beanbag chair for mobile phones is the perfect solution. For a mere $6, Porter's Camera Store (www.porters camerastore.com) will ship you a nifty solution called the Pillow Pod. It's like a beanbag chair for your cameraphone. As simple as it sounds, the Pillow Pod lets you align your phone for just the right composition when using the self-timer.

Part Two:
iPhoto Basics

2

Camera Meets Mac

The Ansel Adams part of your job is over. Your digital camera is brimming with photos. You've snapped the perfect graduation portrait, captured that jaw-dropping sunset over the Pacific, or compiled an unforgettable photo essay of your two-year-old attempting to eat a bowl of spaghetti. It's time to use your Mac to gather, organize, and tweak all these photos so that you can share them with the rest of the world.

This is the core of this book—compiling, organizing, and adjusting your pictures using iPhoto and then transforming this random collection of digital photos into a professional-looking slideshow, set of prints, movie, Web page, poster, email, desktop picture set, or bound book.

But before you start organizing and publishing these pictures using iPhoto, you need to transfer them from your camera to the Mac. This chapter shows you how to get pictures from camera to computer and introduces you to iPhoto.

iPhoto: The Application

iPhoto approaches digital photo management as a four-step process, with each step corresponding to one of the following major areas of the program:

- **Import.** Working with iPhoto begins with feeding your digital pictures into the program. During the import process, iPhoto duplicates your pictures and stores them in its Photo Library folder on the Mac's hard drive. In general, importing is literally a one-click process. This is the part of iPhoto covered in this chapter.

• **Organize.** This step is about sorting and categorizing your chaotic jumble of pictures so that you can easily find them and arrange them into logical groups. You can add searchable keywords like Vacation or Kids to make pictures easier to find. You can change the order of images, and group them into discrete "folders" called albums. Instead of having 4,300 randomly named digital photos scattered about on your three hard drives, you end up with a set of neatly categorized and immediately accessible photo collections. Chapter 5 covers all of iPhoto's organization tools.

Organize mode is also where you share your photo albums onscreen and on paper. In this part of iPhoto, you'll find nine different ways of publishing your pictures. In addition to printing pictures on your own printer (in a variety of interesting layouts and book styles), you can display images as an onscreen slideshow, turn the slideshow into a QuickTime move, order professional-quality prints or a hardback book, email them, apply one to your desktop as a desktop backdrop, select a batch to become your Mac OS X screen saver, or post them on the Web using your .Mac account. If you've already got your own Web site, you can export a collection of photos as a series of ready-to-post Web pages.

Chapters 7 through 12 explain how to undertake each of these self-publishing tasks.

• **Edit.** This is where you fine-tune your photos to make them look as good as possible. iPhoto provides the basic tools you need for rotating, retouching, resizing, cropping, or brightening your pictures. More significant image adjustments—adjusting color balance, sharpening, editing out an ex-spouse—require another image editing program. Editing your photos is the focus of Chapter 6.

• **Book.** iPhoto comes with a built-in page-layout program dedicated to a single purpose: helping you design a linen-covered, acid-free, hardback book of your photos. After you choose a book style, such as Story Book or Portfolio, iPhoto steps you through the process of laying out the photos on each page, complete with titles, captions, and page numbers. When you're done, you can either print out the book yourself, or have it professionally printed and bound using the Order Book feature described in Chapter 10.

Note: Although much of this book is focused on using digital cameras, remember this: You *don't* have to shoot digital photos in order to use iPhoto. You can just as easily use it to organize and publish pictures you've shot with a traditional film camera and digitized using a scanner (or had Kodak convert them to a Photo CD). Importing scanned photos is covered later in this chapter on page 90.

---

iPhoto 4 Requirements

According to Apple, iPhoto 4 requires a Mac that has a USB (Universal Serial Bus) port, a G3 chip or better, 256 megabytes of memory or more, and Mac OS X 10.2.6 or later.

The USB port makes it possible to connect a camera or memory card reader for direct importing of the photos. But technically, you don't need a USB port, since you can always import photos from the hard drive or a CD, as described later in this chapter.

As for processor speed and RAM: iPhoto may be among the most memory-dependent programs on your Mac. It *loves* memory. Memory is even more important to iPhoto than your Mac's processor speed. It makes the difference between tolerable speed and sluggishness, or between a 5,000-photo collection and a 30,000-photo collection. So the more memory and horsepower your Mac has, the happier you'll be.

If you intend to use iPhoto and iDVD together to create your own interactive slideshows, as described in Chapter 12, you need even more oomph: a G4 chip running at 733 MHz or faster. (That's for iDVD, of course.)

Finally, take a look at how much free hard drive space you have. You need at least 250 MB if you're installing only iPhoto 4, iMovie 4, and iTunes 4.2. If you want iDVD and GarageBand too, iLife will eat up 4.3 GB of disk space—and these numbers don't even include the room you'll need for all your photos.

Getting iPhoto

Unlike iPhoto 1 and 2, iPhoto 4 isn't a free download from Apple's Web site; in fact, it's not a download at all. It comes only with Apple's iLife package, or with a new Mac.

Some version of iPhoto has been included free on every Mac sold since January 2002. If your Mac falls into that category, you'll find iPhoto in your Applications folder.

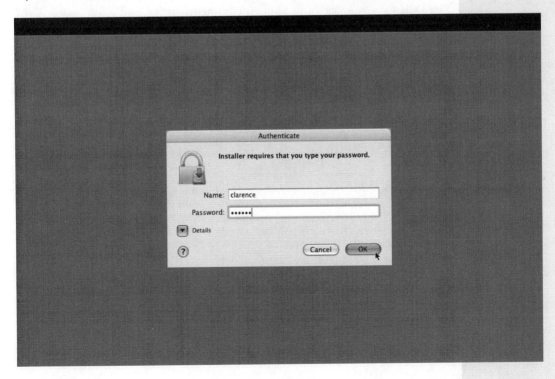

You can tell which version you have by single-clicking its icon and then choosing File→ Get Info. In the resulting info window, you'll see the version number, clear as day.

If you bought your Mac after January 2004, you probably have iPhoto 4 installed. Otherwise, it's available only as part of Apple's iLife '04 software suite—a $50 DVD that includes GarageBand, iTunes, iMovie, iPhoto, and iDVD. iLife will set you back $50 at *www.apple.com,* from mail order Web sites, or at local computer stores.

When you run the iLife installer, you're offered a choice of programs to install. Install all five programs, if you like (4.3 gigabytes of hard drive space required), or just iPhoto 4 by itself.

When the installation process is over, you'll find the iPhoto icon in your Applications folder. (In the Finder, choose Go   Applications, or press Shift-⌘-A, to open this folder.) If you're wise, you'll take a moment to drag the iPhoto icon—the little camera-superimposed-on-palm-tree-scene icon—onto your Dock, so you'll be able to open it more conveniently from now on.

Upgrading from earlier versions

If you've used an earlier version of iPhoto on your Mac, you'd be wise to make a backup of your *iPhoto Library* folder—your database of photos—before running iPhoto 4. That's because iPhoto 4's first bit of business is converting that library into a new, more efficient format that's incompatible with the earlier iPhoto (see Figure 4-1).

Ordinarily, the upgrade process is seamless: iPhoto 4 smoothly converts and displays your existing photos, comments, titles, and albums. But light-

Figure 4-1:
Top: If you're upgrading from an earlier version of iPhoto, this warning is the first thing you see when you launch iPhoto 4. Once you click the Upgrade button, there's no going back—your photo library will no longer be readable with iPhoto 1 or 2.

Bottom: If you upgrade from iPhoto 4.0 to a later version (like 4.0.1), Apple has yet another speed boost to offer you. To take advantage of it, though, you must let iPhoto study your photos and build new, faster-displaying thumbnail representations of them—a process that can take a very long time if you have a lot of pictures.

The Photo Library needs to be upgraded to work with this version of iPhoto.

Your Photo Library will not be readable by previous versions of iPhoto after the upgrade. The upgrade process may take several minutes depending on the number of photos in the library.

Quit   Upgrade

Your thumbnails need to be upgraded.

In this version of iPhoto, the small preview images, or "thumbnails," have been improved. Upgrading the thumbnails will take a while, depending on the number of photos in your library. Do you want to upgrade your thumbnails now?

Later   Upgrade

ning does strike, fuses do blow, and the technology gods have a cruel sense of humor, so having a safety copy is smart.

To perform this backup, open your Home→Pictures folder, and copy or duplicate the iPhoto Library folder. (This folder may be huge, since it contains copies of all the photos you've imported into iPhoto.) Now, if anything should go wrong with the conversion process, you'll still have a clean, uncorrupted copy of your iPhoto Library files.

Running iPhoto 4 for the First Time

Double-click the iPhoto icon to launch the program. After you dismiss the "Welcome to iPhoto" dialog box (which contains a quick recap of the program's benefits), iPhoto checks to see if you have an older version, and if so, offers to convert its photo library (Figure 4-1).

Finally, you arrive at the program's main window, the basic elements of which are shown in Figure 4-2.

Figure 4-2:
Here's what iPhoto looks like when you first open it. The large photo-viewing area is where thumbnails of your imported photos will appear. The pane at the bottom of the window changes depending on which of iPhoto's four modes you're in—Import, Organize, Edit, or Book.

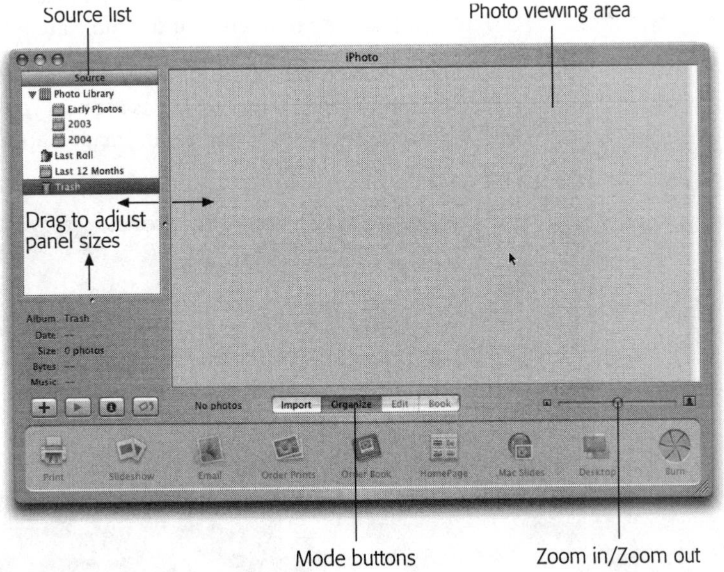

Source list

Photo viewing area

Drag to adjust panel sizes

Mode buttons

Zoom in/Zoom out

Getting Your Pictures into iPhoto

With iPhoto installed and ready to run, it's time for you to import your own pictures into the program—a process that's remarkably easy, especially if your photos are going directly from your camera's memory card into iPhoto.

Of course, if you've been taking digital photos for some time, you probably have a lot of photo files already crammed into folders on your hard drive or on Zip disks or

CDs. If you shoot pictures with a traditional film camera and use a scanner to digitize them, you've probably got piles of JPEG or TIFF images stashed away on disk already, waiting to be cataloged using iPhoto.

This section explains how to transfer files from each of these sources into iPhoto itself.

Connecting with a USB Camera

Every modern digital camera can connect to a Mac using the USB port. If your Mac has more than one USB jack, you can use any of them for your digital camera.

Plugging a USB-compatible camera into your Mac is the easiest way to transfer pictures from your camera into iPhoto. The whole process practically happens by itself.

1. **With your camera turned off, plug it into one of your Mac's USB jacks.**

   To make this camera-to-Mac USB connection, you need what is usually called an *A-to-B* USB cable; your camera probably came with one. The "A" end—the part you plug into your camera—has a small, flat-bottomed plug whose shape varies by manufacturer. The Mac end of the cable has a larger, flatter, rectangular, standard USB plug. Make sure both ends of the cable are plugged in firmly.

   iPhoto doesn't have to be running when you make this connection. The program opens itself and springs into action as soon as you switch on the camera (unless you've changed the factory settings in Image Capture, a little program that sits in your Applications folder).

FREQUENTLY ASKED QUESTION

Is My Camera iPhoto-Friendly?

How can I tell if my digital camera is compatible with iPhoto?

The official answer is: Check Apple's compatibility list. Go to *www.apple.com/iphoto/compatibility*, where you'll find a list of every camera, memory card reader, and printer that Apple has tried with iPhoto. The list includes every recent camera model from Canon, Fuji, Hewlett-Packard, Kodak, Nikon, Casio, Olympus, Sony, Minolta, and others.

If your camera *isn't* on the list, however, don't despair; the list is by no means all-inclusive. Almost any camera released *after* iPhoto works with iPhoto, whether or not it appears on the list. In short, the list includes only camera models that Apple's engineers have personally tested—not every camera on earth that works with iPhoto.

If you have an older, pre-2002 model that *truly* doesn't work with iPhoto, all is not lost. You can always move photos from camera to computer yourself, using whatever software came with the camera—and then *drag* them into iPhoto.

Alternatively, you can load photos into the Mac using a memory card reader that *is* iPhoto compatible (under $30; see page 87). Some professionals prefer this method anyway, because it saves the camera's battery power. (Of course, this tactic doesn't work for camera models that store photos in built-in memory in addition to, or instead of, a removable memory card.)

In other words, as long as your digital photos end up in one of the dozen or so file formats that iPhoto understands, you can use iPhoto—regardless of the make and model of your camera.

Note: If this is the first time you've ever run iPhoto, it asks if you *always* want it to run when you plug in the camera. If you value your time, say yes.

2. Turn on the camera.

If iPhoto is running, it immediately detects that there are new photos available for download and gets ready to import them. If iPhoto isn't running, your Mac is smart enough to detect the presence of the connected camera and launch iPhoto.

Note: There's no danger in plugging in your camera while it's turned on; it's just that the Mac doesn't recognize certain camera models until their power comes on. If, for some reason, iPhoto doesn't "see" your camera after you connect it and turn it on, try turning the camera off, then on again, while it's plugged in.

You can tell whether iPhoto is ready to do its job by checking the information area at the bottom panel, as shown in Figure 4-3. You should see the name of your camera, along with a status line indicating how many pictures iPhoto has detected on it. (The number may be somewhat larger than you expect if you forgot to erase your last batch of photos.)

Figure 4-3:
Top: If you forgot to erase some pictures the last time you imported them to the Mac, iPhoto 4 is smart enough to notice—and to spare you the effort of downloading the duplicate shots.

Bottom: iPhoto keeps you well informed of its progress as it copies and catalogs each of your photos. The tiny preview window in the middle of the status panel at the bottom of the iPhoto window displays a thumbnail of the picture currently being imported. The progress bar beside the preview window counts down the remaining items to be imported.

3. **Turn on the "Erase camera contents after transfer" checkbox, if you like.**

Think about this one for a moment. It's the one big decision you have to make when importing your photos. If you turn on "Erase camera contents after transfer," iPhoto will automatically delete all photos from your camera's memory card once they're safely on the Mac.

The advantage of using this option is that your camera's memory card is instantly and effortlessly wiped clean, making it ready for you to fill with more pictures.

Of course, iPhoto isn't supposed to delete your pictures until *after* it has successfully copied them all to the Photo Library. However, it's not beyond the realm of possibility that a hard disk could fail during an iPhoto import, or that a file could get corrupted when copied, thereby becoming unopenable. If you want to play it safe, leave the "Erase camera contents after transfer" option turned off.

UP TO SPEED

The Memory Card's Back Door

When you connect an older digital camera to the Mac, its memory card shows up as a disk icon at the upper-right corner of your desktop, as shown here.

Newer cameras don't show up this way—but you can get the same effect by inserting your memory card into a card reader attached to your Mac.

Inside the disk window, you'll generally find several folders, each cryptically named by the camera's software. One of them contains your photos; another may contain movies.

Opening this "disk" icon is one way to *selectively* delete or copy photos from the card. (If you do that, though, eject and reconnect the camera before importing into iPhoto, to avoid thoroughly confusing the software.)

Finding the folder that contains the memory card's photos also offers you the chance to copy photos *from* your hard drive *to* your camera—just drag them to the "disk" icon in the Finder.

Finally, more Mac fans are getting into the fun of capturing digital movies with their digital still cameras—but wondering how they're supposed to transfer these movies to the Mac. (iPhoto doesn't muddy up its hands with that job; it handles only still photos.)

Now you know the answer: just open the memory card "disk," find the folder that contains the movie files (they usually bear the file name suffix .AVI or .MOV), and drag them onto your Mac.

The downside of having your card icon show up is that you have to eject it manually after importing your photos into iPhoto. You can drag it to the Trash, Control-click it and choose Eject, click its Eject icon in the Sidebar (Mac OS X 10.3 or later), or use any other disk-ejecting tactic.

P.S.—If your camera *doesn't* show up as an icon, you can always open the Image Capture program in your Applications folder. It's capable of selectively deleting or importing photos and can also import your digital movies.

Then, after you've confirmed that all of your photos have been copied into the iPhoto Library folder, you can use the camera's own command to erase its memory card.

4. **Click the Import button.**

If you chose the auto-erase feature, you'll see a final "Confirm Move" dialog box, affording you one last chance to back out of that decision. Click Delete Originals if you're sure you want the camera erased after the transfer, or Keep Originals if you want iPhoto to import *copies* of them, leaving the originals on the camera.

In any case, iPhoto swings into action, copying each photo from your camera to your hard drive.

The program also creates a *thumbnail* of each picture—a tiny, low-resolution version that appears, like a slide on a slide sorter, in the iPhoto window.

Tip: If you're *not* in the habit of using the "Erase camera contents" option, you may occasionally see the "Import duplicates?" message shown at the top in Figure 4-3. iPhoto notices the arrival of duplicates and offers you the option of downloading them again, resulting in duplicates on your Mac, or ignoring them and importing only the *new* photos from your camera. The latter option can save you a lot of time.

When the process is over, your freshly imported photos will be on display in the main iPhoto window, awaiting your organizational talents.

If your camera is fairly old, you may now have to "eject" the camera's memory card, as described in the box on the facing page. That is, switch to the Finder (pressing ⌘-H is a quick way to hide the iPhoto window momentarily), and then drag the "disk" icon, if you have one, to the Trash. If you fail to do this, then unplugging the camera will produce a nasty onscreen scolding that says, "In the future, please put away the device before removing the device."

5. **Turn off the camera, and then unplug it from the USB cable.**

You're ready to start having fun with your new pictures (page 92).

USB Card Readers

A USB *memory card reader* offers another great way to transfer photos from the camera to iPhoto. Most of these card readers, which look like tiny disk drives, are under $30; some can read more than one kind of memory card.

Instead of connecting the camera to a cable, card-reader owners transfer their photos by removing the camera's memory card and inserting it into the reader, which they leave connected to the Mac all the time. iPhoto recognizes the reader as though it's a camera and offers to import (and erase) the photos, just as described on the previous pages.

This method offers several advantages over the USB-cable method. First, it eliminates the considerable battery drain involved in pumping the photos straight off the camera. Second, it's less hassle to pull a memory card out of your camera and slip it into your card reader (which is always plugged in) than it is to constantly plug and unplug camera cables. Finally, this method lets you use almost *any* digital camera with iPhoto, even those too old to include a USB cable connector.

Tip: iPhoto doesn't recognize most *camcorders,* even though most models can take still pictures. Many camcorders store their stills on a memory card just as digital cameras do, so a memory card reader is exactly what you need to get those pictures into iPhoto.

Connecting with a USB-compatible memory card reader is almost identical to connecting a camera. Here's how:

1. **Pop a memory card out of your camera and insert it into the reader.**

   Of course, the card reader should already be plugged into the Mac's USB jack.

   As when you connect a camera, iPhoto acknowledges the presence of the memory card reader in its status panel and reports the number of images it finds. As described on page 86, you can turn on the "Erase contents after transfer" checkbox if you want iPhoto to automatically clear the memory card after copying the files to your Mac.

2. **Click Import.**

   iPhoto swings into action, copying the photos off the card.

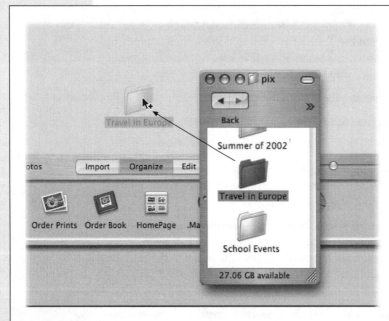

Figure 4-5:
When you drop a folder into iPhoto, the program automatically scans all the folders inside it, looking for pictures to catalog. It creates a new film roll (Chapter 5) for each folder it finds. iPhoto ignores irrelevant files and stores only the pictures that are in a format it can read.

3. **Switch to the Finder. Eject the memory card's icon from the desktop as you would a CD (drag it to the Trash, for example), and then remove the card from the reader.**

Put it back into the camera, so it's ready for more action.

Importing Photos from Non-USB Cameras

If your camera doesn't have a USB connection *and* you don't have a memory card reader, you're still not out of luck.

First, copy the photos from your camera/memory card onto your hard drive (or other disk) using whatever software or hardware came with your camera. Then bring them into iPhoto using one of these two methods:

• Drag the files directly into the main iPhoto window, which automatically starts the import process. You can also drop an entire *folder* of images into iPhoto to import the contents of the whole folder, as shown in Figure 4-5.

Tip: Take the time to name your folders intelligently before dragging them into iPhoto, because the program retains their names. If you drag a folder directly into the main photo area, you get a new *film roll* named for the folder (page 101); if you drag the folder into the album list at the left side of the screen, you get a new *album* named for the folder. And if there are folders *inside* folders, they, too, become new film rolls and albums. Details on all this are in Chapter 5.

• Choose File→Import (or press Shift-⌘-I) in iPhoto and select a file or folder in the Open dialog box (Figure 4-6).

Tip: If your camera or memory card appears on the Mac desktop like any other removable disk, you can also drag its photo icons, folder icons, or even the "disk" icon itself directly into iPhoto.

Figure 4-6:
When the Import dialog box appears, navigate to and select any graphics files you want to bring into iPhoto. You can ⌘-click individual graphics to select more than one simultaneously, as shown here. You can also click one, then Shift-click another one, to highlight both files and *everything in the list in between.*

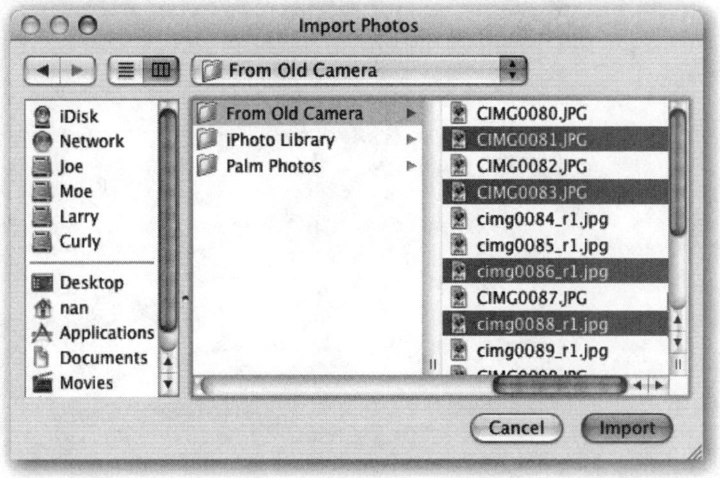

Importing Existing Graphics Files

If you've already got digital photos—or any other kinds of graphics files—stored somewhere on your computer, the easiest way to import them into iPhoto is simply to drag their icons into the main iPhoto window (as described previously), or by using the File→Import command (Figure 4-6).

You can also select and import files from CD-ROMs, DVDs, Jaz or Zip disks, or other disks on the network. If your photos are on a Kodak Photo CD, you can insert the CD (with iPhoto already running) and then click the Import button on the Import pane, just as if you were importing photos from a connected camera. As always, iPhoto makes fresh copies of the files you import, storing them in one centralized photo repository (the iPhoto Library folder) on your hard drive. The program also creates thumbnail versions of each image for display in the main iPhoto window.

Through this process and all other importing processes, remember this: iPhoto *never* moves a file, whether from a memory card or disk. It only copies it.

The File Format Factor

iPhoto can't import digital pictures unless it understands their file format, but that rarely poses a problem. Just about every digital camera on earth saves photos as either JPEG or TIFF files—and iPhoto handles both of these image formats beautifully.

Beware, though, that some of the better digital cameras include an option for saving images in a nonstandard file format that's unique to the camera manufacturer. Kodak, Olympus, and Nikon cameras, for example, can all save images in what's called RAW format, which iPhoto can't read. If you're planning on bringing digital photos straight into iPhoto for editing and organizing, make sure your camera settings have been configured to save photos as JPEGs or TIFFs (as explained in Chapter 2). Otherwise, you'll have to convert the RAW files into JPEG or TIFF files using the camera maker's software.

UP TO SPEED

JPEG and TIFF

Most digital cameras capture photos in a graphics-file format called JPEG. That's the world's most popular file format for photos, because even though it's compressed to take up a *lot* less disk space, the visual quality is still very high.

Some cameras offer you the chance to leave your photos *uncompressed* on the camera, in what's called TIFF format. These files are huge—you'll be lucky if you can fit *one* TIFF file on the memory card that came with the camera—but retain 100 percent of the picture's original quality. (You'd be hard-pressed to detect the quality loss in a JPEG file, but technically speaking, there is some.)

iPhoto recognizes both kinds of files when you import them. (For that matter, iPhoto can also import graphics files in BMP, GIF, MacPaint, PICT, PNG, Photoshop, SGI, Targa, and FlashPix formats, as described later in this chapter.)

Note, however, that the instant you *edit* a TIFF-format photo (Chapter 6), iPhoto converts it into JPEG.

That's fine if you plan to order prints or a hardback book (Chapter 10) from iPhoto, since JPEG files are required for those purposes. But if you took that once-in-a-lifetime, priceless shot as a TIFF file, don't do any editing (even rotating) in iPhoto if you hope to maintain its perfect, pristine quality.

Of course, iPhoto also lets you load pictures that have been saved in a number of other file formats, too—including a few unusual ones. They include:

- **GIF** is the most common format used for non-photographic images on Web pages. The borders, backgrounds, and logos you typically encounter on Web sites are usually GIF files—as well as 98 percent of those blinking, flashing banner ads that drive you insane.

- **PNG** and **FlashPix** are also used in Web design, though not nearly as often as JPEG and GIF. They often display more complex graphic elements.

- **BMP** is a popular graphics file format in Windows.

- **PICT** was the original graphics file format of the Macintosh prior to Mac OS X. When you take a screenshot in Mac OS 9, paste a picture from the Clipboard, or copy an image from the Scrapbook, you're using a PICT file.

- **Photoshop** refers to Adobe Photoshop, the world's most popular image editing and photo-retouching program. iPhoto can even recognize and import *layered* Photoshop files—those in which different image adjustments or graphic elements are stored in sandwiched-together layers.

- **MacPaint** is the ancient file format of MacPaint, Apple's very first graphics program from the mid-1980s. No, you probably won't be working with any MacPaint files in iPhoto. But isn't it nice to know that, if one of these old, black-and-white 8 x 10 pictures, generated on a vintage Mac SE, happens to slip through a wormhole in the fabric of time and land on your desk, you'll be ready?

- **SGI** and **Targa** are specialized graphics formats used on high-end Silicon Graphics workstations and Truevision video-editing systems.

- **PDF** files are Portable Document Format files that open up in Preview or Acrobat Reader, like a user manual, brochure, or Read Me file that you downloaded or re-

---

WORKAROUND WORKSHOP

Import vs. Import

There's plenty about iPhoto that is remarkably straightforward and intuitive—but not the Import command.

There are, in fact, two Import commands: One is a menu command (File→Import) and the other is a big pulsating button in the lower-right corner of the Import screen. They don't do the same thing.

The Import *button* is strictly for importing photos from digital cameras and memory card readers. In fact, if iPhoto doesn't detect the presence of a camera, card reader, or Kodak

Photo CD or Picture CD, the Import button is dimmed out and can't do a thing.

The Import command in the File menu is only for importing digital photos already on disk. Use this command to import photos stored on your hard drive or on disks such as CDs and Jaz disks.

You can effectively ignore the File→Import command, though, since simply dropping the files or folders you want to import into the main iPhoto window accomplishes exactly the same thing.

---

ceived on a CD. Apple doesn't publicize the fact that iPhoto can import PDF files, maybe because iPhoto displays only the first page of multipage documents. (Most of the PDFs you come across probably aren't photos; they're usually multipage documents filled with both text and graphics.)

Note: Most digital photos you work with are probably JPEG files–but they're not always *called* JPEG files. You may also see JPEG referred to as *JFIF* (JPEG File Interchange Format). Bottom line: The terms JPEG, JFIF, JPEG JFIF, and JPEG 2000 all mean the same thing.

If you try to import a file that iPhoto doesn't understand, you see the message shown in Figure 4-7.

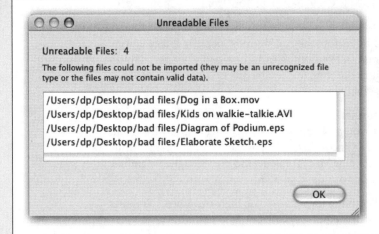

Figure 4-7:
Here's iPhoto's way of telling you that you just tried to feed it a file that it can't digest: an EPS file, an Adobe Illustrator drawing, QuickTime movie, or PowerPoint file, for example.

Of course, you can always open up an EPS or PostScript file in your Preview program, and then export it into a more iPhoto-friendly format from there.

The Post-Dump Slideshow

Once you've imported a batch of pictures into iPhoto, what's the first thing you want to do? If you're like most people, this is the first opportunity you have to see, at full size, the masterpieces you and your camera came up with.

In iPhoto 4, a glorious new feature awaits you: a slideshow with the tools you need to perform an initial screen of the new pictures—like deleting the baddies, rotating the sideways ones, and identifying the best ones with star ratings.

To begin the slideshow, click the Last Roll icon in the Source list at the left side of the screen to identify which pictures you want to look over.

Note: On a freshly installed copy of iPhoto, this icon is labeled Last Roll. If you've fiddled with the iPhoto preference settings, it may say, for example, "Last 2 Rolls" or "Last 3 Rolls," and your slideshow will include more than the most recent batch of photos. If that's not what you want to see, just click the actual photo that you want to begin the slideshow (in the main viewing area).

Now click the Play triangle underneath the Source list. iPhoto fades out of view, and a big, brilliant, full-screen slideshow of the new photos begins, accompanied by music.

You can read more about slideshows in general in Chapter 7. What's useful here, though, is the new iPhoto 4 control bar shown in Figure 4-8. You make it appear by wiggling your mouse as the show begins.

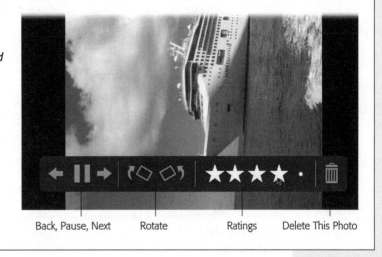

Figure 4-8:
As the slideshow progresses, you can pause the show, go backward, rotate a photo, delete a bad shot, or apply your star rating to a picture, all courtesy of this new control bar.

If you'd rather have it visible during all slideshows of this album or roll, click the Slideshow button at the bottom of the screen—in regular iPhoto, not during a slideshow—and turn on "Display slideshow controls."

Back, Pause, Next   Rotate   Ratings   Delete This Photo

As you can see by the figure, this is the perfect opportunity to throw away lousy shots, fix the rotation, and linger on certain photos for more study—all without interrupting the slideshow. You can even apply a rating by clicking the appropriate star in the band of five; later, you can use these ratings to sort your pictures or create *smart albums*. See Chapter 5 for full detail on rating stars and smart albums.

Here's the full list of things you can do when the onscreen control bar is visible:

- Click the Play/Pause button to start and halt the slideshow. The space bar toggles these controls—and the control bar doesn't have to be visible when you press it.

- Click the left and right arrows to browse back and forth through your photos. The left and right arrow keys on your keyboard do the same thing.

- Press the up or down arrow keys on your keyboard to make the slides appear faster or slower.

- Click the rotation icons to flip photos clockwise or counterclockwise, 90 degrees at a time.

- Click one of the five dots to apply a rating in stars, from one at the left to five all the way at the right. Or use the number keys at the top of the keyboard or on the numeric keypad: press 3 to give a picture three stars, for example.

• Click the Trash can icon to delete a photo from the album you're viewing (but not from the Photo Library). Or simply hit Delete (or Del) on your keyboard.

Tip: There are keyboard shortcuts for all of these functions, too, that don't even require the control bar to be on the screen. See page 170.

Click the mouse anywhere off the control bar to end the slideshow.

This onscreen control bar is a welcome addition in iPhoto 4. In the days of iPhoto 2 and earlier, you had to end the slideshow every time you wanted to delete or rotate a photo, then start the show all over again.

Where iPhoto Keeps Your Files

Having dumped your vast collection of digital photos—from a camera, memory card, hard disk, or anywhere else—into iPhoto, you may find yourself wondering, "Where's iPhoto putting all those files, anyway?"

Most people slog through life, eyes to the road, without ever knowing the answer. After all, you can preview, open, edit, rotate, copy, export, and print all your photos right in iPhoto, without actually opening a folder or double-clicking a single JPEG file.

Even so, it's worthwhile to know where iPhoto keeps your pictures on the hard drive. Armed with this information, you can keep those valuable files backed up and avoid accidentally throwing them away six months from now when you're cleaning up your hard drive.

A Trip to the Library

Whenever you import pictures into iPhoto, the program makes *copies* of your photos, always leaving your original files untouched.

• When you import from a camera, iPhoto leaves the photos right where they are on its memory card (unless you use the "Erase" option).

FREQUENTLY ASKED QUESTION

Moving the iPhoto Library

Do I have to keep my photos in the iPhoto Library folder? What if I want them stored somewhere else?

No problemo! iPhoto has come a long way since the days when it could keep track of photos only if they were in its own folder structure within the iPhoto Library folder.

Just quit iPhoto. Then move the *whole* iPhoto Library folder (currently in your Home→Pictures folder) to another location—even onto another hard drive.

Then open iPhoto again. It will proclaim that it can't find your iPhoto Library folder. Click the Find Library button to show the program where you put the folder. Done deal!

- When you import from the hard drive, iPhoto leaves the originals in whichever folders they're in. As a result, transferring photos from your hard drive into iPhoto *more than doubles* the amount of disk space they take up. In other words, importing 1 GB of photos requires an additional 1 GB of disk space, because you'll end up with two copies of each file—the original, and iPhoto's copy of the photo. In addition, iPhoto creates a separate thumbnail version of each picture, consuming about another 10 K to 20 K per photo.

iPhoto stores its copies of your pictures in a special folder called iPhoto Library, which you can find in your Home→Pictures folder. (To find your Home folder, begin in the Finder and choose Go→Home.) If the short name you use to log into Mac OS X is *mozart,* the full path to your iPhoto Library folder from the main hard drive window would be Macintosh HD→Users→mozart→Pictures→iPhoto Library.

Tip: You should back up this iPhoto Library folder regularly—using the Burn command to save it onto a CD or DVD, for example. After all, it contains all the photos you import into iPhoto—essentially, your entire photography collection. Chapter 14 offers much more on this file management topic.

What all those numbers mean

Within the iPhoto Library folder, you'll find a set of mysteriously numbered files and folders. At first glance, this setup may look bizarre, but there's a method to iPhoto's madness. It turns out that iPhoto meticulously arranges your photos within these numbered folders according to the *creation dates* of the originals, as explained in Figure 4-9.

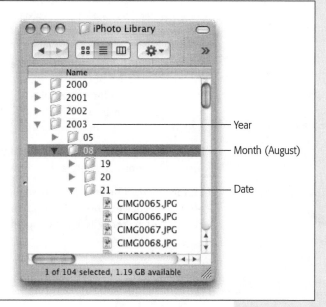

Figure 4-9:
Behold the mysteries of the iPhoto Library. Once you know the secret, this seemingly cryptic folder structure actually makes sense, with all the photos in the library organized by their creation date.

At the top level are the year folders—2004, 2003, and so on. Within those folders are subfolders for each month (01 for January, 02 for February, and so on), and nested within those are subfolders labeled for each day of each month. So a photo that was originally taken on August 21, 2003, is stored in iPhoto Library→ 2003→08→21.

Other folders in the iPhoto Library

In addition to the numbered folders, you'll find several other items nested in the iPhoto Library folder, most of which you can ignore:

- **AlbumData.xml.** Here's where iPhoto stores access permissions for the various *photo albums* you've created within iPhoto. (Albums, which are like folders for organizing photos, are described in Chapter 5.) For example, it's where iPhoto keeps information on which albums are available for sharing across the network (or among accounts on a single machine). Details on sharing are in Chapter 14.

- **Albums folder.** Inside the Albums folder you'll find a set of folders and preference files corresponding to the albums you've made.

   You won't find any actual photo files inside these album folders—only *aliases* that point back to the photos stored elsewhere in the iPhoto Library folder.

- **Data folder.** The iPhoto Library→Data folder contains iPhoto's for-internal-use-only documents. They store information about your Photo Library, such as which keywords you've used.

   But there's also a Data folder inside each year/month/date folder, right alongside your JPEG photo files. Inside this Data folder, numbered files correspond to the photos in your library. These text files are where iPhoto stores the image dimensions, file size, rating, and modification date for each photo.

Note: You might notice that the two Data files (38 and 38.attr, for example) don't correspond to the names of the JPEG photo files themselves (IMG_0023, for example). That's because the photo bears its original file name, but the Data files are given a numeric sequence—234, 235, and so on—based on the order in which they were imported. This file-naming convention is strictly for iPhoto's internal use; you never see these numeric file names within iPhoto.

- **Desktop, Screen Effect.** You'll see these folders only if you've clicked the Desktop or .Mac Slides buttons in iPhoto to turn your photos into desktop pictures (Chapter 13) or online slideshows (Chapter 9). iPhoto keeps track of which photos you've chosen to use with these features by stashing aliases of them in these folders.

- **iDVD.** iPhoto uses this folder for temporary storage of the files it creates while turning your pictures into a slideshow on DVD, as described in Chapter 12.

- **Library.cache, Library.data.** These files are the keys to iPhoto 4's drastically improved speed. They help iPhoto memorize the condition of your current iPhoto library, which greatly accelerates opening iPhoto and scrolling through the photos.

Folders inside the year/month/date folders

A few mysterious icons appear inside each year/month/date photo folder, too, right alongside your JPEG photo files. They include:

- **Thumbs folder.** Here, iPhoto stores the small thumbnail versions of the pictures in your Photo Library—the "slides" that actually appear in the iPhoto window.

  These images are numbered according to the importing sequence, as described in the previous Note.

- **Originals folder.** Some photo folders may contain an Originals folder. It doesn't appear until you use one of iPhoto's editing tools (Chapter 6) to touch up a photo. The Originals folder is the key to one of iPhoto's most remarkable features: the Revert to Original command.

  Before it applies any potentially destructive operations to your photos—like cropping, red-eye removal, brightening, black-and-white conversion—iPhoto *duplicates* the files and stuffs pristine, unedited copies of them in the Originals folder. If you later decide to scrap your changes to a photo using the Revert to Original command—even months or years later—iPhoto moves the unedited file back into its original location, returning your photo to its originally imported state.

Note: Don't confuse the files in the Originals folders with your *true* originals—the files on your hard drive, camera, or memory card that you first imported into iPhoto. As mentioned earlier, iPhoto *never* touches those originals; they stay exactly where they were when you imported them.

Look, don't touch

While it's enlightening to wander through the iPhoto Library folder to see how iPhoto keeps itself organized, don't rename or move any of the folders or files in it. Making such changes will confuse iPhoto to the point where it will either be unable to display some of your photos or will just crash.

The Digital Shoebox

I f you've imported your photos into iPhoto using any of the methods described in the previous chapter, you should now see a neatly arranged grid of thumbnails in iPhoto's main photo viewing area. You're looking at what iPhoto refers to as your *Photo Library*—your entire photo collection, including every last picture you've ever imported. This is the digital equivalent of that old shoebox you've had stuffed in the closet for the last ten years, brimming with snapshots waiting to be sorted and sifted, often never to be seen again.

You're not really organized yet, but at least all your photos are in one place. Your journey out of chaos has begun. From here, you can sort your photos, give them titles, group them into smaller sub-collections (called *albums*) and tag them with keywords so you'll be able to find them quickly. This chapter helps you tackle each of those organizing tasks as painlessly as possible.

The Source List

Even before you start naming your photos, assigning them keywords, or organizing them into albums, iPhoto imposes an order of its own on your digital shoebox.

The key to understanding it is the *Source list* at the left side of the iPhoto window. This list will grow as you import more pictures and organize them—but right off the bat, you'll find icons like Photo Library, Last 12 Months, and Last Roll.

Photo Library
The very first icon in the Source list is called Photo Library. This is a very reassuring little icon, because no matter how confused you may get in working with subsets of

photos later in your iPhoto life, clicking Photo Library takes you back to your entire picture collection. It makes *all* of your photos appear in the viewing area.

Photo Library by Year

In previous versions of iPhoto, the Photo Library was nice enough, although it got a bit unwieldy if you had 2,000 pictures in it (the rough maximum of iPhoto 2). But now that iPhoto can easily handle 25,000 photos, Apple realized that people needed some way to break down this tidal wave of pixels.

Enter the year icons, shown in Figure 5-1. When you click the Photo Library "flippy triangle," iPhoto's Source list now shows small yellow calendar icons, one for each year going back to 2001 (and a catch-all for earlier images).

When you import your entire digital photo collection (or upgrade from an earlier version of iPhoto), the program files each photo by the date you took it. You can click Photo Library to see all your photos amassed in one window, or click, say, the 2003 icon to see just the ones you took in that year.

The year icons are also very helpful when you're trying to put together an iPhoto slideshow or pinpoint one certain photo. After all, you usually can remember what year you took a vacation or when someone's birthday was. The year icons help you narrow down your search without having to scroll through your entire Photo Library.

Photo Library by Month

iPhoto 4 also adds to the Source list the Last 12 Months icon. It's the same idea as the calendar-year icons, except that it puts the most recent photos at your fingertips. The

UP TO SPEED

The Four Faces of iPhoto

iPhoto 4 operates in four different modes: Import, Organize, Edit, and Book. (The original iPhoto program had an extra mode called Share, but those features have since been folded into the Organize mode.) In the previous chapter, you worked in Import mode, bringing your raw digital photos from camera, disk, card, or hard drive into iPhoto's library.

In this chapter, you'll be working in Organize mode, which provides access to iPhoto's various photo-sharing tools and gives you an overview of all the pictures that make up your photo library.

When working in iPhoto, it's important that you're in the right mode for the task at hand—otherwise you may not have access to the iPhoto features that you need.

Here's how to tell what mode the program is in:

- Look at the four mode buttons in the middle of the iPhoto window. The highlighted button indicates the current mode.

- Look at the bottom pane of the iPhoto window, which changes with each mode. In Import mode, for example, the bottom pane displays information about the files you're importing. In Organize mode, the pane contains the buttons you click to publish, print, or share your pictures.

The four mode buttons let you switch from mode to mode at any time. If you're not in Organize mode and you need to be, just click the Organize button to switch over.

| Import | Organize | Edit | Book |

idea, of course, is that most of the time, the freshest photos are the most interesting to you.

Actually, it doesn't even have to say "Last 12 Months." You can specify how many months' worth of photos appear in this heap—anywhere from one month to a year and a half—by choosing iPhoto→Preferences (see Figure 5-1) and going to the General panel. This feature is the ideal way to find the pictures from this past Christmas, photos from your kid's most recent birthday, or wedding pictures from your most recent marriage.

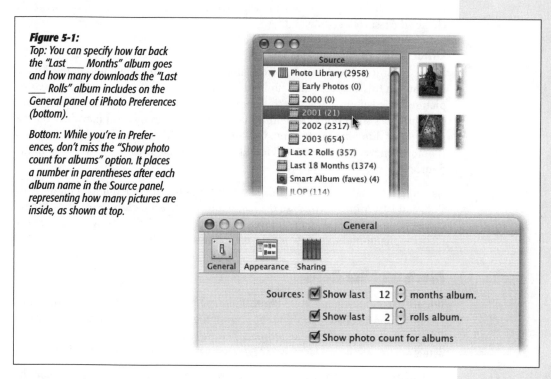

Figure 5-1:
Top: You can specify how far back the "Last ___ Months" album goes and how many downloads the "Last ___ Rolls" album includes on the General panel of iPhoto Preferences (bottom).

Bottom: While you're in Preferences, don't miss the "Show photo count for albums" option. It places a number in parentheses after each album name in the Source panel, representing how many pictures are inside, as shown at top.

Last Roll

Each time you import a new set of photos into iPhoto—whether from your hard drive, a camera, or a memory card—that batch of imported photos constitutes one *film roll*.

Of course, there's no real film in digital photography, and your pictures aren't on a "roll" of anything. But if you think about it, the metaphor makes sense. Just as in traditional photography, where each batch of photos you shoot is captured on a discrete roll of film, in iPhoto, each separate batch of photos you download into the program gets classified as its own film roll.

Most of the time, you'll probably work with the photos that you just downloaded from your camera. Conveniently, iPhoto always keeps track of your most recently added film roll, so you can view its contents without a lot of scrolling.

That's the purpose of the roll-of-film icon called Last Roll in the Source list. With one click, iPhoto displays only your most recent photos, hiding all the others. This feature can save you a lot of time, especially as your Photo Library grows.

In fact, iPhoto 4 lets you specify how *many* film rolls you want listed here; choose iPhoto→Preferences and click the General icon (see Figure 5-1). Simply change the number where it says "Show last __ rolls album." (In the unlikely event that you don't find this icon useful, you can also hide it entirely by turning off the corresponding checkbox.) For example, if you've just gotten back from a three-day Disney World trip, you probably want to see your last *three* imports all at once. In that case, you'd change the last rolls setting to *3*.

Other Icons in the Source List

Library, year icons, and Last Roll icons aren't the only items you'll find in the Source list. Later in this chapter, you'll find out how to create your own arbitrary subsets of pictures called albums. Later in this book, you'll find out how to swipe photos from other people's collections via iPhoto sharing. And later in life, you may discover the geeky joy of dumping photos onto CDs or DVDs—and then loading them back into iPhoto whenever you darned well feel like it. CD and DVD icons can show up in the Source list, too.

As you go, though, remember this key point: Photos in your iPhoto Library, Last Roll, and Last Months icons are the *real* photos. Delete a picture from one of these three collections, and it's gone forever. (That's not true of albums, which store only aliases—phantom duplicates—of the real photos.)

More on Film Rolls

iPhoto starts out sorting your Photo Library by film roll, meaning that the most recently imported batch of photos appears at the bottom of the window. Your main iPhoto window may look like a broad, featureless expanse of pictures, but they're actually in a clear order. Here are a few ways you can change this sort order:

- To change the sort order to reflect the *creation* date of the photos (rather than the date they were imported), choose View→Arrange Photos→by Date.

FREQUENTLY ASKED QUESTION

Your Own Personal Sorting Order

I don't want my photos sorted by creation date or import date—I want to put them in my own order. I tried using View→Arrange Photos→Manually, but the command is dimmed out! Did Apple accidentally forget to turn this on?

No, the command works—but only in an *album*, not in the main Photo Library. If you create a new photo album (as explained later in this chapter) and fill it with photos, you can then drag them into any order you want.

- To view photos sorted alphabetically by their *names*, choose View→Arrange Photos→by Title. (Titles are described on page 112.)

- In a new iPhoto 4 twist, you can sort your pictures by rating, so that your masterpieces are at the top of the window, with the losers way down below. Choose View→Arrange Photos→by Rating. (See page 118 for the full story on ratings.)

- Whether you choose to sort photos by film roll or date, you can *reverse* the sort order so that the most recent items appear at the *top* of the iPhoto window instead of the bottom—an idea that can save you a lot of scrolling through thumbnails. Choose iPhoto→Preferences, go to the Appearance panel, turn on "Place most recent photos at the top," and close the Preferences window. (If you choose this preference in conjunction with the By Title viewing option mentioned in the previous paragraph, your photos appear in *reverse* alphabetical order.)

Tip: If you drag a *folder* of photos into iPhoto, the name of the folder becomes the name of the film roll, so it pays to bring photos into iPhoto from intelligently named folders. In fact, if you import a series of nested folders containing photos, each individual folder of images gets grouped together as its own separately named film roll. By contrast, if you drag a group of individual files into iPhoto, the group gets a generic label like "Roll 45."

Displaying film rolls

If you choose View→Arrange Photos→by Film Roll, iPhoto returns to sorting your photos by film roll, even if you had previously chosen to sort the photos by rating, title, or date. (The Film Roll option in the View menu is dimmed when you're looking at an album or the Last 12 Months collection.)

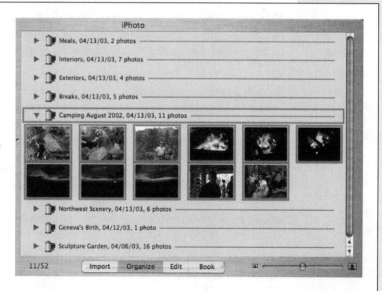

Figure 5-2:
This tidy arrangement is the fastest way to use iPhoto. Display the photos grouped by film roll, and then hide the photo batches you're not working with. Click the triangle beside each header to expand or collapse the film roll, just like a folder in the Finder's list view. Not that the header for each roll lists the date that you imported this batch, along with a count of the pictures in the roll. If you dragged a folder of files into iPhoto—or if you named the roll once the pictures were imported—the film-roll header also lists the name of the enclosing folder.

Tip: To hide or show the film roll dividers, just choose View→Film Rolls. Better yet, use the keyboard shortcut Shift-⌘-F. (The presence or absence of the dividers doesn't affect the sorting order.) You can see these film-roll dividers in Figure 5-2.

You'll probably find this arrangement so convenient that you'll leave it on permanently. As your Photo Library grows, these groupings become excellent visual and mnemonic aids to help you locate a certain photo—sometimes even months or years after the fact.

Furthermore, as your Photo Library becomes ever more massive, you may need to rely on these film-roll groupings just for your sanity: By collapsing the "flippy triangles" next to the groups you're not looking at right now (Figure 5-2), you speed up iPhoto considerably. Otherwise, iPhoto may grind almost to a halt as it tries to scroll through ever more photos. (About 25,000 pictures is its realistic limit for everyday Macs.)

Tip: Click anywhere on the film row divider line—on the film roll's name, for example—to simultaneously select all the photos in a film roll.

Even if you opt not to display the film roll divider lines in the photo viewing area, you can still *sort* the pictures in your Photo Library by film roll. Just choose View→ Arrange Photos→by Film Roll. You won't be able to see where one film roll ends and the next begins, but the photos will be in the right order.

Creating film rolls manually

Film rolls are such a convenient way of organizing your pictures that in iPhoto 4, Apple has given you a radical new feature: You can create film rolls manually, out of any pictures you choose.

This feature violates the sanctity of the original film roll concept—that each importing batch is one film roll, and that *albums* are what you use for arbitrary groupings. Still, in this case, usefulness trumps concept—and that's a good thing.

You just select any bunch of pictures in your Photo Library (using any of the techniques described on page 106), then choose File→New Film Roll From Selection. iPhoto creates and highlights the new roll, like any normal film roll (see Figure 5-2 for an example). iPhoto gives the newborn roll a generic name like "Roll 54" or whatever number it's up to, but you can always rename it, as described on page 105.

Tip: You can *merge* film rolls using this technique, too. Just select photos in two or more existing film rolls before choosing File→New Film Roll From Selection. iPhoto responds by removing the pictures from their existing film rolls, and moving them into a new, unified one. (If you selected all the photos in a couple of film rolls, the original film rolls disappear entirely.) The power and utility of this tactic will become more and more attractive the more you work with big photo collections.

And speaking of cool film-roll tips: You can move any photo into another film roll just by dragging it onto the film roll's row heading!

Renaming and dating film rolls

iPhoto ordinarily labels each film roll with either a roll number (if you imported individual files from a camera or disk) or a folder name (if you imported a folder of photos). In either case, you can easily change the name of the film roll to something more descriptive.

To edit the name of a roll, click the little roll-of-film icon in the film roll divider line. Now the Title text box at the lower-left edge of the window identifies the roll's current name. Just type a new name into this box—ideally, something that helps you remember the batch of photos at a glance.

Using this same technique, you can also change the *date* that appears in the film roll header. This date usually identifies when you imported the photos, but for most purposes, that date is relatively irrelevant. What you probably care more about is the day or month that the photos were actually *taken*.

Once again, start by the clicking roll-of-film icon in the film roll divider. This time, type a new date in the Date text box on the Info pane. You can type the date in a variety of formats—*4 September 2004, September 4, 2004,* and *4/9/04* all work—but you must use a complete date, including day, month, and year. If you don't, iPhoto will take a guess, filling in the missing information for you—and sometimes getting it wrong.

Tip: Another great way to redate a bunch of pictures at once is to use iPhoto 4's new batch processing feature, described on page 114.

Working with Your Photos

All right: You've gotten the hang of the Source list, the Photo Library, and film rolls. Enough learning about iPhoto; it's time to start *using* iPhoto.

Scrolling Through Your Photos

Browsing, selecting, and opening photos is straightforward. Here's everything you need to know:

- Use the vertical scroll bar to navigate through your thumbnails.

Tip: If your photos scroll by too fast for you to find the ones you want, try using iPhoto's Slow Scroll mode. Hold down the Option key while dragging the scroll box in the scroll bar. You get a much slower, smoother scroll, making it easier to navigate to a specific row of thumbnails.

- Scrolling can take awhile if you have a lot of images in your Photo Library, especially if you haven't collapsed the film rolls you're not using, as described earlier. But you can use this standard Mac OS X trick for faster navigation: Instead of dragging the scroll box or clicking the scroll bar arrows, *Option-click* the portion of the scroll bar that corresponds to the location you want in your Photo Library. If you want to jump to the bottom of the Photo Library, Option-click near the bottom of the scroll bar. To find photos in the middle of your collection, Option-click the middle portion of the scroll bar, and so on.

Note: By turning on "Scroll to here" in the General panel of your System Preferences, you can make this the standard behavior for Mac OS X scroll bars—that is, you won't need the Option key.

- Press your Page Up and Page Down keys to scroll one screenful at a time

- Press Home to jump to the very top of the photo collection, or End to leap to the bottom.

- To create the most expansive photo viewing area possible, you can temporarily hide the Source list at the left side of the window. To do so, drag the divider bar (between the Source list and the main photo viewing area) all the way to the left edge of the window. You've just hidden the Source list.

  To reveal that panel again, grab the left edge of the iPhoto window and drag it to the right.

Tip: You can speed up iPhoto's scrolling by turning off the Drop Shadow option in the Appearance section of iPhoto's Preferences window.

Size Control

You can make the thumbnails in iPhoto grow or shrink using the Size Control slider (on the right side of the iPhoto window, just under the photo viewing area). Drag the slider all the way to the left, and you get micro-thumbnails so small that you can fit 200 or more of them in the iPhoto window. If you drag it all the way to the right, you end up with such large thumbnails that you can see only one picture at a time.

Tip: You don't have to *drag* the Size Control slider; just click anywhere along the controller bar to make the slider jump to a new setting. Using this technique, you can instantly change the size of thumbnails from large to small, for example, by clicking once at the left end of the controller.

By the way, you might notice that this Size Control slider performs different functions, depending on what mode iPhoto is in. In Organize mode, it controls the size of thumbnails; in Edit mode, it zooms in and out of an individual image; and in Book mode (Chapter 10), it magnifies or shrinks a single page.

Tip: You may want to adopt a conservative dragging approach when using the size slider, because iPhoto may respond slowly in enlarging or shrinking the photos. Drag in small movements so the program can keep pace with you.

Selecting Photos

To highlight a single picture in preparation for printing, opening, duplicating, or deleting, click the icon once with the mouse.

That much may seem obvious. But many first-time Mac users have no idea how to manipulate *more* than one icon at a time—an essential survival skill.

To highlight multiple photos in preparation for deleting, moving, duplicating, printing, and so on, use one of these techniques:

- **To highlight all the photos.** Select all the pictures in the set you're viewing by pressing ⌘-A (the equivalent of the Edit→Select All command).

- **To highlight several photos by dragging.** You can drag diagonally to highlight a group of nearby photos, as shown in Figure 5-3. You don't even have to enclose the thumbnails completely; your cursor can touch any part of any icon to highlight it. In fact, if you keep dragging past the edge of the window, iPhoto scrolls the window automatically.

Tip: If you include a particular thumbnail in your dragged group by mistake, ⌘-click it to remove it from the selected cluster.

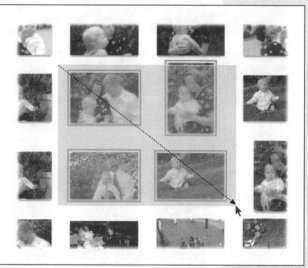

Figure 5-3:
You can highlight several photos simultaneously by dragging a box around them. To do so, start from somewhere outside of the target photos and drag diagonally across them, creating a whitish enclosure rectangle as you go. Any photos touched by this rectangle are selected when you release the mouse.

- **To highlight consecutive photos.** Click the first thumbnail you want to highlight, and then Shift-click the last one. All the files in between are automatically selected, along with the two photos you clicked (Figure 5-4, top). This trick mirrors the way Shift-clicking works in a word processor, the Finder, and many other kinds of programs.

- **To highlight random photos.** If you want to highlight only, for example, the first, third, and seventh photos in a window, start by clicking photo icon No. 1. Then ⌘-click each of the others. Each thumbnail sprouts a colored border to indicate that you've selected it (Figure 5-4, bottom).

If you're highlighting a long string of photos and then click one by mistake, you don't have to start over. Instead, just ⌘-click it again, and the dark highlighting disappears. (If you do want to start over from the beginning, just deselect all selected photos by clicking any empty part of the window.)

The ⌘ key trick is especially handy if you want to select *almost* all the photos in a window. Press ⌘-A to select everything in the folder, then ⌘-click any unwanted photos to deselect them.

Tip: You can also combine the ⌘-clicking business with the Shift-clicking trick. For instance, you could click the first photo, then Shift-click the tenth, to highlight the first ten—and then ⌘-click photos 2, 5, and 9 to *remove* them from the selection.

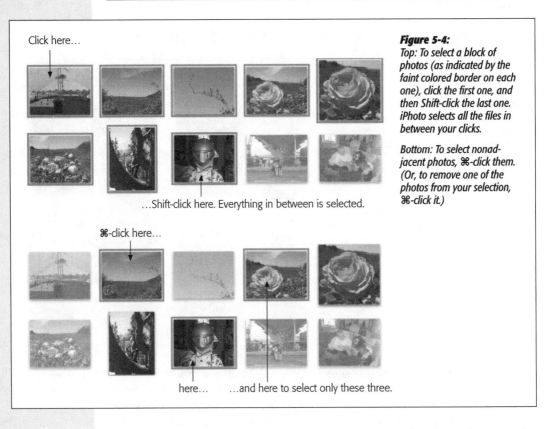

Click here…

…Shift-click here. Everything in between is selected.

⌘-click here…

here…   …and here to select only these three.

Figure 5-4:
Top: To select a block of photos (as indicated by the faint colored border on each one), click the first one, and then Shift-click the last one. iPhoto selects all the files in between your clicks.

Bottom: To select nonadjacent photos, ⌘-click them. (Or, to remove one of the photos from your selection, ⌘-click it.)

Once you've highlighted multiple photos, you can manipulate them all at once. For example, you can drag them en masse out of the window and onto your desktop—a quick way to export them. (Actually, drag them onto a *folder* in the Finder to avoid spraying their icons all over your desktop.) Or you can drag them into an album at the left side of the iPhoto window. Just drag any *one* of the highlighted photos; all other highlighted thumbnails go along for the ride.

In addition, when multiple photos are selected, the commands in the File and Edit menus—such as Duplicate, Print, and Revert To Original—apply to all of them simultaneously.

Opening Photos

iPhoto wouldn't be a terribly useful program if it let you view only postage-stamp versions of your photos (unless, of course, your photos happen to *be* pictures of postage stamps). Fortunately, iPhoto lets you open photos at full size, zoom in on details, and even conduct some basic editing to make them look better. (Editing photos is covered blow-by-blow in the next chapter.)

The easiest way to open a photo is simply to double-click a thumbnail. Unless you've changed iPhoto's settings, the photo opens in the main iPhoto window, scaled to fit into the viewing area.

This is the way most people start out opening pictures using iPhoto, and there's nothing technically wrong with this method. But it does have several drawbacks:

- You can have only one picture open at a time this way.

- Pictures opened by double-clicking are always scaled to fit within the iPhoto window, even if that means scaling them *upward,* over 100 percent of their actual size. As a result, smaller pictures wind up pixellated and distorted as they're stretched to fill the whole window.

   Worse, at this point, there's no way to zoom *out.* You can zoom in further, but you can't reduce the magnification.

- You have no way of knowing if your photo *has* been scaled to fit in the window, since iPhoto doesn't display the magnification level it's using. You can't tell if you're looking at a small photo displayed at 100 percent, or a gigantic photo that's been scaled down to 26 percent.

- Double-clicking a thumbnail catapults you directly into iPhoto's *Edit mode,* hiding all your other thumbnails and transforming the lower panel in the iPhoto window into the Edit pane, with its various cropping, red-eye removal, and color changing tools. That's great if you're ready to start editing photos. But if you opened the picture simply because you wanted to see it at full size, you now have to click the Organize button (just under the photo viewing area), or double-click the big picture, to return to Organize mode so you can view and sort photos.

The better way to open photos

You can avoid all of these problems by using iPhoto's much smarter, but less obvious, method of opening photos: Open each picture *in its own window.*

There are two ways to do this:

- Go to iPhoto→Preferences and change the photo-opening setting. On the General panel, select the "Opens in separate window" button. Then close the window.

Tip: Pressing Option *reverses* whichever choice you make here. That is, if you've chosen "Opens in Edit view" in the Preferences window, then *Option*-double-clicking a thumbnail opens the photo into a separate window instead. Conversely, if you've chosen "Opens in separate window," Option-double-clicking a thumbnail overrides your choice and opens it into the main iPhoto viewing area.

(Option-double-clicking has no effect if you've selected the third Preferences option, "Opens in other," which is described in Chapter 6.)

- Control-click the photo. Choose "Edit in separate window" from the shortcut menu.

When a photo opens in its own window, all kinds of control and flexibility await you. First, you can scale it up *or* down simply by making the window larger or smaller (by dragging its lower-right corner). You can close an open photo from the keyboard by pressing ⌘-W. And best of all, you can open multiple pictures and look at them side by side, as shown in Figure 5-5.

Figure 5-5:
When you open photos in their own windows, you can you look at several at the same time—a critical feature when comparing similar shots. And you can keep your other thumbnails in view, allowing you to easily open additional photos without closing the open ones. Note that the title bar tells you which magnification level iPhoto's using to display each photo.

Another way to zoom

As mentioned earlier, one way to change the magnification level of a photo opened in its own window is to change the size of the window itself. Enlarge the window to zoom in; shrink it to zoom out.

But you can make a window only so big by dragging its corner before you run out of screen, or so tiny before it just can't be shrunk any further. Therefore, to take advantage of iPhoto's full zoom range (5 to 400 percent), you need to use the Zoom *buttons*.

Zoom buttons? Where? They're on iPhoto's *Edit toolbar,* which may be hidden. If you don't see it, make sure you've opened a photo in its own window, and then click the capsule-shaped button in the upper-right corner of the window. You'll find the

Zoom buttons on the left side of the toolbar, as shown in Figure 5-6. (There's much more about using and customizing the Edit toolbar in Chapter 6.)

These buttons let you use iPhoto's full zooming power, regardless of the size of your monitor or the size of your photos.

Tip: Once you've zoomed in, you can ⌘-drag inside the photo area to scroll in any direction. That's more direct than fussing with two independent scroll bars.

Figure 5-6:
Once you've revealed the Edit Toolbar, you can increase or reduce the magnification of photos by using the Zoom buttons on the left. The increments of magnification become progressively smaller with each button-click as you zoom out, and progressively larger as you zoom in.

One interesting phenomenon: Using the Zoom buttons disables iPhoto's zoom-by-changing-the-window-size feature (until you close the photo window and reopen it).

Zoom where you want to zoom

Normally, when you use any of iPhoto's zooming tools—either the Zoom slider in the main iPhoto window or the Zoom buttons in a separate window—iPhoto zooms in toward the *center* of the photo. If you want to view a portion of the photo that's not near the center, you have to scroll to it after zooming.

Here's a way to tell iPhoto exactly which part of a picture you want to blow up, so that you don't have to do any scrolling at all: drag diagonally across the part of the picture you want to enlarge, as shown in Figure 5-7. As you drag out your rectangular target area, the parts of the photo outside the target temporarily dim.

With your target defined, you're ready to zoom. Drag the Zoom slider in the main iPhoto window or click the Zoom button in the Edit toolbar. As iPhoto zooms in on the photo, it automatically steers toward your target rectangle, positioning that part of the photo toward the center of the window.

Tip: If you've equipped your Mac with a mouse that has a scroll wheel on the top, you can scroll images up and down while zoomed in on them by turning that wheel. To scroll the zoomed area *horizontally,* press Shift while turning.

Figure 5-7:
To zoom into a specific portion of a photo, first define your target by dragging out a rectangle with the mouse (top left). Then, when you use any of the standard zooming tools, iPhoto puts your target in the center (lower right), so you can home in on exactly the details you want to see with scrolling.

Titles, Dates, and Comments

Just below the Source list, at the left side of the iPhoto window, you'll find a display of basic information about all the photos in your collection. The information displayed in this Info pane changes depending on what you've selected in the photo viewing area (see Figure 5-8).

Tip: If you don't see the photo information described here, you may have the Info pane hidden. Click the ⓘ button in the main iPhoto window to reveal the info. Click it twice to reveal the Comments field described on page 113.

• When a single photo is selected, iPhoto displays that picture's creation date, dimensions (in pixels), and file size. Beneath that you'll see the name of the Music track that will play when the currently selected Photo Library or album presents a slideshow (see Chapter 7).

• When multiple photos are selected, you see the *range* of their creation dates, plus how many are selected and how much disk space those photos occupy.

- When no photos are selected, the Info area displays the total number of pictures in your Photo Library, the grand total file size of your library, and a range of creation dates taking in *all* your photos. This last statistic is really pretty cool, in that it amounts to a running stopwatch that measures the span of your interest in digital photography (as of the iPhoto era, anyway).

Tip: The file size info can be extremely useful when creating backups, copying photos to another disk, or burning CDs. One glance at the Info panel—with no photos selected—tells you exactly how much disk space you'll need to fit your entire collection.

For each photo in your collection, iPhoto displays two other important chunks of information, both of which you can directly edit right in the Info pane: the Title and Comments.

Photo Titles

Every photo that you import into iPhoto receives a title, a unique name that's used to identify the picture within iPhoto. When importing files from your hard drive, iPhoto assigns titles based on those files' names. But if you're loading photos directly from your digital camera, the names of your files are probably useless numeric tags like CRS000321.JPG, CRS000322.JPG, and so on.

By all means, change these titles to something more meaningful. Just select a thumbnail, click in the Title field (just under that Source list), and type in a new title, as shown in Figure 5-8.

Creating meaningful titles isn't just useful for keeping track of photos within iPhoto. Later, when you publish your digital albums online (Chapter 9) or in print (Chapter 10), iPhoto will use these names as titles on your Web and book pages.

Figure 5-8:
You can make a photo's title as long as you want—but it's smart to keep it short (about ten characters or so). This way, you can see all or most of the title in the Title field (or under the thumbnails, if you turn on the Title checkbox, as explained later in this chapter).

Changing titles en masse

The trouble with naming your photos is that hardly anybody takes the time. Are you really going to sit there and make up individual names for 25,000 photos?

Mercifully, iPhoto 4 now lets you change the names of your photos all at once, thanks to a new "batch processing" command. No, each photo won't have a unique, descriptive name, but at least they can have titles like *Spring Vacation 2* and *Spring Vacation 3* instead of *IMG_1345* and *IMG_1346*.

To use it, choose Photos→Batch Change, or Control-click some selected photos and choose Batch Change from the shortcut menu. The Batch Change sheet drops down from the top of the window (see Figure 5-9).

Tip: Don't be fooled by the command name Batch Change. Photo 4 still can't *edit* a batch of photos. You can't, for example, scale them all down to 640 x 480 pixels, or apply the Enhance filter to all of them at once.

Your options, in the Batch Change pop-up menus, are:

- **Empty.** Set the titles to "empty" if you want to un-name the selected photos, so that they're all blank. You might appreciate this option when, for example, you're working on a photo book (Chapter 10) and you've opted for titles to appear with each photo, but you really want only a few pictures to show up with names under them.

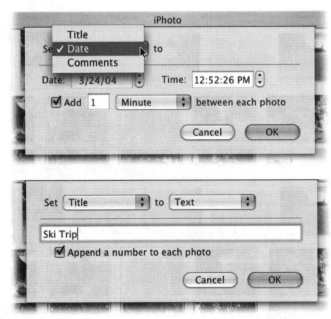

Figure 5-9:
iPhoto 4's new batch processing feature lets you specify Titles, Dates, and Comments for any number of photos you select.

Top: When you assign a date and time to a batch of pictures, turn on "Add ___ minute between each photo" to give each a unique time stamp, which could come in handy later when you're sorting them. Besides, you didn't take them all at the exact same moment, did you?

Bottom: When you title a batch of pictures, turn on "Append a number to each photo" to number them in sequence as well.

- **Text.** This option gives you an empty text box into which you can type, for example, *Ski Trip.* When you click OK, iPhoto names all of the selected pictures to match.

   If you turn on "Append a number to each photo," iPhoto adds digits after whatever base name you choose—for example, *Ski Trip 1, Ski Trip 2,* and so on.

- **Roll Info.** Choose this command to name all the selected photos after the roll's name—"Grand Canyon 2004," for example. iPhoto automatically adds the photo number after this base name.

- **Filename.** If you've been fooling around with naming your photos, and now decide that you want their original, camera-blessed file names to return (IMG_1345 and so on), use this command.

- **Date/Time.** Here's another approach: Name each photo for the exact time it was taken. The dialog box gives you a wide variety of formatting options: long date, short date, time of day, and so on.

Tip: Once you've gone to the trouble of naming your photos, remember that you can make these names appear right beneath the thumbnails for convenient reference. Choose View→Titles to make it so.

Photo Dates

When you select a single photo, you can actually *change* its creation date by editing the Info pane's Date field. You can switch the date from the day the digital file was created to the day the photo was actually taken, for example.

In fact, you can also use the Batch Change command to rewrite history, resetting the dates of a group of photos all at once, as shown in Figure 5-9.

(We trust you won't use this feature for nefarious ends, such as "proving" to the jury that you were actually in Disney World on the day of the office robbery.)

Comments

Sometimes you need more than a one- or two-word title to describe the contents of a photo, an album, or a film roll. If you want to add a lengthier description, you can type it in the Comments field in the Photo Info pane, as shown in Figure 5-10. (If you don't see the Comments field, click the 🔵 button—twice, if necessary—to bring it into view.) Even if you don't write full-blown captions for your pictures, you can use the Comments field to store little details such as the names, places, dates, and events associated with your photos.

The best thing about adding comments is that they're searchable. After you've entered all this free-form data, you can use it to quickly locate a photo using iPhoto's search command.

Tip: If you speak a non-English language, iPhoto 4 just made your life easier. As you're typing comments, you can choose Edit→Special Characters. Mac OS X's Character Palette opens, where you can add international letters like É, ø, and ß. Of course, it's also great for classic phrases like "I ♥ my cat."

Adding comments to photos, albums, or film rolls

To add a comment to a photo, select it, and then click in the Comments field. Keep the following in mind as you squirrel away all those bits and scraps of photo information:

- You don't have to *type* to enter data into the Comments field. You can paste information in using the standard Paste command, or even drag selected text from another program (like Microsoft Word) right into the Comments box.

- If you feel the need to be verbose, go for it; the Comments box holds thousands of words. Careful, though: The field has no scroll bars, so there's a limit as to how much of what you paste or type you'll actually be able to see.

Note: You can't even scroll the Comments box by pressing the arrow keys until the insertion point bumps the top or bottom edge of the box, forcing it to scroll. Even dragging with the mouse all the way to the top or bottom of the box doesn't work. If you've got a lot to say, your best bet is to make the box taller and the Source list wider, as described next.

- You can resize the Comments box by making the Info pane larger, as shown in Figure 5-10. Grab the divider bar above the Title field and drag upward to heighten the Info panel (and the Source list correspondingly shorter). You can also drag the bar between the Source list and the photo viewing area to the right, to widen the Info pane.

- If no photos, or several photos, are selected, the notes you type into the Comments box get attached to the current *album*, rather than to the pictures.

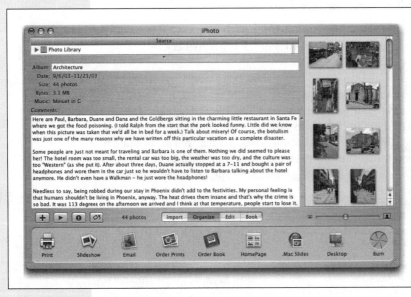

Figure 5-10:
Got a picture that's worth a thousand words? The Comments field can handle it. But you'll have to make iPhoto's Info pane pretty large to see all 1,000 words. By dragging the bars dividing the Info pane, Source list, and photo viewing area, you can adjust the amount of space each takes up in the iPhoto window. In this example, the Info pane dominates the view, with the Album pane and viewing area squished to the edges.

- You can add the same comment to a group of photos using iPhoto 4's Batch Change command. For example, ⌘-click all the pictures of your soccer team, choose Edit→ Batch Change, choose Comments from the first pop-up menu, and type a list of your teammates' names in the Comments field. Years later, you'll have a quick reminder of everyone's name.

You can just as easily add comments for an album (click it in the Source list, making sure that no individual photos are selected) or a film roll whose name you've highlighted.

Comments as captions

While the Comments field is useful for storing little scraps of background information about your photos, you can also use it to store the *captions* that you want to appear with your photos when you publish them. In fact, some of the book layouts included with iPhoto's book-creation tools (Chapter 10) automatically use the text in the Comments field to generate a caption for each photo.

(On the other hand, you don't *have* to use the Comments box text as your captions. You can always add different captions when you're editing the book.)

The Photo Info Window

The small Info pane in the main iPhoto window displays only the most basic information about your photos: title, date, and size. For more detailed information, use the Show Info command. It opens the Photo Info window, where iPhoto displays a surprisingly broad dossier of details about your photo: the make and model of the digital camera used to take it, for example, and even exposure details like the f-stop, shutter speed, and flash settings.

To open the Photo Info window (Figure 5-11), select a thumbnail and then choose File→Show Photo Info (or press ⌘-I). (If more than one photo is selected, you'll get only a bunch of dashes in the info window.)

The Photo Info window contains two tabs: Photo and Exposure. The Photo panel contains information about the image file itself—when it was originally created, when it was first imported, and when it was last modified. If the image was shot with a digital camera (as opposed to being scanned or imported from disk), the make and model of the camera appear at the bottom of the window (see Figure 5-11).

Tip: Comparing the details on the Exposure panel with the advice in Chapters 2 and 3 can be eye-opening. For example, if you put your camera into its automatic mode and take a few pictures, this is a great way to find out—and learn from—the shutter and lighting settings the camera used.

How on earth does iPhoto know so much about how your photos were taken? Most digital cameras embed a wealth of image, camera, lens, and exposure information in the photo files they create, using a standard data format called *EXIF* (Exchangeable Image Format). iPhoto automatically scans photos for EXIF data as it imports them.

Note: Some cameras do a better job than others at embedding EXIF data in photo files. iPhoto can extract this information only if it has been properly stored by the camera when the digital photo is created. Of course, most (if not all) of this information is missing altogether if your photos didn't come from a digital camera (if they were scanned in, for example).

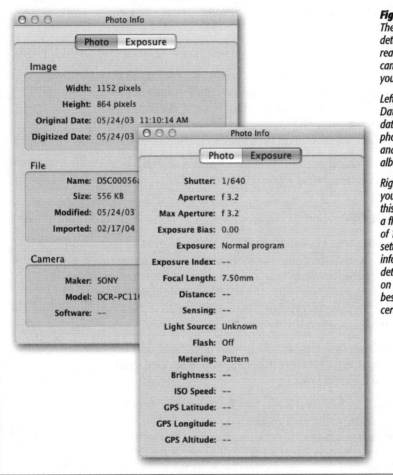

Figure 5-11:
The Photo Info window reports details about your photos by reading the EXIF tags that your camera secretly embeds in your files.

Left: iPhoto uses the Original Date (or lacking that, Modified date) information to sort your photos in the Photo Library and place them in the year albums.

Right: On the Exposure panel, you can tell at a glance that this photo was shot without a flash, at a shutter speed of 1/640, and with an f-stop setting of 3.2. Tracking this information can be useful in determining which settings on your camera produce the best-quality digital photos in a certain set of conditions.

Rate Your Photos

iPhoto 4 offers a great new way to categorize your pictures—by how great they are. You can assign each picture a rating of 1 to 5 stars, then use the ratings to sort your Photo Library (page 102), or gather only the cream of the crop into a slideshow (Chapter 7), smart album (page 127), or photo book (Chapter 10).

Here are the ways you can rate your digital masterpieces:

- In Edit or Organize mode, select a photo (or several) and choose Photo→My Rating; from the submenu, choose one through five stars.

Tip: If the top of the screen is just too far away, you can also Control-click any one of the selected thumbnails (or, in Edit mode, anywhere on the photo) and choose the My Rating command from the shortcut menu. Its submenu is exactly the same as what you'd find in the Photo→My Rating command.

- In Edit or Organize mode, select a photo (or several) and press ⌘-1 for one star, ⌘-2 for two stars, and so on. Press ⌘-0 to strip away any existing ratings.

- During a slideshow, twitch the mouse to bring up the onscreen control bar. In the bar, click the row of dots to turn them into rating stars (click the third dot to give the current photo three stars, for example). Or just press the number keys on the keyboard to bestow that number of stars as the slides go by.

- To remove a rating, select the photo and choose Photo→My Ratings→None. You're saying, in effect, "This photo has not yet been rated." *Keyboard shortcut:* ⌘-0.

Tip: Once you've applied your star ratings, you can view the actual little stars right under the corresponding thumbnails by choosing View→My Ratings (or pressing Shift-⌘-R).

Deleting Photos

As every photographer knows—make that every *good* photographer—not every photo is a keeper. At some point, you'll probably want to delete some of your photos.

The iPhoto Trash

iPhoto has a private Trash can that works just like the Finder's Trash. (You can see it nestled at the bottom the Source list as shown in Figure 5-12.) When you want to purge a photo from your Photo Library, you drag it to the Trash. Instead of deleting

---

FREQUENTLY ASKED QUESTION

Undeletable Photos?

iPhoto won't delete photos of my sister. I thought I got rid of a bunch of unflattering pictures of her the other day, and then I found them again when browsing through my Photo Library. Why aren't they staying deleted?

Possibility 1: You deleted the pictures from an *album* instead of the Photo Library itself (the first icon in the list). When you remove a photo from an album, it removes only a *reference* to that picture from the album, leaving the photo itself untouched in the Photo Library.

If the pictures of your sister are really horrendous, click the Photo Library icon in the Source list, move the offending photos to the Trash, and then empty the Trash. That'll get rid of them once and for all.

Possibility 2: You're trying to delete the photo from inside a smart album (page 127). You have to delete such photos from the Photo Library itself, or the Last ___ Months or Last ___ Rolls collections.

---

the photo immediately, iPhoto lets it sit there in the Trash "album," awaiting permanent disposal via the Empty Trash command. This feature gives you one more layer of protection against deleting some precious picture accidentally.

You can relegate items to the Trash by selecting one or more thumbnails in the Photo Library and doing one of the following:

- Drag the thumbnails into the Trash.

- Control-click a photo and choose Move to Trash from the shortcut menu.

- Press ⌘-Delete or choose Photos→Move to Trash.

To view the photos that you have piling up in the Trash, awaiting their journey to the great Fotomat in the sky, click the Trash icon, as shown in Figure 5-12. If you decide you don't really want to get rid of any of these trashed photos, it's easy to resurrect them: Just drag the thumbnails out of the Trash and onto the Photo Library icon in the Source list, or else choose Photos→Restore to Photo Library. You've just rescued them from photo-reject limbo and put them back into your main photo collection.

Tip: You can also move photos from the Trash back into your Photo Library by selecting them—yes, in the Trash "album"—and then pressing ⌘-Delete. Think of it as the un-Trash command.)

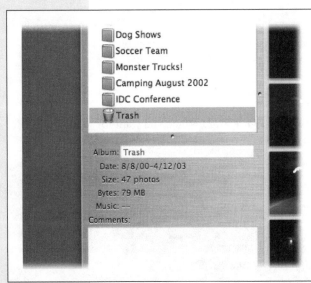

Figure 5-12:
When you dump a photo into iPhoto's Trash, it's not really gone—it's just relocated to the Trash folder. Clicking the Trash icon in the Source list displays all the photos in the Trash and makes the Info panel show the total number of trashed photos, their date range, and their sizes.

To *permanently* delete the photos in the Trash, choose File→Empty Trash, or Control-click the Trash icon to access the Empty Trash command via a shortcut menu. iPhoto displays an alert message, warning you that emptying the Trash removes these photos permanently and irreversibly. (Of course, if you imported the photos from files on disk or haven't deleted them from your camera, you can still recover the original files and reimport them.)

Note: As you might expect, dragging photos into the Trash doesn't reduce the total size of your Photo Library by a single byte, because iPhoto is still storing a copy of each photo in its Trash folder. Only when you *empty* the Trash does the iPhoto Library folder actually shrink in size.

Whatever pictures you throw out by emptying the trash also disappear from any albums you've created. (Deleting a photo from an *album* is different, as described in the box on page 125. More on albums later in this chapter.)

Tip: If you'd rather delete a photo instantly and permanently, without all of this Trash foolishness, drag it clear out of the iPhoto window and onto the Trash icon on your *Dock*.

Albums

No matter how nicely you title, sort, and arrange photos in your digital shoebox, it's still a *shoebox* at this point, with all your photos piled together in one vast collection. To really get organized and present your photos to others, you need to arrange your photos into *albums*.

In iPhoto terminology, an album is a subset of pictures from your Photo Library. It's a collection of photos that you group for easy access and viewing. Represented by a little album-book icon in the Source list at the left side of the screen, an album can consist of any photos that you select, or it can be a *smart album* that iPhoto assembles by matching certain criteria that you set up—all pictures that you took in 2003, for example, or all photos that you've rated four stars or higher. (If you've used smart playlists in iTunes, you'll recognize the concept.)

While your Photo Library as a whole might contain thousands of photos from a hodgepodge of unrelated family events, trips, and time periods, a photo album has a focus: Steve & Sarah's Wedding, Herb's Knee Surgery, and so on.

As you probably know, mounting snapshots in a *real* photo album is a pain—that's why so many of us still have stacks of Kodak prints stuffed in envelopes and shoeboxes. But with iPhoto, you don't need mounting corners, double-sided tape, or scissors to create an album. In the digital world, there's absolutely no excuse for leaving your photos in hopeless disarray.

Technically, you're not required to group your digital photos in albums with iPhoto, but consider the following advantages of doing so:

- It makes finding photos much faster. By opening only the relevant photo album, you can avoid scrolling through thousands of thumbnails in the Photo Library to find a picture you want—a factor that takes on added importance as your photo collection expands.

Note: The Search feature in iPhoto 2 that let you search your Photo Library by titles and comments has been removed from iPhoto 4. As you'll see in the next section, the smart album feature now does the same thing.

• Only in a photo album can you drag your photos into a different order. To change the order of photos displayed in a slideshow or an iPhoto hardbound book, for example, you need to start with a photo album (see Chapters 7 and 10).

Creating an Album by Clicking

Set up a new photo album in iPhoto using any of the following methods:

• Choose File→New Album.

• Press ⌘-N.

• Control-click in a blank area of the Source list and choose New Album from the shortcut menu.

• Click the + button in the iPhoto window, below the Source list.

A dialog box appears, prompting you to name the new album. Type in a descriptive name (*Summer in Aruba, Yellowstone 2004, Edna in Paris,* or whatever), click OK, and watch as a new photo album icon appears in the Source list (Figure 5-13). Now you can add photos to your newly spawned album simply by dragging in thumbnails from your Photo Library.

Figure 5-13:
There's no limit to the number of albums you can add, so make as many as you need to logically organize all the photos in your Photo Library. New albums are always added to the end of the list, but you can change the order in which they appear by simply dragging them up or down in the list.

Creating an Album by Dragging

You can also drag a thumbnail (or a batch of them) from the photo viewing area directly into an empty portion of the Source list. In a flash—well, in about three seconds—iPhoto creates a new album for you, named Album-1 (or whatever number it's up to). The photos you dragged are automatically dumped inside.

Similarly, you can drag a bunch of graphics files *from the Finder* (the desktop behind iPhoto) directly into the Source list. In one step, iPhoto imports the photos, creates a new photo album, names it after the folder you dragged in, and puts the newly imported photos into that album.

Tip: Remember that you can drag photos directly from the Finder onto a photo album icon in the Source list, forcing iPhoto to file them there in the process of importing.

Creating an Album by Selecting

This quick album-creation technique takes advantage of a new command in iPhoto 4: File→New Album From Selection. Scroll through your Photo Library and select any pictures you like using the methods described on page 106; they don't have to be from the same film roll, or even the same year. When you're done, choose New Album From Selection, type a name for the new album, and click OK.

Adding More Photos

To add photos to an existing album, just drag them onto its icon. Figure 5-14 illustrates how you can select multiple photos (using any of the selection techniques described on page 106) and drop them into an album in one batch.

Figure 5-14:
When you drag multiple photos in iPhoto, a little red numeric badge appears next to the pointer telling you exactly how many items you've got selected. In this example, 21 pictures are being dragged en masse into a photo album.

The single most important thing to understand about adding photos to an album is this: Putting photos in an album doesn't really *move* or *copy* them. It makes no difference where the thumbnails start out—whether it's the Photo Library or another album. You're just creating creates *references*, or pointers, back to the photos in your master Photo Library. This feature works a lot like Macintosh aliases; in fact, behind the scenes, iPhoto actually does create aliases of the photos you're dragging. (It stashes them in the appropriate album folders within the iPhoto Library folder.)

What this means is that you don't have to commit a picture to just one album when organizing. One photo can appear in as many different albums as you want. So, if you've got a great shot of Grandma in Hawaii and you can't decide whether to drop the photo into the Hawaiian Vacation album or the Grandma & Grandpa album, the answer is easy: Put it in both. iPhoto just creates two references to the same original photo in your Photo Library.

Tip: To rename an existing photo album, double-click its name or icon in the Source list. A renaming rectangle appears around the album's name, with text highlighted and ready to be edited.

Viewing an Album

To view the contents of an album, click its name or icon in the Source list. All the photos included in the selected album appear in the photo viewing area; the other photos in your Photo Library are hidden.

You can even browse more than one album at a time by highlighting their icons simultaneously:

- To view the contents of several adjacent albums in the list, click the first one, then Shift-click the last.

- To view the contents of albums that aren't consecutive in the list, ⌘-click them.

Tip: Viewing multiple albums at once can be extremely useful when it's time to share your photos. For example, you can make prints or burn an iPhoto CD archive (as explained in Chapters 8 and 14) with the contents of more than one album at a time.

Remember, adding photos to albums doesn't remove them from the Photo Library itself, your master collection. So if you lose track of which album contains a particular photo, just click the Photo Library icon at the top of the Source list to return to the overview of your *entire* photo collection.

Tip: You can put your albums in any order. Just drag them up or down in the Source list.

Moving Photos Between Albums

There are two ways to transfer photos from one photo album to another.

- To *move* a photo between albums, select it and then choose Edit→Cut (or press ⌘-X), removing the photo from the album. Click the destination photo album's name or icon, and then choose Edit→Paste (or press ⌘-V). The photo is now a part of the second album.

- To *copy* a photo into another album, drag it onto the icon of the destination album in the Source list. That photo is now a part of both albums.

Removing Photos from an Album

If you change your mind about how you've got your photos organized and want to remove a photo from an album, open the album and select the photo. (Be sure that you're viewing the contents of a photo *album* in the photo viewing area and not the main Photo Library, the Last 12 Months collection, or the Last Roll collection. Deleting a photo from those sources really does delete it for good.)

Then do one of the following:

- Choose Edit→Cut, or press ⌘-X.

- Choose Edit→Clear.

- Press the Delete key.

- Press the Del (forward-delete) key.

- Control-click the photo, and then, from the shortcut menu, choose Remove from Album.

The thumbnail disappears from the album, but of course it's not really gone from iPhoto. It's still in your Photo Library.

Duplicating a Photo

You can't drag the same photo into an album twice. When you try, the thumbnail simply leaps stubbornly back into its original location, as though to say, "Nyah, nyah, you can't drag the same photo into an album twice."

It's often useful to have two copies of a picture, though. As you'll discover in Chapter 8, a photo whose dimensions are appropriate for a slideshow or desktop picture (that is, a 4:3 proportion) are inappropriate for ordering prints (4 x 6, 8 x 10, or whatever). To use the same photo for both purposes, you really need to crop them independently.

In this case, the old adding-to-album trick isn't going to help you. This time, you truly must duplicate the file, consuming more hard drive space behind the scenes. To do that, highlight the photo and choose File→Duplicate (⌘-D). iPhoto switches briefly into Import mode, copies the file, and then returns to your previous mode. The copy appears next to the original, bearing the same name plus the word "copy."

Note: If you duplicate a photo in an album, you'll see the duplicate both there and in the Photo Library, but not in any other albums. If you duplicate it only in the Photo Library, that's the only place you'll see the duplicate.

Putting Photos in Order

If you plan to turn your photo album into an onscreen slideshow, a series of Web pages, or a printed book, you'll have to tinker with the order of the pictures, arranging them in the most logical and compelling sequence. Photos in the main Photo Library or in a smart album (page 127) are locked into a strict sort order—either by creation date, rating, or film roll—but once they're dragged into a photo album, you can shuffle them manually into a new sequence.

To custom-sort photos in an album, simply drag and drop, as shown in Figure 5-15.

Figure 5-15:
Arrange photos in any order you want by dragging them to a new location within a photo album. In this example, two selected photos from the top-left corner are being dragged to a new location in the next row. The 2 indicates the number of photos being moved; the black vertical bar indicates where iPhoto will insert them when you release the mouse.

Duplicating an Album

It stands to reason that if you have several favorite photos, you might want to use them in more than one of iPhoto's presentations (in a slideshow and a book, for example). That's why it's often convenient to *duplicate* an album: so that you can create two different sequences for the photos inside.

Just highlight an album and then choose File→Duplicate. iPhoto does the duplicating in a flash—after all, it's just duplicating a bunch of tiny aliases. Now you're free to rearrange the order of the photos inside, to add or delete photos, and so on, completely independently of the original album.

Tip: For quick duplicating, you can also Control-click an album in the list and choose Duplicate from the shortcut menu. Duplicating a smart album creates an identical album, which you can then edit as described on the preceding pages.

Merging Albums

Suppose you have three photo albums that contain photos from different trips to the beach, called Spring Break at Beach, Summer Beach Party, and October Coast Trip. You'd like to merge them into a single album called Beach Trips 2003. No problem.

Select all three albums in the Source list (⌘-click each, for example). The photos from all three albums now appear in the photo viewing area. Now create a new, fourth album, using any of the usual methods; select all of the visible thumbnails; and drag them into the new album.

You've now got one big album containing the photos from all three of the original albums. You can delete the three source albums, if you like, or keep all four around. Remember, albums contain only references to your photos—not the photos themselves—so you're not wasting space by keeping the extra albums around. The only penalty you pay is that you have a longer list of albums to scroll through.

Deleting an Album

To delete an album, select its icon in the Source list, and then choose Edit→Clear or press the Delete (or Del) key. You can also Control-click an album and choose Delete Album from the shortcut menu. iPhoto asks you to confirm your intention.

Deleting an album doesn't delete any photos—just the references to those photos. Even if you delete *all* your photo albums, your Photo Library remains intact.

Tip: If you're a person of steely nerve and unshakable confidence, there *is* a way to make iPhoto delete an album for good—including all the photos inside it. See page 295.

Smart Albums

Albums, as you now know, are the primary organizational tool in iPhoto. Since the dawn of iPhoto, you've had to create them yourself, one at a time—by clicking the + button beneath the Source list, for example, and then filling up the album by dragging photo thumbnails.

iPhoto 4, though, can create albums *for* you, thanks to *smart albums.* These are self-updating folders that always display pictures according to certain criteria that you set up—all pictures that you took in 2003, for example, or all photos that you've rated four stars or higher. (If you've ever used smart playlists in iTunes, you'll recognize the idea immediately.)

To create a smart album, choose File→New Smart Album (Option-⌘-N), or Option-click the + button below the Source list. Either way, the Smart Album sheet slides down from the top of the window (Figure 5-16).

The controls here are designed to set up a search of your Photo Library. Figure 5-16 illustrates how you'd find pictures that you took in the last two months of 2003—but only those that have four- or five-star ratings and mention your friend Casey in the title or comments.

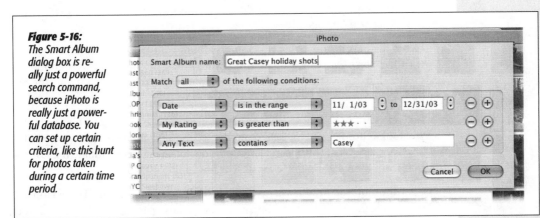

Figure 5-16:
The Smart Album dialog box is really just a powerful search command, because iPhoto is really just a powerful database. You can set up certain criteria, like this hunt for photos taken during a certain time period.

Click the + button to add a new criterion row to be even more specific about which photos you want iPhoto to include in the smart album. Use the first pop-up menu to choose a type of photo feature (keyword or date, for example) and the second pop-up menu to tell iPhoto whether you want to match it ("is"), eliminate it ("is not"), and so on. The third part of the criterion row is another pop-up menu or a search field where you finally tell iPhoto what to look for.

- You can limit the smart album's reach by limiting it to a certain **Album,** or, by choosing "is not" from the second pop-up menu, *eliminate* an album from consideration. All your albums are listed in the third pop-up menu.

- **Any Text** searches your Photo Library for words or letters that appear in the title, comments, or keywords (page 129) that you've assigned to your photos.

Tip: If you can't remember how you spelled a word or whether you put it in the Comments or Title field, choose "Any Text," choose "contains" from the second pop-up menu, and in the search field type just the first few letters of the word ("am" for Amsterdam, for example). You're bound to find some windmills.

- **Comments, Filename, Keyword,** and **Title** work the same way, except they search *only* that part of the photo's information. Search for "Keyword" "is" "Family" (choose "Family" from the third pop-up menu) to find only those pictures that you specifically assigned the keyword "Family," for example, and not just any old photos where you've typed the word "family" somewhere in the comments.

- **Date** is one of the most powerful search criteria. By choosing "is in the range" from the second pop-up menu, you can use it to create an album containing, for example, only the pictures you took on December 24 and 25 of last year, or for that five-day stretch two summers ago when your best friends were in town. Or if you've been on an extended picture-snapping spree, you can choose "is in the last" from the second pop-up menu and choose a limited number of days, weeks, or months from the third pop-up menu.

- The **My Rating** option on the first pop-up menu really puts the fun into smart albums. Suppose you've been dutifully giving your pictures star ratings from 1 to 5, as described on page 118.

  Here's the payoff. You can use this smart album feature to collect, say, only those with five stars to create a quick slideshow of just the highlights. Or choose "is greater than" two stars for a more inclusive slideshow that leaves out only the real duds.

- **Roll** lets you make iPhoto look only in, for example, the last five film rolls that you took (choose "is in the last" from the second pop-up menu and type 5 in the box). Or, if you're creating an album of old shots, you can eliminate the last few rolls from consideration by choosing "is not in the last."

- Click the – button next to a criterion to take it out of the running. For example, if you decide that date shouldn't be a factor, delete any criterion row that tells iPhoto to look for certain dates.

When you click OK, your smart album is ready to show off. When you click its name in the Source list (it has a little gear icon), the main window shows you the thumbnails of the photos that match your criteria. The best part is that iPhoto will keep this album updated whenever your collection changes—as you change your ratings, as you take new photos, and so on.

Tip: To change the parameters for a smart album, click its icon in the list and then choose Photos→Show Info (⌘-I). The Smart Album sheet reappears.

Keywords

Keywords are descriptive words—like *family*, *vacation*, or *kids*—that you can use to label and categorize your photos, regardless of which photo album they're in.

The beauty of keywords in iPhoto is that they're searchable. Want to comb through all the photos in your library to find every close-up taken of your children during summer vacation? Instead of browsing through multiple photo albums, just perform an iPhoto search for photos containing the keywords *kids*, *vacation*, *close-up*, and *summer*. You'll have the results in seconds.

Keywords are also an integral part of iPhoto 4's new smart albums feature, as described on the previous pages.

Note: The Keywords feature, which was such an important part of iPhoto 2, has been stripped down a bit in iPhoto 4. The Keywords window shown in Figure 5-17 used to let you search for words found in your titles and captions as well as keywords. Since that function has been taken over by smart albums (page 127), the Keywords window is now all keywords, all the time.

Editing Keywords

To start working with iPhoto's Keywords feature, choose Photos→Show Keywords (or press ⌘-K) to open the Keywords window (Figure 5-17). This is where you edit your keyword list, assign keywords to specific photos, and search for photos using keywords. (You can edit and assign keywords in any of iPhoto's four modes, but it makes the most sense to do it in Organize mode, where you can see thumbnails of all your photos.)

Apple gives you five sample entries in the Keywords list to get you rolling: Favorite, Family, Vacation, Kids, and Birthday. But these are intended only as a starting point. You can add as many new keywords as you want—or delete any of Apple's—to create a meaningful, customized list:

- To add a new keyword, choose New from the Keywords pop-up menu at the top of the window. A new entry called "untitled" appears in the Keywords list, ready to be edited. Just type in your new keyword name.

- To delete a keyword, select it in the list and then choose Delete from the Keywords pop-up menu. As you might expect, you can delete multiple keywords by Shift-clicking or (for noncontiguous selections) ⌘-clicking any number of keywords in the list before choosing the Delete command.

- To rename a keyword, select it in the list, choose Rename from the Keywords popup menu, and edit the name.

***

Note: Be careful about renaming keywords after you've started using them; the results can be messy. If you've already applied the keyword *Fishing* to a batch of photos, but later decide to replace the word *Fishing* with *Romantic* in your keyword list, all the Fishing photos automatically inherit the keyword Romantic. Depending on you and your interests, this may not be what you intended.

***

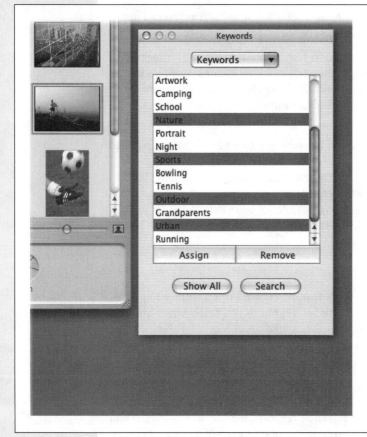

Figure 5-17:
The second photo here has been assigned four keywords. You can tell which ones—Nature, Sports, Outdoor, and Urban—because when you select the photo, the corresponding keywords appear highlighted in gray in the Keywords list.

To remove all these keywords after assigning them to a photo, click Remove. To get rid of a specific keyword, click that word in the list first, and then click Remove.

It may take some time to develop a really good master set of keywords. The idea is to assign labels that are general enough to apply across your entire photo collection, but specific enough to be meaningful when conducting searches.

Here's a general rule of thumb: Use *albums* to group pictures of specific events—a wedding, family vacation, or beach party, for example. (In iPhoto 4, you can use *film rolls* for the same purpose, if you prefer; see page 101.) Use *keywords* to focus on general characteristics that are likely to appear through your entire photo collection—words like Mom, Dad, Casey, Robin, Family, Friends, Travel, and Vacation.

Suppose your photo collection includes a bunch of photos that you shot during a once-in-a-lifetime trip to Rome last summer. You might be tempted to assign *Rome* as a keyword. Don't…because you probably won't use *Rome* on anything other than that one set of photos. It would be smarter to create a photo album or film roll called *Trip to Rome* to hold all those Rome pictures. Use your keywords to tag the same pictures with descriptors like Travel or Family. It also might be useful to apply keywords that describe attributes of the photos themselves, such as Close-up, Landscape, Portrait, and Scenic—or even the names of the people *in* the photos, like Harold, Chris, and Uncle Bert.

Assigning Keywords

To use keywords to perform searches, you must first assign them to your photos. Here's how the process works:

1. **Choose Photos→Show Keywords, or press ⌘-K.**

   The Keywords window appears.

2. **Select a photo, or several, in the photo viewing area.**

   You can assign keywords when viewing thumbnails in the main Photo Library, or in a specific photo album. Use any of the selection techniques described on page 106.

3. **Click the entries in the Keywords list that you would like to assign to the selected photo(s).**

   You can click as many of the keywords as you want, thereby assigning multiple keywords, as shown in Figure 5-17. Shift-click to select several consecutive keywords in the list, or ⌘-click to select multiple, nonadjacent entries.

4. **Click Assign.**

   iPhoto assigns the keywords to the selected photos.

Tip: Instead of clicking Assign, you can simply Option-double-click a keyword to assign it to the selected photos.

You can see which keywords you've applied to each photo by looking at the Keywords window. When you select a photo, its assigned keywords show up highlighted in the Keywords list, as shown in Figure 5-17.

Better yet, if you have iPhoto set up to show keywords in the main photo viewing area (choose View→Keywords or press Shift-⌘-K), you'll immediately see the assigned keywords underneath each photo, as shown in Figure 5-18.

If you want to remove any of these keywords after assigning them, use the Remove button in the Keywords window, as explained in Figure 5-17. But don't confuse *remov-*

ing keywords with *deleting* keywords. Removing a keyword strikes it from a specific photo; deleting it (using the pop-up menu in the Keywords window) removes the word permanently from the keywords list—and, of course, from all photos to which you've assigned it.

Figure 5-18:
You might find it easier to keep track of which keywords you've assigned by displaying them right in the photo viewing area. Choose View→Keywords, or press ⌘-Shift-K, to make them appear.

The Checkmark "Keyword"

You may have noticed that one entry in the keyword list is not a word, but a symbol—a small checkmark. You can't edit this particular entry; it's always just a checkmark.

The checkmark works just like the other keyword entries. But instead of assigning a particular keyword to photos, it flags them with a small checkmark symbol, as shown in Figure 5-19. You'll find this marker extremely useful for temporary organizational tasks.

For example, you might want to cull only the most appropriate images from a photo album for use in a printed book or slideshow. As you browse through the images, use the checkmark button to flag each shot you want. Later, you can use the Search function (described next) to round up all of the images you checkmarked, so that you can drag them all into a new album en masse.

You remove checkmarks from photos just as you remove keywords: With the Keywords window open, select a checkmarked photo, click the checkmark in the Keywords list, then click Remove. (If you click Remove without first clicking the checkmark, iPhoto will remove not just the checkmark, but any other keywords you had assigned to the photo.)

Tip: Just after moving your checkmarked photos to an album, remember to remove the checkmark from all of them while they're still selected. That way, you won't get confused the next time you want to use the checkmark button for flagging a batch of photos.

Figure 5-19:
The idea behind the checkmark button is to provide an easy, uncomplicated way of earmarking a series of photos while sifting through your collection.

Searching by Keyword

Whether you tag photos with the checkmark symbol or a series of keywords, the big payoff for your diligence arrives when you need to get your hands on a specific set of photos, because iPhoto lets you *search* for them.

To perform a keyword search, open the Keywords window (⌘-K). Then double-click a keyword in the Keywords list. (Or, if you're charging by the hour, click the word and then click Search.)

iPhoto immediately rounds up all photos labeled with that keyword, displays them in the photo viewing area, and hides all others.

Here are the important points to remember when using iPhoto's keyword searches:

- To search for photos that match multiple keywords, select all keywords you want—by Shift-clicking (to select a range of consecutive keywords) or ⌘-clicking (for noncontiguous entries) in the Keywords list—and *then* click Search.

Note: When you use multiple keywords, iPhoto finds only the photos that match *all* of those criteria. In other words, if you select *Friends, Candid,* and *Vacation* in a keyword search, iPhoto displays only those photos that contain *all three* keywords.

If you want to find photos tagged with the word Friend *or* Candid *or* Vacation, you have to perform those searches individually, using a single keyword each time.

- You can confine your search to a single album by selecting it before searching. Similarly, clicking the Photo Library in the list before searching (or Last Roll, or Last 12 Months) means that you want to search that photo collection. (You cannot, however, select multiple albums and search only in those.)

- Remember, double-clicking a keyword performs a search; Option-double-clicking *assigns* the word to the selected photo(s).

- Click Show All to restore the view to the whole album or whole Photo Library you had visible before you performed the search.

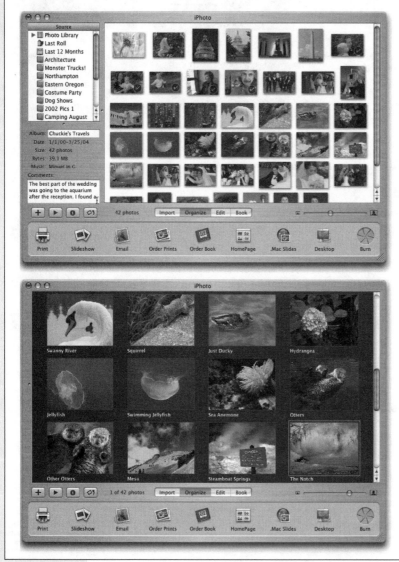

Figure 5-20:
Here's the same Photo Library with two very different customized views.

Top: In the first example, the thumbnails are set to a very small size, with drop shadows, against a white background. The Source list, Information panel, and Comments are displayed.

Bottom: The second view features large thumbnails, with borders, against a dark gray background. The Source list is hidden, but the titles for each photo are displayed.

Customizing the Shoebox

iPhoto starts out looking just the way you see it in Figure 5-4, with each of your pictures displayed as a small thumbnail against a plain white background. This view makes it easy to browse through photos and work with iPhoto's various tools. But hey, this is *your* digital shoebox. With a little tweaking and fine-tuning, you can completely customize the way iPhoto displays your photos.

Start with a visit to iPhoto→Preferences and click the Appearance button.

Tip: You can open the iPhoto Preferences window at any time by pressing ⌘-; (semicolon).

Changing the View

The controls in the Appearance panel of the Preferences window lets you change the overall look of your Photo Library (see Figure 5-20). Here are your options:

- **Add or remove a border or shadow.** The factory setting, Drop Shadow, puts a soft black shadow behind each thumbnail in the photo viewing pane, a subtle touch that gives your Photo Library an elegant 3-D look.

  As pretty as this effect is, however, there's one great reason to turn it *off*: It slows iPhoto down slightly, as the program has to continually redraw or resize those fancy shadows behind each thumbnail whenever you scroll or zoom. Switch to either the Border or No Border setting and you'll be rewarded with faster scrolling and smoother zooming whenever you change the size of thumbnails (as described in the next section). The Border setting puts a thin white frame around each picture. You won't see this border unless you change the background color, as explained in the next paragraph.

- **Change the background color.** Right under the No Border radio button, a slider lets you adjust the background color of the photo viewing pane. Actually, the term "color" is a bit of an overstatement, since your palette of color choices includes white, black, or any shade of gray in between.

- **Adjust the Alignment.** Turn on the "Align photos to grid" checkbox if you want the thumbnails in your Photo Library to snap into evenly spaced rows and columns, even if your collection includes thumbnails of varying sizes and orientations, as shown in Figure 5-21.

- **Change the date order.** Turning on "Place most recent photos at the top" puts them at the top of the main iPhoto window. It's sort of like seeing your most recent email messages at the top of your inbox. If you turn this checkbox off, you'll have to scroll all the way down to see your most recent pictures.

- **Choose text size.** The pop-up menu at the bottom of the Appearance panel lets you choose Small or Large for the album names in the Source list, depending on your eyesight. As for keywords and the other text in the iPhoto window, you're stuck with one size—tiny.

Showing/Hiding Keywords, Titles, and Film Roll Info

If you want to display thumbnails along with the titles and keywords you assign your pictures using iPhoto, you can switch these view options on or off by choosing View→ Titles (Shift-⌘-T) and View→Keywords (Shift-⌘-K). Titles and keywords appear under each thumbnail (see Figure 5-18).

As with most of iPhoto, your formatting options are limited. You can't control the font, style, color, or size of this text. Your only choice is to either display the title and keywords or to keep them hidden.

Figure 5-21:
The "Align to grid" option is insignificant if all your photos are the same size and orientation. But with a variety of horizontal and vertical images, as shown here, photos stay in strict rows and columns (right) despite their size and shape differences. The window on the left shows an "unaligned" version of the same thumbnails.

FREQUENTLY ASKED QUESTION

Return of the Find Command

Hey—where's the Find command?

It's not there any more. You're supposed to use the smart album feature to find photos according to certain criteria.

Still, the Find command of iPhoto 2 had charms of its own—and you can recreate it for nostalgia's sake.

Create a new smart album and name it Find. Set up the criteria as shown here: the first row says "Any Text "contains," and the next couple say "Keyword contains." Click OK.

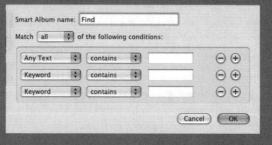

At the moment, your new smart album doesn't contain any pictures, of course. But when you want to find certain photos, click the Find album and press ⌘-I, which re-opens the smart album sheet. Type the phrase you're looking for into the text box (to search among comments or titles), or specify the keyword you want, and then press the Return or Enter key. Presto: the matching pictures appear in the smart album.

The next time you open this homemade Find dialog box, the same search term will still be in the text box; just type over it, if necessary, to perform a new search.

Editing Your Shots

F resh from the camera, digital snapshots often need a little bit of help. A photo
may be too dark or too light. The colors may be too bluish or too yellowish.
The focus may be a little blurry, or the composition may not be quite right.

Fortunately, one of the great things about digital photography is that you can fine-tune
images in ways that, in the world of traditional photography, would require a fully
equipped darkroom, several bottles of smelly chemicals, and an X-Acto knife.

iPhoto isn't a full-blown photo editing program like Adobe Photoshop. But it does
include a handful of tools that you can use to improve your digital photos. This chapter shows you how to use each of the tools in iPhoto's digital darkroom to spruce up
your photos—and how to edit your photos in other programs if more radical image
enhancement is needed.

Editing in iPhoto

You can't color-correct photos, paint in additional elements, mask out unwanted
backgrounds, or apply any special effects filters in iPhoto, as you can with editing
programs like Photoshop and GraphicConverter. Nonetheless, iPhoto is designed to
handle seven basic photo fix-up tasks:

- **Enhance.** With one click, this tool endeavors to make photos look more vibrant
  by tweaking the brightness and contrast settings and adjusting the saturation to
  compensate for washed-out or oversaturated colors.

- **Cropping.** The cropping tool lets you cut away the outer portions of a photo to
  improve its composition or to make it the right size for a printout or Web page.

- **Retouch.** This little brush lets you paint out minor imperfections like blemishes, freckles, and scratches.

- **Brightness/Contrast.** These sliders can tone down bright, overexposed images or lighten up those that look too dark and shadowy. While the Enhance button takes an all-or-nothing approach to fixing a photo, the Brightness and Contrast controls let you make tiny adjustments to the settings.

- **Red-Eye.** This little filter gets rid of one very common photo glitch—those shining red dots that sometimes appear in a person's eyes as the result of flash photography.

- **Black & White.** Turns your color photos into a moody black-and-white art shots.

- **Sepia.** Makes new photos look faded and brownish, for that old-time daguerreotype look. It's the only new editing tool in iPhoto 4.

For anything beyond these simple touch-up tasks, you need to open your photos in a more powerful editing program—which you can easily do from within iPhoto, as explained later in this chapter.

Using the Editing Tools

All iPhoto editing is done in a special editing mode, which you can open up by any of the following methods:

- With a photo selected, click the Edit button in the middle of the main iPhoto window. iPhoto's editing tools appear in the lower pane.

- Double-click a thumbnail. If you have iPhoto set to open photos right in the main window (which is the factory setting), iPhoto jumps into Edit mode and enlarges the selected photo to fill the window. The tools appear, once again, at the bottom.

- If you've instructed iPhoto to open a photo in a separate window when you double-click its thumbnail (as suggested on page 109), the Edit tools appear in a top-mounted toolbar, as shown in Figure 6-1. (If the toolbar isn't visible, click the

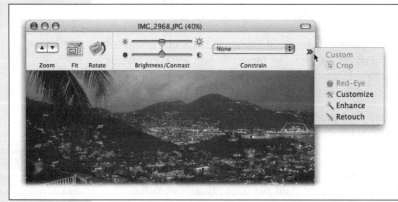

Figure 6-1:
iPhoto's editing tools appear in the toolbar when you open a photo in its own window. A >> symbol at the right end of the toolbar (as shown here) means that the window is too narrow to display all the tools. Just drag the window wider to show all tools, or click the double-arrow to access the tools via a pop-up menu.

capsule-shaped button in the upper-right corner of the window to make it appear, or choose Window→Show Toolbar.)

- Control-click a thumbnail or a photo in its own window; from the shortcut menu, choose "Edit" (to edit right in iPhoto's main window) or "Edit in separate window." (If you've bought a two-button mouse for your Mac, you can right-click instead.)

One-Click Fixups: The Enhance Button

The Enhance button provides a simple way to improve the appearance of less-than-perfect digital photos. You click one button to make colors brighter, skin tones warmer, and details sharper. (If you've used Photoshop, the Enhance button is a lot like the Auto Levels command.)

But if you want to know *exactly* what the Enhance button does, good luck. Apple guards that information as though it's a top-secret meatloaf recipe. iPhoto's online help makes only a nebulous statement about it "improving colors," but provides no explanation as to *how* they're improved.

What's clear is that the Enhance button analyzes the relative brightness of all the pixels in your photo and attempts to "balance" the image by dialing the brightness or contrast up or down and intensifying dull or grayish-looking color. In addition to this overall adjustment of brightness, contrast, and color, the program makes a particular effort to identify and bring out the subject of the photo. Usually, this approach at least makes pictures look somewhat richer and more vivid.

Using the Enhance Button

If you're editing a photo in iPhoto's main window, you'll find the Enhance button on the lower pane of the window, along with iPhoto's other editing tools. To enhance a photo, just click the Enhance button. There's nothing to select first, and no controls to adjust. (It's something like Photoshop's Auto Levels command in that regard.)

Tip: You can also Control-click a photo to choose Enhance from the shortcut menu.

Figure 6-2:
The Enhance command works particularly well on photos that are slightly dark and that lack good contrast, like the original photo on the left. Using iPhoto's Brightness and Contrast sliders alone helped a little, as shown in the middle photo, but the Enhance button produced the best results, as shown at right.

If you've opted to open a photo in a separate window for editing, you won't see the Enhance button in the toolbar. To bring it out of hiding, add the button to the Editing toolbar, as explained on page 150. (Or just invoke the command using the Tip above.)

Tip: After using the Enhance button, you can hold down the Control key to see your unenhanced "before" photo. Release the key to see the "after" image.

By pressing and releasing the Control key, you can toggle between the two versions of the photo in order to assess the results of the enhancement.

As you use the Enhance button, remember that iPhoto's image-correcting algorithms are simply best guesses at what your photo is supposed to look like. It has no way of knowing whether you've shot an overexposed, washed-out picture of a vividly colored sailboat, or a perfectly exposed picture of a pale-colored sailboat on an overcast day.

Consequently, you may find that Enhance has no real effect on some photos, and only minimally improves others. Remember, too, that you can't enhance just one part of a photo. When you click the Enhance button, iPhoto runs its enhancement routine on the whole picture. If you want to selectively adjust specific portions of a picture, you need a true photo editing program like GraphicConverter or Photoshop Elements.

Tip: If using the Enhance command does improve your photo, but just not enough, you can click it repeatedly to amplify its effect—as many times as you want, really. It's just that applying Enhance more than three times or so risks turning your photo into digital mush.

If you go too far, remember that you can press ⌘-Z (or choose Edit→Undo) to backtrack. In fact, you can take back as many steps as you like, all the way back to the original photo.

In some cases, you'll have to do more than click the Enhance button to coax the best possible results from your digital photos. You may have to do further tweaking with the Brightness and Contrast sliders as explained later in this chapter.

Cropping

iPhoto's cropping tool is a digital paper cutter. It neatly shaves off unnecessary portions of a photo, leaving behind only the part of the picture you really want.

You'd be surprised at how many photographs can benefit from selective cropping. For example:

- **Eliminate parts of a photo you just don't want.** This is a great way to chop your brother's ex-girlfriend out of an otherwise perfect family portrait, for example (provided she was standing at the end of the lineup).

- **Improve a photo's composition.** Trimming a photo allows you to adjust where your subject matter appears within the frame of the picture. If you inspect the professionally shot photos in magazines or books, for example, you'll discover that many pros get more impact from a picture by cropping tightly around the subject, especially in portraits.

- **Get rid of wasted space.** Huge expanses of background sky that add nothing to a photo can be eliminated, keeping the focus on your subject.

- **Fit a photo to specific proportions.** If you're going to place your photos in a book layout (Chapter 10) or turn them into standard size prints (Chapter 8), you may need to adjust their proportions. That's because there's a substantial discrepancy between the *aspect ratio* (length-to-width proportions) of your digital camera's photos and those of film cameras—a difference that will come back to haunt you if you order prints. The following discussion covers all the details.

How to Crop a Photo

Here are the steps for cropping a photo:

1. **Open the photo for editing.**

   You can use any of the methods mentioned earlier in this chapter.

2. **Make a selection from the Constrain pop-up menu, if you like (Figure 6-3).**

   The Constrain pop-up menu controls the behavior of the cropping tool. When the menu is set to None, you can draw a cropping rectangle of any size and proportions, in essence going freehand.

   When you choose one of the other options in the pop-up menu, however, iPhoto constrains the rectangle you draw to preset proportions. It prevents you from coloring outside the lines, so to speak.

   This feature is especially important if you plan to order prints of your photos (Chapter 8). When you attempt to do so, you'll notice that you can order prints only in standard photo sizes: 4 x 6, 5 x 7, 8 x 10, and so on. Most digital cameras, however, produce photos whose proportions are 4 to 3 (width to height). That's great for onscreen slideshows, DVDs, and iPhoto books (Chapter 10), because your Mac screen, television, and iPhoto book layouts use 4 to 3 dimensions, too—but that doesn't divide evenly into standard print photograph sizes.

   That's why the Constrain pop-up menu offers you canned choices like 4 x 6, 5 x 7, and so on. Limiting your cropping to one of these preset sizes guarantees that your cropped photos will fit perfectly into Kodak prints. (If you don't constrain your cropping this way, Kodak will decide how to crop them to fit instead of you.)

Note: Even though the Constrain menu ensures the right *proportions*, it doesn't in any way guarantee that the total *size* of the final photos is adequate. See the box "When Cropping Problems Crop Up" on page 144 for more about properly sizing your photos.

Other crop-to-fit options in the Constrain menu let you crop photos for use as a desktop picture ("1024 x 768 [Display]," or whatever your actual monitor's dimensions are), as a 4 x 6-inch print, to fit into one of the Book layouts available in iPhoto's Book mode (Chapter 10), and so on.

Tip: Opening a photo into its own separate editing window (by Control-clicking its thumbnail and choosing "Edit in separate window") triggers a bonus feature: two boxes in the toolbar labeled Custom. Into these text boxes, you can type any proportions you want: 4 x 7, 15 x 32, or whatever your eccentric design needs happen to call for.

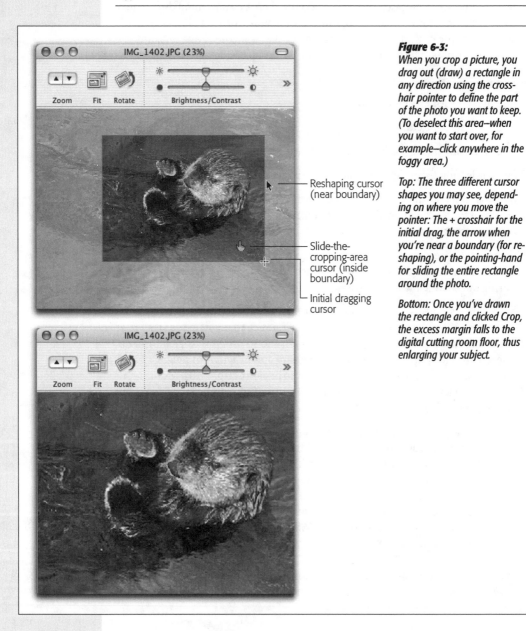

Figure 6-3:
When you crop a picture, you drag out (draw) a rectangle in any direction using the cross-hair pointer to define the part of the photo you want to keep. (To deselect this area—when you want to start over, for example—click anywhere in the foggy area.)

Top: The three different cursor shapes you may see, depending on where you move the pointer: The + crosshair for the initial drag, the arrow when you're near a boundary (for re-shaping), or the pointing-hand for sliding the entire rectangle around the photo.

Bottom: Once you've drawn the rectangle and clicked Crop, the excess margin falls to the digital cutting room floor, thus enlarging your subject.

Reshaping cursor (near boundary)

Slide-the-cropping-area cursor (inside boundary)

Initial dragging cursor

As soon as you make a selection from this pop-up menu, iPhoto 4 draws a preliminary cropping rectangle—of the proper dimensions—on the screen, turning everything outside it dim and foggy.

In general, this rectangle always appears in landscape (horizontal) orientation. To make it vertical, open the pop-up menu a second time and choose Constrain as Landscape. (The exception is the constrain choice called "4 x 3 (DVD)," which starts you out with a horizontal rectangle as a time-saving convenience.)

Tip: Actually, there's a quicker way to rotate the selection from horizontal to vertical (or vice versa): Option-drag across the photo to draw a new selection rectangle, as described in the next step. The selection rectangle crisply turns 90 degrees.

Now, the cropping area that iPhoto suggests with its foggy-margin rectangle may, as far as you're concerned, be just right. In that case, skip to step 5.

More often, though, you'll probably want to give the cropping job the benefit of your years of training and artistic sensibility by *redrawing* the cropping area:

3. **Click anywhere in the foggy area to get rid of the rectangle. Then position the mouse pointer (which appears as a crosshair) at one corner of your photo. Drag diagonally across the portion of the picture that you want to *keep*.**

As you drag a rectangle across your photo, the portions *outside* of the selection—the part of the photo that iPhoto will eventually trim away—get dimmed out once again (Figure 6-3).

Tip: Even if you've turned on one of the Constrain options in step 2, you can override the constraining by pressing ⌘ after you begin dragging.

Don't worry about getting your selection perfect, since iPhoto doesn't actually trim the photo until you click the Crop button.

4. **Adjust the cropping, if necessary.**

If the shape and size of your selection area is OK, but you want to adjust which part of the image is selected, you can move the selection area without redrawing it. Position your mouse over the selection so that the pointer turns into a hand icon. Then drag the existing rectangle where you want it.

You can even change the *shape* of the selection rectangle after you've released the mouse button, thanks to an invisible quarter-inch "handle" that surrounds the cropping area. Move your cursor close to any edge or corner so that it changes from the + shape to an arrow. Now you can drag the edge or corner to reshape the rectangle (see Figure 6-3).

If you get cold feet, you can cancel the operation by clicking once anywhere outside the cropping rectangle (to remain in Edit mode) or by double-clicking anywhere on the photo (to return to Organize mode). Or, if the photo is open in its own window, just close the window.

Note: Despite its elaborate control over the *relative* dimensions of your cropping rectangle, iPhoto offers no indication at all over its *actual* size in pixels. If you want to crop a photo to precise pixel dimensions, you'll have to do the job in another program, like GraphicConverter or Photoshop Elements. (See page 152 for instructions on flipping into a different program for editing.)

5. **When the cropping rectangle is set just the way you want, click the Crop button.**

   Alternatively, Control-click the photo and choose Crop from the shortcut menu. (That method is handy if the Crop button on the toolbar isn't visible.)

   If throwing away all those cropped-out pixels makes you nervous, relax. When you click Crop, iPhoto, behind the scenes, makes a duplicate of the original photo before doing the deed—a handy safety net for the day you decide to revert back to the uncropped version, months or years later.

   If you realize immediately that you've made a cropping mistake, you can choose Edit→Undo Crop Photo to restore your original.

   If you have regrets *weeks* later, on the other hand, you can always select the photo and choose File→Revert to Original. iPhoto reinstates the original photo from its backup, discarding every change you've ever made.

Note: When you crop a photo, you're cropping the photo in *all albums* in which it appears (Chapter 5). If you want a photo to appear cropped in one album but not in another, you must first duplicate it (highlight it and then choose File→Duplicate), then edit each version separately.

UP TO SPEED

When Cropping Problems Crop Up

Remember that cropping always *shrinks* your photos. Take away too many pixels, and your photo may end up too small (that is, with too low a resolution to print or display properly).

Here's an example: You start with a 1600 x 1200 pixel photo. Ordinarily, that's large enough to be printed as a high-quality, standard 8 x 10 portrait.

Then you go in and crop the shot. Now the composition is perfect, but your photo only measures 800 x 640 pixels. You've tossed out nearly a million and a half pixels.

The photo no longer has a high enough *resolution* (pixels per inch) to produce a high-quality 8 x 10. The printer is forced to

blow up the photo to fill the specified paper size, producing visible, jaggy-edged pixels in the printout. The 800 x 640 pixel version of your photo would make a great 4 x 5 print (if that were even a standard size print)—but pushing the print's size up further noticeably degrades the quality.

Therein lies a great advantage of using a high-resolution digital camera (5 or 6 megapixels, for example). Because each shot starts out with such a high resolution, you can afford to shave away a few hundred thousand pixels and still have enough left over for good-sized, high-resolution prints.

Moral of the story: Know your photo's size and intended use—and don't crop out more photo than you can spare.

Painting Out Freckles, Scratches, and Hairs

Sometimes an otherwise perfect portrait is spoiled by the tiniest of imperfections—a stray hair or an unsightly blemish, for example. Professional photographers, whether working digitally or in a traditional darkroom, routinely remove such minor imperfections from their final prints—a process known as *retouching,* for clients known as *self-conscious.*

iPhoto's Retouch brush lets you do the same thing with your own digital photos. You can paint away scratches, spots, hairs, or any other small flaws in your photos with a few quick strokes.

The operative word here is *small.* The Retouch brush can't wipe out a big blob of spaghetti sauce on your son's white shirt or completely erase somebody's mustache. It's for tiny fixups that don't involve repainting whole sections of a photo. (For that kind of photo overhaul, you need a real photo editing program like the ones described at the end of this chapter.)

The Retouch brush works its magic by blending together the colors in the tiny area that you're fixing. It doesn't cover the imperfections you're trying to remove, but *blurs* them out by softly blending them into a small radius of surrounding pixels.

Tip: The Retouch brush is particularly useful if your photo library contains traditional photographs that you've scanned in. You can use it to wipe away the dust specks and scratches that often appear on film negatives and prints or that are introduced when you scan the photos.

Figure 6-4:
The key to using the Retouch brush is to target small areas and use restraint so that you don't overblur the area you're working on. Notice how the Retouch brush was used on the original photo (top) to subtly soften wrinkles around the eye and remove imperfections in the upper left corner (bottom).

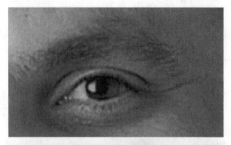

Using the Retouch Brush

The Retouch brush appears in the lower pane of the main iPhoto window as soon as you enter Edit mode. If you've opted to open a photo in a separate window for editing, use the Customize Toolbar command to add the Retouch brush to the Editing toolbar, as shown in Figure 6-7.

Alternatively, when in Editing mode, you can select the Retouch brush by Control-clicking a photo and choosing Retouch from the shortcut menu.

Once you've selected the Retouch brush, your pointer turns into a small crosshair with a hole in the middle. Using the center of the crosshair, target the imperfection and "paint" over it, using a series of short strokes to blend it with the surrounding portion of the picture. Don't overdo it: If you apply too much retouching, the area you're working on starts to look noticeably blurry and unnatural, as if someone smeared Vaseline on it.

Fortunately, you can use the Edit→Undo command (⌘-Z) to take back as many of your brush strokes as necessary.

Note: On high-resolution photos, it can take a moment or two for iPhoto to process each individual stroke of the Retouch brush. If you don't see any results, wait a second for iPhoto to catch up with you.

Brightness/Contrast

No software can rescue a photo that was taken with very poor lighting, but a little time spent with the Brightness and Contrast sliders can make many photos look much more vivid, with deeper, more saturated colors. If the Enhance command (described earlier in this chapter) doesn't produce quite the results you were hoping for, you may be able to further improve the quality of your photo by adjusting these controls.

Figure 6-5:
These sliders allow you to make incremental adjustments in brightness and contrast, but they can be sluggish on large photos.

You can save some time by clicking anywhere along a slider bar to make the controller jump directly to that point. Click the sun or circle icon at the ends of the sliders to crank the brightness or contrast all the way up or down.

The Sliders

These controls are easy to use. Just drag each slider to the left or right to decrease or increase the overall brightness and contrast of a photo (see Figure 6-5). The results appear almost instantly, so you can experiment freely.

The brightness and contrast controls can also salvage shots that were either too light or too dark when they were taken. Again, you can't add details that simply aren't there, but brightening a dark shadowy image, or deepening the contrast on a washed-out image, can coax out elements that were barely visible in the original photo.

Tip: When your adjustments are subtle, it's sometimes hard to tell how much you've really improved a photo without comparing the results directly to the original, unedited one. Remember that pressing the Control key temporarily restores the photo to its pre-edited condition. By pressing and releasing Control, you can toggle back and forth as much as you want, comparing the two versions before deciding to keep the changes permanently.

As long as you remain in Edit mode, you can back out of your changes no matter how many of them you've made. For example, if you've adjusted the Brightness and Contrast sliders, you can remove those changes using the Edit→Undo Brightness/Contrast command (⌘-Z).

In fact, you can remove these changes even after you've performed other editing functions, like cropping or rotating. The only catch is that you must back out of the changes one at a time. In other words, if you change the contrast on a photo, then crop it, and then rotate it, you'll have to use the Undo command three times—first to unrotate, then to uncrop, and finally, to undo the contrast setting.

But once you leave Edit mode—either by closing the photo's window or by double-clicking it, thereby returning to Organize mode—you lose the ability to undo your edits. At that point, the only way to restore your photo is to choose the File→Revert to Original, which removes all the edits you've made to the photo since importing it.

Red-Eye

You snap a near-perfect family portrait. The focus is sharp, the composition is balanced, everyone's relaxed and smiling. And then you notice it: Uncle Mitch, standing dead center in the picture, looks like a vampire bat. His eyes are glowing red, as though illuminated by the evil within.

You've been victimized by *red-eye*, a common problem in flash photography. That creepy possessed-by-aliens look has ruined many an otherwise great photo.

Red-eye is actually light reflected back from your subject's eyes. The bright light of your camera's flash passes through the pupil of each eye, illuminating the blood-red retinal tissue at the back of the eye, which is reflected back into the camera lens. Red-eye problems worsen when you shoot pictures in a dim room, because your subject's pupils are dilated wider, allowing even more light from the flash to illuminate the retina.

Page 62 offers advice on avoiding red-eye to begin with. But if it's too late for that, and people's eyes are already glowing evilly, iPhoto's Red-Eye tool lets you alleviate red-eye problems by digitally removing the offending red pixels. Here's how:

1. **Open your photo in Edit mode.**

   Change the zoom setting, if necessary, so that you have a close-up view of the eye that has the red-eye problem.

2. **Use the crosshair pointer to select the face (by dragging a box across it).**

   The more face you select, the better the tool does, since it distinguishes red from almost-red by comparing the eyes with the facial tones. So grab a generous number of pixels, including the eyes.

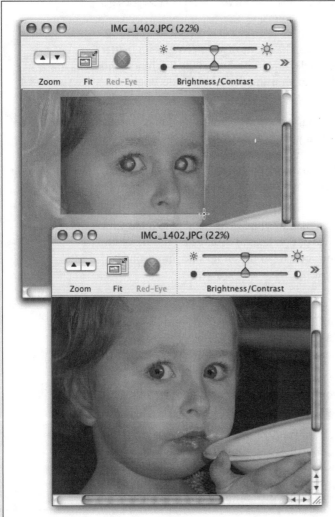

Figure 6-6:
Top: Anything even slightly red in your photo gets blackened out by iPhoto's Red-Eye tool. Select a good chunk of the face, omitting anything else that's visibly red (lips, clothing, furniture, and so on).

Bottom: Truth be told, the Red-Eye tool doesn't know an eyeball from a pinkie toe. It just turns any red pixels black, regardless of what body part they're associated with. Friends and family members look more attractive—and less like Star Trek characters—after you touch up their phosphorescent red eyes with iPhoto.

3. **Click the Red-Eye button.**

(The Red-Eye button is dimmed until you've actually selected a portion of the photo. If you're editing in a separate window, as shown in Figure 6-6, you may have to use the >> menu at the right end of the toolbar to find the Red-Eye command.)

iPhoto neutralizes the red pixels, painting the pupils solid black.

Of course, this means that everybody winds up looking like they have *black* eyes instead of red ones—but at least they look a little less like the walking undead.

B & W, Sepia

The B & W (Black and White) and Sepia tools don't correct anything. They simply drain the color from your photos. B & W converts them into moody grayscale images (a great technique if you're going for that Ansel Adams look); Sepia repaints them entirely in shades of antique brown (as though they were 1865 daguerreotypes).

Open a photo in Edit mode, and then click the Black & White or Sepia button. That's all there is to it. If you change your mind, you can use File→Undo to restore the color immediately, or choose File→Revert to Original at any point to return to your original file.

Tip: If you don't see the B & W or Sepia buttons, you can always Control-click the photo and choose the corresponding command from the shortcut menu.

Rotate

Unless your digital camera has a built-in orientation sensor, iPhoto imports all photos in landscape orientation (wider than they are tall). The program has no way of knowing if you turned the camera 90 degrees when you took your pictures. Once you've imported the photos, just select the sideways ones and rotate them into position (if indeed you didn't do so during your first slide show, as described on page 92).

You don't have to be in Edit mode to rotate photos. Remember, you can select thumbnail images when you're in Organize mode and then use one of the following methods to turn them right-side up:

- Choose Edit→Rotate→Counter Clockwise (or Clockwise).

- Click the Rotate button in the main iPhoto window, just under the Info pane (it's the rightmost of the four buttons on the pane). (Option-click this button to reverse the direction of the rotation.)

- Press ⌘-R to rotate selected photos counter-clockwise, or Shift-⌘-R to rotate them clockwise.

- Control-click a photo and choose Rotate→Clockwise (or Counter Clockwise) from the shortcut menu.

Tip: After importing a batch of photos, you can save a lot of time and mousing if you select *all* the thumbnails that need rotating first (by ⌘-clicking each, for example). Then use one of the rotation commands above to fix all the selected photos in one fell swoop.

Incidentally, clicking Rotate (or pressing ⌘-R) generally rotates photos counterclockwise, and Option-clicking (Shift-⌘-R) generally rotates them clockwise. But you can swap these directions by choosing iPhoto→Preferences and changing the Rotate setting on the General tab of the Preferences dialog box.

Note: When you rotate an image saved in GIF format in iPhoto, the resulting rotated picture is saved as a JPEG file. The original GIF is stored unchanged in an Originals folder in the iPhoto Library folder (see Chapter 4).

Customizing the Toolbar

Like the toolbar in all Mac OS X Finder windows, the Editing toolbar—the one that appears when you open a photo in its own window—can be customized to contain the particular editing tools you use the most.

With at least one photo open in its own window, start by choosing Window→Customize Edit Toolbar. (Alternatively, you can click the Customize button on the toolbar, or Control-click a toolbar button and choose Customize Toolbar from the shortcut menu.) The toolbar's customization panel fills the window (Figure 6-7). You now have a dozen more icons at your disposal, ready to be installed on the toolbar.

To put a new item on the toolbar, just drag it into position. To remove an existing tool, drag it off the toolbar. It vanishes in a puff of smoke, Mac OS X–style. Here are some of the changes you might consider making:

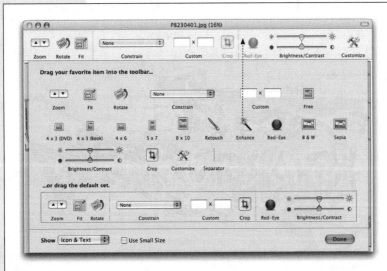

Figure 6-7:
This toolbar is handy, especially if you tend to use the same Constrain settings for most of your cropping. Just drag the proposed tool candidates upward into place, and then click Done. And now, a tip: If you find that the toolbar takes up too much space, Control-click anywhere on it and choose Text Only from the shortcut menu.

- Several tools—including the Enhance button and the Retouch brush—don't come factory-installed in the Editing toolbar. It's up to you to add them.

- iPhoto offers buttons for each of the constrained cropping options described earlier. If there's one cropping size that you find yourself using frequently, put it in the toolbar.

- Get rid of the tools you never use, in order to keep the toolbar free from clutter. If you never crop to a custom size, for example, you can drag the Custom constraining fields out of the way. (You can always restore tools later.)

- Even if you don't add or remove any buttons, you can drag the ones that are already there into a new order, putting them exactly where you want them. (You can do this at any time, even when the customization panel isn't open, by ⌘-dragging the buttons on the toolbar.)

- Drop separator lines between the various tools to group them visually on the toolbar according to your preference.

Tip: You can restore the toolbar to its original condition by dragging the default set of tools at the bottom on the customization panel to the toolbar.

No need to worry about adding too many items to this toolbar. If you keep piling on the icons, it sprouts a fly-out menu on the right side, listing every button, as shown in Figure 6-1.

When you're finished dragging extra buttons to the toolbar, click Done to close the Customize panel and activate your new icons.

Tip: While your mind is on fiddling with the toolbar, remember that you can control the size of its icons and their labels, just as in many other Apple programs. The trick is to ⌘-click the white, capsule-shaped Toolbar button in the upper-right corner of the window. With each click, you cycle through to the next smaller configuration of the toolbar. You can keep going until the icons themselves disappear, and only button labels in tiny type remain.

Beyond iPhoto

If you're serious about digital photographs, iPhoto's tools by themselves aren't going to cut it. You'll have to spring for a more full-featured image-editing program, such as Adobe Photoshop, Photoshop Elements, Canvas, GraphicConverter, or a similar program.

Photoshop is by far the most popular tool for the job, but at about $600, it's also one of the most expensive. Unless you intend to perform sophisticated image-editing and compositing (sandwiching together parts of different photos into one image), save yourself some money and buy Photoshop Elements. It's a trimmed-down version of Photoshop with all the basic image-editing stuff and just enough of the high-end features. It costs less than $100, and a free trial version is available online. (Your digital camera may even have come with Photoshop Elements right in the box.)

Before you go software shopping, though, check out your own hard drive. If you bought your Mac recently, you may already have the image-editing software you need. Apple includes GraphicConverter—a simple but powerful editing program with Photoshop-like tools—on some Mac models.

Opening Photos in Other Programs

To open a photo in a "real" editing program, first open that program so that its icon appears in the Dock. Then drag a thumbnail from iPhoto's window directly onto the program icon. (Of course, you can also drag a picture from iPhoto's window onto the application's *desktop* icon, or an alias of it.) In fact, you can even drag several thumbnails at once to open all of them simultaneously.

If you've already been working in, say, Photoshop, you might be tempted to use its File→Open command to open an iPhoto photo directly. But the drag-and-drop method is far more efficient; if you use File→Open, you'll have to navigate through the oddly numbered folders of the labyrinthine iPhoto Library folder (page 94) to locate the picture you want.

Tip: When you edit a photo in another program, you're essentially going behind iPhoto's back; the program doesn't have a chance to make a safety copy of the original. Therefore, you're sacrificing your ability to use the Revert to Original command to restore your photo to its original state in case of disaster (page 154).

The sneaky workaround: Just make one tiny change to the photo *in iPhoto* before you drag its thumbnail onto another program's icon. Rotate it all the way around, for example—anything to force iPhoto to create a backup. Thereafter—whether you edit the photo in another program or not—you can restore the photo to its original condition at any time.

Setting up a default editing program

The drag-and-drop approach is great if you *occasionally* want to open a photo in another program. But if you find yourself routinely editing your photos in another program, there's a much easier method: Just set up iPhoto to open your photos in that program automatically when you double-click. You set up this arrangement as follows.

1. Choose iPhoto→Preferences.

   The Preferences window opens.

2. Click the General button, if necessary. For the "Double-click photo" preference settings, select the "Opens photo in" radio button, then click Select Application.

   A standard Open dialog box appears so you can navigate to your favorite photo editing program.

3. **Choose the program you want to use for editing, then click Open.**

When you're done, close the Preferences window.

Now, whenever you double-click a thumbnail, iPhoto launches the designated editing program and uses it to open your photo.

One big advantage of this method is that it lets iPhoto track your editing activity—yes, even in other programs. iPhoto can therefore update its thumbnail versions of your photos to reflect the changes. It can also preserve the original version of the photos you edit externally, so that you can later use the Revert to Original command if disaster should strike any time later, as explained later in this chapter.

Freedom of choice

It's nice to be able to edit photos in external programs, but it's a lot of trouble to switch that feature on and off; a trip to iPhoto→Preferences is involved every time. If you're like many photo fans, what you want is to use iPhoto's convenient editing features *most* of the time, ducking out to other programs only when you need more industrial-strength features.

Fortunately, iPhoto offers a couple of tricks that let you switch to an external editor only on demand:

- Clicking the Edit button below the photo-viewing area *always* opens a selected photo for editing right in iPhoto, regardless of your Preferences setting.

- Better yet: If you Control-click a thumbnail, the shortcut menu offers you three choices: "Edit" (in the main iPhoto window), "Edit in separate window," or "Edit in external editor." (The last option is available only if you've selected an editing program as described above.) No matter what your settings in Preferences may be, this route always gives you the choice of all three editing modes.

Fixing Digital Photos

Once you've moved beyond the world of iPhoto, there's plenty that you can do to improve the quality of your digital photos. Programs like Photoshop and Photoshop Elements let you make dozens of different enhancements to your photos and apply a seemingly endless variety of wild special effects.

Still, you'll probably find yourself using only a handful of such features for most photo-fixing work. Here are some of the operations that are worth tackling.

Color correction

One of the most common failings of digital cameras (and many flatbed scanners, too) is that they don't capture color very accurately. Digital photos often have a slightly bluish or greenish tinge, producing dull colors, lower contrast, and sickly looking skin tones. Most image-editing programs let you bump up or lower each of the individual color channels in your photos, adding red values or decreasing green values, so that your photos have more balanced, lifelike color.

Sharpness

Another frequent complaint about digital cameras is that they don't produce the sharpest images. Programs like Photoshop, Photoshop Elements, and GraphicConverter can apply a sharpening filter that brings out edges and adds definition to a slightly blurry photo.

Saturation

Another way to improve dull, washed-out colors is to increase the *saturation* of a photo, making colors deeper, richer, and less "gray"—a standard operation in most image-editing programs. You can also improve photos that have harsh, garish colors by dialing *down* the saturation, so that the colors end up looking a little less intense than they appeared in the original snapshot.

If you're using GraphicConverter, you can access the Saturation slider by choosing Picture→Brightness/Contrast.

(iPhoto's Enhance command automatically adjusts saturation when "enhancing" your photos, but provides no way to control the *degree* of its adjustment.)

Reverting to the Original

iPhoto includes built-in protection against overzealous editing—a feature that can save you much grief. If you end up cropping a photo too much, or cranking up the brightness of a picture until it seems washed out, or accidentally turning someone's lips black with the Red-Eye tool, you can undo all your edits at once with the Revert to Original command. Revert to Original strips away *every change you've ever made* since the picture arrived from the camera. It leaves you with your original, unedited photo.

The secret of the Revert to Original command: Whenever you use any editing tools, iPhoto—without prompting and without informing you—instantly makes a duplicate of your original file. With an original version safely tucked away, iPhoto lets you go wild on the copy. You can remain secure in the knowledge that in a pinch, iPhoto can always restore an image to the state it was in when you first imported it.

Note: The unedited originals are stored in an Originals folder inside the photo folder for each date (see page 96), deep in your Home→Pictures→iPhoto Library folder. (The Originals folder doesn't exist until you edit at least one photo.)

To restore an original photo, undoing all cropping, rotation, brightness adjustments, and so on, select a thumbnail of an edited photo or open the photo in Edit mode. Then choose File→Revert to Original. iPhoto swaps in the original version of the photo—and you're back where you started.

As noted earlier, iPhoto does its automatic backup trick whenever you edit your pictures (a) within iPhoto or (b) using a program that you've set up to open when you double-click a picture. It does not make a backup when you drag a thumbnail onto the icon of another program. In that event, the Revert to Original command will be dimmed when you select the edited photo.

Bottom line: If you want the warmth and security of Revert to Original at your disposal, don't edit your pictures behind iPhoto's back. Follow the guidelines in the previous two paragraphs so that iPhoto is always aware of when and how you're editing your pictures.

FREQUENTLY ASKED QUESTION

In iPhoto, Less Is More

I just finished editing a batch of photos, cropping each picture to a much smaller size. But now my iPhoto Library folder is taking up more space on my hard drive! How can making the photos smaller increase the size of my photo collection? Shouldn't throwing away all those pixels have the opposite effect—shrinking things down?

Your cropped photos do, in fact, take up much less space than they did. Remember, though, that iPhoto doesn't let you monkey with your photos without first stashing away a copy of each original photo, in case you ever want to use the Revert to Original command to restore a photo to its original condition.

So each time you crop a picture (or do any other editing) for the first time, you're actually creating a new, full-size file on your hard drive, as iPhoto stores both the original *and* the edited versions of the photo. Therefore, the more photos you edit in iPhoto, the more hard drive space your photo collection will take up.

Incidentally, it's worth noting that iPhoto may be a bit overzealous when it comes to making backups of your originals. The simple act of rotating a photo, for example, creates a backup (which, considering how easy it is to re-rotate it, you might not consider strictly necessary). If you've set up iPhoto to open a double-clicked photo in another program like Photoshop, iPhoto creates a backup copy *even if you don't end up changing it* in that external program.

If this library-that-ate-Cleveland effect bothers you, you might investigate the free program iPhoto Diet (available from the "Missing CD" page of *www.missingmanuals.com*, for example). One of its options offers to delete the backups of photos that have simply been rotated. Another deletes perfect duplicates that iPhoto created when you opened those photos in another program without editing them.

There's even an option to delete *all* backups—a drastic option for people who believe that their photos will never be better than they are right now.

Part Three:
Meet Your Public

3

The iPhoto Slideshow

i Photo's slideshow feature offers one of the world's best ways to show off your digital photos. Slideshows are easy to set up, they're free, and they make your photos look fantastic. This chapter details not only how to put together an iPhoto slideshow, but how to give presentations that make you and your photos look their absolute best.

About Slideshows

When you run an iPhoto slideshow, your Mac presents the pictures in full-screen mode—no windows, no menus, no borders—with your images as big as they'll go within the confines of your monitor. Professional transitions take you from one picture to the next, producing a smooth, cinematic effect. If you want, you can even add a musical soundtrack to accompany the presentation. The total effect is incredibly polished, yet creating a slideshow requires very little setup.

The One-Click Slideshow

If you haven't already tried iPhoto's slideshow feature, give it a whirl right now. It requires only a single click.

With either a photo album or your entire Photo Library displayed in the iPhoto window, click the Play button under the Info pane (see Figure 7-1). A moment later, your Mac's screen fades to black, and then the show begins. Each photo is displayed full screen for two seconds, and then softly fades out as the next one dissolves into view. The default musical soundtrack—J. S. Bach's "Minuet in G"—plays in the background. (You'll always find the currently selected soundtrack listed in the Info panel at the left side of the iPhoto window.)

As noted in Chapter 4, this is a great feature for reviewing photos you've just dumped into the Mac from the camera. In fact, that delicious moment when you first see the pictures at full-screen size—after having viewed them only on the camera's two-inch screen—is just what Apple's engineers had in mind when they designed the Play button.

Remember to wiggle your mouse during the slideshow when you want to summon iPhoto 4's new onscreen control bar (page 92).

When you've had enough, click the mouse or press any letter or number key to end the show and return to the iPhoto window. (Otherwise, iPhoto will run the show in a continuous loop forever.)

Figure 7-1:
The quickest way to kick off a slideshow in iPhoto is to click the Play button in the main iPhoto window, shown by the cursor here. There's no keyboard shortcut, but you can hit any key except the arrow keys, modifier keys (like Shift and Option), and the Space bar to stop a show once it's running.

Setting Up the Show

Of course, this canned slideshow is just a starting point. To put together a presentation that will dazzle friends and family, you're invited to select the most impressive photos, choose the perfect background music, and even control how fast or slow the show moves along. Best of all, you can save different slideshow settings for *each album,* as described later in this chapter.

Choose Your Photos

When putting together a slideshow, your first task is choosing the photos you want to include.

As a starting point, here's how iPhoto determines which photos *it* includes:

- If no photos are selected, iPhoto shows all the pictures currently in the photo viewing area, starting with the first photo in the album or Photo Library.

Most people, most of the time, want to turn one album into a slideshow. That's easy: just click the album before starting the slideshow. It can be any album you've created, a smart album, the Last Roll album, or one of iPhoto's built-in monthly yearly albums. As long as no individual pictures are selected, iPhoto will reveal all the pictures in the currently open album.

Note: You can run a slideshow from a photo album, or from your entire Photo Library—but not from *multiple* albums. You can select more than one album simultaneously (by ⌘-clicking them), but when you click Play, iPhoto uses only the first album for the slideshow.

- If only one photo is *visible* (but not selected) in the photo viewing area, then the slideshow consists of that one picture. The music still plays—you just end up with a one-picture show.

- If one photo is *selected,* iPhoto uses that picture as its starting point for the show, ignoring any that come before it. Of course, if you've got the slideshow set to loop continuously, iPhoto will eventually circle back to display the first photo in the window.

- If you've selected more than one picture, iPhoto includes *only* those pictures in its slideshow.

Not all pictures are good pictures

Choosing photos for your slideshow involves more than just picking the photos you like the best. You also have to make sure you've selected pictures that are the right size.

Why is the size so important? Because iPhoto always displays slideshow photos at full-screen dimensions—and on most of today's monitors, that means at least 1024 x 768 pixels. If your photos are smaller than that, iPhoto stretches them to fill the screen, often with disastrous results. If you include a tiny 320 x 240 pixel snapshot in a slideshow, for example, the resulting image, blown up to more than ten times its normal size, turns into a blurry, blocky-looking mess.

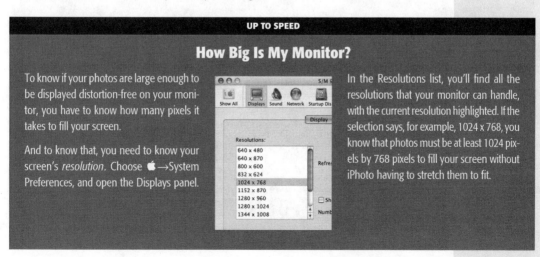

UP TO SPEED

How Big Is My Monitor?

To know if your photos are large enough to be displayed distortion-free on your monitor, you have to know how many pixels it takes to fill your screen.

And to know that, you need to know your screen's *resolution*. Choose →System Preferences, and open the Displays panel.

In the Resolutions list, you'll find all the resolutions that your monitor can handle, with the current resolution highlighted. If the selection says, for example, 1024 x 768, you know that photos must be at least 1024 pixels by 768 pixels to fill your screen without iPhoto having to stretch them to fit.

Note: Although iPhoto blows up images to fill the screen, it always does so proportionally, maintaining each photo's vertical-to-horizontal aspect ratio. As a result, photos often appear with vertical bars at the left and right edges when viewed on long rectangular screens like the Apple Cinema Display, the 17-inch iMac or PowerBook, and so on. For one way to solve this problem, see "Scale photos to fill screen" (page 165).

Figure 7-2:
Here's an example of what happens when a 240 x 180 pixel photo ends up in a slideshow. Projected at full-screen dimensions, a portrait that looks great at its normal size becomes jaggy-edged and fuzzy—unflattering to both the subject and the photographer. If you plan to use your photos in a slideshow, make sure your digital camera is set to capture pictures that are at least 1024 x 768 pixels.

WORKAROUND WORKSHOP

Small Photos, Big Show

You can't control the size of your pictures as they appear during a slideshow, as they always fill the screen. To ensure that the results look good, you need to make sure all your photos are sized to fill the screen *properly,* as mentioned earlier in this chapter.

But what if you're *stuck* with photos that are simply not big enough? Suppose you're charged with putting together a slideshow for the family reunion, and the only pictures you have of Uncle Rodney happen to be scanned photos that are only 640 x 480 pixels?

You can't cut Rodney out of the slideshow, but at the same time, you know Aunt Lois won't take kindly to having her husband appear onscreen hideously distorted. ("Why does Rod look so jagged?" you can imagine her saying. "What did you do to him?") Here's one simple way to have smaller photos displayed perfectly in a slideshow and keep everyone happy:

Using a program like GraphicConverter or Photoshop Elements, create a new document that's exactly the right size for your screen. If your monitor's set to 1024 x 768 pixels, create a document that's 1024 x 768 pixels. Fill the background of the blank document so that it's black, to match the black between slides. (Actually, you can use whatever background you like.)

Now open the small photo that you want to include in your slideshow. Paste a copy of it into the center of your blank document. Save the results and then import the image file into iPhoto.

You now have a new picture, perfectly sized for your slideshow. Your small photo will appear onscreen at the proper size, with a black border around it. No, the photo won't fill the screen, but at least it will appear just as clear and distortion-free as the larger photos.

Determining the size of your photos

If you're not sure whether your photos are big enough to be slideshow material, iPhoto provides two easy ways to check their sizes:

- Click a thumbnail in the photo viewing area, and then look at the Size field in the Info pane. You'll see something like "1600 x 1200." That's the width and height of the image, measured in pixels.

- Select a thumbnail and choose Photos→Show Info, or press ⌘-I to open the Show Info window. The width and height of the photo are the first two items listed in the Image section of the Photo pane.

Putting photos in the right order

iPhoto shows your pictures in the same order you see them in the photo viewing area. In other words, to rearrange your slides, drag the thumbnails around within their album. Remember that you can't drag pictures around in the Photo Library, a smart album, the Last 12 Months collection, or the Last Roll folder—only within a photo album.

Note: If iPhoto appears to be shamelessly disregarding the order of your photos when running a slideshow, it's probably because you've got the "Present slides in random order" option turned on in the Slideshow dialog box, as described in the following section.

Slideshow Settings

With your photos selected, you're ready to configure the settings for your slideshow. In Organize mode, click the Slideshow icon at the bottom of the iPhoto window to explore your options. The Slideshow dialog box has two panels—Settings and Music—as shown in Figure 7-3. In iPhoto 4, you have more ways than ever to customize your slideshow:

Transitions

In previous versions of iPhoto, you were stuck with one type of transition—the crossfade or *dissolve*, in which one slide gradually fades away as the next "fades in" to take its place. In iPhoto 4, you have a choice of five transition effects:

- **None.** An abrupt switch—a simple cut—to the following image.

- **Cube.** Imagine that your photos are pasted to the sides of a box that rotates to reveal the next one. If you've ever used the Fast User Switching feature in Mac OS 10.3, you've got the idea.

- **Dissolve.** This classic crossfade should be familiar to users of previous versions of iPhoto or the screen saver feature in Mac OS X.

- **Mosaic Flip.** The screen is divided into a bunch of squares, each of which rotate in turn to reveal part of the new image, like puzzle pieces turning over.

- **Wipe.** The new image sweeps across the screen, pushing the old one off the other side.

If you choose a transition other than Dissolve or None, a pop-up menu and slider below the pop-up menu offer you the chance to choose a direction and speed for the effect.

- **Direction.** Determines the direction the new image enters from. Choose Right to Left, Top to Bottom, or vice versa. (Most people find Left to Right the most comfortable way to experience a transition, but a slow top-to-bottom wipe is pleasant, too.)

- **Speed.** Move the slider to the right for a speedy transition, or to the left for a leisurely one. Take into account your Timing setting, described below. The less time your photo is onscreen, the better off you are with a fast transition speed, so that your audience has time to see the picture before the next transition starts. However, moving it *all* the way to the right produces a joltingly fast change.

Tip: For a smooth, but unobtrusive transition, choose Dissolve, with the Speed slider moved almost all the way to the right. It's less abrupt than None, but it puts all the emphasis on the pictures, not the transition.

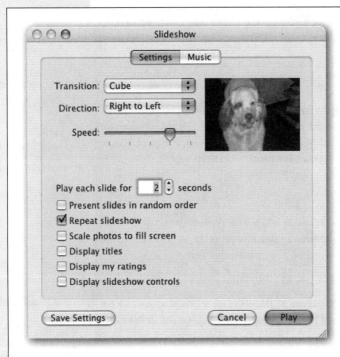

Figure 7-3:
The Slideshow dialog box is where you set slideshow timing for each show. You can go as fast as one second per slide, or bump the number up to 60 seconds each for a very leisurely presentation. (You can type a number larger than 60 in the "Play each slide…" field, but iPhoto will ignore you. It refuses to spend any more than one minute on each shot, no matter how good a photographer you are.)

Using the pop-up menus and Speed slider at the top of this dialog box, you can choose from five transition effects and decide how quickly you want them to go by. If you chooose Wipe, Cube, or Mosaic Flip, in fact, you can also use the Direction pop-up menu to specify whether the change proceeds left to right, top to bottom, or whatever.

Slide timing

If left to its own devices, iPhoto advances through your pictures at the rate of one photo every two seconds. If that seems too brisk or too slow, you can change the rate.

In the Slideshow dialog box, use the "Play each slide for __ seconds" controls to specify a different interval, as shown in Figure 7-3.

Tip: You can also speed up or slow down a show that's already under way, just by pressing the up or down arrow keys. Behind the scenes, iPhoto adjusts the number of seconds in the Slideshow dialog box accordingly.

The timing you choose here doesn't affect the timing or speed of the *transitions*, as it did in iPhoto 2. You set the transition speed independently using the slider, as described above.

Note: You can't set different timings for different pictures. It's one-timing-fits-all—within each show, anyway. You *can* set a different timing for each album.

Present slides in random order

An iPhoto slideshow normally displays your pictures in the order they appear in the photo viewing area. But if you'd like to add a dash of surprise and spontaneity to the proceedings, turn on the "Present slides in random order" checkbox. iPhoto will shuffle the pictures into whatever order it pleases.

Repeat slideshow

When iPhoto is done running through all your photos in a slideshow, it ordinarily circles back and starts playing the whole sequence from the beginning again. If you want your photos to play just once through, turn off the "Repeat slideshow" checkbox.

Scale photos to fill screen

What happens when photos in your slideshow don't match your screen's proportions? For example, suppose your slideshow contains photos in portrait orientation—that is, pictures taken with the camera rotated. Ordinarily, iPhoto shrinks the picture to fit the screen, and fills up the unused screen space on each side with vertical black bars.

But if you turn on "Scale photos," iTunes enlarges the picture so much that it completely fills the screen. This solution, however, comes at a cost: Now the top and bottom of portrait-oriented pictures are lost beyond the edges of the monitor. (You can lose the left and right edges instead if the photo's proportions don't match your screen.)

When the middle of the picture is the most important part, this option works fine. If the black bars bother you, the only other alternative is to crop the odd-sized pictures in the slideshow album so that they match your monitor's shape. (See "Cropping" on page 140.)

Display titles

Every photo in your collection can have a name—a title. If you turn on this option, iPhoto superimposes each photo's title during the slideshow, in a small white-on-black box in the upper-right corner of the screen.

Needless to say, the cryptic file names created by your digital camera (IMG00034. JPG) usually don't add much to your slideshow. But if you've taken the time to give your photos helpful, explanatory names ("My dog age 3 mos"), then by all means turn on the "Display titles" checkbox.

Display slideshow controls

You can always summon iPhoto's new onscreen control bar by twitching the mouse during a slideshow; then, if a few seconds go by without any mouse activity, the bar politely fades away again.

If you turn on "Display slideshow controls," however, then the control bar appears automatically every time this slideshow begins—no mouse wiggling required—and remains onscreen all the time.

Display my ratings

As described on page 118, you can differentiate your stunning award-winners from the photographic dogs by adding ratings to each, on a one-to-five-star scale. If you turn on this option, iPhoto superimposes a small ratings bar on the bottom of each slideshow picture. (You can't change the rating using this mini-bar; it's for display purposes only. Of course, a quick mouse wiggle summons the full-blown control bar, complete with its own star-rating panel that you *can* change.)

Note: The control bar and the star-rating panel occupy the same space near the bottom of the slideshow "canvas," so they can't both be on the screen at the same time. That's why the "Display my ratings" checkbox is grayed out when "Display slideshow controls" is turned on.

---

iTunes: The Soundtrack Store

Perhaps more than any other single element, *music* transforms a slideshow, turning your ordinary photos into a cinematic event. When you pair the right music with the right pictures, you do more than just show off your photos; you create a mood that can stir the emotions of your audience. So if you really want your friends and family to be transfixed by your photos, add a soundtrack.

That's especially easy if, like many Mac OS X fans, you've assembled a collection of your favorite music in iTunes, the free music-playing software that comes with every Mac. (It's also included with the $50 iLife package, or you can download it from *www. apple.com*.) In iPhoto 4, for the first time, you have the choice of an individual song from your iTunes Library or an entire *playlist*. Gone are the days of listening to the same tune repeating over and over again during a lengthy slideshow—a sure way to go quietly insane (unless, of course, you really like that song...a *lot*).

The possibilities of this new feature are endless, especially combined with iPhoto's new smart albums feature. You can create a smart album that contains, say, only photos of your kids taken in December, and give it a soundtrack composed of holiday tunes, created effortlessly using a smart playlist in iTunes. Instant holiday slideshow!

Your first iPhoto slideshow is born with a ready-to-use soundtrack—J. S. Bach's "Minuet in G." In fact, Apple sends iPhoto to you equipped with *two* Bach classics—the Minuet and "Jesu, Joy of Man's Desiring."

Not to knock Bach, but it's fortunate that you're not limited to two of his greatest hits. To switch to a soundtrack of your own choosing, click the Music button at the top of the Slideshow dialog box (Figure 7-4). If you use iTunes, every track in your iTunes Library automatically appears here. You can search and sort through your songs and playlists, just as though you were in iTunes itself.

Figure 7-4:
The Music tab of the Slideshow dialog box lets you choose a playlist (or your entire iTunes Library). By clicking the column headings, you can sort the list by Song, Artist (as shown here), or Time.

If you have a long slideshow (600 photos, say), use the pop-up menu to choose an iTunes playlist rather than an individual song. iTunes will repeat the song (or playlist) for as long as your slideshow lasts.

UP TO SPEED

About MP3 Files

Many of the tracks in your iTunes Library are probably MP3 files. But what exactly does that mean?

MP3 is short for *MPEG-1 Audio Layer -3*, a highly compressed file format that lets you store near-CD-quality music in remarkably small files. In recent years, MP3 has become a standard format for storing and playing back digital music. iTunes is set up to store music in MP3 format, for example, as does the portable iPod music player and virtually all the other Walkman-size digital music players.

There are at least two ways to get your hands on MP3 files

for use as slideshow soundtracks:

- Convert tracks from your favorite CDs into MP3 files using iTunes. Once the songs are in your iTunes Library, you can access them using iPhoto.

- Perform a search on the Internet for *MP3*. You'll find literally thousands of Web sites offering downloads of free music. Just download the tracks you want—and use iTunes to play them and keep them organized.

To get started, click the Music button near the top of the Slideshow dialog box. As shown in Figure 7-4, a pop-up menu reads Sample Music; the two Bach pieces mentioned above appear in a list below. If you have songs of your own in iTunes, choose iTunes Music Library from this pop-up menu to access them (this option is grayed out if you don't have any music files in iTunes).

Your iTunes playlists appear on this menu, too. (A playlist is, for iTunes songs, what an album is in iPhoto: a hand-picked subset of the larger collection.) In other words, you can use this pop-up menu either to select an entire playlist to use as your soundtrack, or to call up a playlist for the purpose of listing the songs in it, thereby narrowing your search for the one song you seek.

- To listen to a song before committing to it as a soundtrack, click its name in the list and then click the triangular Play button. (Click the same button, now shaped like a square Stop button, when you've heard enough.)

- To use an entire playlist as a soundtrack for your slideshow, select it from the pop-up menu. At slideshow time, iPhoto will begin the slideshow with the first tune in the playlist, and continue through all the songs in the list before starting over.

- To use an individual song as a soundtrack, click its name in the list. That song will loop continuously for the duration of the slideshow.

- Rather than scroll through a huge list, you can locate the tracks you want by using the capsule-shaped Search field near the bottom of the window. Click in the

---

POWER USERS' CLINIC

Screen Saver: The Other Slideshow

As good as iPhoto's slideshow feature is, there's an even more impressive way to display your photos onscreen: turn an album into a Mac OS X *screen saver*.

In some ways, iPhoto's Slideshow feature and Mac OS X's screen saver module are very similar. Both completely fill the screen with your photos, and both crossfade one image into the next for a very smooth, polished presentation. But the screen saver module adds another subtle effect—gently zooming in and out of each picture. When combined with the crossfades between shots, the result is a less static, more cinematic slideshow.

The downside of showing photos in screen saver mode is that you have no control over the speed (photos change every eight to ten seconds), you can't override the timing or advance photos manually, and there's no sound.

Still, photos look so good when displayed via the screen saver module that you might consider showing your photos this way and just playing the accompanying music on a CD player stuck under the desk.

See page 283 for instructions on setting up a photo album as a screen saver.

Search field, and then type a word (or part of a word) to filter your list. iPhoto searches the Artist, Song, and Album fields of the iTunes Library and displays only the matching entries. To clear the search and view your whole list again, click the X in the search field.

- Click one of the three headers—Artist, Song, or Time—to sort the iTunes music list alphabetically by that header.

- You can also change the arrangement of the three columns by grabbing the headers and dragging them into a different order.

Once you've settled on (and clicked) an appropriate musical soundtrack for the currently selected album, click Save Settings (to memorize that choice without starting the slideshow) or Play (to begin the slideshow right now). From now on, that song or playlist will play whenever you run a slideshow from that album. (It also becomes the *proposed* soundtrack for any new slideshows you create.)

Alternatively, if you decide you don't want any music to play, turn off the "Play music during slideshow" checkbox on the Music panel of the Slideshow dialog box.

FREQUENTLY ASKED QUESTION

Slideshow Smackdown: iPhoto vs. iMovie

I've read that iMovie makes a great slideshow program, too. Supposedly I can import my photos, add music, and play it all back full-screen with cool cross-dissolves, just like you're saying here. Which program should I use?

The short answer: iPhoto for convenience, iMovie for control.

In iMovie, you can indeed import photos. You can add them to the timeline at the bottom of the window in any order. What's more, you have individual control over their timing (1 second for the first slide, 3 seconds for the second, or whatever) and the crossfades between them (dissolve between slides 1 and 2, a left-to-right "wipe" between slides 2 and 3, and so on). You can even add what Apple calls the Ken Burns Effect: slow, elegant pans and zooms for certain photos, much like the Mac OS X screen saver.

The music options are much greater in iMovie, too. Not only can you import music straight from a music CD (without having to use iTunes as an intermediary), but you can actually record a narration into a microphone as the slideshow

plays. And, of course, you have a full range of title and credit-making features at your disposal, too.

When the show looks good, you can export it to a QuickTime movie just as described in Chapter 11—or, for the absolute finest in picture quality, to Apple's iDVD software for burning onto a real DVD. (A Mac with a DVD burner, called an Apple SuperDrive, is required.)

But iPhoto has charms of its own. Creating a slideshow is *much* less work in iPhoto, for one thing. If you want a slideshow to loop endlessly—playing on a laptop at somebody's wedding, for example, or at a trade show—iPhoto is also a much better bet. (iMovie can't loop.)

Remember, too, that iPhoto is beautifully integrated with your various albums. Whereas building an iMovie project is a serious, sit-down-and-work proposition that results in *one* polished slideshow, your Photo Library has as many different slideshows as you have albums—all ready to go at any time.

Note: You can't select multiple songs from the song list in the Slideshow dialog box. The Shift-click and ⌘-click keystrokes that work in so many Mac lists and dialog boxes are useless here. If you have in mind a group of several songs that would make a perfect backdrop for your slideshow, the solution is to create a new playlist in iTunes, taking care to drag into it the desired songs from your Music Library, in the order that you want them to play. Switch back to iPhoto, and choose that playlist from the pop-up menu in the Slideshow dialog box (see Figure 7-4).

In addition to MP3 files, iTunes (and therefore, iPhoto) can also play music stored in common sound file formats, like AIFF, WAV, and AAC. The first two are considerably less popular then MP3, in part because they take up much more disk space (and require much more time to download). You can convert AIFF and WAV files into MP3s using iTunes.

AAC is the format for songs you buy from Apple's iTunes Music Store (*www.itunes. com*) and download directly into iTunes 4 or later.

Different Shows, Different Albums

You can save different slideshow settings for each album in your Photo Library, something you couldn't do in the program's earliest incarnations.

To save settings for a specific photo album, first choose the album from the Source list, then click the Slideshow icon in the lower pane of the iPhoto window to open the Slideshow dialog box (you have to be in Organize mode to see the button). Pick the speed, order, repeat, and music settings you want, then click Save Settings. The settings you saved will automatically kick in each time you launch a slideshow from that album.

You'll never have to remember which song you've chosen for a given album, either. When you click the album's name, the name of the saved iTunes track appears right in the Info panel of the main iPhoto window, as shown in Figure 7-1.

Running the Show

Once you've picked your photos, set your options, and selected a music track, your show is ready to run. Click the Play button (the triangular button beneath the Source list) in the main iPhoto window. The slideshow begins instantly.

Control Over the Show

iPhoto slideshows run themselves, advancing from photo to photo according to the timing you set in the Slideshow dialog box. However, you can control a slideshow after it starts running in a number of ways. Some of these functions are also represented by icons on the control bar (see page 92), but it's nice to know that you can also trigger them from the keyboard, with or without the control bar:

- **Pause it.** Press the Space bar at any point to pause a slideshow. The music keeps playing, but the photos stop advancing. If the control bar isn't onscreen, a glowing Pause indicator briefly appears in the lower portion of the picture. When you're ready to move to the next slide and resume the auto-advancing of pictures, press Space again. A small Play indicator appears onscreen momentarily to confirm that iPhoto has understood your command.

- **Manual advance.** Press the right or left arrow keys to advance to the next or previous photo, overriding the preset timing. In fact, once you hit either arrow key, the slideshow shifts into manual mode and stops advancing the photos altogether. A small translucent bar with arrows and a Play button appears onscreen to indicate that iPhoto is listening to your key presses.

  At this point, you can continue to use the arrow keys to move through all the photos—or stay on one photo for the rest of your life, for all iPhoto cares. As with the pause command, the music track keeps on playing. (To stop the music, you must end the slideshow.)

  In short, this is a terrific setup for a slideshow that you're narrating in person.

- **Back to auto-advance.** To put a slideshow back into autoplay mode after you've used one of the arrow keys, press the Space bar. The photos advance automatically once again. Or, just wait a moment. As the onscreen arrows or control bar fade away, auto-advancing will resume.

- **Speed it up or slow it down.** Press the up or down arrow keys to speed up or slow down the slideshow on the fly. You'll discover that iPhoto can't create a stroboscopic, three-frames-per-second effect; one picture per second is about its maximum speed. (Give the poor thing a break—it's got a *lot* of data to scoop off the hard drive and throw onto your screen.)

Note: The changes you make manually are temporary. The next time you run a slideshow, you'll start again with the timing set in the Slideshow dialog box.

- **Rate the photos.** Even if you haven't summoned the control bar, you can rate photos as they flash by just by tapping the corresponding number keys on your keyboard: 1, 2, 3, 4, or 5 for the corresponding number of stars, or 0 to remove the rating.

- **Rotate the photos.** If a photo appears sideways, press ⌘-R to rotate it counterclockwise, or Option-⌘-R to rotate it clockwise. (Or vice versa, if you've fooled around with iPhoto's Preferences dialog box.)

- **Delete the duds.** When a forgettable photo appears, press the Delete or Del key on your keyboard to move it to the iPhoto Trash (page 119), without even interrupting the show. (Unless you have very understanding family and friends, you may want to do this *before* you show the pictures to others for the first time.)

Slideshow Tips

The following guidelines will help you build impressive slideshows that truly showcase your efforts as a digital photographer:

- Very small photos are ugly when blown up to full-screen size. Very large ones look fine, but iPhoto takes longer to display them, and the crossfade transitions might not look smooth. For the best possible results, make your photos the same pixel size as your screen.

- To whatever degree possible, stick with photos in landscape (horizontal) orientation, especially if you have a wide monitor screen. With portrait-oriented (vertical) photos, iPhoto displays big black borders along the sides.

- For similar reasons, try to stick with photos whose proportions roughly match your screen. If you have a traditionally shaped screen (iBook, 12-inch PowerBook, 15-inch iMac, and so on), use photos with a 4:3 (width to height) ratio, just as they came from the camera. However, if you have a widescreen monitor (Cinema Display, 17-inch iMac, and so on), photos cropped to 6 x 4 proportions are a closer fit.

Tip: If you don't have time to crop all your odd-sized or vertically oriented photos, consider using the "Scale photos" feature described on page 165. It makes your pictures fill the screen nicely, although you risk cutting off important elements (like heads and feet).

- Preview images at full size before using them. You can't judge how sharp and bright an image is going to look based solely on the thumbnail.

- Keep the timing brief when setting the playing speed—maybe just a few seconds per photo. Better to have your friends wanting to see more of each photo than to have them bored, mentally rearranging their sock drawers as they wait for the show to advance to the next image. Remember, you can always pause a slideshow if someone wants to take a longer look at one picture.

- Give some thought to the order of your photos. A good slideshow can tell a story. You might want to start with a photo that establishes a location—an overall shot of a park, for example—and then follow it with close-ups that reveal the details.

- If your viewers fall in love with what you've shown them, you have four options: (a) save the slideshow as a QuickTime movie that you can email them or burn onto a CD for their at-home enjoyment (Chapter 11); (b) turn the show into an interactive DVD using Apple's iDVD software (see Chapter 12); (c) create a .Mac slideshow (page 212); or (d) make your admirers buy their own Macs.

Slideshows and iDVD

If you have a Mac equipped with a DVD-burning SuperDrive, you have yet another slideshow option: Instead of running a presentation directly from iPhoto, you can send your slideshow—music and all—from iPhoto to iDVD, Apple's simple DVD-authoring software. Using iDVD, you can transform the pictures from your album into an interactive slideshow that can be presented using any DVD player. (Just picture the family clicking through your photos on the big-screen TV in the den!)

Learn how to do the iPhoto-to-iDVD conversion in Chapter 12.

Making Prints

There's a lot to love about digital photos that remain digital. You can store hundreds of them on a single CD; you can send them anywhere on earth by email; and they won't wrinkle, curl, or yellow until your monitor does.

Sooner or later, though, most people want to get at least some of their photos on paper. You may want printouts to paste into your existing scrapbooks, to put in picture frames on the mantle, to use on homemade greeting cards, or to share with your Luddite friends who don't have computers.

Using iPhoto, you can create such prints using your own printer. Or, for prints that look, feel, and smell like the kind you get from a photo finishing store, you can transmit your digital files to Kodak Print Services, an online photo processing service. In return, you receive an envelope of professionally printed photos on Kodak paper that are indistinguishable from their traditional counterparts.

This chapter explains how to use each of iPhoto's printing options, including the features that let you print greeting cards, contact sheets, and other special items from your digital photo collection.

Making Great Prints

Using iPhoto to print your pictures is pretty easy. But making *great* prints—the kind that rival traditional film-based photos in their color and image quality—involves more than simply hitting the Print command.

One key factor, of course, is the printer itself. You need a good printer that can produce photo-quality color printouts. Fortunately, getting such a printer these days is pretty easy and inexpensive. Even some of the cheapo inkjet printers from Epson, HP, and

Canon can produce amazingly good color images—and they cost less than $100. (Of course, you make it up to the printer company on the back end when you buy more ink cartridges. Depending on how many prints you make, what you spend on these expensive cartridges can easily double or triple the cost of the printer in a year.)

Tip: If you're really serious about producing photographically realistic printouts, consider buying a model that's specifically designed for photo printing, such as one of the printers in the Epson Stylus Photo series or the slightly more expensive Canon printers. What you're looking for is a printer that uses *six* or even *seven* different colors of ink instead of the usual "inkjet four." The extra colors do wonders for the printer's ability to reproduce a wide range of colors on paper.

Even with the best printer, however, you can end up with disappointing results if you fail to consider at least three other important factors when trying to coax the best possible printouts from your digital photos. These factors include the resolution of your images, the settings on your printer, and your choice of paper.

Resolution and Shape

Resolution is the number of individual pixels squeezed into each inch of your digital photo. The basic rule is simple: The higher your photo's resolution, or *dpi* (dots per inch), the sharper, clearer, and more detailed the printout will be. If the resolution is too low, you end up with a printout that looks blurry or speckled.

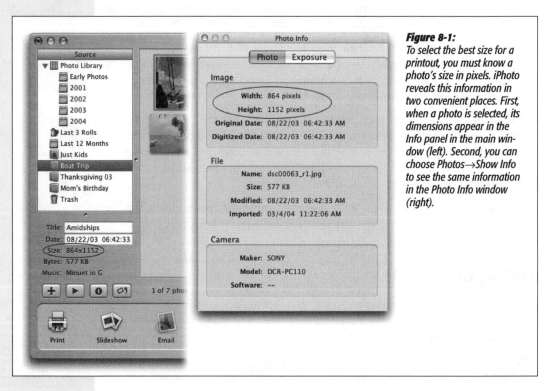

Figure 8-1:
To select the best size for a printout, you must know a photo's size in pixels. iPhoto reveals this information in two convenient places. First, when a photo is selected, its dimensions appear in the Info panel in the main window (left). Second, you can choose Photos→Show Info to see the same information in the Photo Info window (right).

Low-resolution photos are responsible for more wasted printer ink and crumpled photo paper than any other printing snafu, so it pays to understand how to calculate a photo's dpi when you want to print it.

Calculating resolution

To calculate a photo's resolution, divide the horizontal or vertical size of the photo (measured in pixels) by the horizontal or vertical size of the print you want to make (usually measured in inches).

Suppose a photo measures 1524 x 1016 pixels. (How do you know? See Figure 8-1.) If you want a 4 x 6 printout, you'll be printing at a resolution of 254 dpi (1524 pixels divided by 6 inches = 254 dpi), which will look fantastic on paper. Photos printed on an inkjet printer look their best when printed at a resolution of 220 dpi or higher.

But if you try to print that same photo at 8 x 10, you'll get into trouble. By stretching those pixels across a larger print area, you're now printing at just 152 dpi—and you'll see a noticeable drop in image quality.

While it's important to print photos at a resolution of 250 to 300 dpi on an inkjet printer, there's really no benefit to printing at higher resolutions—600 dpi, 800 dpi, or more. It doesn't hurt anything to print at a higher resolution, but you probably won't notice any difference in the final printed photos—at least not on inkjet printers. Some inkjets can spray ink at finer resolutions—720 dpi, 1440 dpi, and so on—and using these highest settings produces very smooth, very fine printouts. But bumping the resolution of your *photos* higher than 300 dpi doesn't have any perceptible effect on their quality.

Aspect ratio

You also have to think about your pictures' *aspect ratio*—their proportions. Most digital cameras produce photos with 4-to-3 proportions, which don't fit neatly onto standard print paper (4 x 6 and so on). You can read more about this problem on page 141. (Just to make sure you're completely confused, print paper is measured *height by width,* whereas digital photos are measured *width by height.*)

If you're printing photos on letter-size paper, the printed images won't have standard Kodak dimensions. (They'll be, for example, 4 x 5.3.) You may not particularly care. But if you're printing onto, say, precut 4 x 6 photo paper (which you choose in the File→Page Setup dialog box), you can avoid ugly white bands at the sides by first cropping your photos to standard print sizes (see page 140).

Tweaking the Printer Settings

Just about every inkjet printer on earth comes with software that adjusts various print quality settings. Usually, you can find the controls for these settings right in the Print dialog box that appears when you choose File→Print. To reveal these printer-specific controls in iPhoto, click the Advanced Options button in the Print dialog box, and then choose an additional command from the pop-up menu (Figure 8-2).

Before you print, verify that you've got these settings right. On most printers, for example, you can choose from several different quality levels when printing, like Draft, Normal, Best, or Photo. There might also be a menu that lets you select the kind of paper you're going to use—plain paper, inkjet paper, glossy photo paper, and so on.

Choose the wrong settings, and you'll be wasting a lot of paper. Even a top-of-the-line Epson photo printer churns out awful photo prints if you feed it plain paper when it's expecting high-quality glossy stock. You'll end up with a smudgy, soggy mess. So each time you print, make sure your printer is configured for the quality, resolution, and paper settings that you intend.

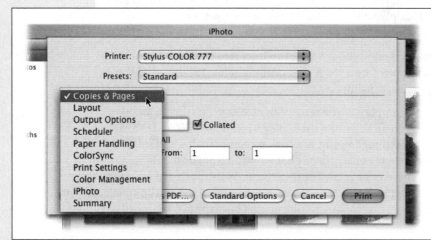

Figure 8-2:
Click Advanced Options in the standard iPhoto Print dialog box to open this important box. Here, choose Print Settings, Quality & Media, or a similar command from the pop-up menu (depending on your printer type) to see the controls for paper type, print quality, and so on.

Paper Matters

When it comes to inkjet printing, paper is critical. Regular typing paper—the stuff you'd feed through a laser printer or copier—may be cheap, but it's too thin and absorbent to handle the amount of ink that gets sprayed on when you print a full-color digital photo. If you try to print large photos on plain paper, you'll end up with flat colors, slightly fuzzy images, and paper that's rippled and buckling from all the ink. For really good prints, you need paper designed expressly for inkjets.

Most printers accommodate at least five different grades of paper. Among them:

- Plain paper (the kind used in most photocopiers)

- High Resolution paper (a slightly heavier inkjet paper—not glossy, but with a silky-smooth white finish on one side)

- Glossy Photo paper (a stiff, glossy paper resembling the paper that developed photos are printed on)

- Photo Matte paper (a stiff, non-glossy stock)

- Most companies also offer an even more expensive glossy *film*, made of polyethylene rather than paper (which feels even more like traditional photographic paper)

These better photo papers cost much more than plain paper, of course. Glossy photo paper, for example, might run $25 for a box of 50 sheets, which means you'll be spending about 60 cents per 8 x 10 print—not including ink.

Still, by using good photo paper, you'll get much sharper printouts, more vivid colors, and results that look and feel like actual photographic prints. Besides, at sizes over 4 x 6 or so, making your own printouts is still less expensive than getting prints from the drugstore, even when you factor in printer cartridges and photo paper.

Tip: To save money and avoid wasting your high-quality photo paper, use plain inkjet paper for test prints. When you're sure you've got the composition, color balance, and resolution of your photo just right, load up your expensive glossy photo paper for the final printouts.

Printing from iPhoto

When you choose File→Print (⌘-P) in iPhoto, you don't see the standard Mac OS X Print dialog box—the one that asks you how many copies you want to print, which pages you want included, and so on. (As shown in Figure 8-2, you must click Advanced Options to see these controls.)

POWER USERS' CLINIC

Advanced Printing Options

As mentioned earlier, the "advanced" printing options that appear when you click the Advanced Options button in the Print dialog box aren't really advanced. They're the standard, everyday options that you find in the Print dialog box when printing from any other Mac OS X program, as shown in Figure 8-2.

You can safely ignore many of these options, which vary depending on which printer you're using. For example, unless you're using a fancy printer equipped with multiple paper trays and double-sided printing capabilities, there's no need to concern yourself with the Duplex and Paper Feed options. The Error Handling panel, which appears if you're using a PostScript printer, controls arcane details about how your printer reports PostScript errors; you'll be happier if you don't even think about it. And the Summary panel is just a window showing your current printer settings, with nothing to turn on or off.

Some of these other printing options are more useful:

- **Copies & Pages.** You don't have to use this panel to choose the number of copies you want printed; you do that using the standard iPhoto print options. However, this panel does allow you to set a specific *range* of pages for printing, which can be helpful. You can print just the first page or two of a 26-page contact sheet, for example, to test your print settings.

- **Output Options.** This panel offers another way to save your print job as a PDF file, exactly like the one described on page 186.

- **Printer Features.** This panel is important, since it's where you can make adjustments that are specific to *your* particular printer. Depending on the make and model of your printer, this might be where you set print resolution, quality, and speed settings.

Instead, you're presented with iPhoto's own private version of the Print command, with six photo-specific printing options at your disposal: Standard Prints, Full Page, Greeting Cards, Contact Sheet, N-Up, and Sampler.

Each of these six printing styles is discussed in detail below.

Standard-Sized Prints

Use this method to print out photos that conform to standard photo sizes, like 5 x 7 or 8 x 10. This is especially useful if you intend to mount your printed photos in store-bought picture frames, which are designed to handle photos in these standard dimensions.

1. **Select the thumbnail(s) of the photo(s) you want to print.**

   Alternatively, you can open the photo in Edit mode before you print it; the Print command is accessible in all of iPhoto's modes. You can also select more than one photo—a good idea if you want to get the most out of your expensive inkjet paper (see step 5). Just highlight the ones you want, using the techniques described on page 106.

2. **Choose File→Print, or press ⌘-P.**

   The iPhoto Print dialog box appears.

3. **From the Style pop-up menu, choose Standard Prints.**

   This is the factory setting, but if you've been printing other formats, you may have to switch it back.

4. **Using the Size pop-up menu, choose the print size you want.**

   You have several standard photo sizes to choose from—4 x 6, 5 x 7, and so on. Remember, though, that choosing a larger size stretches the pixels of your photo across a larger area, reducing the photo's resolution and potentially degrading its print quality. For best results, don't choose 8 x 10 unless the picture you're print-

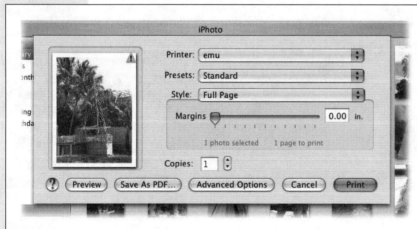

Figure 8-3:
See that warning icon on the top right corner of the preview? That's iPhoto's warning that the selected print size is too large, given the resolution of your photo. If you ignore the warning, your printout will likely have jagged edges or fuzzy detail.

ing is at least 1200 x 1800 pixels. (A yellow triangle warns you if the resolution is too low; see Figure 8-3.)

The Preview panel displays how your photo will be positioned on the paper, as shown in Figure 8-3.

5. **Select the number of photos you want printed on each page.**

When the "One photo per page" checkbox is turned off, iPhoto fits as many photos as it can on each page, based on the paper size (which you select using the File→ Page Setup command) and the photo size that you've chosen. Conversely, when the checkbox is turned on, you get one photo at the center of each page.

On letter-size paper, iPhoto can fit nine 2 x 3, four 3 x 5, two 4 x 6, or two 5 x 7 pictures on each page. (If you're printing one photo per sheet—on 4 x 6 paper, for example—use the Full Page option described below, not "One photo per page.")

6. **Choose the number of copies you want to make.**

You can either type the number into the Copies field or click the arrows to increase or decrease the number.

7. **Click the Print button (or press Enter).**

Your printer scurries into action, printing your photos as you've requested.

Tip: Printing photos using these standard sizes works best if your digital photos are trimmed so that they fit perfectly into one of the three preset dimensions—4 x 6, 5 x 7, or 8 x 10. Use iPhoto's Constrained Cropping tool, explained on page 141, to trim your photos to precisely these sizes.

Greeting Cards

When you choose Greeting Card from the Style pop-up menu of the Print dialog box, iPhoto automatically rotates and positions your photo (Figure 8-4). You could conceivably print out cards on standard letter-size paper and then fold it into halves

Figure 8-4:
iPhoto's Greeting Card printing doesn't create any actual greeting card content—no titles, holiday-themed icons, fancy borders, or pithy verses here. All you get is a printout of your photo on an otherwise blank sheet of paper, ready to be folded into a greeting card–shaped configuration.

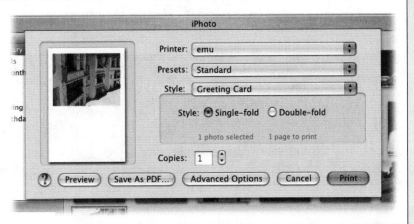

or quarters, but this option is actually designed for printing on special inkjet greet-ing-card paper. This kind of glossy or matte paper stock, made by Epson and others, comes prescored and perforated for tidy edge-to-edge printing and crisp folding.

Here's how you print out a greeting card:

1. **Select or open the photo(s) you want to print.**

   Only one photo goes on each card. If you've selected more than one picture, you'll see only the first one illustrated in the preview.

2. **Choose File→Print, press ⌘-P, or click the Print button at the bottom of the Organize-mode iPhoto window.**

   The Print dialog box appears.

3. **From the Style menu, choose Greeting Card. Pick a greeting card style using the radio buttons.**

   You have two choices: Single-fold, which prints your photo onto a half sheet of paper; or Double-fold, which fits your photo into a quarter-page printing area. The Preview panel on the left side of the Print dialog box illustrates how each of these options will appear in the final printout.

4. **In the Copies field, enter the number of copies you want to make.**

   If you selected multiple photos in Step 1, iPhoto will print multiple greeting cards, one per photo. The number you enter here is different, in that it tells iPhoto how many *duplicates* of each one to print.

5. **Click the Print button (or press Enter).**

   Print, fold, sign, and mail.

Printing Full Page Photos

iPhoto's Full Page printing option reduces or enlarges each photo so that it completely fills a single page.

To make Full Page prints, select the photo(s) you want to print, press ⌘-P, and then choose Full Page from the Style pop-up menu in the Print dialog box (Figure 8-5).

FREQUENTLY ASKED QUESTION

Changing Page Sizes

iPhoto's Print command lets me choose the size of the pho-tos I want to print, but not the size of the paper I'm printing them on. Can't I pick a different paper size?

Yes, but remember that you change this kind of setting in the Page Setup dialog box, not the Print dialog box. Choose File→Page Setup, and then select the paper size you want using the Paper Size pop-up menu.

With Full Page printing, it takes ten pages to print ten photos, of course—but when you make Standard, N-Up, Sampler, or Contact Sheet prints, iPhoto can fit more than one photo on each page.

Tip: iPhoto's print dialog box tells you how many photos you've selected and how many pages it will take to print them all. However, this information is easy to miss because it appears in dim, grayed-out text near the center of the dialog box, under the Margins slider (Figure 8-5).

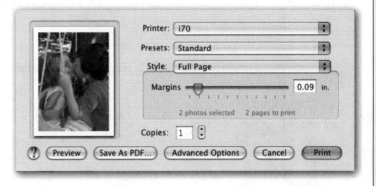

Figure 8-5:
Use the Margins slider to change the width of the margins around your photo. You can add margins of up to one inch. You can also specify zero margins, although that doesn't mean you'll get edge-to-edge printing. You will, however, get the smallest margins your particular printer can muster.

Contact Sheets

The Contact Sheet option prints out a *grid* of photos, tiling as many as 120 different pictures onto a single letter-size page (eight columns, fourteen rows, for example).

Photographers use contact sheets as a quick reference tool when organizing photos—a poor man's iPhoto, if you think about it. But this printing option is also handy in some other practical ways:

- By printing several pictures side by side on the same page, you can easily make quality comparisons among them without using two sheets of paper.

- Use contact sheet printing to make test prints, saving ink and paper. Sometimes a 2 x 3 print is all you need to determine if a picture is too dark or if its colors are wildly off when rendered by an inkjet printer. Don't make expensive full-page prints until you're sure you've adjusted your photo so that it will print out correctly.

- You can easily print multiple copies of a *single* picture if you want to produce lots of wallet-sized (or smaller) copies. (You can also do this using the N-Up option described on page 182.)

Contact Sheet printing options

To make Contact Sheet prints, choose Contact Sheet from the Style pop-up menu in the Print dialog box. Your printing options vary:

- If no photos are selected, the Contact Sheet option will print *all* the photos in the current album (or Photo Library, if that's what's selected). Use the Across slider (Figure 8-6) to change the size of the grid and, therefore, the number of photos that will appear on each printed page. iPhoto will print as many pages as needed to include all the photos in your current view.

- If several photos are selected, iPhoto will print a contact sheet containing only the selected photos.

- When only *one* photo is selected, iPhoto clones that one photo across the whole grid, printing one sheet of duplicate images at whatever size you specify using the slider control.

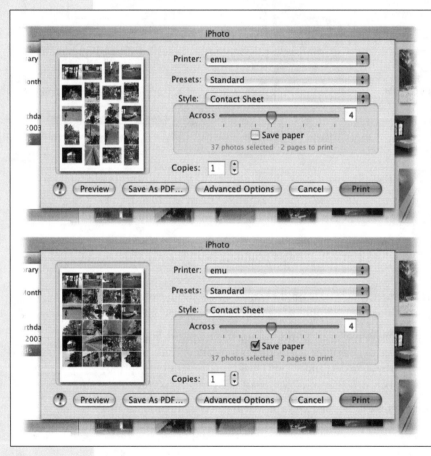

Figure 8-6:
To fit even more pictures on a contact sheet, turn on the Save Paper checkbox, which appears only when you're printing more than one photo. It not only squishes the pictures closer together on the page, but also automatically rotates vertical photos so that they fit into an evenly spaced grid, again reducing white space. With more photos squeezed onto each page (bottom), you end up using less paper than you would otherwise (top).

N-Up

With the N-Up option, you can tell iPhoto exactly how many photos you want printed on each page. The five preset grid configurations let you tile 2, 4, 6, 9, or 16 pictures on each sheet of paper. iPhoto automatically rotates photos as needed to make them fit perfectly into the grid size you choose.

N-Up printing may sound an awful lot like the Contact Sheet option just described, but it's slightly different. When printing Contact Sheets, you specify how many *columns* you want in your photo grid and, based on your choice, iPhoto crams as many photos on the page as it can—even if they end up the size of postage stamps. With N-Up Printing, you control the total number of pictures printed on each page, with a maximum of 16 photos in a 4 x 4 grid.

Tip: If you need your photos to be printed at a specific size—to fit in a 5 x 7 picture frame, for example—use the Standard Prints option instead of N-Up. With Standard Prints, you can specify the exact *size* of the photos; with N-Up, you can't.

N-Up printing options

As with printing contact sheets, your N-Up printing options depend on what you've got selected in the iPhoto window when you choose the Print command and choose N-Up from the Style menu.

• If no photos are selected, iPhoto will print *all* the photos in the current album (or the Photo Library, if that's what's selected). Use the "Photos per page" pop-up menu to set the number of photos that will appear on each printed page, as shown in Figure 8-7. iPhoto will print as many pages as needed to include all the photos in your current view.

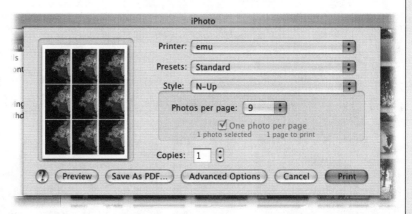

Figure 8-7:
Need a sheet of wallet-sized photos to send to relatives? One way to make them is via the N-Up printing option. Just turn on the "One photo per page" checkbox so that you have two, three, or four rows of duplicate pictures. You can print up to sixteen copies of a photo on each sheet.

• If you select several photos, iPhoto will print a grid containing only those.

• When only *one* photo is selected, iPhoto prints one sheet of duplicate images at whatever grid size you specify.

Sampler Pages

While the Contact Sheet and N-Up options produce a straight grid of evenly-sized photos on each printed page, the Sampler option lets you print a grouping of photos at *different sizes* on a single page—just like the portrait galleries you might get from a professional photographer. For example, you can print a sheet that contains a combination of one large photo and five smaller photos, as shown in Figure 8-8.

Once you choose Sampler from the Style menu in the Print dialog box, you can choose from two different Sampler templates from the Template pop-up menu. Sampler 1 puts three pictures on each page—one large photo on the top, with two smaller ones beneath it. Sampler 2 produces the six-photo layout shown in Figure 8-8.

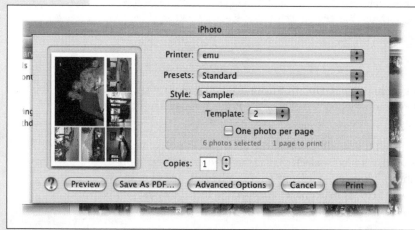

Figure 8-8:
You can print a neatly arranged combination of large and small photos on each page using one of the Sampler templates.

GEM IN THE ROUGH

Portraits & Prints

iPhoto's Sampler option prints *combination* templates like the portrait galleries delivered by professional photographers, but it doesn't offer much flexibility. You can't specify exactly which photos you want where, for example.

Fortunately, a $20 companion program called Portraits & Prints nicely compensates for iPhoto's printing weaknesses. (You can download it from, for example, the "Missing CD" page at *www. missingmanuals.com*.)

Once again, the idea is that you'll drag selected photos directly out of the iPhoto window and, in this case, into the Portraits & Prints window. There, you can boost or reduce

color intensity, sharpen, crop, rotate, add brightness, and remove red-eye. (If you designate Portraits & Prints as your preferred external photo editing program, any changes you make while in Portraits & Prints will be reflected in iPhoto's thumbnails.)

But all that is just an appetizer for the main dish: a delicious variety of printing templates, like the one shown here. The program comes with six "portrait sets" that let you arrange different pictures at different sizes on the same sheet. You can even save your layouts as *catalogs*, so that you can reuse them, or reprint them at a later date.

Tip: For even more flexibility when printing a combination of photo sizes on a single page, see the box on the facing page.

The Sampler option offers the same "One photo per page" checkbox available with N-Up printing (explained in Figure 8-7). Turn it on to fill each page with multiple copies of a single photo, just like the school photos brought home by fourth-graders worldwide each year.

Positioning photos in Sampler templates

You can pick exactly which of the photos from your collection are included in Sampler printouts by selecting them in the iPhoto window *before* choosing the Print command. If you have no photos selected, iPhoto will build Sampler pages using *all* the photos currently visible in the iPhoto window. If you have just one photo selected, iPhoto will fill the Sampler page with duplicates of the single photo. The order of the photos in your Photo Library determines how they're positioned in the printout, as explained in Figure 8-9.

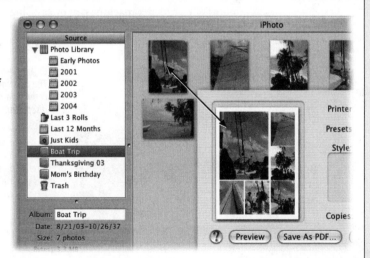

Figure 8-9:
The thing to keep in mind when setting up Sampler pages is that the first photo in your current selection is always the one that iPhoto picks as the "large" photo in the layout. If you want a specific photo to end up in the jumbo photo slot, make sure it's either the first one in the album or first among those you select. If you decide to rearrange the photos on the soon-to-be-printed page, close the Print dialog box, drag the thumbnails into a different order in the main iPhoto window, and then choose Print again.

The Preview Button

A mini-preview of your printout-to-be is always visible on the left side of the Print dialog box. But this postage stamp preview is far too small to show much detail. Worse, it shows you only the *first page* of a multipage job.

For a better preview, click Preview. iPhoto processes the print job, just as if you had hit Print—a "Print" progress bar appears at this point, indicating that the job is "on its way" to the printer. Instead of transmitting the job to your printer hardware, however, iPhoto creates a temporary PDF (Acrobat) file. It opens in Preview, the free graphics-viewing program that comes with Mac OS X.

Tip: Depending on the size of your print job, building a preview can take awhile. iPhoto must process all the image data involved, just as if it were really printing.

You end up with a full-size, full-resolution electronic version of your printout. Using the commands in Preview's Display menu, you can zoom in or out to view details, scroll across pages, and move from page to page (to preview every page of a contact sheet, for example). You're seeing exactly how iPhoto is going to render your printout when it actually hits the printer, using the print options you selected.

If you like what you see in the PDF preview, you have the following two choices:

- Close the Preview window, return to iPhoto, and choose File→Print again (the Print dialog box will have closed itself automatically). Now, confident that you're going to get the results you expect, click the Print button and send the printout to your printer.

- If you want to *keep* the preview—in order to distribute an electronic version of a contact sheet, for example—you can save it, using one of the options shown in Figure 8-10. You can save it, for example, as a PDF file, which anyone with a Mac, Windows PC, or Unix machine can open using the free Acrobat Reader program that comes on every computer.

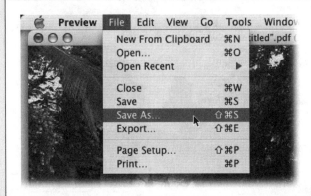

Figure 8-10:
The documents generated by the Preview command are temporary. If you close one, it disappears without even asking if you want to save it.

To save a preview document permanently, choose File→Save As or File→Export. The difference between the two commands: Save As lets you save only as a PDF document; Export lets you choose other formats, like JPEG or TIFF. Save As can create a multipage PDF from a bunch of selected pictures. Export saves only the first page in a selection.

Save As PDF

The Save As PDF button, a standard part of all Mac OS X Print dialog boxes, lets you save a printout-in-waiting as a PDF file instead of printing it on paper. Any type of iPhoto printout—greeting card, contact sheet, sampler, and so on—can be converted to PDF. After opening the Print dialog box, set up your print options the way you want, click the Save As PDF button, name the PDF in the Save to File dialog box, and click Save. (Saving the file can take awhile if you're converting several pages of photos into the PDF.)

Tip: You can also save a print job as a PDF file *after* you've previewed the results, as shown in Figure 8-10.

Ordering Prints Online

Even if you don't have a high-quality color printer, traditional prints of your digital photos are only a few clicks away—if you have an Internet connection and you're willing to spend a little money, that is.

Thanks to a deal between Apple and Kodak, you can order prints directly from within iPhoto. After you select the size and quantity of the pictures you want printed, one click is all it takes to have iPhoto transmit your photos to Kodak Print Services and bill your credit card for the order. The rates range from 39 cents for a single 4 x 6 print to about $23 for a jumbo 20 x 30 poster. Your finished photos, printed on high-quality glossy photographic paper, are sent to you within two days.

Tip: If you plan to order prints, first crop your photos to the proper proportions (4 x 6, for example), using the Crop tool as described in Chapter 6. Most digital cameras produce photos whose shape doesn't quite match standard photo-paper dimensions. If you send photos to Kodak uncropped, you're leaving it up to Kodak to decide which parts of your photo will be lopped off to fit. (More than one Mac fan has opened the envelope to find loved ones missing the tops of their skulls.)

By cropping the pictures to photo-paper shape before you place the order, *you* decide which parts get eliminated. (You can always restore the photos to their original uncropped versions using the Revert to Original command described on page 154.)

Here's how the print-buying process works:

1. **Select the photos you want to print.**

   Click an album in the album list to order prints of everything in it, or select only the specific photos you want. Only the photos you select will appear in the Order Prints window.

2. **Click the Organize button below the main iPhoto window. Then click the Order Prints icon on the bottom panel.**

   Now the Mac must go online to check in with the Kodak processing center. If you have a dial-up connection, your Mac dials out automatically. (If the Mac can't make an Internet connection at all, the Order Prints window, shown in Figure 8-11, doesn't open.)

3. **Click Set Up Account, if necessary.**

   The Set Up Account button appears at the lower-right corner of the dialog box if you've never before ordered an iPhoto book or iPhoto prints. It guides you through several dialog boxes where you surrender your identity and credit-card info. You'll also see the option to turn on "1-Click Ordering system," which is mandatory if you want to order prints. All of this is a one-time task designed to save you time when you make subsequent orders.)

   For details on the process, see page 246. When the Summary screen finally appears, click Done to return to the Order Prints window.

---

4. Select the sizes and quantities you want.

If you want 4 x 6 or 5 x 7 prints of every photo you've selected, just use the Quick Order pop-up menu at the top of the dialog box.

For more control over sizes and quantities of individual photos, ignore that pop-up menu. Instead, fill in the numbers individually for each photo, scrolling down through the dialog box as necessary. The total cost of your order is updated as you make selections.

Tip: If you want *mostly* prints of one size—5 x 7's, for example—type the quantity into the "5 x 7 prints, quantity" box at the top of the window, so that iPhoto fills in that number for every photo. Now you're free to *change* the quantity for the few photos that you *don't* want to order at 5 x 7.

As you order, pay heed to the alert icons (little yellow triangles) that may appear on certain lines of the order form (visible, in spades, in Figure 8-11). These are iPhoto's standard warnings, declaring that certain photos don't have a high enough resolution to be printed at the specified sizes. A photo that looks great at 5 x 7 may look terrible as a 16 x 20 enlargement. Unless you're the kind of person who thrives on disappointment, *never* order prints in a size that's been flagged with a low-resolution alert.

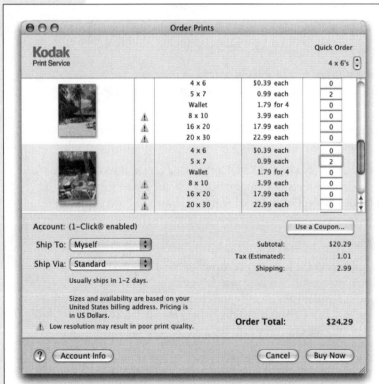

Figure 8-11:
The Order Prints window lets you order six different types of prints from your photos—from a set of four wallet-sized prints to mammoth 20" x 30" posters. Use the scroll bar on the right to scroll through all the photos you've selected to specify how many copies of each photo you want to order. If you need to change your shipping, contact, or credit card information, click the Edit 1-Click Settings button to modify your Apple ID profile.

Tip: You'll see the same warning icon when you print your own photos and order photo books (Chapter 10). As always, you have few attractive choices: order a smaller print, don't order a print at all, or order the print and accept the lower quality that results.

5. **Click the "Buy Now" button to order the prints.**

   "Buy Now" means just that. You don't receive an "Are you sure?" message. Your photos are transferred, your credit card is billed, and you go sit by the mailbox.

   A dialog box appears, showing the reference number for your order and a message saying that you'll be receiving a confirmation via email.

At first glance, you might not consider ordering prints online the most economical method. A batch of 24 standard 4 x 6 snapshots costs about $9, plus shipping, which is more than you'd pay for processing a roll of film at the local drugstore.

Still, this service is economical in other ways. For example, you get to print only the prints that you actually want, rather than developing a roll of 36 prints only to find that only two of them are any good. It's far more convenient than the drugstore method, and it's a handy way to send top-notch photo prints directly to friends and relatives who don't have computers. Furthermore, it's ideal for creating high-quality enlargements that would be impossible to print on the typical inkjet printer.

UP TO SPEED

How Low Is Too Low?

When you order photos online, the Order Prints form automatically warns you when a selected photo has a resolution that's too low to result in a good-quality print. But just what does Kodak consider too low? Here's the list of Kodak's official minimum resolution recommendations.

To order this size picture:	Your photo should be at least:
Wallet-sized	640 x 480 pixels
4 x 5	768 x 512 pixels
5 x 7	1152 x 768 pixels
8 x 10	1536 x 1024 pixels

These are *minimum* requirements, not suggested settings. Your photos will look better in print, in fact, if you *exceed* these resolution settings.

For example, a 1536 x 1024 pixel photo printed at 8 x 10 inches meets Kodak's minimum recommendation, but has an effective resolution of 153 x 128 dpi—a relatively low resolution for high-quality printing. A photo measuring 2200 x 1760 pixels, printed at the same size, would have a resolution of 220 dpi—and look much better on paper, with sharper detail and subtler variations in color.

Sharing Online— and on Your Network

Holding a beautifully rendered glossy color print created from your own digital image is a glorious feeling. But unless you have an uncle in the inkjet cartridge business, you could go broke printing your own photos. Ordering high-quality prints with iPhoto is terrific fun, too, but it's slow and expensive.

For the discerning digital photographer who craves both instant gratification and economy, the solution is to put your photos *online*—either by emailing them to others or posting them on the Web.

Fortunately, transferring your pictures from iPhoto to the Web doesn't require that you buy a Web server, register a domain (dot-com) name, or even design HTML pages. With minimal setup, iPhoto can connect directly to Apple's own Mac.com Web site and publish your photos automatically.

Emailing photos is even easier. And sharing your iPhoto library across a home or office network is easiest of all—and it's one of the nicest new perks in iPhoto 4.

Emailing Photos

Emailing from iPhoto takes just a few clicks and doesn't require that you sign up for anything (that is, assuming that you already have an email account). It's perfect for quickly sending off a single photo—or even a handful of photos—to friends, family, and co-workers. (If you have a whole *batch* of photos to share, on the other hand, consider using the Web-publishing feature described later in this chapter.)

The most important thing to know about emailing photos is this: *full-size photos are usually too big to email.*

Suppose, for example, that you want to send three photos along to some friends—terrific shots you captured with your 4-megapixel camera.

First, a little math: A typical 4-megapixel shot might consume a megabyte of disk space. So sending along three shots would make at least a 3-megabyte package.

Why is that bad? Let us count the ways:

- It will take you 12 minutes to send (using a standard dial-up modem).

- It will take your recipients 12 minutes to download. During that time, the recipients must sit there, not even knowing what they're downloading. And when you're done hogging their time and account fees, they might not consider what you sent worth the wait.

- Even if they do open the pictures you sent, the average high-resolution shot is much too big for the screen. It does you no good to email somebody a 4-megapixel photo (2272 x 1704 pixels) when his monitor's maximum resolution is only 1024 x 768. If you're lucky, his graphics software will intelligently shrink the image to fit his screen; otherwise, he'll see only a gigantic nose filling his screen. But you'll still have to contend with his irritation at having waited 12 minutes for so much superfluous resolution.

- The typical Internet account has a limited mailbox size. If the mail collection exceeds 5 MB or so, that mailbox is automatically shut down until it's emptied. Your massive 3-megabyte photo package might be what pushes your hapless recipient's mailbox over its limit. She might miss out on important messages that get bounced as a result.

For years, this business of emailing photos has baffled beginners and enraged experts—and for many people who haven't yet discovered iPhoto, the confusion continues.

It's all different when you use iPhoto. Instead of unquestioningly attaching a multi-megabyte graphic to an email message and sending the whole bloated thing off, its first instinct is to offer you the opportunity to send a scaled-down, reasonably sized version of your photo instead (see Figure 9-1). If you take advantage of this feature,

Figure 9-1:
The Mail Photo dialog box not only lets you choose the size of photo attachments, it also keeps track of how many photos you've selected and estimates how large your attachments are going to be, based on your selection.

your modem-using friends will savor the thrill of seeing your digital shots without enduring the agony of a half-hour email download.

The Mail Photo Command

iPhoto doesn't have any emailing features of its own. All it can do is get your pictures ready and hand them off to your existing email program. iPhoto's Mail Photo command works with four of the most popular Mac email programs—Microsoft Entourage, America Online, Qualcomm's Eudora, and Apple's own Mail (the free email program that came with your copy of Mac OS X).

If you currently use Apple's Mail program to handle your email, you're ready to start mailing your photos immediately. But if you want iPhoto to hand off to AOL, Entourage, or Eudora, you have to tell it so. Choose iPhoto→Preferences (or press ⌘-comma), and then choose the email program you want from the Mail pop-up menu.

Once iPhoto knows which program you want to use, here's how the process works:

1. **Click the Organize button in the main iPhoto window.**

   In order to email photos, you have to be in Organize mode, with its expanse of buttons at the bottom of the window.

2. **Select the thumbnails of the photo(s) you want to email.**

   You can use any of the picture-selecting techniques described on page 106. (If you fail to select a thumbnail, you'll get an error message asking you to select a photo and try again.)

3. **Click the Email icon on the pane at the bottom of the iPhoto window.**

   The dialog box shown in Figure 9-1 appears.

4. **Choose a size for your photo(s).**

   This is the critical moment. As noted above, iPhoto offers to send a scaled-down version of the photo. The Size pop-up menu in the Mail Photo dialog box, shown in Figure 9-1, offers four choices.

   Choose **Small (240x320)** to keep your email attachments super small—and if you don't expect the recipient of your email to print the photo. (A photo this size can't produce a quality print any larger than a postage stamp.) On the other hand, your photos will consume less than 100 K apiece, making downloads quick and easy for those with dial-up connections.

Note: Don't be weirded out by the fact that iPhoto, for the first and only time, displays these dimensions backwards (height x width). What it should say, of course, is "Small (320x240)."

Choosing **Medium (640x480)** yields a file that will fill a nice chunk of your recipient's screen, with plenty of detail. It's even enough data to produce a slightly larger print—about 2 x 3 inches. Even so, the file size (and download time) remains reasonable; this setting can trim a 2 MB, 4-megapixel image down to an attachment of less than 150 K.

The **Large (1280x960)** setting downsizes even your large photos to about 450 K, preserving enough pixels to make good 4 x 6 prints and completely fill the typical recipient's screen. In general, send these sparingly. Even if your recipients have a cable modem or DSL, these big files may still overflow their email boxes.

Despite all the cautions above, there may be times when a photo is worth sending at **Full Size (full quality)**, like when you're submitting a photo for printing or publication. This works best when both you and the recipient have high-speed Internet connections and unlimited-capacity mail systems.

In any case, this option attaches a copy of your original photo at its original dimensions.

Note: iPhoto retains each picture's proportions when it resizes them. But if a picture doesn't have 4:3 proportions (maybe you cropped it, or maybe it came from a camera that wasn't set to create 4:3 photos), it may wind up *smaller* than the indicated dimensions. In other words, think of the choices in the Size pop-up menu as meaning, "this size or smaller."

---

5. Include Titles and Comments, if desired.

Turn on these checkboxes if you want iPhoto to copy the title of the photo and any text stored in the Comments field into the body of the email. When Titles is turned on, iPhoto also inserts the photo's title into the Subject line of the email message.

Note: If multiple photos are selected when you generate an email message, the Titles option produces a generic Subject line: "5 great iPhotos" (or whatever the number is). You can edit this proposed text, of course, before sending your email.

FREQUENTLY ASKED QUESTION

Using iPhoto with PowerMail, QuickMail Pro, MailSmith...

Hey, I don't use Entourage, Eudora, AOL, or Apple Mail! How can I get iPhoto to send my photos via QuickMail? It's not listed as an option in the iPhoto's Mail Preferences.

You're right. Even if you have a different email program selected in the Internet panel of System Preferences, iPhoto won't fire up anything but Entourage, Eudora, or Mail when you click the Compose button.

There's a great workaround, though, thanks to the programming efforts of Simon Jacquier. Using his free utility, iPhoto Mailer Patcher, you can make iPhoto work obediently with MailSmith, PowerMail, QuickMail Pro, or even the aging Claris Emailer. It replaces the Mail button on iPhoto's bottom-edge panel with the icon of your preferred email program. You can download iPhoto Mailer Patcher from *http://homepage.mac.com/jacksim/software.*

6. **Click Compose.**

At this point, iPhoto processes your photos—converting them to JPEG format and, if you requested it, resizing them. It then launches your email program, creates a new message, and attaches your photos to it. (Behind the scenes, iPhoto uses AppleScript to accomplish these tasks.)

7. **Type your recipient's email address into the "To:" box, and then click Send.**

Your photos are on their merry way.

Tip: iPhoto always converts photos into JPEG format when emailing them. If you to want preserve a file's original format when emailing a Photoshop file or a PDF, *don't* use the Mail Photo feature. Instead, create a new email message manually, and then drag the thumbnails from iPhoto directly into the message window to attach them. (If you want to resize the photos, export them first using the File→Export command, which offers you a choice of scaling options.)

Publishing Photos on the Web

Putting your photos on the Web is the ultimate way to share them with the world. If the idea of enabling the vast throngs of the Internet-using public to browse, view, download, save, and print *your* photos sounds appealing, read on; it's amazingly easy to get your photos from iPhoto to the Internet.

Before you can post your photos online—and on your network using iPhoto's built-in Web tools—you need a *.Mac* account. That's Apple's suite of Internet services: email accounts, secure file-backup, Web-site hosting, and a few other extras. If you don't already have a .Mac account, see the "Getting a .Mac Account" box on the next page. Follow the directions, and you'll have one in less than five minutes. (A .Mac membership costs $100 per year; a two-month trial account is free.)

Three Roads to Webdom

iPhoto actually provides three different Web-publishing routes (two of which require a .Mac account), offering varying degrees of sophistication and complexity.

- **The easiest, most hands-off approach:** Use the HomePage feature within iPhoto. With only a couple of mouse clicks, this feature lets you construct Web pages, transfer them to the Internet, and make them available to the public. (A .Mac account is required.)

What's especially nice about the resulting Web page is that it presents a tidy collection of thumbnail images—a gallery that downloads relatively quickly into your audience's browsers. Then, when visitors click one of the thumbnails, a new window opens up to display the picture at full size (see Figure 9-2).

- **More effort, more design and layout options:** Copy photos from iPhoto to the Pictures folder of your iDisk (a 100 MB Internet-based "virtual hard drive" that comes with a .Mac account). Then use the HomePage features at Apple's Web site (instead of the layout tools in iPhoto) to set up your pages.

- **For the experienced Web page designer:** If you already have a Web site, you can use iPhoto's Export command to generate Web pages (HTML documents) that already contain your photos. You can upload these files, with the accompanying graphics, to your Web site, whether that's a .Mac account or any other Web-hosting service. (Most Internet accounts, including those provided by America Online, Earthlink, and other service providers, come with free space for Web pages uploaded in this way.)

This is the most labor-intensive route, but it offers much more flexibility if you know how to work with HTML to create more sophisticated pages. It's also the route you should take if you hope to incorporate the resulting photo gallery into an existing Web site (that is, one in which the photos aren't the only attraction).

All three of these methods are detailed in the following pages.

UP TO SPEED

Getting a .Mac Account

.Mac, Apple's subscription online service, provides everything you need to put a collection of your photos online—and on your network. Unfortunately, the service isn't free (as it was when it was called iTools and didn't include as many features). A .Mac membership will set you back $100 per year.

The good news is that Mac OS X makes it incredibly easy to sign up for an account, and a two-month trial account is free. (There are a few limitations on the trial account; it grants you 20 MB of iDisk space instead of 100 MB, for example.) If you don't already have an account, here's how you get one:

Choose →System Preferences. When you click the Internet icon, the .Mac tab is staring you in the face. Click Sign Up.

Now you go online, where your Web browser opens up to the .Mac sign-up screen. Fill in your name and address, make up an account name and password, and, if you like, turn off the checkbox that invites you to receive junk mail.

You're also asked to make up a question and answer (such as, "First grade teacher's name?" and "Flanders"). If you ever forget your password, the .Mac software will help you—provided you can answer this question correctly. Click Continue.

An account summary screen now appears (print it or save it). On the next screen, the system offers to send an email message to your friends letting them know about your new email address (which is *whatever-name-you-chose@mac.com*).

The final step is to return to the Internet pane of System Preferences. On the .Mac tab, fill in the account name and password you just composed. You're now ready to use your .Mac account.

Method 1: Use HomePage in iPhoto

Web publishing doesn't get any easier than it is with iPhoto's built-in HomePage feature. Your photos end up on a handsome-looking Web page in just a few quick steps—and you don't have to know the first thing about HTML.

1. **In iPhoto, select the photos you want to put on the Web, or click the album that contains them.**

   Make sure you've got iPhoto in Organize mode. If you don't, click the Organize button on the row of mode buttons just under the main photo viewing pane. The album can be one you've dragged pictures into, a smart album, the Last Roll(s) album, a year album, and so on. Use the selection techniques described on page 106 to isolate a bunch of photos within an album.

Note: The HomePage feature in iPhoto can't handle more than 48 photos per Web page. If you want to "publish" more than that, you'll have to create a series of separate pages.

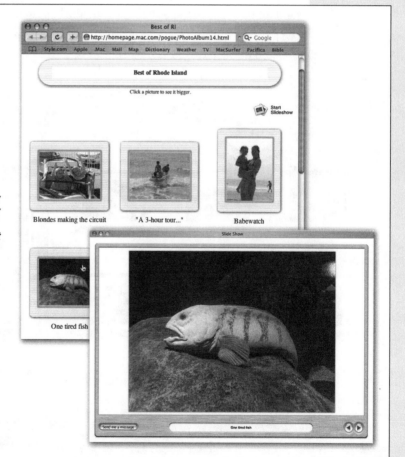

Figure 9-2:
You'd be nuts to stuff your full-size pictures onto the Web; the 70 percent of the population that uses dial-up modems would come after you with a lynch mob.

Fortunately, iPhoto adopts a respectful approach: It uploads only a gallery of small-ish thumbnails (top). When visitors click one of them, a larger version of it opens (bottom right). This way, they wait only for the pictures they really want to see at full size. At this point, the left and right arrow buttons conduct a tour of the larger photos.

2. Click the HomePage button.

After it connects to the Internet, iPhoto opens its Publish HomePage window, which offers a visual menu of predesigned frame styles for your photos (see Figure 9-3).

Note: If iPhoto can't detect an Internet connection or can't find your .Mac account, you get an error message.

In the latter case, click Open .Mac Preferences to enter your existing .Mac name and password, or click Join Now and follow the steps in "Getting a .Mac Account" box on page 196 to create an account.

---

3. Click a frame style.

The Publish HomePage window immediately displays a mock-up of how your finished Web page is going to look (Figure 9-3), displaying the thumbnails in whatever order they appear in iPhoto. You can choose from 14 different frame and text styles by clicking the photo thumbnails in the drawer alongside the window.

4. Edit the page title, subtitle, and individual photo titles.

Just click inside a text block to edit it. You can use iPhoto's spelling checker, if you need the help (page 242).

Figure 9-3:
Before you even open a Web browser, iPhoto shows you what your yet-to-be-created Web page is going to look like in the Publish HomePage window. In iPhoto 4, you can choose from among 14 canned Web designs, complete with frame styles, background colors, font schemes, and so on. Better yet, you're not looking at a page of HTML code.

If you don't bother changing the photo names, iPhoto will simply use whatever titles the photos have in the program itself. (On the other hand, be careful: Any changes you make to the photo titles here are reflected in iPhoto.)

5. **Select the layout options you want.**

Use the Layout radio button in the lower-left corner of the window to switch between a two-column or three-column layout.

The "Send Me a Message" option lets you include a link on your Web pages that lets your fans send their gushing admiration via email to your .Mac address. Turning on the Counter option adds an odometer-style counter to your page, so you can marvel (or despair) at the number of visitors who hit your pages once you publish them. You can see how both of these options look in Figure 9-4.

Figure 9-4:

Top: When you've got your titles and captions looking good, click Publish to upload the photos to your .Mac account. Depending on the size and number of the photos you've selected, and the speed of your connection, this can take some time.

Bottom: Once iPhoto has copied the photos to your .Mac account, you see this message, indicating that your new Web page has been born. You can see your finished page on the Web by clicking the Visit Page Now button, but pay heed to the URL listed above the buttons; that's the Web address you need to give out if you want others to visit the page. (You can either click this address to visit the page, or drag across it to copy it.)

6. **Click Publish.**

This is the big moment: iPhoto connects to the .Mac Web site, scales down your photos to a reasonable size, and then transfers them to the server (Figure 9-4, top).

When the process is complete, as indicated by the alert dialog box (Figure 9-4, bottom), you can go to the page and see your results.

Note: If you include larger photos in your Web page, iPhoto automatically scales them down to 800 x 600 pixel JPEG files, so that they can be more easily loaded and displayed in a Web browser. If you want your Web pages to include *exact* copies of your original photos—regardless of size or file format—you must copy them to your iDisk yourself and then use the online HomePage tools to create your Web pages, as described later in this chapter. Or use the Export to the Web option described on page 204.

In any case, beware: Your iDisk holds only 100 MB of data—a limit that's easy to hit once you're addicted to self-publishing. (If you're *really* addicted, Apple is happy to raise the ceiling to 200 MB or even a gigabyte—for an additional annual fee.)

What you get when you're done

When you see what you've created with iPhoto, you'll be impressed: It's a professional-looking, stylishly titled Web page with thumbnails neatly arranged in a two- or three-column grid. Clicking a thumbnail opens an enlarged version of the picture, complete with Previous and Next buttons (Figure 9-2). You can return to your main index page at any time, or use the buttons in the slideshow window to navigate through the larger versions of your pictures.

Tip: In the URLs for your .Mac-hosted Web sites (such as *http://hompage.mac.com/yackell/PhotoAlbum2.html*), capitalization counts—a point not to be forgotten when you share the site's address with friends. If you type one of these addresses into a Web browser with incorrect capitalization, you'll get only a "missing page" message.

Then again, maybe it's better to send your friends a much shorter, easier to remember address. You can convert long URLs into shorter ones using a free URL redirection service. At *www.kickme.to,* for example, you can sign up to turn *http://hompage.mac.com/gladys/PhotoAlbum22.html* into *www.gladys.kickme.to.* (And if the kickme.to service isn't working as you read this, do your own shopping for free redirection services by searching Google for *free URL redirection.*)

Editing the text of the Web page

To touch up the picture names or page title, visit *www.mac.com,* click the HomePage icon, click the name of the page you want to edit (in the list depicted in Figure 9-5), and then click the Edit button beneath it. You wind up right back in the page-editing mode shown in Figure 9-3, where you're free to change the text in any of the title or caption boxes.

Editing the pictures on a Web page

Remember that your photo gallery Web page depicts *all* of the photos in a specific folder in your iDisk's Pictures folder. Adding, rearranging, or deleting photos from your Web page is therefore something of a hassle.

On the other hand, why bother? Publishing Web pages like this is easy and relatively quick. In many cases, the simplest way to make changes to a page is simply to republish it from within iPhoto.

Of course, then you'll want to delete the original Web page. To do so, visit *www. mac. com,* click the HomePage icon, and then proceed as shown in Figure 9-5.

Note: Deleting a Web page doesn't delete the photos that were on it; they remain in your iDisk's Pictures folder. If .Mac ever reports that your iDisk is out of room, you may want to burrow into that Pictures folder (specifically, into its Photo Album Pictures folder) for some housecleaning. See the box on page 202 for more on this folder's contents.

Figure 9-5:
Deleting a Web page is easy once you've signed onto the .Mac Home Page Web site. Click the name of the page you want to delete, and then click the Delete button. When asked, "Are you sure?" click Yes.

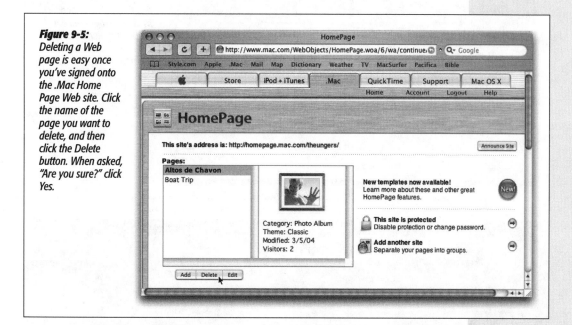

Method 2: Use .Mac

Although using iPhoto's HomePage feature is incredibly simple, there's another way to go about creating, editing, and managing your photo galleries online: visit your .Mac Web site. Here, you're offered a few more templates, a quick way to edit your titles and captions, and the freedom to drag your photos into a new sequence without having to fiddle around in iPhoto. As a bonus, you can use your photos in Web pages that aren't necessarily photo-gallery designs—baby announcement pages, for example.

To get started with HomePage, you first must copy the photos you want to publish from iPhoto to the Pictures folder of your iDisk—in fact, into a *new folder* in the Pictures folder, one folder per Web page. (If your iDisk isn't already onscreen, just choose Go→iDisk or Go→iDisk→My iDisk in the Finder, so that its icon appears on your desktop.) You can drag thumbnails directly out of iPhoto and into the Pictures folder on the iDisk.

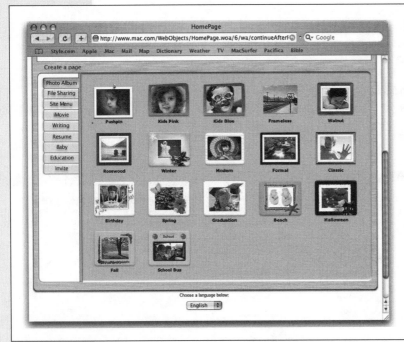

Figure 9-6:
Your Web-publishing options multiply considerably once you hit HomePage. In addition to the photo album themes shown here, you can also create résumés, personal newsletters, baby announcements, and party invitations. You can find these other options by clicking the "Create a page" tabs along the left side of the screen in the main HomePage screen.

FREQUENTLY ASKED QUESTION

Where Did All the Photos Go?

When iPhoto transfers my photos to the .Mac Web site, where are they going?

Everything gets stored on your iDisk, the 100 MB virtual disk that comes with your .Mac account. (Your iDisk looks and behaves like a miniature hard drive, but it's really just a privately reserved chunk of space on one of Apple's secure servers.)

The HTML pages generated by HomePage automatically go in the Sites folder on your iDisk. (In fact, if you know how to use a Web page creation program like Dreamweaver, you can make changes to your Web pages by editing these documents.)

The photos themselves get dumped into Pictures→Photo Album Pictures on the iDisk, where you'll find each separately exported group of Web page pictures housed in its own time-stamped folder.

Once your photos are in the iDisk's Pictures folder, you're ready to create your Web pages. Go to *www.mac.com,* sign in, click the HomePage icon, then click one of the "Create a page" tabs on the HomePage screen to view the styles of pages you can create. Some of the formatting options available are shown in Figure 9-6.

The first tab, Photo Album, offers much the same photo-gallery layouts that you find in iPhoto itself (except that you get a few bonus layout designs). But you're free to use your photos in the other Web page designs here, too, like the baby announcements, writing samples, invitations, and so on.

If you choose Photo Album, click the miniature image of the design you want. HomePage next asks which photos folder in your Pictures folder you want to place on your new Web page, as shown in Figure 9-7. Select a folder of pictures, and then click Choose. After a few moments, your new photo album page appears with photos already inserted in the appropriate spots.

(If you choose any other Web page design, like Baby, the routine is pretty much the same, except that you have to click Edit at the top of the page in order to choose the photo you want.)

To finish the project, click Edit at the top of the page to change the chunks of dummy text on the page. (Make an effort to avoid misspellings and typos, unless you want an audience of 400 million to think you slept through fourth-grade English.)

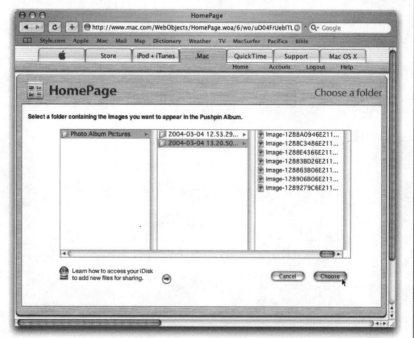

Figure 9-7:
Tell HomePage which photos to use. Two things to remember here: First, the pictures you choose must be in the Pictures folder of your iDisk, or HomePage won't see them; second, you can only choose a folder, not individual files. To include specific photos on a page, put them into a folder of their own in your Pictures folder before you start building the page.

Finally, click Preview to see how the Web page will look. When everything is just the way you want it, click Publish. The page goes live, as indicated by the confirmation dialog box shown at the bottom of Figure 9-4.

Tip: You can create as many Web pages as your iDisk will hold, by the way. When you return to the main HomePage screen, a list of your existing Web pages appears, complete with New Page, Edit Page, and Delete Page buttons.

Corporations and professional Web designers may sniff at the simplicity of the result, but it takes *them* a lot longer than two minutes to do their thing.

Method 3: Export Web Pages

If you already have your own Web site, you don't need .Mac or HomePage to create an online photo album. Instead, you can use iPhoto's Export command to generate HTML pages that you can upload to any Web server. You're still saving a lot of time and effort—and you still get a handy, thumbnail gallery page like that shown back in Figure 9-2.

The Web pages you export directly from iPhoto don't include any fancy designs or themed graphics. In fact, they're kind of stark; just take a look at Figure 9-11.

POWER USERS' CLINIC

Password Protection

When you publish your photos using HomePage, the pages you create become accessible to the whole Web-browsing world. Specifically, anyone with a Web browser and an Internet connection can view, and even download, your pictures.

If you don't feel comfortable sharing your photos quite so freely, you can add a password to your Home-Page–generated sites, thereby controlling access to your photos. All right, you may not particularly care who sees your dog photos–indeed, you may be trolling for a dog-photo agent. But if you'd rather eliminate the possibility that your boss might see your bachelor party shots, or that your husband might see shots of your old boyfriend, password-

protect the page, and then distribute the password only to those who need to know.

To password-protect your site, access the screen shown in Figure 9-5. Select the name of your site from the Site list at the left side of the page, and then click the "Protect this site" button. On the "Edit your site" screen, turn on the Password On checkbox, insert the password of your choice, and then click Apply Changes.

After you've turned on password protection, anyone who comes to one of your .Mac-hosted Web pages will be prompted to enter the password (as shown here) before gaining access to your photos.

But they offer more flexibility than the pages made with HomePage. For example, you can select the background color (or image) that appears on each page, specify the dimensions of thumbnails and images, and choose exactly how many thumbnails you want included on each page.

This is the best method if you plan to post the pages you create to a Web site of your own—especially if you plan on tinkering with the resulting HTML pages yourself.

Preparing the export

Here are the basic Web exporting steps:

1. In iPhoto, select the photos you want to include on the Web pages.

Unlike the HomePage feature, the Export command puts no limit on the number of photos you can export to Web pages in one burst. Select as many photos as you want; iPhoto will generate as many pages as needed to accommodate all the pictures into your specified grid.

Tip: If you don't select any photos, iPhoto assumes you want to export all the photos in the current album (including the Photo Library or Last Roll(s) album).

---

2. Choose File→Export, or press Shift-⌘-E.

The Export Photos dialog box now appears.

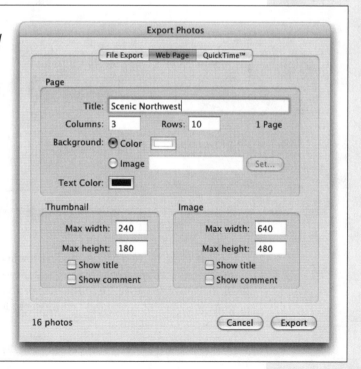

Figure 9-8:
As you change the size of the thumbnail grid or the size of the thumbnails, the number of pages generated to handle the images changes. The page count, based on your current settings, appears just to the right of the Rows field. The total count of the photos you're about to export appears in the lower-left corner of the window.

3. **Click the Web Page tab.**

You see the dialog box shown in Figure 9-8.

4. **Set the Page attributes, including the title, grid size, and background.**

The title you set here will appear in the title bar of each exported Web page, and as a header in the page itself.

Tip: For maximum compatibility with the world's computers and operating systems, use all lowercase letters and no spaces.

Use the Columns and Rows boxes to specify how many thumbnails you want to appear across and down your "index" page. (The little "1 page" indicator tells you how many pages this particular index gallery requires.)

If you'd like a background page color other than white, click the rectangular swatch next to the word Color, and follow the instructions in Figure 9-9. You can also pick a color for the text that appears on each page by clicking the Text Color swatch.

Figure 9-9:
Left: Drag the right-side slider all the way up to see the spectrum of colors available to you. Drag downwards to view darker colors.

Right: Alternatively, click one of the other color-picking buttons at the top of the dialog box. The crayon picker delights with both ease of use and creative color names, like Spindrift to describe a pale sea green.

You can even choose a background *picture* instead of a solid background color. To make it so, click the Image button, and then the Set button to select the graphics file on your hard drive. Be considerate of your audience, however. A background graphic will make your pages take longer to load, and a busy background pattern can be very distracting.

5. **Specify how big you want the thumbnail images to be, and also specify a size for the expanded images that appear when you click them.**

The sizes iPhoto proposes are fine *if* all of your photos are horizontal (that is, in landscape orientation). If some are wide and some are tall, however, you're better off specifying *square* dimensions for both the thumbnails and the enlarged photos—240 x 240 for the thumbnails and 640 x 640 for the biggies, for example.

6. **Turn on "Show title" and "Show comment," if desired.**

Even though "Show title" may sound like your Web pages will sprout *show titles* ("Phantom of the Opera," "Oklahoma!," "Mame"), this option actually draws upon the *photo* titles you've assigned in iPhoto, centering each picture's name underneath its thumbnail. The larger version of each picture will also bear this name when it opens into its own window.

Turning on the "Show comment" option displays any text you've typed into the Comments field for each picture in iPhoto. Depending on which checkboxes you turn on, you can have the comments appear under each thumbnail, under each larger-size image, or both.

7. **Click Export.**

The Save dialog box appears.

8. **Choose (or, by clicking New Folder, create) a folder to hold the export files and then click OK.**

The export process gets under way.

Examining the results

When iPhoto is done with the export, you end up with a series of HTML documents and JPEG images—the building blocks of your Web-site-to-be. A number of these icons automatically inherit the name of the *folder* into which you've saved them. If you export the files into a folder named Tahiti, for example, here's what you'll find (see Figure 9-10):

- **Tahiti.html.** This is the main HTML page, containing the first thumbnails in the series that you exported. It's the home page, the index page, and the starting point for the exported pages.

- **Page1.html, Page2.html...** You see these only if you exported enough photos to require more than one page of thumbnails—that is, if iPhoto required *multiple* "home" pages.

- **Tahiti-Thumbnails.** This folder holds the actual thumbnail graphics that appear on each of the index pages.

- **Tahiti-Pages.** This folder contains the HTML documents (named Image1.html, Image2.html, Image3.html, and so on) that open when you click the thumbnails on the index pages.

- **Tahiti-Images.** This folder houses the larger JPEG versions of your photos. Yes, these are the *graphics* that appear on the Image HTML pages.

Tip: Some Web servers require that the default home page of your site be called *index.html.* To force your exported Web site to use this name for the main HTML page, save your exported pages into a *folder* called index. Now the home page will have the correct name (index.html) and all the other image and page files will be properly linked to it. (After exporting, feel free to rename the folder. Naming it *index* was only necessary during the exporting process.)

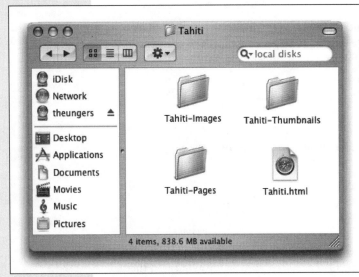

Figure 9-10:
This is what a Web site looks like before it's on the Internet. All the pieces are here, filed exactly where the home page (called, in this example, Tahiti. html) can find them.

Once you've created these pages, it's up to you to figure out how to *post* them on the Internet where the world can see them. To do that, you'll have to upload all the exported files to a Web server, using an *FTP* program like the free RBrowser Lite (available from the "Missing CD" page of *www.missingmanuals.com*).

Only then do they look like real Web pages, as shown in Figure 9-11.

Enhancing iPhoto's HTML

If you know how to work with HTML code, you don't have to accept the unremarkable Web pages exported by iPhoto. You're free to tear into them with a full-blown Web authoring program like Adobe GoLive, Macromedia Dreamweaver, or the free Netscape Composer (*www.netscape.com*) to add your own formatting, headers, footers, and other graphics (Figure 9-12). (Heck, even Microsoft Word lets you open and edit HTML Web pages—plenty of power for changing iPhoto's layout, reformatting the text, or adding your own page elements.)

If you're a hard-core HTML coder, you can also open the files in a text editor like BBEdit or even TextEdit to tweak the code directly. With a few quick changes, you can make your iPhoto-generated Web pages look more sophisticated and less generic. Some of the changes you might want to consider making include:

- Change font faces and sizes.

- Change the alignment of titles.

- Add a footer with your contact information and email address.

- Add *metadata* tags (keywords) in the *page header,* so that search engines can locate and categorize your pages.

- Insert links to your other Web sites or relevant sites on the Web.

If you're *not* an HTML coder—or even if you are—you can perform many of these adjustments extremely easily with the free BetterHTMLExport plug-in for iPhoto, described next.

Figure 9-11:
Here's what a Web page exported straight from iPhoto looks like. The no-frills design is functional, but not particularly elegant. The links that let you navigate from page to page are always anchored to the top of the page, and you have no control over fonts or sizes. On the other hand, the HTML code behind this page is 100 percent editable.

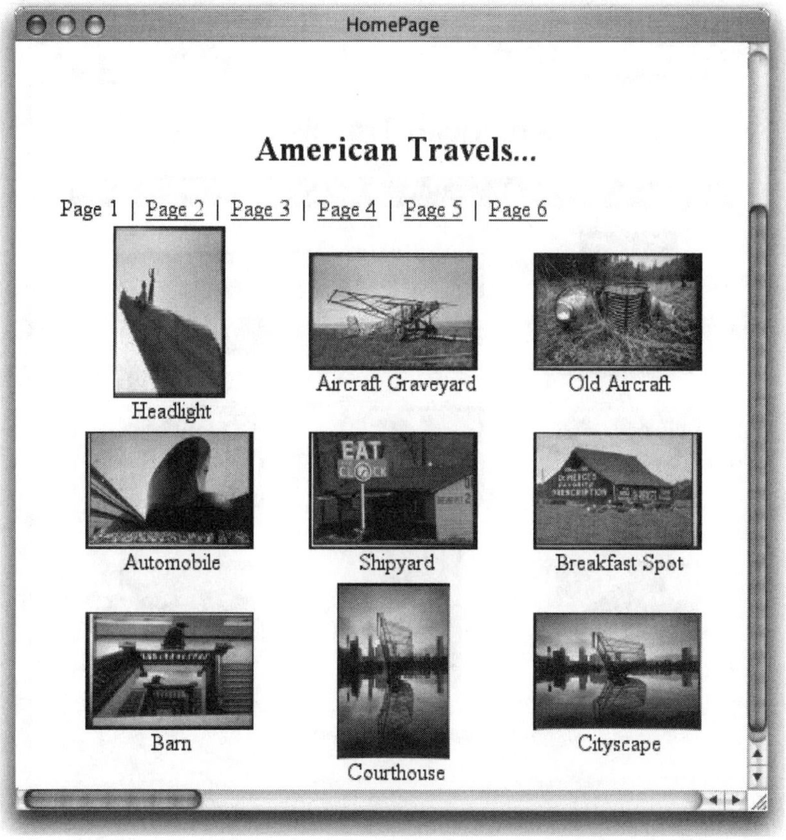

Better HTML

iPhoto's Export command produces simple, serviceable Web page versions of your photo albums. Most people assume that if they want anything fancier, they need either HTML programming chops or a dedicated Web design program.

Actually, though, you can add a number of elegant features to your photo site using an excellent piece of add-on software that requires no hand coding—or special editing software—at all.

It's the fittingly named BetterHTMLExport, an inexpensive iPhoto 4 plug-in that extends the features of iPhoto's own HTML Exporter. (See page 291 for more on plug-ins.)

You can download a copy of BetterHTMLExport from the "Missing CD" page of *www.missingmanuals.com,* among other places. The version for iPhoto 4 is a $20 shareware program.

Here are some of the great things you can do with BetterHTMLExport:

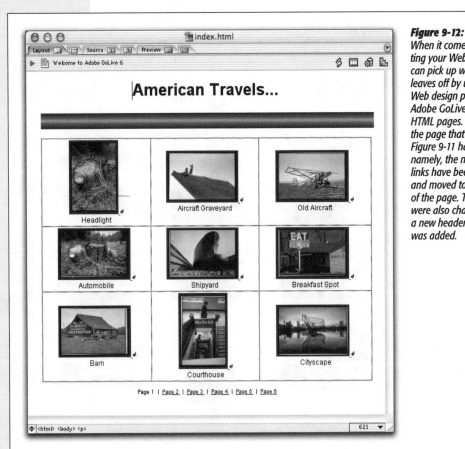

Figure 9-12:
When it comes to formatting your Web pages, you can pick up where iPhoto leaves off by using a Web design program like Adobe GoLive to edit the HTML pages. Here's what the page that began in Figure 9-11 has become; namely, the navigational links have been shrunk and moved to the bottom of the page. The fonts were also changed, and a new header graphic was added.

Burning Pro Caliber Photo CDs

iPhoto's ability to export complete Web sites into a folder is the first step in creating a terrific, self-contained photo gallery *on a CD*. This, by the way, is exactly the way many professional photographers distribute their own catalogs. Their clients insert the CD into their own computers, double-click the "Double-click Me" icon, and then view the main "gallery" page of thumbnails in their Web browsers—even though these Web pages and graphics are actually right there on the CD. There's nothing to stop you from stealing this technique for use with your own photo gallery.

But wait, you might protest: Why bother publishing your photos as Web pages on a CD, when iPhoto 4 itself has a built-in CD burning feature (covered in Chapter 14) that requires only one click?

The answer is simple: The CDs that iPhoto creates can be read only by iPhoto. The pictures wind up in an iPhoto Library folder containing an unalterable hierarchy of nested folders, as required by iPhoto (see page 94). If, for example, you pop an iPhoto CD into a Windows computer, you'll have to dig through cryptically named nested folders to find the photos. You'll have no way to view a page of thumbnails or to read the comments accompanying each photo.

But by exporting your photo collection as a series of HTML pages, you can create galleries of photos on CD that your admirers can navigate and view using any computer equipped with a Web browser, even when they're not online. Here's what you need to do:

After exporting a Web page as described on these pages, insert a blank CD and give it a descriptive name. Then, onto

the CD's icon, drag the three folders and index file (the HTML file that shares its folder's name, such as the one called Tahiti.html in Figure 9-10).

If you think your audience might need a little hint as to how to get started, you have three options. You might create a simple Read Me text file that says nothing more than, "To get started, double-click the document called *Tahiti.html*" (or whatever your index page is called).

If that seems a bit inelegant, you could instead add a similarly named empty folder to the CD window. (You could even paste a more attractive icon onto that folder icon. You might swipe the iPhoto icon for this purpose, for example. To do that, highlight the iPhoto program icon, choose File→Get Info, click the iPhoto icon in the corner of the dialog box, choose Edit→ Copy, click your empty folder on the CD, click *its* icon in the Get Info window, and then choose Edit→Paste.)

The third option for giving your viewers a clue is to display the CD window in Icon view. Then choose View→Show View Options. When the View Options dialog box appears, click the Picture radio button; then click the Select button next to it. Now you can choose a graphics file that you've carefully designed to be the same size and shape as the CD window itself—a graphic image that not only forms a lovely backdrop for the CD window, but (at least on Mac OS X machines) contains typographically attractive instructions for getting started with it, as shown here.

Finally, burn the CD (choose File→Burn Disc).

Web pages: they're not just for the Internet anymore.

- Add comments (not just titles) on index and image pages.

- Insert "Previous" and "Next" links on each individual image page, so that you can jump from picture to picture without returning to the index (thumbnail) page.

- Control the JPEG quality/compression setting used to create copies of your photos.

- Create links to your *original* images instead of just JPEG versions of them.

- Choose where on the page you want to include navigation hyperlinks.

See Figure 9-13 for a quick tour of this valuable add-on, and Figure 9-14 for an example of what it can do.

Figure 9-13:
BetterHTMLExport works by adding a new panel called Better Web Page to the standard Export Photos dialog box. It in turn offers panels of features for customizing the Web pages you export from iPhoto. For instance, you can have your pages display your titles and comments beneath all thumbnail images. Other gems include the "Links On Bottom" and "Links On Top" checkboxes, which add a row of links to the top of every page of your Web catalog, as shown in Figure 9-14.

The .Mac Slideshow

iPhoto 4 also gives you perhaps the weirdest and wildest way to share your photos online—and on your network: publish them as a *.Mac slideshow*.

When you send your photos out into the world as .Mac slides, other Mac OS X users can *subscribe* to your show, displaying *your* pictures as *their* screen saver—without having to manually download any files or launch a Web browser. (They do, of course, need an Internet connection.) In a minute or so, your latest photos can appear as full-screen slides on the Macintosh of a friend, family member, co-worker, or anyone else who knows your .Mac membership name.

Note: Creating and viewing a .Mac slideshow requires Mac OS X 10.2 or later.

Note, too, that if your aim is to turn your photos into a screen saver only on *your* Mac (and not make them available to the world at large), you don't need a .Mac account, and you don't need to follow the steps below. Instead, use the Desktop button (page 283). It's quicker and cheaper, and it doesn't require an Internet connection.

Creating a .Mac slideshow

Before any other Mac users can connect to your slideshow pictures, you have to make them available via your .Mac account. (If you don't have a .Mac account, you'll be prompted to sign up for one when you attempt to use the .Mac feature. See the box on page 196.) Here are the steps for publishing your slideshow:

Figure 9-14:
Thanks to these numbered links, your viewers won't have to keep ducking back to the index page to jump to a different photo; they'll have a row of underlined number buttons (1 2 3 4 5) to click at the top of each page. Also shown here: the "index" link that returns you to the main thumbnail page and the Original Photo link that loads the original photo file—at full, multi-megapixel size. All of these grace notes are brought to you by BetterHTMLExport.

1. **In iPhoto, select the photos you want to make available as screen saver slides.**

   If you don't select any specific photos, iPhoto creates your .Mac slideshow from whatever pictures are currently displayed in the iPhoto window—either the whole Photo Library, a specific album, or a combination of albums.

2. **With iPhoto in Organize mode, click the .Mac Slides button in the lower pane of the window.**

   A dialog box opens, asking if you're sure you really want to publish your personal photos to the Internet. It's a question that deserves some consideration. Once you create .Mac slides, your pictures will be freely available to hundreds of thousands of Internet-connected Mac OS X fans around the world. (They do, however, need to know—or guess—your .Mac membership name.) If you have any reservations about making these glimpses of your life available to the world at large, now's the time to click Cancel.

   Otherwise, read on:

3. **Click Publish to begin uploading your photos.**

   One by one, iPhoto grabs your photos and copies them to your iDisk, dropping them into a special location in the Pictures→Slideshows→Public folder.

   When all the photos are safely online, a confirmation dialog box appears, letting you know that your slideshow is now available. (If you look at the uploaded files

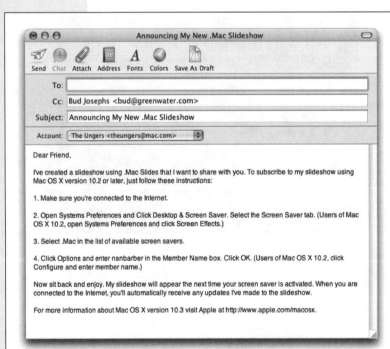

Figure 9-15:
Once you've made your photos available to the whole world for use as a screen saver, iPhoto can help you tell everyone about it, too. Click the Announce Slideshow button in the confirmation dialog box to launch your email program and generate an announcement email. As you can see here, the announcement contains complete instructions for accessing the slideshow using the Screen Effects panel of the System Preferences.

on your iDisk, you'll notice that iPhoto has renamed your pictures according to its own private naming scheme. It's only the uploaded copies that have been renamed, however, not the photos on your Mac.)

Note: You can publish any number of Web sites on your .Mac account, but only *one* set of .Mac slides. Each time you upload photos for a .Mac slideshow, you *replace* any earlier slideshow photos you've uploaded.

---

4. **Click Announce Slideshow, if you like (see Figure 9-15).**

   If you'd rather not email your friends to let them know about your slides, click Quit instead. Then use your Mac's screen saver feature, as outlined in the next section, to see the fruits of your labor.

Subscribing to a .Mac slideshow

After you've uploaded your photos as .Mac slides, you, or anyone else with Mac OS X 10.2 (or later) and an Internet connection, can subscribe to the show and make it into a screen saver. Here's how:

1. **Choose →System Preferences. Click the Screen Effects (Mac OS X 10.2) or Desktop & Screen Saver icon (Mac OS X 10.3) to open the panel.**

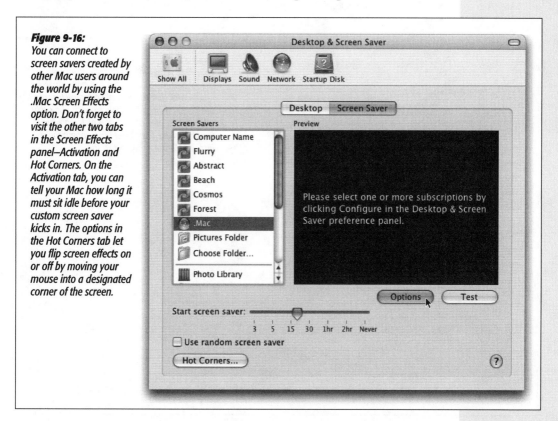

Figure 9-16:
You can connect to screen savers created by other Mac users around the world by using the .Mac Screen Effects option. Don't forget to visit the other two tabs in the Screen Effects panel—Activation and Hot Corners. On the Activation tab, you can tell your Mac how long it must sit idle before your custom screen saver kicks in. The options in the Hot Corners tab let you flip screen effects on or off by moving your mouse into a designated corner of the screen.

Switch to the Screen Effects (Mac OS X 10.2) or Screen Saver (Mac OS X 10.3) tab of the window, if it's not already displayed. This is where you choose the particular effect that your Mac will use as a screen saver.

2. **Click .Mac in the Screen Effects list.**

A message appears on the little black Preview screen, as shown in Figure 9-16, prompting you to click the Configure (Mac OS X 10.2) or Options (Mac OS X 10.3) button so that you can select a slideshow and set up the playback options.

3. **Click the Configure (or Options) button.**

The Subscriptions window appears. The controls here determine which slideshows you can see on your Mac and how they're displayed.

4. **In the .Mac Membership Name box, enter the name of the .Mac member whose slideshow you want to see.**

There's no way to *get* this name. Unless you find the creator's name at the *www. dotmac.info* Web page (see the box on the facing page), you just have to know it.

Tip: You can subscribe to as many different .Mac slideshows as you want. As you do, their names accumulate in the Subscriptions window.

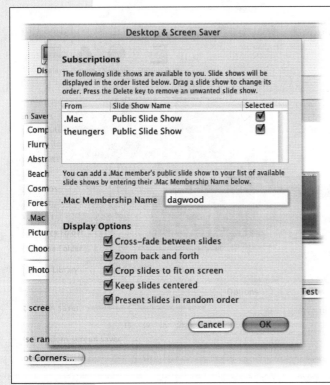

Figure 9-17:
Your Mac remembers each show you've subscribed to—though you can have it use or ignore any combination of shows by turning the Selected checkbox next to each title on or off. You can also change the order in which the shows are presented by dragging them into a different order in this list.

5. Choose your Display Options.

Adjust the checkboxes in the lower portion of the window to change the way the slides are to be presented on your screen. You can control zooming, crossfades, and other options, as shown in Figure 9-17.

6. Click OK to return to the main Screen Effects window.

This is the big moment: The Mac hooks up to the .Mac site(s) you've specified and finds the shared slideshow. Seconds later, you see the results of your tinkering: The slides you've subscribed to appear on the little Preview screen in a miniature version of the slideshow, complete with zooming effects and crossfades.

Note: If the slideshow you've subscribed to is very large, the Preview screen may remain black for a minute or two as the images get downloaded to your Mac.

---

7. Click the Test button to preview the slideshow at full size.

Your screen goes black, and then the first of the slides you've subscribed to fills the screen. Depending on the options you've selected, the slideshow progresses with photos slowly zooming and cross-fading into each other. To end the test, just click your mouse.

You've now got a remote slideshow that will play back on your screen according to the rules you've set up in the Activation and Hot Corners tabs of the Screen Effects panel. Of course, at any time, you can go back into Screen Effects and reconfigure the .Mac slide settings: add additional slideshows to your subscriptions, rearrange

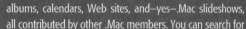

FREQUENTLY ASKED QUESTION

Trolling for .Mac Slides

The idea of sharing .Mac slides with friends sounds great, and I would do it in a heartbeat—if I had more friends. As it turns out, I don't know another soul running Mac OS X. Am I destined to watch my same boring photos cross-fade into each other, day after day, in utter solitude?

Fortunately, no. Thousands of .Mac members have already made their slideshows available to the world, and they're just waiting for you to subscribe to them.

The trick is to visit *www.dotmac. info/index.html,* where you'll find a listing of movies, photo

albums, calendars, Web sites, and—yes—.Mac slideshows, all contributed by other .Mac members. You can search for specific items or just browse the listings, then subscribe to any number of slideshows. Thanks to the miracle of modern technology, you can now fill your screen with the photos of total strangers.

Want to give the world access to *your* slideshow, too? Click the Add a Page button on the *dotmac.info* home page. Add a description of your slides along with your membership name, so that anyone who wants to can subscribe to your slides from their Mac.

---

their playback order, or (when the kid in your cousin's new-baby slideshow turns 21, perhaps) delete .Mac slideshows from the list.

Photo Sharing on the Network

One of the coolest features of iTunes is the way you can "publish" certain playlists on your home or office network, so that other people in the same building can listen to your tunes. Why couldn't iPhoto do the same thing with pictures?

In iPhoto 4, it can.

For this example, suppose that you're the master shutterbug who has all the cool shots.

On your Mac, choose iPhoto→Preferences and click Sharing. Turn on "Share my photos" (Figure 9-18).

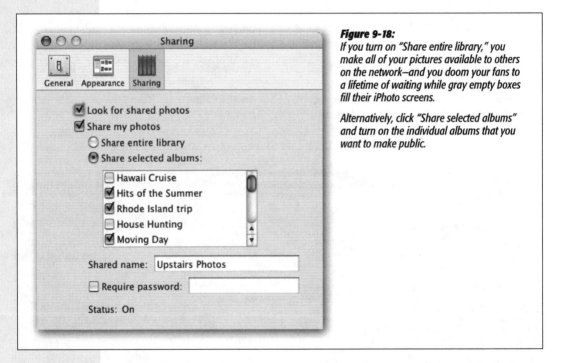

Figure 9-18:
If you turn on "Share entire library," you make all of your pictures available to others on the network—and you doom your fans to a lifetime of waiting while gray empty boxes fill their iPhoto screens.

Alternatively, click "Share selected albums" and turn on the individual albums that you want to make public.

You might be tempted to turn on "Share entire library," so that no crumb of your artistry will go unappreciated—but don't. Even the fastest Macs on the fastest networks will grind to a halt if you try to share even a medium-sized photo library. You are, after all, attempting to ram gigabytes of data through your network to the other Macs.

It's far more practical to turn on the checkboxes for the individual albums you want to share, as shown in Figure 9-18.

Unless you also turn on "Require password" (and make up a password), everyone on the network with iPhoto 4 can see your shared pictures.

Finally, close the Sharing window.

At this point, other people on your network will see *your* albums show up in *their* Source lists, above the list of their own albums; see Figure 9-19. (Or at least they will if they have "Look for shared photos" turned on in their iPhoto Preferences, also shown in Figure 9-18.)

As you may know, when you share iTunes music over a network, other people can only *listen* to your songs—they can't actually *have* them. (The large, well-built lawyers of the American record companies have made sure of that.)

But iPhoto is another story. Nobody is going to issue you a summons for freely distributing your own photos. So once you've jacked into somebody else's iPhoto pictures via the network, feel free to drag them into your own iPhoto albums, thereby copying them onto your own Mac. Now you can edit them, print them, and otherwise treat them like your very own photos.

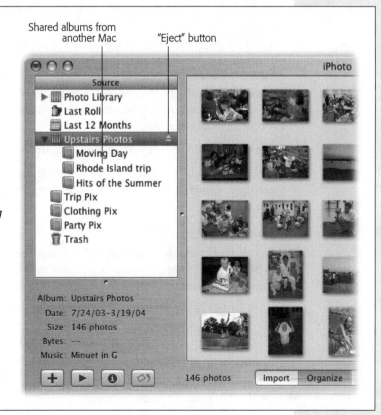

Figure 9-19:
You can't delete or edit the photos you've summoned from some other Mac. But you can drag them into your own albums (or your own Photo Library) to copy them.

When you've had enough, click the Eject button. The flippy triangle, the list of albums, and the Eject button itself disappear. The name of the shared collection ("Upstairs Photos" in this example) remains on the screen, though, in case you want to bring them back for another look later.

Shared albums from another Mac

"Eject" button

Photo Sharing Across Accounts

Mac OS X is designed from the ground up to be a *multiple-user* operating system. You can set up Mac OS X with individual *user accounts* so that everyone must log in (that is, you have to click your name and type a password) when the computer turns on.

Upon doing so, you discover the Macintosh universe just as you left it, including *your* icons on the desktop, Dock configuration, desktop picture, screen saver, Web browser bookmarks, email account, fonts, startup programs, and so on. This accounts feature adds both convenience (people don't have to wade through other people's stuff) and security (people *can't* wade through other people's stuff). As you can imagine, this feature is a big deal in schools, businesses, and families.

This feature also means that each account holder has a separate iPhoto Library folder. (Remember, it lives inside your own Home folder.) The photos *you* import into iPhoto are accessible only to you, not to anyone else who might log in. If you and your spouse each log into Mac OS X with a different account, you each get your own Photo Library—and neither of you has access to the other's pictures in iPhoto.

But what if the two of you *want* to share the same photos? Ordinarily, you'd be stuck, since iPhoto can't make its library available to more than a single user.

There are three relatively easy solutions to this common conundrum.

Easiest: Share Your Library

iPhoto 4's new sharing feature, as described on the previous pages, isn't just useful for sharing photos across the network. It's equally good at sharing photos between *accounts* on the same Mac.

Log in as, say, Dad. Share some albums (Figure 9-18).

When Mom logs in, she'll find that Dad's albums show up in her copy of iPhoto, exactly as shown in Figure 9-19. She can copy whichever pictures she likes into her own albums.

Pretty Easy: ShareAlike

The problem with the Share Your Library method is that you wind up with *copies* of the pictures. In some situations, you may want to work on exactly the same set of pictures. You want, in other words, to share the *same iPhoto Library.*

For this trick, download the free ShareAlike program (from, for example, the "Missing CD" page at *www.missingmanuals.com*). This program is designed exclusively to share your iPhoto and iTunes libraries with other account holders, shown in Figure 9-20.

Tip: iPhoto Library Manager, described on page 314, can also share your library with other accounts. It's not quite a one-click affair, though, as it is with ShareAlike.

Geekiest of All: Move the Library

If you're just not in the mood to download some freeware, here's another way to share your entire photo collection across accounts: Move the actual iPhoto Library folder (currently in your Home→Pictures folder) into the Users→Shared folder on your hard drive.

Then put one alias of that iPhoto Library folder into the Home→Pictures folder of each account holder. Now everybody can log in and work with the same iPhoto Library folder. (Note that if you try this stunt using Fast User Switching in Mac OS X 10.3, only the first person to open iPhoto can import and edit pictures. Subsequent account holders can only look at them.)

Tip: Of course, you can also share the contents of a Photo Library by burning an iPhoto CD, as described on page 307. Once you've put your Photo Library on CD using the Burn command, any account holder—on your own Mac or any other—can open and view it within iPhoto. Other people can copy individual photos or whole albums from your CD to their own Photo Libraries.

Figure 9-20:
To share your Photo Library with other user-account holders on your Mac, select the name of the account holder to be your sharee from the pop-up menu, and then click Begin Sharing. For best results, click Fix Permissions before and after each sharing session.

(This program can also share your iTunes collection across accounts—but that's another book.)

Publishing a Photo Book

A t first, gift-giving is fun. During those first 20, 30, or 40 birthday, anniversary, Christmas, thank you, welcome-to-the-neighborhood, good-luck-in-your-new-location, sorry-about-the-car, or I-think-you're-the-cutest-one-in-the-whole-tenth-grade-class events, you might actually *enjoy* picking out a present, buying it, wrapping it, and delivering it.

After a certain point, however, gift-giving becomes exhausting. What the heck do you get your dad after you've already given him birthday and holiday presents for 15 or 35 years?

If you have iPhoto, you've got an ironclad, perennial answer. The program's Book feature lets you design and order (via the Internet) a gorgeous, linen-covered, 9 x 11-inch hardbound book, printed at a real bindery and shipped back to you in a slipcover. Your photos are printed on the glossy, acid-free, single-sided pages, complete with captions, if you like.

A ten-page book costs $30 (extra pages are $3 each). That's about the least you could hope to pay for a handsome, emotionally powerful gift *guaranteed* never to wind up in an attic, at a garage sale, or on eBay. In short, it's a home-run gift every time.

But the iPhoto book is not *only* a gift. You should also consider ordering them for yourself—one each for your vacation, wedding, child, or whatever. These books are amazing keepsakes to leave out on your coffee table—the same idea as most families' photo albums, but infinitely classier, longer lasting, less messy to assemble—and not much more expensive.

Phase 1: Pick the Pix

The hardest part of the whole book-creation process is winnowing down your photos to the ones you want to include. Many a shutterbug eagerly sits down to create his very first photo book—and winds up with one that's 49 pages long (that is, $147).

As a general rule, each page of your photo book can hold a maximum of six pictures. (iPhoto also offers canned book designs called Catalog and Yearbook, which hold up to 32 tiny pictures per page in a grid. At that size, however, your pictures don't exactly sing. Instead, the whole thing more closely resembles, well, a catalog or yearbook.)

Even the six-per-page limit doesn't necessarily mean you'll get 60 photos into a ten-page book, however. The more pictures you add to a page, the smaller they have to be, and therefore the less impact they have. The best-looking books generally have varying numbers of pictures per page—one, four, three, two, whatever. In general, the number of pictures you'll fit in a ten-page book may be far lower than 60—25, for example.

The first step is to create an album (page 121) filled with the pictures you really want in the book. In Organize mode, you can drag pictures in, which can be an excruciating experience, especially if you and a collaborator are trying to work together. ("You can't get rid of that one! It's adorable!" "But honey, we've already got 139 pictures in here!" "I don't care. I *love* that one.")

As you work, constantly keep in mind the photo *sequence*. Drag them around in the album to determine a preliminary order. You'll have plenty of opportunity to fine-tune each page of the book (and rearrange the pictures on it) later in the process. When you're still in Organize mode, the only critical task is to place the two most sensational or important photos first and last (for the cover and the last page of the book).

Tip: Using a smart album (page 127) to help you ferret out just the pictures that belong in the book—for example, only the four-star photos from this year—is a good idea, in principle. However, remember that you can't rearrange the pictures in a smart album. In other words, you can't pick a different picture for the cover (page 229), and you can't drag photos from one page to another.

If you're sneaky, though, you can use the power of the smart album and still retain the freedom to reorganize. Just open the smart album—and drag all the thumbnails inside it into a *regular* album. Build the book from the pictures in the regular album.

Phase 2: Choose a Theme

Once you've corralled the book's pictures into an album of their own, click the album, and then click the Book button below the main picture area (Figure 10-1). (If you forget to click an album before clicking Book, iPhoto will scold you.)

Now you see something like Figure 10-1: a large preview page at top, and a scrolling bank of thumbnails below, representing the book's pages. iPhoto has just turned into a page-layout program.

Tip: Light blue lines surround each photo and text box. These *guides,* as they're called, won't appear in the printed book. They're there just for convenience, to help you visualize how the finished layout will look. Still, if they bother you, turn off the Show Guides checkbox in the lower-left corner of the window.

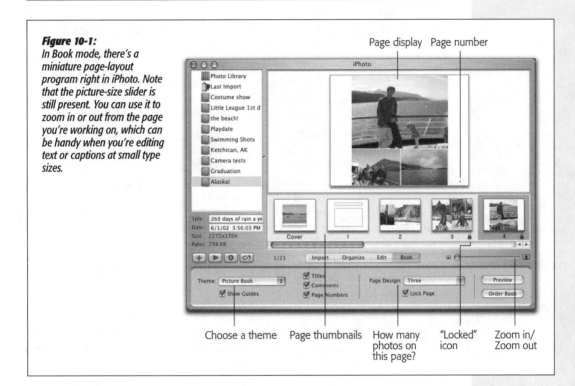

Figure 10-1:
In Book mode, there's a miniature page-layout program right in iPhoto. Note that the picture-size slider is still present. You can use it to zoom in or out from the page you're working on, which can be handy when you're editing text or captions at small type sizes.

Page display   Page number

Choose a theme   Page thumbnails   How many photos on this page?   "Locked" icon   Zoom in/ Zoom out

---

Before you dive in, take a moment to get your bearings. Note that the thumbnails are numbered—an early-warning system that shows you how many pages long your book will be (read: how expensive). If you're like most people, your initial layout will be much too long. Not to worry; you'll fix that in a moment.

In book-design mode, you can't add photos to your album, take any photos out, or rearrange them into a master sequence. You can perform tasks like these as you work on your book—but you must click the Organize button to do so.

What you can do, however, is design your book pages, and that process begins when you choose a *theme* for the book—a canned design. Use the Theme pop-up menu at the lower-left corner of the iPhoto screen for this purpose (Figure 10-1). Before you begin fiddling with individual pages, try each of the themes in turn, studying the thumbnails and page previews to get a feeling for the effect.

Caution: Choose carefully. You can switch to a different theme for this album later, but you'll lose *all the custom text and photo groupings* you've performed so far.

You won't lose your captions, because those are the Comments stored with every photo in your collection. "Custom text" refers to the text you type into Introduction pages and onto every page of the Story Book design (described below). (If you have, in fact, typed any custom text, iPhoto warns you about this loss when you try to switch layout themes.)

If you want to experiment with a different theme once you've spent some time with one, *duplicate the album first.* (With the album highlighted in the list, choose File→Duplicate.) Now you can change the theme on the duplicate without destroying the work you've done on the original.

Your choices are:

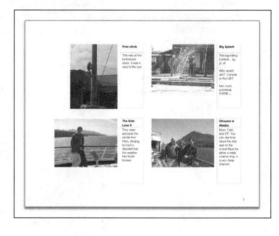

- **Catalog.** This design looks exactly like a mail order catalog: a picture on the left, and a name and description on the right—eight times per page (or one, or four). It's neatly aligned and somewhat conservative. For example, there's a page design called Introduction, where you can pour a lot of text, such as your shipping policies, a letter from the founder, what this season's catalog offers, and so on.

It's also good for more than just designing catalogs, however. It would be an ideal "face book" (with mini biographies) for, say, a dating agency or personnel director. It's also a candidate for a regular photo album, in the event you're the kind of person who wants it to look square and gridlike, like a *real* photo album book from Office Max.

- **Classic.** It's easy to deduce the philosophy behind this conservative, clean design: maximum photos, minimum text. Photos are as large as possible on the page (up to six per page), and each offers only enough room for a title and a very short caption.

• **Collage.** New in iPhoto 4, this design is a wacky, energetic layout in which *no* photos are square with the page. Everything falls at a tilt, as though tossed onto a coffee table helter-skelter. If there's more than one photo per page, they may even *overlap*.

It's actually not that new in iPhoto 4; it's exactly like Story Book, except without captions. (The one exception: A page design called "One with Text" gives you the flexibility to insert an occasional single photo with a tall, skinny text block next to it.)

• **Picture Book.** This design is as stark as it gets: maximum photos, period. There's no text, and only minimum margins. Thus, on one-photo-per-page pages, the photo stretches gloriously from one edge of the page to the other—a *full bleed,* as publishers say.

This dramatic design can be emotionally compelling in the extreme. The absence of text and minimization of white space seems to make the photos speak—if not shout—for themselves.

As you build your first book, you may be compelled to choose a theme that offers space for captions. But if your text is no more illuminating than, "Timmy doing a belly-flop" or "Dad falls asleep at the bar," consider the Picture Book theme instead. This is, after all, a *photo* album, so it may be worth giving the photos all the space they deserve. You don't need to eat into their space by restating the obvious.

Tip: Keeping in mind that the book is published *horizontally,* in landscape mode, will help you maximize page coverage. For example, on pages with only one photo, a horizontal shot looks best. It will fill the page, edge to edge. On pages with two photos, two side-by-side vertical (portrait-mode) shots look best. They'll appear side by side, filling the page top to bottom. And on three-photo layouts, one vertical shot with two horizontal ones is ideal.

• **Portfolio.** Modeled after a photographer's portfolio, this design has elements of both Catalog and Picture Book. Like Catalog, it provides text boxes that accommodate a title and description for each photo. But as with Picture Book, the photos are otherwise displayed at maximum size, with very little white space between them.

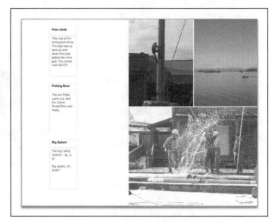

The whole effect is a tad industrial-looking, so you probably wouldn't want to use it as a "memory book" for some trip or event. It's useful in situations where Catalog would be right, except that it's more interesting to look at, thanks to the varied photo sizes.

• **Story Book.** This layout is the big brother to Collage. Once again, you get a zany layout of crooked, overlapping photos. The difference: In this design, text boxes appear on each page for captions, which are always parallel to the page edges and therefore anchor the design. Like Collage, this theme works best when fun, craziness, or lightheartedness is your desired effect.

• **Year Book.** This theme lets you fit up to 32 photos on each page—just as in a high school yearbook. Of course, if you choose greater quantities, the photos themselves get smaller—but iPhoto always leaves you enough room for a title ("Chris Jones") and a little description ("Swim team '02; voted Most Likely to Enter the Priesthood").

Tip: Make an effort to choose a quantity of photos that neatly fills the final page, or at least a row of it. Otherwise, the final page can look a bit half-finished.

Try choosing each of these themes in turn from the Themes pop-up menu. The thumbnails of your pages give you immediate feedback about the suitability of each design for your book project.

Phase 3: Design the Pages

Once you've selected an album and a theme, the most time-consuming phase begins: designing the individual pages.

It's important to understand that iPhoto thinks of the pictures in your book as a *continuous stream* that flows from left to right, in precisely the same order as in the album you've selected. You can drag your page thumbnails around with the mouse to rearrange them—but behind the scenes, you're simultaneously rearranging the photos in the album. Similarly, if you drag photos around in the Organize window for your album, you'll wind up rearranging the pages of your book. Figure 10-2 should drive this point home.

Tip: You'll soon discover that designing a book is a much happier experience if you work on your pages strictly from *left to right.* Doing so reduces the likelihood that your photos will sproing out of order unexpectedly, as described on page 233.

To begin work on a page, click its thumbnail. Now you have three decisions to make: how many photos should appear on the page, what text should appear, and what the text should look like.

Tip: Even in Book mode, you can still rotate photos, rename them, change their dates, or delete them, just as you would thumbnails in Organize mode (see Chapter 5).

The Cover

Start with the Cover page—the first thumbnail in the row. When it's selected, the cover photo appears in the main picture area. This is the picture that will be pasted

---

FREQUENTLY ASKED QUESTION

Cover = Page in the Album

I want to use my cover photo as one of the pages in the book, just like they do in real coffee-table photo books. How do I do it?

In Organize mode, click the photo and then choose File→ Duplicate (⌘-D).

Now you have two copies of the photo. Drag one to the front of the line in the album (to use as the cover). Drag the other into the mass of other photos, so that you can now use it in one of the interior page layouts.

(and centered) on the linen cover of the actual book. (The cloth cover of your book will be one of several handsome dark colors, *not* white as it appears here.)

You can't do much with the cover except to change the title or subtitle; see "Edit the Titles and Captions," on page 236. You'll choose the cover color in a later step.

Tip: The picture you see here is the *first picture* in the album. If it's not the photo you want on the cover, click the Organize button and drag a different photo to the beginning of your album.

Pictures per Page

Click the thumbnail for page 2. If you did some preliminary arranging work in your album, your photos should already be in roughly the right *order* for the book pages—but not necessarily the right *groupings*.

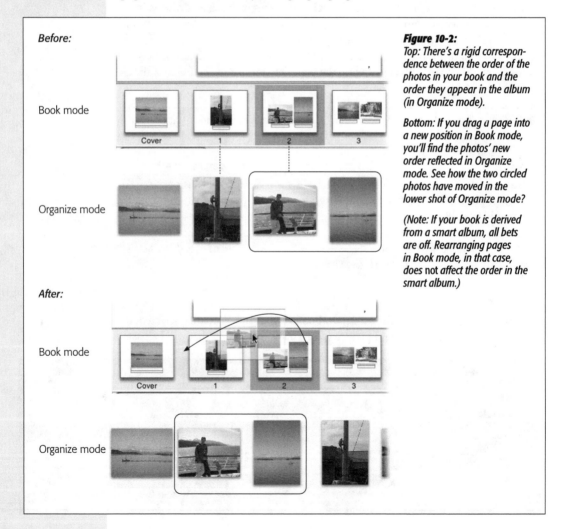

Figure 10-2:
Top: There's a rigid correspondence between the order of the photos in your book and the order they appear in the album (in Organize mode).

Bottom: If you drag a page into a new position in Book mode, you'll find the photos' new order reflected in Organize mode. See how the two circled photos have moved in the lower shot of Organize mode?

(Note: If your book is derived from a smart album, all bets are off. Rearranging pages in Book mode, in that case, does not affect the order in the smart album.)

You control how many pictures appear on a page—and, to an extent, their layout—by choosing a number from the Page Design pop-up menu. Your choices are:

- **Cover.** The first thumbnail in your book *must* have the Cover design.

  On the other hand, subsequent pages can *also* have the Cover layout. You can use this quirk to your advantage. For example, in a book that documents your trip to three countries, a "cover" layout can introduce each country's batch of photos.

- **Introduction.** Not all themes offer this page design, but on those that do, this special page has no photos at all. It's just a big set of text boxes that you can type (or paste)

FREQUENTLY ASKED QUESTION

Case of the Hideous Layout

Oh my gosh, you can't believe how ragged my book pages look. They don't look anything like the tidy illustrations in this chapter, or the examples on the Apple Web site. What's going on?

iPhoto's design templates operate on the simple premise that all of your photos have a *4:3 aspect ratio.* That is, the long and short sides of the photo are in four-to-three proportions (four inches to three inches, for example).

In most cases, that's what you've already got, since those are the standard proportions of standard digital photos. If all your pictures are in 4:3 (or 3:4) proportions, they will fit neatly and beautifully into the page-layout slots iPhoto provides for them.

A few cameras produce photos in the more traditional 3:2 film dimensions (1800 x 1200 pixels, for example), and some cameras let you choose. That feature will make you very happy when it comes time to order Kodak prints of your pictures (Chapter 8)—but will cause you nothing but headaches when you want to lay out a photo book. They won't align with the canned iPhoto designs, and full-bleed (edge-to-edge) pictures won't go edge to edge. They'll leave unsightly strips of white along certain edges.

Another possibility: You may have made the mistake of *mis-cropping* your photos in iPhoto. When you arbitrarily chop out excess portions of your pictures, you lose the tidy 4:3 aspect ratio they were born with. You wind up with one picture that's 4:2.5, another that's 5:3, and so on. These photos won't line up when placed into a book layout, either.

The simple way to avoid these problems is to crop your non-4:3 photos using the Constrain pop-up menu (page 141). From this menu, choose "4 x 3 (Book)" to crop safely.

Now, even though you're chopping away edges of your photo, you're maintaining the ideal book proportions.

If you've already done unconstrained cropping—if you're reading this advice too late, and you've got uneven layouts in your book—you have only one recourse. Click Organize, click the pictures you cropped, and choose File→Revert to Original. Thanks to iPhoto's secret backup system, you now have the photos as they were when they first arrived from the camera.

You can now re-crop them, this time using the Constrain menu to keep the proportions pure.

---

into. Here's where you can let the audience know about the trip, the company, or the family; tell the story behind the book; praise the book's lucky recipient; scare off intellectual-property thieves with threatening copyright notices; and so on.

Tip: An Introduction page (one of the choices in the Page Design pop-up menu) doesn't have to be the first page of the book (after the cover). You can turn *any* page into an Introduction page. Such pages make great section dividers.

They're especially useful in designs that use the Picture Book theme that otherwise have no text at all. An Introduction page can set the scene and explain the following (uncaptioned) pages of pictures.

- **One, Two, Three, Four...** These commands let you specify how many photos appear on the selected page. iPhoto automatically arranges them according to its own internal sense of symmetry. (Most themes offer up to six photos per page in iPhoto 4—a welcome bit of flexibility. The limit was four in iPhoto 2.)

  Use these options to create a pleasing overall layout for the book and give it variety. Follow a page with one big photo with a page of four smaller ones, for example.

  You can also use these commands to fit the number of photos you have to the length of your book. If you have lots of pictures and don't want to go over the $30 ten-page limit, then choose higher picture counts for most pages. Conversely, if iPhoto warns you that you have blank pages at the end of your book, spread your photos out by choosing just one or two photos for some pages.

- **One with Text.** Unique to the Collage theme (page 227), this choice on the Page Design pop-up menu places one picture on the left side of a page with a long, narrow text box to the right. It's like a vertical alternative to the Introduction page layout.

- **End.** The Page Design pop-up menu for the Story Book theme offers a bonus page design called End. Use it for the last page of the book.

  The End page is designed to hold three pictures, and you'd be well advised to fiddle with your album until the last page does, in fact, have three photos on it. Otherwise, you'll wind up with a strange, half-filled look on the End page. For example, if there's only one photo on it, that picture will sit halfway off the left

---

FREQUENTLY ASKED QUESTION

The Save Command

Yo...where's the Save command?

There isn't one. iPhoto automatically saves your work as you go.

If you want to make a safety copy along the way—a fallback version—highlight the *album* from which the book is derived

and choose File→Duplicate. This process takes virtually no extra memory or disk space, but it's good insurance. If you change the layout or theme of a book, iPhoto vaporizes all the text you've entered (and often a lot of the layout work). If that happens, you'll be glad you had a backup.

---

margin, as though sailing off to the left ("Later, dude!"), and the rest of the page will be blank.

Tip: Normally, your selection from this pop-up menu affects only the page you're working on. But if you want all the pages to look the same, hold down Option as you pick a design. iPhoto applies that design to all pages in the book. (This business involves laying out all of your pages again, even those that you've locked.)

Each time you change the number of photos on a page, something happens that you may find disconcerting: Pictures on the *following* pages slide onto earlier or later pages. Figure 10-3 illustrates this phenomenon.

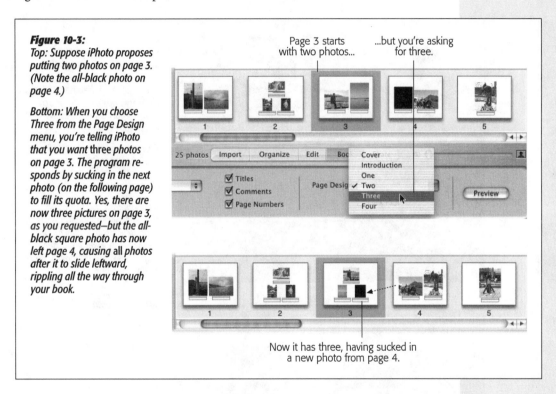

Figure 10-3:
Top: Suppose iPhoto proposes putting two photos on page 3. (Note the all-black photo on page 4.)

Bottom: When you choose Three from the Page Design menu, you're telling iPhoto that you want three photos on page 3. The program responds by sucking in the next photo (on the following page) to fill its quota. Yes, there are now three pictures on page 3, as you requested—but the all-black square photo has now left page 4, causing all photos after it to slide leftward, rippling all the way through your book.

Page 3 starts with two photos... ...but you're asking for three.

Now it has three, having sucked in a new photo from page 4.

This syndrome can drive you wiggy if it winds up disrupting a page that you've already tweaked to perfection—a problem you'll almost certainly encounter if you don't work on your pages from left to right.

The solution is simple. Once a page has the right photos on it (and the right *number* of photos), lock it by turning on the Lock Page checkbox at the lower edge of the window. (A tiny padlock icon appears on the page's thumbnail, as shown in Figure 10-1.)

From now on, even if you change the number of shots on an earlier page, the page you locked will remain undisturbed.

Even this trick, though, requires some caution. Keep in mind the following gotchas:

- Once you've locked a page, the Page Design pop-up menu no longer functions for that page. You have to unlock a page before you can change the number of pictures on it.

- If you do unlock a page, watch out…you're taking the muzzle off a spring-loaded design. Because iPhoto is maintaining a picture group that, in its head, is out of sequence (relative to Organize mode), unlocking a page may cause its pictures to explode into other locations. As a result, you'll witness a ripple effect that's likely to scramble *all* unlocked pages in your book.

Before

After

Figure 10-4:
In some ways, you are at the mercy of iPhoto's design templates. You can't dictate how the photos overlap their neighbors (in Story Book), or how much space separates pictures in Picture Book, shown here.

And yet—ring them bells! Fire them flares! In iPhoto 4, you can, at last, drag to swap photos on a single page.

If the photos have the same shape, they simply swap positions, which sometimes means that you can swap a quarter-page photo with the half-page picture next to it.

If they have different proportions, swapping photos sometimes means that you can flip the tall one from one side of the page to the other, as shown here.

- If you use the Theme pop-up menu to change themes, all bets are off. Changing themes blasts *all* layout work into oblivion, locked or not.

Photo and Page Sequence

As you work, continue to consider the overall effect of your layout. You can't drag pictures from one page to another, but—thanks to a new iPhoto 4 feature—you can drag them around *within each page*. Just click the photo you want to move, wait for a thin yellow border to appear, and then drag until it's *over* the photo (or photo spot) where you want it to go. When the existing picture sprouts a pink border, let go of the mouse button; the two pictures swap places (Figure 10-4).

You still can't drag a photo from one page to the next. You can, however, rearrange entire *pages*. Just drag the page thumbnails left or right in their track. If you return to Organize mode, you'll see that the photos have shifted there, too, to reflect their new order in the book; again, see Figure 10-2.

In fact, if using a combination of dragging pictures on pages and dragging whole pages around turns into an exercise in frustration for you, you can always switch into Organize mode, drag the photos into the exact order you want, then switch back into Book mode for the finishing touches.

And give thanks: Before iPhoto 4, Organize mode was the *only* way to rearrange pictures in a book. Now you have a choice.

Note: The exception to all this: Dragging pictures in Organize mode doesn't work in smart albums.

Sometimes chronological order is the natural sequence, especially for books that will be mementos of special events like trips, parties, and weddings. But there's nothing to stop you from cheating a bit—rearranging certain scenes—for greater impact and variety.

As you drag your pictures into order, consider these effects:

- Intersperse group shots with solo portraits, scenery with people shots, vertical ones with horizontals.

- On multiple-photo pages, exploit the direction your subjects face. On a three-picture page, for example, you could arrange the people in the photos so that they're all looking roughly toward the center of the page, for a feeling of inclusion (Figure 10-5). You might put a father looking upward to a shot of his son diving on a photo higher on the page, or a brother and sister back-to-back facing outward, signifying competition.

- Group similar shots together on a page.

Page Limits

The book can have anywhere from 10 to 50 pages. If you create fewer pages, you'll be warned during the book-ordering process that you're about to pay for a ten-page book with blank pages at the end. If you create more than 50 pages, you won't be allowed to place the order at all.

There's nothing to stop you from creating multiple books, however. ("Our Trip to New Jersey, Vol. XI," anyone?)

Figure 10-5:
Variety is good—but thematic unity is good, too. Here, two photos taken at the same event, moments apart, feel good together. They tell a little scene and add a little action to your book.

Hiding Page Numbers

Each built-in theme includes page numbers stamped on the lower-right corner of each page. You never have to worry about a page number winding up superimposed on one of your pictures, though. A picture *always* takes priority, covering up the page number.

Even so, you may feel that page numbers intrude on the mood your book creates. If so, just eliminate them by turning off the Page Numbers checkbox at the lower-left corner of the window.

Tip: As you work, you may discover photos here and there that need a little editing—cropping, brightening, and so on (Chapter 6). No problem: Just double-click a picture in the book-page display window to open it in either Edit mode or an external photo-editing program, as described on page 152. Close the editing window, or click the Book button again, when you're finished.

Phase 4: Edit the Titles and Captions

In every theme, iPhoto offers you text boxes that you can fill with titles, explanations, and captions. Most layouts have space for this kind of text on every page. Only the Picture Book design is text-free (except for the cover and introduction page).

In any case, taking the time to perfect this text is extremely important. A misspelling or typo you make here may haunt you (and amuse the book's recipient) forever.

In general, iPhoto offers the following four kinds of text boxes:

- **The book title.** This box appears on the book's cover and, if you've added one, Introduction page. When you first create a book, iPhoto proposes the *album's* name as the book name, but you're welcome to change it.

  A second text box, all set with slightly smaller-type formatting, appears below the title. Use it for a subtitle: the date, "A Trip Down Memory Lane," "Happy Birthday Aunt Enid," "A Little Something for the Insurance Company," or whatever.

- **The introduction.** Applying the Introduction page design to a page gives you a huge text block that you can fill with any introductory text you think the book needs.

Tip: An Introduction page doesn't have to be the first page of the book (after the cover). You can turn *any* page into an all-text Introduction page. Such pages make great section dividers.

They're especially useful in Picture Book designs that otherwise have no text at all. Whatever you type or paste into the Introduction page can set the scene and explain the following (uncaptioned) pages of pictures.

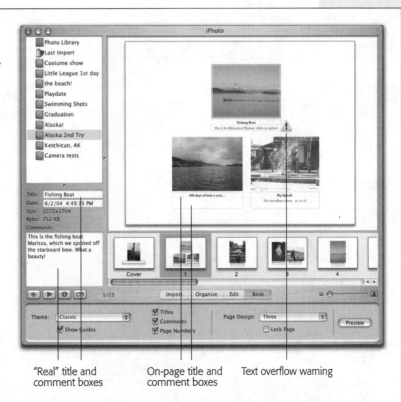

Figure 10-6:
iPhoto offers two different places to enter text. Using the boxes at the left side of the screen is usually faster, since you don't have to wait for iPhoto to zoom in to the text box. A yellow, nonprinting warning sign appears if the text box is too small to display all of the comment text (or the full photo name).

"Real" title and comment boxes

On-page title and comment boxes

Text overflow warning

- **Photo titles.** In most layouts, iPhoto displays the name of each photo. If you haven't already named each picture, you'll get only the internal iPhoto name of each picture—"IMG_0030.JPG," for example. You can edit this name either in the text box on your page preview, or in the Title text box at the left side of the iPhoto window (Figure 10-6).

- **Comments.** The larger text box that appears for each photo (in some layouts) is for a caption. It automatically displays any comments you've typed into the Comments box for a photo at the left side of the iPhoto screen (see page 112). Or, to be precise, it displays the first chunk of that text.

Note, by the way, that some of the layouts don't show nearly as much text as the "real" Title or Comments box does. In these cases, iPhoto has no choice but to chop off the excess, showing only the first sentence or two. A yellow, triangular

---

UP TO SPEED

The Heartbreak of the Yellow Exclamation Point

As you work on your book design, you may encounter the dreaded yellow-triangle-exclamation point like the one shown here. It appears everywhere you want to be: on the corresponding page thumbnail, on the page display, on the page preview (which appears when you click Preview), and so on.

If you actually try to order the book without eliminating the yellow triangles: you even get a warning in the form of a dialog box. "Low Quality Warning: One or more photos in your book may print at too low a quality based on the design you have chosen. Do you want to continue?"

All of this boils down to one heartbreaking problem: At least one of your photos doesn't have enough resolution (enough pixels) to reproduce well in the finished book. If you ignore the warning and continue with the ordering process, you're likely to be disappointed by the blotchy, grainy result in the finished book.

You may remember from Chapter 1 that the resolution of your digital camera is relatively irrelevant if you'll only be showing your pictures onscreen. It's when you try to *print* them that you need all the megapixels you can get—like

now.

The easiest solution is to shrink the photo on its page. And the easiest way to do *that* is to increase the *number* of pictures on that page. (Some layouts put both large and small photos on the same page. In that case, you may have to click Organize and drag photos around so that your low-res, problem-child picture lands in one of the smaller slots.)

Decreasing a picture's size also squeezes its pixels closer together, improving the dots-per-inch shortage that iPhoto is warning you about.

If even that dramatic step doesn't eliminate the yellow warning emblems, try to remember if you ever cropped this photo. If so, your last chance is to click Organize, click the photo, and then choose File→Revert To Original. Doing so will undo any *cropping* you did to the photo, which may have thrown away a lot of pixels that you suddenly find yourself needing. (If Revert To Original is dimmed, then you never performed any cropping, and this last resort is worthless.)

Finally, if nothing has worked so far, your only options are to eliminate the photo from your book or to order the book anyway.

---

exclamation point appears next to any text box that has overflow of this kind—your cue to edit down the text to fit the text box on the layout (Figure 10-6).

Note: On the other hand, iPhoto may give you "false positives," showing a yellow triangle (and text visually wrapping on the screen) when, in fact, the text will look just fine when it's printed. (This problem is especially apparent with small text and a reduced-size display of the page.) To find out what you'll *really* get, make a final proofreading pass using one of the techniques described on page 244.

Editing Text

You're welcome to edit the photo titles or comments in either place: right here in the layout, or back in the Info box for the individual photos. In general, the editing process is straightforward:

- Click inside a text box to activate the insertion-point cursor, so you can begin typing. iPhoto zooms in on the page and scrolls it, if necessary, so that the type is large enough to see and edit. When you click outside a text box—on another part of the page, for example—the page shrinks again to fit the window.

- You can select text and then use the Edit menu's Cut, Copy, and Paste commands to transfer text from box to box.

- You can also move selected text *within* a text box by dragging it and dropping it. The trick is to *hold down* the mouse button for a moment before dragging. Add the Option key to make a *copy* of the selected text instead of moving it.

- Double-click a word, or triple-click a paragraph, to neatly highlight it.

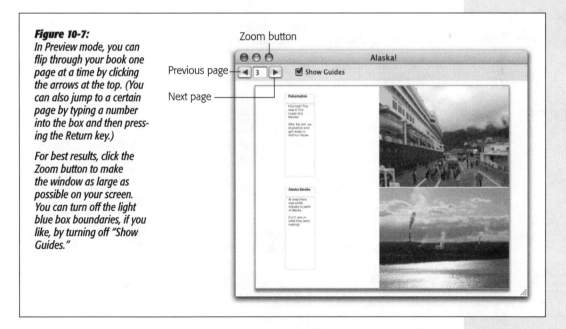

Figure 10-7:
In Preview mode, you can flip through your book one page at a time by clicking the arrows at the top. (You can also jump to a certain page by typing a number into the box and then pressing the Return key.)

For best results, click the Zoom button to make the window as large as possible on your screen. You can turn off the light blue box boundaries, if you like, by turning off "Show Guides."

Zoom button

Previous page

Next page

- Press Control-right arrow or Control-left arrow to make the insertion point jump to the beginning or end of the line.

- To make typographically proper quotation marks ("curly like this" instead of "this"), press Option-[and Shift-Option-[, respectively. And to make a true long dash—like this, instead of two hyphens—press Shift-Option-hyphen.

But here's the biggest tip of all: *Edit your text in Preview mode.* (Click the Preview button at the lower-right corner of the window, or just double-click one of the book's page thumbnails; see Figure 10-7.)

In Preview mode, each page appears in its own window, which you can make as large as you like. iPhoto therefore doesn't have to zoom and unzoom as you click each text box, which makes the editing go faster. And because you can see the whole page (instead of only the portion that fits within the photo viewing area), you have a better sense of your text block's look and proportions relative to the picture.

Tip: Can't seem to get the size, placement, or variety of type that you want? Then the heck with iPhoto and its straitjacketed text boxes—you can use whatever type you want.

All you have to do is jump into a graphics program, like Photoshop Elements, AppleWorks, or GraphicConverter. Create a JPEG graphic document that's 1350 x 1800 pixels, with a resolution of 150 dots per inch. Now fill it with text, using the graphic software's text tools. You have complete freedom of fonts and placement.

Finally, bring this graphic into iPhoto. Use it as a single "photo" on the page where you want the text to appear. It's crude and crazy, but it works!

Hiding Text

As noted earlier, the Picture Book theme is especially dramatic because it *lacks* text. The pictures spill across the pages, strong and big.

Bear in mind, though, that you can turn off the text for *any* of the layout themes, adding more white space (not more room for photos). Just turn off the corresponding checkbox (Titles or Comments) in the lower-left corner of the iPhoto window. (You can also leave *individual* boxes empty, of course.)

Note: You can't *add* titles or comment boxes to a theme that doesn't have them, however. The pages in the Picture Book theme don't have any text on them, and no amount of turning the Titles and Comments checkboxes on or off can change that.

Formatting Text

To a certain extent, you can change the fonts, sizes, and styles of type in your book. To begin, choose Edit→Font→Show Fonts (or press ⌘-T). As shown in Figure 10-8, Mac OS X's standard Font panel appears.

Now click inside the kind of text box you want to change, and then click any font you like.

All right, "any" may be stretching it. The truth is:

- You can't change the *size* of the type—only the font and style.

- In general, whatever changes you make apply to *every* title or comment box in the entire book. There's no way to make one caption look different from other captions, or to format only part of a sentence (so that you can italicize a single word, for example).

- There are two exceptions to the previous point. If you select some words and then Control-click them, a shortcut menu appears. Choosing Italic or Bold from its Font submenu affects all text in all boxes—but choosing *Underline* affects only the selected words. (It looks pretty crude, but that's a different conversation.)

  The Font submenu even offers a Show Colors command. It opens a color palette; using it, you can apply different colors, too, to individual text selections. Yes, the bright, multicolored result might look a little bit like it was designed by Barney the Dinosaur, but the Color option is worth keeping in mind when you're preparing books about, for example, someone's fourth birthday party.

- Most people have good luck using almost any font in the Font panel. You should know, though, that Apple *officially* recommends only these fonts: Helvetica, Helvetica Neue, Century Gothic, Papyrus, GillSans, MarkerFelt, Baskerville, and Brushscript, without any variations of them (bold, italic, and so on).

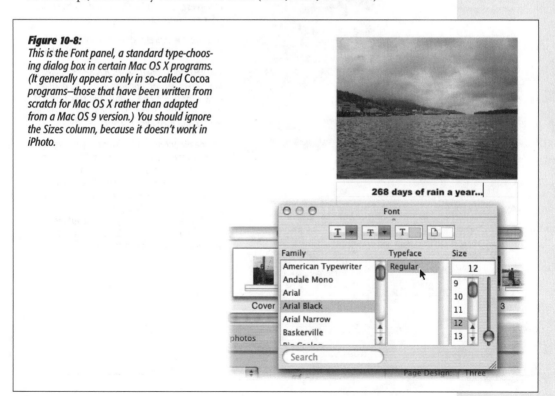

Figure 10-8:
This is the Font panel, a standard type-choosing dialog box in certain Mac OS X programs. (It generally appears only in so-called Cocoa programs–those that have been written from scratch for Mac OS X rather than adapted from a Mac OS 9 version.) You should ignore the Sizes column, because it doesn't work in iPhoto.

Check Your Spelling

Ordinarily, you might scoff at the overkill—what difference does a typo make in a photo-organizing program, for goodness' sake? But your tune will change the very day you get your $30 (or $150) hardbound photo book in the mail, proudly titled, "Our Trip to the Grand Canyin."

As in a word processor, you can ask iPhoto to check your spelling several ways:

- **Check a single word or selection.** Highlight a word, or several, and then choose Edit→Spelling→Check Spelling (⌘-semicolon). If the word is misspelled in iPhoto's opinion, a red, dashed line appears under the word. Proceed as shown in Figure 10-9.

- **Check a whole text block.** Click inside a title or comment box and then choose Edit→Spelling→Spelling (⌘-colon). The standard Mac OS X Spelling dialog box appears, also shown and described in Figure 10-9.

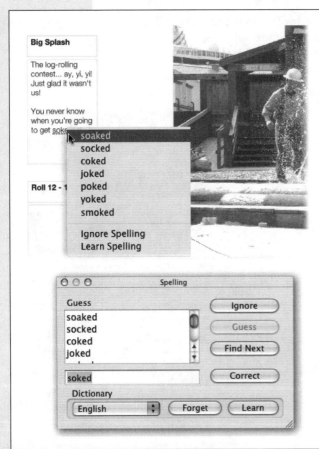

Figure 10-9:
Top: Control-click any word that's underlined with a red, dashed line. If the resulting shortcut menu contains the correct spelling, choose it. Otherwise, choose Ignore or Add (to teach Mac OS X that word for future spell checks).

Bottom: If you prefer a more word processor–like spelling check, you can summon this box.

The first "misspelled" word already appears. If the correct version appears in the list, double-click it (or single-click it and then click Correct). If not, type the correct word into the box below the list and then click Correct.

On the other hand, if the word in your caption is fine as it is, click either Ignore ("Stop under-lining this, iPhoto. It's a word I want spelled this way; let's go on") or Add ("This is a name or word that not only is correctly spelled, but I may use again. Add it to your dictionary so you'll never flag it again"). Alas, iPhoto forgets everything you've told it to Ignore as soon as you click into a different text box.

- **Check as you type.** The trouble with the spelling commands described here is that they operate on only a single, tiny text block at a time. To check your entire photo book, you must click inside each title or caption and invoke the spelling command again. There's no way to have iPhoto sweep through your entire book at once.

Your eyes might widen in excitement, therefore, when you spot the Edit→ Spelling→Check Spelling As You Type command. You'd expect it to make iPhoto flag words it doesn't recognize *as you type them.*

Sure enough, when this option is turned on, whenever you type a word not in iPhoto's dictionary, iPhoto adds a colorful dashed underline. (Technically, it underlines any word not in the *Mac OS X* dictionary, since you're actually using the standard Mac OS X spelling checker—the same one that watches over you in Mac OS X's Mail program, for example.)

To correct a misspelling that iPhoto has found in this way, Control-click it. A shortcut menu appears. Proceed as shown in Figure 10-9.

There's only one problem: This option turns itself *off* every time you click into a new text box. Using the mouse (there's no keyboard shortcut), you have to turn it on again for every title and caption. The regular Check Spelling command looks positively effortless by comparison.

Listen to Your Book

Unfortunately, even a spelling checker won't find missing words, inadvertently repeated words, or awkward writing. For those situations, what you really want is for iPhoto to *read your captions aloud* to you.

No problem: Just highlight some text by dragging through it, and then Control-click the highlighted area. As shown in Figure 10-10, a shortcut menu appears, containing the Speech command.

Figure 10-10:
Control-clicking highlighted text produces this secret shortcut menu, which includes commands that make iPhoto start and stop reading the text aloud. It uses whatever voice you've selected in Mac OS X's System Preferences→Speech control panel.

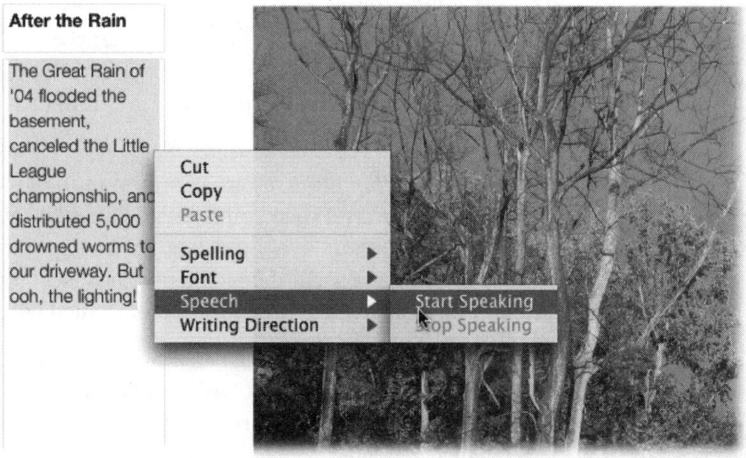

Phase 5: Preview the Masterpiece

Ordering a professionally bound book is, needless to say, quite a commitment. Before blowing $30 or more on a one-shot deal, you'd be wise to proofread and inspect it from every possible angle.

Preview It Onscreen

One easy way to inspect your book is to click the Preview button in the lower-right corner of the screen—or just double-click the thumbnail for any page. iPhoto fills your screen with an electronic version of the selected page for your inspection, as shown in Figure 10-7.

Print It

As any proofreader can tell you, though, looking over a book on paper is a sure way to discover errors that somehow elude detection onscreen. That's why it's a good idea to print out your own, low-tech edition of your book at home before beaming it away to Apple's bindery.

While you're in Book mode, choose File→Print. After the Mac OS X Print dialog box appears, fire up your printer and click Print when ready. The result may not be linen-bound, and it uses up a lot of inkjet ink. But it's a tantalizing preview of the real thing—and a great way to give the book one final look.

Turn It into a PDF File

Sooner or later, almost everyone with a personal computer encounters PDF (Portable Document Format) files. Many a software manual, Read Me file, and down-loadable "white paper" comes in this format, for many of the following reasons:

- **Other people see your layout.** When you distribute PDF files to other people, they see precisely the same fonts, colors, page design, and other elements that you did in your original document. They get to see all of this even if they don't *have* the fonts or the software you used to create the document. (Now contrast this with the alternative: sending somebody, for example, a Microsoft Word document. In this scenario, if your correspondents don't have precisely the same fonts as you, then they'll see a screwy layout. And if they don't have Microsoft Word, they'll see nothing at all.)

- **It's universal.** PDF files are very common in the Macintosh, Windows, and even Unix/Linux worlds. When you create a PDF file, you can distribute it (by email, for example) without ever worrying about what kind of computers your correspondents are using. All the recipient needs is a copy of the free Adobe Acrobat Reader program, which now comes preinstalled with every computer.

- **It has very high resolution.** PDF files print at the maximum quality of any printer. A single PDF file prints great both on cheapo inkjets and on high-quality image-setting gear at professional print shops. (You're looking at a PDF file right now, in fact, which was later printed at a publishing plant.)

- **You can search it.** Although you may be tempted to think of a PDF file as something like a captured graphic of the original document, it has several key differences. Behind the scenes, its text is still text. You can search it using a Find command.

If you suspect other people might want to have a look at your photo book before it goes to be printed—or if they'd just like to have a copy of their own—a PDF file makes a convenient package.

Here's how to create a PDF file:

1. **With your book design on the screen in front of you, choose File→Print.**

   The print dialog box appears.

2. **Click the Save as PDF button.**

   The Save sheet appears.

3. **Type a name for the file, choose a folder location for it, and click Save.**

   Your PDF file is ready to distribute. (Fortunately, the recipients will be able to correct the rotation within Adobe Acrobat using its View→Rotate Counterclockwise command, or within Preview using View→Rotate Left.)

Figure 10-11:
Bottom left: Choose a color, a quantity, and a recipient.

Top right: You won't be allowed to choose a quantity or recipient, though, until you've first signed up for an Apple account, which you'll enjoy using over and over again to order books and stuff from the Apple online stores.

To sign up for an account, click the Set Up Account button (not shown here, but it would appear in place of Buy Now if this were your first time). To correct or update your account info later, click the Account Info at the bottom of the first dialog box (lower left).

Phase 6: Send the Book to the Bindery

When you think your book is ready for birth, click the Organize button. In the row of icons at the bottom of the screen, click Order Book.

After several minutes of converting your screen design into an Internet-transmittable file, iPhoto offers you a screen like the one shown in Figure 10-11. (If your book is *shorter* than ten pages, iPhoto first warns you that you're about to pay for a bunch of blank pages. Ten pages is the *minimum* for a book.)

Note: If you receive a Low Quality Warning at this stage, see the box on page 238.

At this stage, your tasks are largely administrative.

- **Choose a cover color.** Use the Cover Color pop-up menu to choose Black, Burgundy (red), Light Gray, or Navy (blue). The books in the illustration, including

POWER USERS' CLINIC

The Secret, Really Really Final PDF

Looking over your final book as a PDF file in Preview is a pretty darned effective way to give it a final look-over.

Incredibly enough, though, even this PDF doesn't show you *exactly* what you're about to submit to Apple. It doesn't show you exactly the final type layout, for example, which is why some people wind up with chopped-off text boxes even though they looked fine in Preview. Nor does it show whether any photo files are corrupted, resulting in blank pages.

When a book doesn't print out quite right, Apple is generally very forgiving, and will invite you to resubmit the book's file to try again. But sometimes, you don't have the time to wait for a second attempt—for example, when it's December 21 and you really need that book for Christmas.

In such cases, you'll be glad that you know how to inspect the actual, secret PDF book file that iPhoto sends to Apple. Here's how to find it (these directions are for Mac OS X 10.3, but the 10.2 procedure is similar):

Assemble your book, and click the Order Book button. Just af-

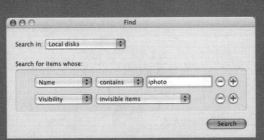

ter the "Assembling Book" progress window disappears, you arrive at the Order Book screen shown in Figure 10-10.

Switch back to the Finder. Choose File→Find. Set the first row of pop-up menus to read, "Name" "contains" iPhoto.

Click the + button to create a new row. Set its pop-up menus to read, "Visibility" "invisible items," as shown here.

Click Search.

On the Search Results screen, you'll find a folder named iPhoto. Double-click it to find a secret file named something like Book-107690896.pdf. When you open this PDF, you'll find it filled with wacky crop marks and other oddities, but it shows exactly, precisely what you'll get when that handsome volume arrives at your house in hardback form. This is your last chance to look it over for imperfections.

This is the actual file that you'll send to Apple's printing plant.

If it looks good, close the document, return to iPhoto, specify how many copies you want, and click Buy Now.

the handy magnified swatch, change color to show you what you're getting. (If you're ordering more than one book, they must all have the same color.)

- **Inspect the charges.** If you've gone beyond ten pages, you'll see that you're about to be charged $3 per additional page.

- **Indicate the quantity.** You can order additional copies of the same book. Indeed, after you've spent so much time on a gift book for someone else, you may well be tempted to order yourself a copy.

Your Apple ID—and One-Click Ordering

You can't make any additional progress until you've signed up for an Apple account and turned on "1-Click Ordering."

You may well already have an Apple account if you've ever bought something from an online Apple store or the iTunes Music Store, for example. Whether you do or not, ordering your first iPhoto book requires completing some electronic paperwork like this:

1. **Click Set Up Account.**

   This button appears only if you've never ordered an iPhoto book before (Figure 10-11). In any case, an Apple Account Sign-In screen appears. If you already have an Apple account, type in your Apple ID and account password here by all means.

   An Apple ID is your email address. As noted above, it's the same ID you use to customize the look of Apple's help Web site (if you've ever done that) or to buy something from Apple online. It's your .Mac address, if you have that.

   When you're finished, click Sign In. On the next screen, make sure 1-Click Ordering is turned on. Click Edit Shipping, if you like, to supply any addresses you plan to use repeatedly for shipping books and Kodak prints to. Finally, click Done. Skip to step 7.

   If you've never established such an account, go on:

2. **Click Create Account.**

   The Create an Apple Account screen appears (top right in Figure 10-11).

3. **Fill in your email address, a password (twice), a question (which you'll be asked if you forget your password) and its answer, and your date of birth.**

   Unless you enjoy receiving junk email, turn off "I would like to receive Apple news, software updates, special offers, and information…from other companies."

4. **Click the Step 2 button; on the Terms of Use screen, click Accept.**

   Now you're asked for your billing information. This is how you'll pay for the book, and all books to come.

5. **Fill in your billing information, and then click Continue.**

iPhoto lets you set up a number of addresses for people you may want books shipped to. The next screen proposes that you add *yourself* to this list.

6. **Click the Step 3 button.**

You wind up right where you started: at the Order Book screen. This time, however, the controls at the bottom are "live" and operational.

7. **From the Ship To pop-up menu, choose the lucky recipient of this book.**

If it's you, choose Myself. If not, you can choose Add New Address from this pop-up menu.

Note: You can order books if you live in Europe, Japan, or North America, but Apple offers shipping only to people in the same region (Europe, Japan, or North America).

If you wind up at the 1-Click Account Summary screen following this detour, click Done.

8. **From the Ship Via pop-up menu, indicate how you want the finished book shipped.**

WORKAROUND WORKSHOP

Secrets of the Apple Book Publishing Empire

It's no secret that when you order prints of your photos via the Internet, Kodak makes the prints. But neither temptation nor torture will persuade Apple to reveal who makes the gorgeous iPhoto photo books.

It didn't take long for Mac fans on the Internet, however, to discover some astonishing similarities between the iPhoto books and the books created by a firm called MyPublisher.com. The pricing, timing, and books themselves are all identical. (When asked if it's Apple's publishing partner, MyPublisher.com says, "We don't discuss our partner relationships," which means "Yes.")

The truth is, iPhoto-generated books are more elegantly designed than the ones you build yourself at MyPublisher.com. And it's certainly easier to upload books directly from

iPhoto, rather than uploading photo files one at a time using your Web browser.

Still, you should know that building your books directly at MyPublisher.com offers greater design freedom than iPhoto does. You have greater choices of cover colors and materials (even leather), you can add a glossy dust jacket, you can add borders around the pages, you have your choice of lightly patterned backgrounds, and you have much more flexibility over the placement of photos and text.

In fact, it's easy to get carried away with these options and produce something absolutely ghastly, which is probably why Apple chose to limit your options so you simply can't go wrong.

"Standard" shipping takes about four days and costs $8. "Express" means over-night or second-day shipping (depending on when you place the order) and costs $15. An additional book sent to the same address costs another $1 for Standard shipping, or $2 for Express.

9. **Indicate how many copies of this book you want, using the Quantity control.**

You'll see the Order Total updated.

10. **Click "Buy Now."**

You've already stored your credit card information, so there's nothing to do now but wait for your Mac to upload the book itself. After a few minutes, you'll see a confirmation message.

11. **Go about your life for a few days, holding your breath until the book arrives.**

You'll certainly be impressed by the linen-covered cover and the heavy, glossy pages. The photos are printed on Indigo digital presses (fancy digital four-color offset machines), but aren't what you'd call Kodak quality—or even photo-inkjet-on-glossy-paper quality.

But the book itself is classy, it's handsome…and it smells good!

From iPhoto to QuickTime

A s Chapter 7 makes clear, once you select your images and choose the music to go with them, iPhoto orchestrates the production and presents it live on your Mac's screen as a slideshow.

Which is great, as long as everyone in your social circle lives within six feet of your screen.

The day will come when you want friends and family who live a little farther away to be able to see your slideshows. Sure, you could pack up your Mac and fly across the country, but wouldn't it be easier to simply send the slideshow as a file attachment that people can play on their own computers?

That's the beauty of QuickTime, a portable multimedia container built into every Mac. Even if the recipient uses a Windows PC (every family has its black sheep), your photos will meet their public; QuickTime movies play just as well on HPs and Dells as they do on iMacs and PowerBooks.

The trick is to convert your well-composed iPhoto slideshow into a standalone QuickTime movie: a file on your hard drive that you can email to other people, post on your Web page for downloading, burn onto a CD, and so on.

Exporting a Slideshow to QuickTime

Fortunately, iPhoto makes creating the movie as simple as creating the original show itself. You just have to know which buttons to click.

Step 1: Perfect the Slideshow

Before you pack up your slideshow for release to the public, review it to make sure it plays the way you want it to. You'll probably find it easiest to create a new album just for your QuickTime slideshow (Chapter 5), so that you can fool around with the sequence and photo selection without messing up the album designed for such purposes as photo books and *onscreen* slideshows.

Thinking like a focus group

As you review your presentation, place the pictures into the proper sequence, remembering that you won't be there to verbally "set up" the slideshow and comment as it plays. Look at it with fresh eyes and ask yourself, "If I knew nothing about this subject, would this show make sense to me?"

During this exercise, you might decide that your presentation could use a few more descriptive images to better tell the story. If that's the case, go back through your master photo library and look for pictures of landmarks and signs that are easily recognizable. Put one or two at the beginning of the show to set the stage. For example, if your slideshow is about a vacation in Washington, D.C., then you might want to open with a picture of the Capitol, White House, or Lincoln Memorial.

Tip: If you don't have any suitable opening shots in your library, or even if you do, another option is to begin your show with a few words of text, like opening credits. To do so, create a JPEG graphic containing the text in a program like AppleWorks, Photoshop, or GraphicConverter. (Make sure this graphic matches the pixel dimensions of your slideshow, as described in the following section.) Then drag the file right into your slideshow album, placing it first in the sequence. You've got yourself an opening title screen.

Which photos make the cut

If you're used to the slideshow feature described in Chapter 7, the method for specifying which photos are exported to your QuickTime movie might throw you.

- If *one* thumbnail is selected, that's all you'll get in the finished QuickTime movie—the world's shortest slideshow. (This is the part that might throw you: An iPhoto slideshow would begin with that one selected photo and then move on from there, showing you all the rest of the photos in the album.)

- If *several* thumbnails are selected, only they make it into the QuickTime slideshow movie.

- If *no* thumbnails are selected, the entire album's worth of photos wind up in the show.

When you're ready to convert your presentation to a QuickTime movie, choose File→ Export.

The Export Photos dialog box appears, as shown in Figure 11-1. Click the QuickTime tab, where you have some important decisions to make.

Step 2: Choose the Movie Dimensions

Specifying the width and height for your movie affects not only how big it is on the screen during playback, but also its file size, which may become an issue if you plan to email the movie to other people. iPhoto generally proposes 640 x 480 pixels.

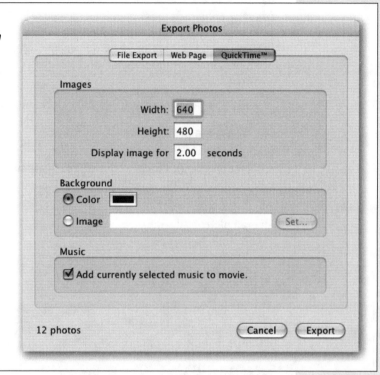

Figure 11-1:
Here's the Export dialog box with the QuickTime tab selected. This is the airlock, the womb, the last time you'll be able to affect your movie before it's born.

That's an ideal size: big enough for people to see some detail in the photo, but not so big that the resulting movie won't play from, say, a CD. (CDs are much slower than hard drives.)

You're free to change these dimensions, however. If the movie will be played back from a hard drive, you may want to crank up the dimensions close to the size of the screen itself: 800 x 600 is a safe bet if you're not sure. Remember, though, you have to leave some room for the QuickTime Player controls, so that your viewers can start and stop the movie.

Proportion considerations

All of these suggestions assume, by the way, that your photos' dimensions are in a 4:3 ratio, the way they come from most cameras (see page 141). That way, they'll fit nicely into the standard QuickTime playback window.

But there's nothing to stop you from typing other numbers into the Width and Height boxes. If most of the shots are vertical, for example, you'll want to reverse the proposed dimensions so that they're 480 x 640, resulting in a taller, thinner playback window.

In any case, it would be hard to imagine why you'd want to choose dimensions other than those in a 4:3 ratio unless:

- You've cropped the photos for use in ordering prints (page 187).

- Your camera doesn't produce 4:3 images. (A few produce photos with a 3:2 width-to-height ratio instead, in which case you'd want your movie dimensions to match.)

- You're going for a bizarre, distorted look in your finished film.

Size considerations

As you choose dimensions, however, bear in mind that they also determine the *file size* of the resulting QuickTime movie. That's not such an issue if you plan to play the movie from a CD, DVD, or hard drive. But if you plan to send the movie by email or post it on a Web page, watch out.

For example, consider the slideshow movie shown in Figure 11-2. It contains 24 slides and has an MP3 music soundtrack.

Figure 11-2:
This sample QuickTime movie has dimensions of 320 x 240 pixels. This is not what you'd call an IMAX movie; it will play in a fairly small window on your audience's screens.

At 640 x 480 pixels, this movie would take up 3 MB on your hard drive—and at least that much in your recipients' email inboxes. Scaling it down to a quarter of that size (320 x 240) would shave off about a third of that, resulting in a 2.1 MB file.

But 2.1 MB is a very big file to send as an email attachment to anyone who connects with a dial-up modem. You could, of course, reduce the dimensions even further. At some point, though, you'd reach a point of diminishing returns. The pictures would be so microscopic that the project wouldn't be worth doing.

In that case, you might want to start whittling down the music rather than the photos (see the box below).

Managing Music

In the Music section of your QuickTime export dialog box, you have the option of including the soundtrack you originally selected for your slideshow (page 166) by turning on the box labeled, "Add currently selected music to movie." (If you want a different soundtrack, click Cancel, click the Slideshow icon, and choose a different song from your iTunes collection.)

POWER USERS' CLINIC

Musical Liposuction

If you're struggling with the size of a QuickTime movie slideshow that's too big for emailing, consider shrinking the size of the music track. By cutting its *bit rate* (a measure of its sound quality) from 192 to 128 kbps, for example, the file size for a hypothetical 320 x 240–pixel movie would shrink from 2.1 MB to 1.5 MB—and your ears would hardly be able to hear the difference.

This kind of surgery requires iTunes, the music-management software that comes with every Mac (and came with your copy of iLife). In addition, it requires that you import, or reimport, the desired song from its original CD. (If it's a song that's already in your iTunes collection, you might want to rename the existing, high-quality version to differentiate it from the new one you're about to create. Highlight it and then choose File→Get Info to rename it.)

In iTunes' Preferences dialog box, click the Importing icon. Choose MP3 Encoder from the Import Using pop-up menu, if it's not already selected, and choose, for example, "Good Quality (128 kbps)" from the Configuration pop-up menu. (A lower Custom number will result in even smaller files,

although the sound quality may suffer.) Click OK to close the dialog box.

Put your music CD into your Mac and wait for iTunes to display its contents. (Hint: If iTunes doesn't automatically fill in the actual names of the tunes in place of Track 1, Track 2, and so on, make sure you're connected to the Internet and choose Advanced→Get CD Track Names.) Now highlight the track you want to add to your slideshow, and then choose Advanced→Convert Selection to MP3.

iTunes imports the song at the new, lower *sample rate* (quality setting). The song's name appears in your iTunes Music Library list.

Now return to iPhoto. Click Organize, if necessary, then click the Slideshow icon. Navigate to, and open, your new resampled song from the list of titles in the dialog box.

When you export the slideshow to QuickTime, you'll find that it's much more svelte, but sounds practically identical to the puffier version.

To save file size, you could turn off this box. That 320 x 240 movie would shrink to a mere 440 K—less than one-fourth the size of the presentation with the original soundtrack—but, of course, you'd wind up with a silent movie.

Fortunately, there is a middle road. It involves some work in iTunes and a slight reduction in sound quality, but reducing the file size of the music track can result in a substantial file shrinkage. See the box on the previous page for details.

Step 3: Seconds per Photo

How many seconds do you want each picture to remain on the screen before the next one appears? You specify this number using the "Display image for ___ seconds" box in the QuickTime Export dialog box.

When you first open the dialog box, iPhoto proposes whatever frame rate you used in your original slideshow. You're free to change it to other timings. (Although you can *type* a frame rate shorter than one second, iPhoto won't actually create the show with a rate any faster than one image per second. So much for artistic license.)

Step 4: Background Colors

The color or image you choose in the Background section of the dialog box will appear as the first and last frames of the export. It will also fill in the margins of the frame when a vertically oriented or oddly proportioned picture appears.

Figure 11-3:
Here's a custom background created in AppleWorks and saved in JPEG format. This is the underlying "placemat" that will show through from behind when photos in the QuickTime slideshow don't quite fill the frame.

Solid colors

To specify a solid color, click the color swatch next to the Color button. The color picker described in the figure on page 206 appears.

White, light gray, dark blue, and black makes excellent backgrounds.

Background graphics

If you click the Image button and then the Set button next to it, you can navigate your hard drive in search of a *graphics* file to use as the slideshow background. This is where a graphics program like AppleWorks, Photoshop, or GraphicConverter comes in handy. By designing a picture there (in dimensions that match your movie) and exporting it as a JPEG file, you have complete freedom to control the kind of "movie screen" your QuickTime slideshow will have (Figure 11-3).

Step 5: Export the Movie

Having specified the dimensions, frame rate, music, and background for your movie, there's nothing left but to click the Export button in the dialog box. You'll be asked to

---

POWER USERS' CLINIC

When Photos and Backgrounds Match

If you're getting seriously hooked on this iPhoto thing, here's a trick that will make you the envy of your nerd friends: Use the Color background option to create an illusion that your photos are appearing and disappearing on a constant background.

For example, consider this photo of a moon jelly jellyfish swimming in an aquarium tank. It was photographed so there were no distracting elements in the background—just the subject in blue water.

If you create a background the same color as the water, the movie will begin by showing your solid color—and then moon jelly will just *blink* into existence, without an apparent frame change or background shift. It looks really cool.

What's the trick to creating a backdrop that matches the water? First, choose File→Export, go to the

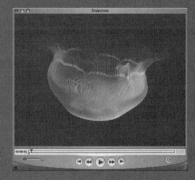

QuickTime panel, then click the rectangular swatch for background color. When the Color Picker dialog box appears, click the magnifying glass icon at the bottom of the box.

Now your cursor is, in fact, a functional magnifying glass that you can move to any part of the screen. The trick now is to position it over the actual iPhoto photo whose background color you want to clone, as shown here. Click the mouse button to capture that color, and then click Apply in the color picker box. You'll notice that the rectangle next to the color radio button has now changed to the color of the background you cloned.

When you export the movie, this custom color will fill in the first and last frames—and your jellyfish (or whatever the first photo is) will seem to pop into existence on top of it.

---

specify a name and folder location for the movie (leaving the proposed suffix *.mov* at the end of the name), and then click Save. After a moment of computing, iPhoto returns to its main screen.

Press ⌘-H to hide iPhoto; then navigate to the folder you specified and double-click the movie to play it in QuickTime Player (a program that comes with every Mac). When the movie opens, click the Play triangle or press the Space bar to enjoy your newly packaged slideshow (Figure 11-4).

Whenever playback is stopped, you can even "walk" through the slides manually by pressing the right-arrow key twice (for the next photo) or the left-arrow key once (for the previous one).

Tip: Even Windows PC users can enjoy your QuickTime movies—if they visit *www.apple.com/quicktime/ download* to download the free QuickTime Player program for Windows.

Figure 11-4:
Once you're in QuickTime Player, you can control the playback of the slideshow in a number of ways. If you don't feel like clicking and dragging onscreen controls, the arrow keys adjust the volume (up and down) or step through the photos one at a time (right and left).

Fun with QuickTime

The free version of QuickTime Player is, well, just a player. If you're willing to pay $30, however, you can turn it into QuickTime Player Pro, which offers a few special features relevant to iPhoto movie fans.

- **Play movies in full-screen mode.** QuickTime Player Pro can play slideshows in full-screen mode—no menu bar, Dock, window edges, or other distracting elements—in effect turning your laptop screen into a portable theater (among other advantages).

- **Edit your flicks.** QuickTime Player Pro lets you trim off excess footage or add an additional soundtrack, or even a text track for subtitles (captions).

- **Adjust video and audio.** Only the Pro version lets you fine-tune your video and audio controls—Brightness, Treble, Bass, and so on—and then save those settings with your movie.

- **No more nagware.** Upgrading eliminates the persistent "Upgrade Now" dialog box that appears when you open the regular Player program.

If you don't care much about customizing your movies after you export them from iPhoto, then apply that $30 to another memory card for your digital camera.

But if you decide that the upgrade is worthwhile, visit *www.apple.com* and click the QuickTime tab. There you'll find the links that let you upgrade your free QuickTime player to the Pro version. In exchange for $30, you'll be given a registration number that "unlocks" QuickTime's advanced features. (To input the serial number in QuickTime Player, choose QuickTime Player→Preferences→Registration, and then click the Registration button.)

Then you'll be ready for the following tricks.

Play Movies at Full Screen

If you've upgraded to QuickTime Player Pro, here's how to create a full-screen cinematic experience.

First, use a black background when you export your movie from iPhoto. That way, there will be no frame marks or distracting colors to detract from your images. Furthermore, the black bars on the sides of vertically oriented photos will blend in seamlessly with the rest of the darkened monitor, so that nobody is even aware that the photo has been rotated. Those black bars will also fill in the gap between the standard monitor shape and the nonstandard ones preferred by Apple these days (such as the screens on the extra-wide Cinema Display, 17-inch iMac, or 15-inch PowerBook).

Second, export your movie in as large a size as will fit on your screen. That means dimensions of 1024 x 768, or whatever matches your monitor's current setting. (To find out, choose →System Preferences and click the Display icon.) Your images will occupy more of your Mac's display area, imparting greater impact.

Once you've exported your movie, presenting it in "theater mode" is as simple as choosing Movie→Present Movie. Then set up the dialog box as shown in Figure 11-5.

To end a self-playing show, click the mouse; to end a show in Slideshow mode, press ⌘-period.

Once you've created a slideshow movie, keep in mind that nothing's etched in stone—at least not if you have QuickTime Player Pro. Suppose you don't care for the empty frames of background color (or background picture) that iPhoto adds automatically at the beginning and end of your movie. Or what if, thanks to an unforeseen down-sizing, a graduation, or a romantic breakup, you want to delete a photo or two from an existing movie? Using QuickTime Player Pro, you can snip unwanted photos or frames right out.

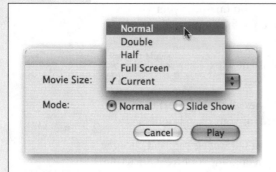

Figure 11-5:
From the Movie Size pop-up menu, choose Normal or Current. (Yes, you could choose Full Screen—but that would stretch your photos to fill the screen, often resulting in distortion.) Click Play, sit back, and enjoy.

Selecting footage

Before you can cut, copy, or paste footage, QuickTime Player needs to provide a way for you to specify *what* footage you want to manipulate. Its solution: the two tiny black triangles that sprout out of the left end of the horizontal scroll bar, as shown in Figure 11-6. These are the "in" and "out" points; by dragging these triangles, you can enclose the scene you want to cut or copy.

Figure 11-6:
To select a particular scene, drag the tiny black triangles apart until they enclose the material you want, or use the clicking/Shift-clicking trick shown here. As you drag or click, QuickTime Player updates the movie picture to show you where you are. The material you select is represented by a gray strip in the scroll bar.

Everything between them is selected.

Click in this bar
to place starting handle.

Shift-click in the bar
to place the ending handle.

Tip: You can gain more precise control over the selection procedure shown in Figure 11-6 by clicking one of the black triangles and then pressing the right or left arrow key to adjust the selection a frame at a time.

Or try Shift-clicking the Play button. As long as you hold down the Shift key, you continue to select footage. When you release Shift, you stop the playback; the selected passage then appears in gray on the scroll bar.

Once you've highlighted a passage of footage, you can proceed as follows:

- Jump to the end or beginning of the selected footage by pressing Option-right arrow or -left arrow key.

- Deselect the footage by dragging the two triangles together again.

- Play only the selected passage by choosing Movie→Play Selection Only. (The other Movie menu commands, such as Loop, apply only to the selection at this point.)

- Drag the movie picture out of the Player window and onto the desktop, where it becomes a *movie clipping* that you can double-click to view.

- Cut, copy, or clear the highlighted material using the commands in the Edit menu.

Tip: Here's a great way to add opening credits or other titles to your slideshows. If you paste some copied text directly into QuickTime Player Pro, you get a two-second title at the current frame, professionally displayed as white type against a black background. QuickTime Player automatically uses the font, size, and style of the text that was in the text clipping. You can paste a graphic image, too; once again, you get a two-second "slide" of that still image.

If you find it easier, you can also drag a text or picture *clipping file* directly from the desktop into the QuickTime Player window; once again, you get a two-second insert. To make the text or picture appear longer than two seconds, drag or paste it several times in a row.

In either case, you need to specify the fonts, sizes, and styles for your low-budget titling feature by formatting the text the way you want it *before* you copy it from your word processor.

Exporting Edited Movies

After you've finished working on a sound or movie, you can send it back out into the world by choosing File→Save As. At this point, you can specify a new name for your edited masterpiece. You must also choose one of these two options:

- **Save normally.** The term "normally" is a red herring. In fact, you'll almost never want to use this option, because it produces a very tiny file that contains no footage at all; it's like an alias of the movie you edited. A file that you save "normally" works only as long as the original, *unedited* movie remains on your drive. If you try to email the newly saved file, your unhappy recipient won't see anything at all.

- **Make movie self-contained.** This option produces a new QuickTime movie—the one you've just finished editing. Although it consumes more disk space, it has none of the drawbacks of a "save normally" file. This is the option you should choose.

Advanced Audio and Video Controls

One of the difficulties of creating multimedia productions is that there's no standard calibration for all the various computers that might play them. For example, a slideshow that your friend creates on his Dell computer might look washed-out on your Mac.

Should you inherit movies with poor audio and video, QuickTime Player Pro gives you some useful audio and video controls to compensate.

To summon these controls, open a movie in QuickTime and choose Movie→Show Sound Controls (or Movie→Show Video Controls). See Figure 11-7.

Figure 11-7:
You can adjust the brightness, balance, bass, or treble using these generally hidden controls. The trick is to show and hide them as needed via the Movie menu.

Burning a QuickTime Movie CD

If your QuickTime slideshow lasts more than a minute or two, it's probably too big to send to people by email. In those situations, the ideal distribution method for your masterpiece may be a CD that you burn yourself. Here's how the process goes:

1. **Prepare your QuickTime movie.**

   Since file size isn't as much of an issue, you can make your slideshow dimensions 640 x 480, 800 x 600, or any other size that will fit on the computer screen. There's no need to throttle down the music quality (page 239), either.

Tip: To make things easy for the audience (even if it's only you), you can turn on the Auto Play feature, which will make the movie play immediately after being double-clicked. (Savings: One click on the triangular Play button.)

To turn on Auto Play, start by opening the movie in QuickTime Player Pro. Choose Movie→Get Movie Properties. In the Properties dialog box, choose Auto Play from the pop-up menu on the right, and then turn on the Auto Play Enabled checkbox. Save the movie as usual.

2. **Put a blank CD in your burner.**

   A few seconds after you insert the CD-R (recordable) or CD-RW (rewritable) disc, it appears on your desktop as "untitled CD." You can rename it by clicking its name and then typing away.

3. **Drag the QuickTime movie(s) onto the CD's icon.**

   These are, of course, the slideshow movies you've exported from iPhoto.

4. **Click once on the CD icon and then choose File→Burn Disc.**

   A confirmation dialog box appears (Figure 11-8).

5. **Click Burn.**

   The Mac saves the movies onto the CD.

   When the process is complete, eject the disc. It will play equally well on Mac OS 9, Mac OS X, and Windows computers that have QuickTime Player installed.

Tip: If you have the software called Toast Titanium *(www.roxio.com),* an additional option awaits. You can open your exported iPhoto slideshow movie and then export it as a *VCD-compatible MPEG* file.

If you burn the MPEG movie file onto a CD, you'll have yourself what's known as a *Video CD.* It's something like a low-rent, VHS-quality DVD. It will play on most modern DVD players, thus offering you a handy way for computer-less people to watch your slideshow on TV.

Of course, if your fans have DVD players, you might have even more fun making a full-blown, commercial-style DVD for them, as described on page 269. The beauty of VCD discs, though, is that you don't need a Mac with a SuperDrive (DVD burner) to create one.

Figure 11-8:
You have one last chance to change your mind before you burn the CD. If everything's a go, then click Burn.

Slideshow Movies on the Web

Chapter 9 offers complete details for posting individual photos on the Web. But with just a few adjustments in the instructions, you can just as easily post your slideshow movies on the Web, too, complete with music.

Preparing the Movie for Web Use

You could, of course, just make a slideshow movie as described on the previous pages, and then slap it up on the Web. Unfortunately, a movie like that would involve quite a wait for your Web visitors. They would click the movie's icon to view it—and wait while the entire 3 MB movie downloads to their computers. Only then could they begin watching it.

But if you have QuickTime Player Pro, you can create movies that start playing almost immediately when Web visitors click them. Here's how to pre-process your finished slideshow movie so that it will start faster online. Open your movie in QuickTime Player Pro, and then follow these steps:

1. **Choose File→Export.**

   The "Save exported file as" dialog box appears. Make sure that the Export pop-up menu says "Movie to QuickTime Movie," and the Use pop-up menu says Most Recent Settings.

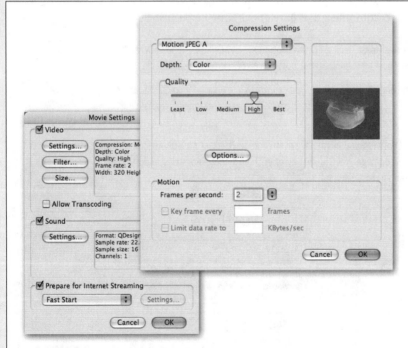

Figure 11-9:
Bottom left: These settings will help you prepare your movie for Web serving. After you've tried an export or two, you can play with the adjustments to customize your slideshow even further.

Top right: These are good video settings for an exported slideshow Web movie.

2. **Click Options.**

   The Movie Settings dialog box appears (Figure 11-9, bottom). Your job is to format the movie so that it will look good without taking a long time to download.

3. **Under Video, click Settings. In the Compression Settings dialog box (Figure 11-9, top), choose "Photo – JPEG" from the first pop-up menu.**

   This format is compact and high quality, making it a good choice for slideshows.

4. **In the "Frames per second" box, type whatever frame rate you used when you originally exported your movie from iPhoto.**

   For example *1* equals one frame (photograph) per second.

5. **Drag the Quality slider to High or Best, and then click OK.**

   You return to the Movie Settings dialog box.

6. **Click the Size button. Enter *320* in the Width field and *240* in the Height field; click OK.**

   Use a larger size only if you're sure that your audience members all have high-speed Internet access. Note, though, that if you post your movie to a .Mac account using Apple's HomePage service, it will get squished down to 320 x 240 anyway, possibly resulting in distortion.

7. **Under Sound, click Settings. In the Sound Settings dialog box, choose QDesign Music 2 from the Compressor pop-up menu, and then click OK.**

   The QDesign Music format produces high-quality music at very small file sizes, which is just what you'd hope for in Web-played movies. (If your movie has a spoken dialog track rather than music, use the Qualcomm PureVoice codec instead.)

   You return once again to the Movie Settings box. Here, confirm that the "Prepare for Internet Streaming" checkbox is turned on, and that Fast Start is selected in its pop-up menu. These settings are responsible for the fast-playback feature described above, in which your viewers don't have to wait for the *entire* movie to download before playback starts. Instead, they'll only have to wait for a quarter or half of it, or whatever portion is necessary to play the entire movie uninterrupted while the latter part is still being downloaded.

8. **Click OK, then Save.**

   Your slideshow takes a few minutes to export. But once the process is complete, you're ready to upload the file to your Web site.

Note: Once you've optimized and exported your slideshow in QuickTime Pro, don't use the File→Save or File→Save As command after making changes to the movie. If you do, you'll automatically turn *off* the Fast Start option you built in when you exported the movie.

It's OK to make further changes. But when you're finished, use the File→Export command again, repeating the previous steps, to preserve the movie's Web-optimized condition.

Uploading to a .Mac account

If you maintain your own Web site, upload the movie as you would any graphic. Create a link to it in the same way. Your movie will start to play in your visitors' Web browsers when they click that link.

If you have a .Mac account, though, posting the movie online is even easier. When your movie file is ready, bring your iDisk onto the screen as described on page 202. Drag your movie file into the Movies folder, as shown in Figure 11-10.

Now open your Web browser. Go to *www.mac.com,* sign in, and then click the HomePage tab. You're now looking at the Web page shown in Figure 11-11.

Then create a movie-playing page like this:

1. **Click the iMovie tab, and then click one of the movie templates (Figure 11-11).**

    Now a "big-screen" version of that template thumbnail appears.

2. **At the top of the page, click the Edit icon.**

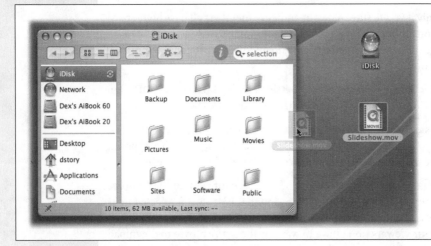

Figure 11-10:
Once you've brought your iDisk icon to the screen, drag your slideshow movie into its Movie folder. Be prepared to wait a long time for both steps; the iDisk is not what you'd call a speedy mechanism.

Figure 11-11:
Choose a design template from among the iMovie ones. This is idiot-proof Web design at its finest.

A "Choose a file" Web page appears, featuring a tiny list of movies you've dragged into your iDisk's Movies folder. Whichever one is first in the list begins to play immediately, just to remind you of what it is.

3. **Click the name of the movie you want, and then click Choose (Figure 11-12, inset).**

You return to the Edit page. Ignore the fact that your actual movie doesn't yet appear in the placeholder frame.

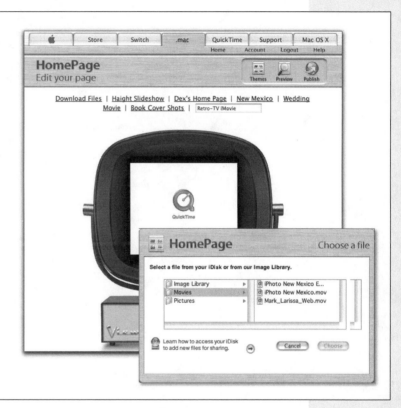

Figure 11-12:
Left: Here's your basic Web-page construction zone. Fill in the movie's name (two different places) and a caption at the bottom, if you want one.

Right: If you click Choose, you open the screen shown in the inset. Every movie you've ever dragged to your Movies folder (Figure 11-10) appears here, ready for selection.

4. **In the text boxes at the bottom of the dialog box, type a title and caption for your movie, if you like.**

If you'd like a self-updating counter that shows how many people have viewed your movie, turn on the Show checkbox at the very bottom of the window.

5. **Name the movie page by typing a title into the text box just above the movie, and then click Publish.**

Finally, a Congratulations page appears, letting you know the Web address of the finished movie page. Note the little button that offers to email this address to your friends, family, and agent, too—a handy feature, considering that this case-sensitive address is none too easy to remember (*http://homepage.mac.com/your name/iMovieTheater1.html*).

You can also click the blue lettering of the address to view the movie yourself, right then and there—an almost irresistible offer. (For an example of a movie-on-the-Web made just this way, visit *http://homepage.mac.com/dstory* and click the "Haight St. Movie" link.)

iDVD Slideshows

L et's face it. Most of the methods iPhoto gives you to show off your prize photos are geek techniques like sending them by email, posting them on a Web page, turning them into a desktop picture, and so on. All of these methods involve making your audience sit, hunched and uncomfortable, around a computer screen.

Now imagine seating them instead in front of the big-screen TV in the family room, turning down the lights, cranking up the surround sound, and grabbing the DVD remote to show off the latest family photos.

You can do it—if you have a DVD-burning drive and iDVD, Apple's DVD-creation software. (iDVD 4 came with your iLife package, if indeed it wasn't already aboard your Mac when you bought it.) With iDVD, you can create DVD-based slideshows from your photo collection, complete with soundtracks and navigational menus and screens just like the DVDs you rent from Blockbuster.

This chapter covers the basics of how to bring your photos from iPhoto to iDVD and how to customize, preview, and burn your slideshows once you've exported them to iDVD.

The iDVD Slideshow

You don't actually need iPhoto to create a slideshow in iDVD. By itself, iDVD has all the tools you need to create interactive DVDs that include movies and soundtracks as well as slideshows.

But using iPhoto can save you a lot of time and trouble. You can use iPhoto to preview, edit, and organize all your photos into albums. Then, once your photos are arranged into neatly organized albums, one click hands them off to iDVD, which converts them into a DVD-readable format. iDVD also hooks up all the navigational links and menus needed to present the show.

Creating an iDVD Slideshow

Creating a DVD of your own photos entails choosing the photos that you've organized in iPhoto, selecting a theme, building menus, and configuring the settings that determine how your slideshow will look and operate. Finally, you can preview the entire DVD without actually burning a disc to test navigation, pacing, and other settings. When the whole thing looks right, you burn the final disc.

You can begin in either of two ways: from inside iPhoto or from inside iDVD. The following pages walk you through both methods.

Starting in iPhoto

You can save a few steps by beginning your odyssey in iPhoto.

1. **If you want a musical soundtrack, select one for each selected album (or for the whole Photo Library).**

   Music is optional, of course. See Chapter 7 for complete instructions on how to add a soundtrack to a slideshow. Whatever music you've assigned to your slideshows in iPhoto will automatically carry over into iDVD.

2. **In Organize mode, select the photo album(s) you want to turn into a slideshow.**

   You can select either a single photo album or multiple albums in the Source list. If you want to include your *entire* Photo Library in the slideshow, click the Photo Library icon (although you can't have more than 99 photos in a slideshow).

Tip: Remember that any photos that aren't in a 4:3 aspect ratio (page 141) will wind up flanked by black bars when displayed on a standard TV set.

Figure 12-1:
If you don't see an iDVD button in your copy of iPhoto (bottom right, next to the Burn button), it's probably because you don't have a copy of iDVD installed on your Mac. The iDVD icon doesn't appear in iPhoto's Organize pane unless you've got iDVD 3 installed.

3. **Click the iDVD icon in the lower pane of the iPhoto window (Figure 12-1).**

This is the big hand-off. iDVD opens up a default presentation window (see Figure 12-2). See how the names of your selected albums are already listed as menu items that can be "clicked" with the DVD's remote control?

If you included your whole photo collection when exporting to iDVD, the sole menu item is called Photo Library.

Technically, at this point, your slideshow is ready to meet its public. If you're looking for some instant gratification, click Preview on the bottom of the window to flip iDVD into presentation mode. Then click the name of your album as it appears on the DVD menu page to make the show begin. Use the iDVD remote control shown in Figure 12-7 to stop, pause, or rewind the show in progress.

To really make the finished show your own, though, you'll want to spend a few minutes adding some custom touches. See "Customizing the show" on page 273.

Starting in iDVD

You can also begin building the show right in iDVD. To see how, click the Customize button (shown in lower left of Figure 12-2). The slide-out Customize "drawer"

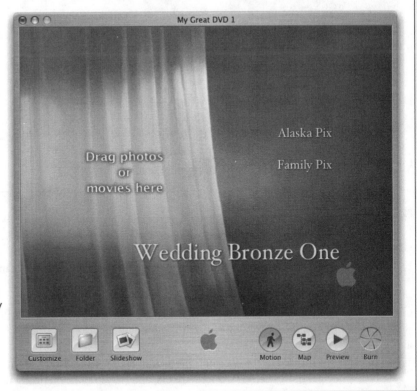

Figure 12-2:
Here's what you see when iDVD first opens. The name of each iPhoto album you exported appears on the main menu page of the DVD. Click a name once to select it, and (after a pause) click again to edit and change it. Double-click a menu title quickly to open a window where you can view thumbnails of the included pictures and change their order (Figure 12-5).

Oh—and if your DVD is not, by chance, going to be about a wedding, read on to find out how to change this starter design.

opens. Click the Media tab, and from the pop-up menu, choose Photos (see Figure 12-3); if you don't see this drawer, click the Customize button. You now see a little tiny iPhoto window, right there in iDVD, complete with thumbnails, your Source list, and even a Search box.

Figure 12-3:
All the hard work you've done in iPhoto titling your photos and organizing them into albums pays off when it's time to use those pictures in iDVD. Clicking the Photos tab gives you instant access to your whole Photo Library. You can even use the Search box to find photos by name or comments.

Each album you drag out of the list and onto the main iDVD stage area becomes another menu name that your audience will be able to click with their remotes. (If the album won't "stick" and bounces back to the Source list, it's because that album or that menu screen is too full. iDVD doesn't like albums that hold more than 99 photos, or menu screens with more than 12 buttons.)

Tip: You can also drag photos, or folders full of them, right off of your Finder desktop and onto the main menu screen to install them there as slideshows.

If you'd selected a single piece of music to accompany the slideshow of that album in iPhoto, then iDVD remembers, and plays it automatically when you play the DVD slideshow. As of iDVD 4.0.1, however, iDVD does not remember whatever *playlist* of music you'd chosen.

To fix that, or to assign different music altogether, choose Audio from the pop-up menu at the top of the Customize drawer and survey your iTunes collection. When you find a song or playlist that seems right, double-click the name of your slideshow to reveal the Slideshow Editor window shown in Figure 12-4. Drag the playlist or song onto the little square Audio "well," also shown in Figure 12-4. (Click the Return button to return to the menu-design page.)

Figure 12-4:
In the Media panel of the Customize drawer, choose Audio. You see your entire list of iTunes music—in fact, you even see your playlists here. To avoid the music-ending-too-soon syndrome, drag an entire playlist into the little Audio well beneath the slide display. Your DVD will play one song after another according to the playlist.

Customizing the Show

iDVD provides an impressive number of options for customizing the look, feel, and sound of the slideshows you create, including its overall design scheme. That's merciful, because otherwise, every DVD you create would look like a bronze Wedding album.

1. **Choose a Theme.**

   With the Customize drawer open as shown in Figure 12-5, click the Themes button at the top to reveal the list of ready-to-use visual themes that you can apply to your slideshow. (Several are shown in Figure 12-5.) Click a theme to select it and apply it to your DVD's main-menu screen.

2. **Add your own background graphics, if you like.**

   All themes let you drop in a background photo. (Click Settings in the Customize drawer, and drag the picture into the Background "well.") Some let you drop a photo into more interesting, animated *regions* of the background called *drop zones*, as described in Figure 12-5.

3. Add, remove, and reorder your pictures.

When you bring albums into iDVD directly from iPhoto, your photos arrive in the same sequence as they appeared within their iPhoto albums. Once you're in iDVD, however, you can change the order of these photos, remove them from the show, or add others.

To edit a slideshow in this way, double-click its title on the DVD menu page ("Alaska Pix" in Figure 12-5, for example).

Figure 12-5:
In this animated main-menu screen (the theme called Fish One), the fish actually swims around the screen. As for the photo in the frame: That's a "drop zone," an area that you can fill with a photo or movie of your choosing. (Click the Media button at top, choose Photos or Movies, and drag the picture or movie you want directly into the drop zone.)

The editing window shown in Figure 12-6 appears. In this window, you can also set up other options, like switching between automatic and manual advancing of photos, selecting a different soundtrack, and adding navigation buttons to a slideshow.

You can rearrange the slides by dragging them (the other slides scoot aside to make room), delete selected slides by pressing the Delete key, or add more pictures to them by dragging new photos out of the Customize drawer or from the Finder.

Then, of course, there are the controls at the bottom of the window. They offer a great deal of control over the show. For example:

Loop slideshow makes the slideshow repeat endlessly.

Display < > during slideshow adds navigation arrows to the screen as your slideshow plays. Your audience can click these buttons with their remote controls to move back and forth within your slideshow.

They're not technically necessary, of course. If you set your slides to advance automatically (read on), you won't need navigation arrows. And even if you set up the slideshow for manual advance, your audience can always press the arrow buttons on their DVD remote to advance the slides. But if you think they need a visual crutch, this option is here.

Add original photos on DVD-ROM is an interesting one. When iDVD creates a slideshow, it scales all of your photos to 640 by 480 pixels. That's ideal for a standard television screen, which, in fact, can't display any resolution higher than that.

But if you intend to distribute your DVD to somebody who's computer savvy, you may want to give them the original, full-resolution photos. They won't see these photos when they insert the disc into a DVD player. But when they insert your DVD into their computers, they'll see a folder filled with the original, high-res photos, suitable for printing, using as Desktop wallpaper, paying you for, and so on. (In other words, you've created a disc that's both a DVD-video disc and a DVD-ROM.)

Slide Duration, of course, lets you specify how much time each slide spends on the screen before the next one appears: 1, 3, 5, 10 seconds, or Manual. Manual means that your audience will have to press the Next button on the remote control to change pictures.

Then there's the Fit to Audio option, which appears in the pop-up menu only after you've added a sound file to your slideshow (Figure 12-4). In this case, iDVD will determine the timing of your slides automatically—by dividing the length of the

Figure 12-6:
Changing the sequence of slides involves little more than dragging them up or down in the list. As in iPhoto, you can select multiple slides at once and then drag them en masse.

Don't miss the tiny icon at the top-right corner of the window. It switches to a list view that reveals the names of the photos—and still lets you drag them up or down to rearrange them.

Click Return to go back to your main-menu design screen.

soundtrack by the number of slides in your show. If the song is 60 seconds long, and you've got 20 slides in the show, each slide will sit on the screen for three seconds.

Transition lets you specify any of several graceful transition effects—Dissolve, Cube, and so on—to govern how one slide morphs into the next. Whatever transition you specify here affects all slides in the show.

4. **Add more menu pages and slideshows, if you like.**

The "home page" (main menu) for your DVD can show no more than 12 buttons. If you have more than 11 slideshows to store, you can create a secondary menu page to hold the overflow. It will be represented on the main menu by a "More Shows…" button, for example.

If you're making a "Family Photos 2004" DVD, for instance, you might want to create a separate menu page called Holidays with its own theme. On that page, you can add slideshows like Halloween, Labor Day Weekend, and so on.

To add a new menu page in iDVD, click the Folder button in the main iDVD window; a corresponding menu button called My Folder appears on the main "home page." Double-click "My Folder" to open your secondary, empty menu page. Then add slideshows to it by dragging albums onto it from the mini-iPhoto browser shown in Figure 12-3.

At any time, you can return to the main menu by clicking the Back button (a left-pointing arrow). Once you're there, don't forget to rename the My Folder menu button to say, for example, "More Shows."

6. **Click the Return button to go back to the menu-design screen.**

FREQUENTLY ASKED QUESTION

Crazy-Fast Slideshows

I turned a photo album into a slideshow in iDVD and it came out perfect—except that when I preview the slideshow, iDVD acts like it's on amphetamines and races frantically through the photos, flashing each one so briefly that you can hardly see it. What's going on?

What's going on is the Fit to Audio feature. You turn it on or off in the editing window, shown in Figure 12-6.

This option is designed to assist you with making your photos and your music end tidily together. It essentially divides the song length by the number of photos you've

selected. If you've selected a one-minute soundtrack and have 99 photos in your album, iDVD will try to flash one photo every six-tenths of a second to make the pictures "fit" the soundtrack!

You'll have the same problem if you've chosen a more reasonable number of slides but a very short soundtrack.

You can solve the problem when editing a slideshow in iDVD by changing the Slide Duration setting from Fit to Audio to a specific interval, like 3 Seconds or 5 Seconds.

Previewing the DVD

Your last step is to test your DVD presentation (without burning a disc) to check navigation, timing, photo sequences, and so on.

1. **Click the Preview button.**

   iDVD switches into Preview mode, which simulates how your disc will behave when inserted into a DVD player. This is a great chance to put your DVD-in-waiting through its paces before wasting an expensive blank disc.

2. **Use the iDVD remote control to click your menu buttons, stop, pause, or rewind the show in progress.**

   See Figure 12-7.

Figure 12-7
When you put iDVD in Preview mode (by clicking the Preview button) a small remote control panel appears next to the main window. It works just like your real DVD player's remote control. You can pause, rewind, or fast-forward slideshows. Clicking the Menu button takes you out of a slideshow and back to the main menu page of the DVD, where you can select other slideshows or movies to view.

3. **From the View menu, choose Show TV Safe Area. Click through your slides looking for decapitations.**

   In its early days, the little cathode-ray guns inside the TV worked by painting one line of the TV picture, then turning around and heading back in the opposite direction. To make sure that the screen was painted edge to edge, these early TVs were programmed to overshoot the edges of the screen—or, to use the technical term, to *overscan* the screen.

   TV technology is much better now, but even modern TVs exhibit some overscanning. The amount varies, but you may be missing as much as 10 percent of the picture beyond the edges of the glass.

   The overscanning effect means that when you show your slides on a TV, you'll lose anything that's very close to the edges of the frame. Avoiding this problem, fortunately, is supremely easy, thanks to the Show TV Safe Area command. Using a dimmed, gray frame, it shows you exactly how much of your photos might get lopped off by overscanning. See Figure 12-8 for instructions on how to proceed.

4. Click the Exit button on the "remote" when you're finished.

When everything in the DVD looks good, you're ready to master your disc. Insert a blank disc in your SuperDrive and click the Burn button.

Figure 12-8:
When checking for decapitations, you may discover that nothing important is lost (top), that in fact the cropping of the average TV helps focus attention on your photos' subjects. If you discover too many scalps missing, on the other hand, choose iDVD→Preferences, click the Slideshow icon, and turn on "Always scale slides to TV Safe area" (bottom). Doing so makes iDVD shrink the pictures enough so that they won't get chopped off on a TV—guaranteed.

Extra Credit: Self-Playing Slideshows

As you work on your DVD menu structure, behind the scenes, iDVD builds a handy map. You can't add to it, or drag or delete any elements you see there, but you can double-click one of the icons to open the corresponding menu, movie, or slideshow.

To view the map, just click the Map button at the bottom of the main iDVD window (see Figure 12-9). The element you were working on appears with colored highlighting. (Click the Map button again to return to the menu screen you were working on.)

But the map is more than just a pretty navigational aid. It also makes possible a self-playing slideshow, one that plays automatically when the DVD is inserted, before your viewers even touch their remote controls.

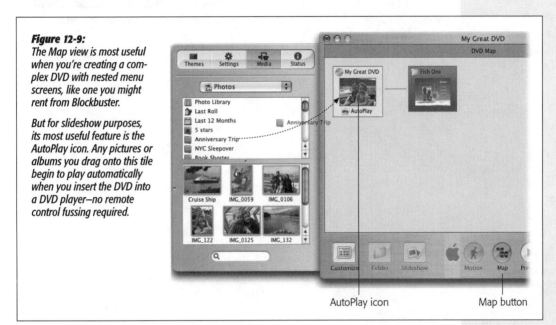

Figure 12-9:
The Map view is most useful when you're creating a complex DVD with nested menu screens, like one you might rent from Blockbuster.

But for slideshow purposes, its most useful feature is the AutoPlay icon. Any pictures or albums you drag onto this tile begin to play automatically when you insert the DVD into a DVD player—no remote control fussing required.

AutoPlay icon   Map button

Once you've got the Photos list open in the Customize drawer, as described on page 272, you can also drag an entire iPhoto album onto the Autoplay icon. Alternatively, you can click and ⌘-click just the photos you want in the Customize panel, and then drag them en masse onto the Autoplay icon. In fact, you can even drag photos—as a group or in a folder—right out of the Finder and onto this icon.

To control how long your still image remains on the screen, or how quickly your Autoplay slideshow plays, double-click the AutoPlay tile. You arrive at the slideshow editor shown in Figure 12-6, where you can adjust the timing, transition, and even the audio that plays behind the picture(s).

If you decide to replace your Autoplay material, just drag new stuff right onto it. Or, to eliminate the Autoplay segment, drag it right off the Autoplay tile. It disappears in a little puff of Mac OS X cartoon smoke.

You can design a project that way for the benefit of, for example, technophobic DVD novices whose pupils dilate just contemplating using a remote control. They can just insert your Autoplay-only DVD and sit back on the couch as the pictures flash by automatically.

It's even possible to create a DVD that never even gets to the menu screen—a DVD consisting only of Autoplay material, a slideshow that repeats endlessly during, say, your cocktail reception. Just highlight the Autoplay tile and then choose Advanced→ Loop Slideshow. You've got yourself a self-running, self-repeating slideshow of digital photos that plays on a TV at a party or wedding reception. The DVD will loop endlessly—or at least until it occurs to someone in your audience to press the Menu or Title button on the remote, which displays your main menu at last. The Menu button redisplays the previous menu screen; the Title button causes a return to the main menu.

Part Four: iPhoto Stunts

4

Screen Savers, AppleScript, and Cameraphones

Y
ou've assembled libraries of digital images, sent heart-touching moments to friends and family via email, published your recent vacation on the Web, authored a QuickTime movie or two, and even boosted the stock price of Canon and Epson single-handedly through your consumption of inkjet printer cartridges. What more could there be?

Plenty. This chapter covers iPhoto's final repertoire of photo stunts, like turning your photos into one of the best screen savers that's ever floated across a computer display, plastering one particularly delicious shot across your desktop, calling upon AppleScript to automate photo-related chores for you, extracting pictures from a cameraphone, and even exporting your shots to a Palm organizer.

Building a Custom Screen Saver

Mac OS X's screen saver feature is so good, it's been the deciding factor responsible for pushing more than one Mac fan over the edge into making the upgrade to Mac OS X. When this screen saver kicks in (after several minutes of inactivity on your part), your Mac's screen becomes a personal movie theater. The effect is something like a slideshow, except that the pictures don't simply appear one after another and sit there on the screen. Instead, they're much more animated. They slide gently across the screen, zooming in or zooming out, smoothly dissolving from one to the next.

Mac OS X comes equipped with a few photo collections that look great with this treatment: forests, space shots, and so on. But let the rabble use those canned screen savers. You, a digital master, can use your own photos as screen saver material.

Meet the Screen Saver

When you're ready to turn one of your own photo collections into a screen saver, collect the photos in an album, if they're not in one already (Chapter 5). Or, if you're using Mac OS X 10.3, simply highlight the photos you want to use as screen saver fodder, whether they're in an album or not.

Then, in Organize mode, click the album to highlight it, and then click the Desktop icon on the bottom panel.

- If you're using Mac OS X 10.2 (Jaguar), the dialog box shown at top in Figure 13-1 appears. Click OK.

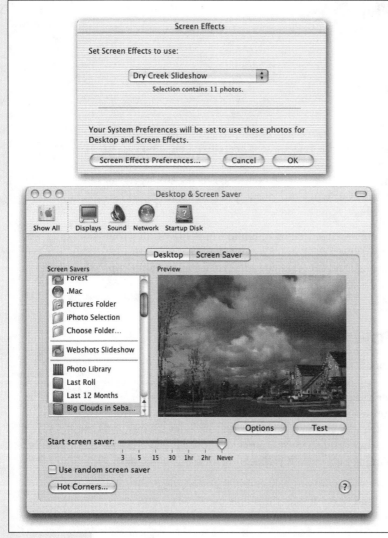

Figure 13-1:
Top: In Mac OS X 10.2, you get to choose which album to use for your Mac's screen saver. Or, click Screen Effects Preferences to open the proper pane of System Preferences, where you can specify when the screen saver should kick in.

Bottom: In Mac OS X 10.3, all of your custom albums within iPhoto are listed in the Screen Saver panel of the Desktop & Screen Saver preferences window. Just pick the one you want to use as a screen saver, or click iPhoto Selection (in the upper part of the list) to "play" whatever pictures you've selected in iPhoto, even if they weren't in an album.

Either way, Mac OS X turns your photos into a smoothly flowing, full-screen slideshow.

- If you're using Mac OS X 10.3 (Panther), you go straight to the Desktop & Screen Saver panel of System Preferences (shown at bottom in Figure 13-1).

Tip: Horizontal shots fill your monitor better than vertical ones—the verticals have fat black bars on either side to fill the empty space.

If you have an oddball camera (one whose photos have a 3:2 width-to-height ratio instead of 4:3) or an oddball screen (like the extra-wide titanium PowerBook G4 screen or many Apple Cinema displays), there's one more step. You might want to crop the photos, or copies of them, accordingly to maximize their impact.

Ready to view the splendor of your very own homemade screen saver? If you have the patience of a Zen master, you can now sit there, motionless, staring at your Mac

---

UP TO SPEED

Screen Saver Basics

You don't technically need a screen saver to protect your monitor from burn-in. Today's energy-efficient CRT monitors wouldn't burn an image into the screen unless you left them on continuously for two years, and flat-panel screens *never* burn in.

No, screen savers are about entertainment, pure and simple.

In Mac OS X, when you click a module's name in the screen saver list, you see a mini version of it playing back in the Preview screen.

You can control when your screen saver takes over your monitor. For example, the "Start screen saver" slider lets you specify when the screen saver kicks in (after what period of keyboard or mouse inactivity).

When you click the Hot Corners button, you're presented with a pane that lets you turn each corner of your monitor into a *hot spot.* Whenever you roll your cursor into that corner, the screen saver either turns on instantly (great when you happen to be shopping on eBay at the moment your boss walks by) or stays off permanently (for when you're

reading onscreen or watching a movie). If you use Mac OS X 10.3, you can use two corners for controlling the screen saver and the other two to activate Exposé (Panther's anti-window-clutter feature).

In any case, pressing any key or clicking the mouse always removes the screen saver from your screen and takes you back to whatever you were doing.

The Options button reveals the additional settings illustrated here, some of which are very useful. Turn *off* "Crop slides to fit on screen," for example, if you want the Mac to show each photo, edge to edge (even if it has to use black bars to fill the rest of your monitor); otherwise, it enlarges each photo to fill the screen, often lopping off body parts in the process. (If "Crop slides" is on, you can also turn on "Keep slides centered" to prevent the Mac from panning across each photo.)

And turning off "Zoom back and forth," of course, eliminates the majestic, cinematic zooming in and out of successive photos that makes the screen saver look so darned cool.

---

for the next half an hour or so—or as long as it takes for Mac OS X to conclude that you're no longer working and finally begin displaying your images on the screen.

If, however, you feel that life is too short as it is, click the Test button shown in Figure 13-1. See the box on page 285 for details on setting up and triggering the screen saver function.

Tip: Your screen saver slideshows look best if your pictures are at least the same resolution as your Mac's monitor. (In most cases, if your digital camera has a resolution of 1 megapixel or better, you're all set.)

If you're not sure what your screen resolution is, go to System Preferences and click the Displays icon (or just consult the Displays mini-menu next to your menu bar clock, if it appears there).

Figure 13-2:
Top: Folder and icons may occasionally mar a desktop photo's full-screen magnificence, but look at the bright side: The fact that you're getting documents in your children's eyes will be all the more incentive for you to become a better housekeeper.

Bottom: In System Preferences, use this pop-up menu to tell the Mac how you want to handle desktop pictures that don't precisely match the dimensions of your screen.

One-Click Desktop Backdrop

iPhoto's desktop-image feature is the best way to drive home the point that photos of your children (or dog, or mother, or self) are the most beautiful in the world. You pick one spectacular shot to replace the standard Mac OS X swirling blue desktop pattern. It's like refrigerator art on steroids (Figure 13-2).

Creating wallpaper in iPhoto is so easy that you could change the picture every day—and you may well want to. In Organize mode, click a thumbnail. (In Mac OS X 10.3, you can even select several, or a whole album.)

Then click the Desktop button on the bottom panel. Even though the iPhoto window is probably filling your screen, the change happens instantly behind it. Your desktop is now filled with the picture you chose.

Mac OS X 10.3 even drives home the point by switching to the proper panel of System Preferences automatically. Whatever pictures or albums you selected show up in the iPhoto Selection category; click the one you want to plaster on the desktop first.

Just three words of advice. First, choose a picture that's at least as big as your screen (1024 x 768 pixels, for example). Otherwise, Mac OS X will stretch it to fit, distorting the photo in the process.

Tip: If you're really fussy, you can even crop the photo first to the exact measurements of the screen; in fact, the first command in iPhoto's Constrain pop-up menu (page 141) lists the exact dimensions of your screen, so you can crop the designated photo (or a copy of it) to fit precisely.

Second, horizontal shots work much better than vertical ones; iPhoto blows up vertical shots to fit the width of the screen, potentially chopping off the heads and feet of your loved ones.

Finally, if a photo doesn't precisely match the screen's proportions, note the pop-up menu shown at bottom in Figure 13-2. It lets you specify how you want the discrepancy handled. Your choices include:

- **Fill screen.** This option enlarges or reduces the image so that it fills every inch of the desktop. If the image is small, the low-resolution stretching can look awful. Conversely, if the image is large and its dimensions don't precisely match your screen's, parts get chopped off. At least this option never distorts the picture, as the "Stretch" option does (below).

- **Stretch to fill screen.** Use this option at your peril, since it makes your picture fit the screen exactly, come hell or high water. Unfortunately, larger pictures may be squished vertically or horizontally as necessary, and small pictures are drastically blown up and squished, usually with grisly-looking results.

- **Center.** This command centers the photo neatly on the screen. If the picture is larger than the screen, you see only the middle; the edges of the picture are chopped off as they extend beyond your screen.

But if the picture is smaller than the screen, it won't fill the entire background; instead it just sits right smack in the center of the monitor at actual size. Of course, this leaves a swath of empty border all the way around your screen. As a remedy, Apple provides a color-swatch button next to the pop-up menu. When you click it, the Color Picker appears (page 206), so that you can specify the color in which to frame your little picture.

- **Tile.** This option makes your picture repeat over and over until the multiple images fill the entire monitor. (If your picture is larger than the screen, no such tiling takes place. You see only the top center chunk of the image.)

And one last thing: If public outcry demands that you return your desktop to one of the standard system backdrops, open System Preferences, click the Desktop & Screen Saver (or Screen Effects) icon, click the Desktop button if necessary, choose Apple Backgrounds in the list box at the left of the window, then take your pick.

Tip: Want to really blow onlookers' minds? Then turn on the Mac feature that automatically *changes* your desktop picture every 5, 15, or 30 minutes, rotating from one iPhoto photo to the next within its album. It's the wallpaper for the easily bored.

To pull this off, open System Preferences; click Desktop & Screen Saver (10.3) or Screen Effects (10.2). Turn on the Change Picture checkbox and specify the timing for the picture-changing, using the pop-up menu next to it. Stand by for applause.

While you're in the Desktop & Screen Saver or Screen Effects preferences pane, you might notice that all of your iPhoto albums are listed below the collection of images that came with your Mac. You can navigate through those albums to find a new desktop image. This approach isn't as fast (or fun) as picking pictures in iPhoto, but if for some reason iPhoto isn't open on your Mac (heaven forbid!), you can take care of business right there in System Preferences.

Exporting and Converting Pictures

The whole point of iPhoto is to provide a centralized location for every photo in your world. That doesn't mean that they're locked there, however; it's as easy to take pictures out of iPhoto as it is to put them in. Spinning out a photo from iPhoto can be useful in situations like these:

- You're creating a Web page outside of iPhoto and you need a photo in a certain size and format.

- You shot a bunch of 6-megapixel photos, you're running out of disk space, and you wish they were all 4-megapixel shots instead. They'd still have plenty of resolution, but not so much wasted space.

- You're going to submit some photos to a newspaper or magazine, and the publication requires TIFF-format photos, not iPhoto's standard JPEG format.

- Somebody else on your network loves one of your pictures and would like to use it as a desktop background on *that* machine.

- You want to use one of your iPhoto photos in a document you're creating (in a word processor, for example).

- You want to set free a few of the photos so that you can copy them *back* onto the camera's memory card. (Some people use their digicams as much for *showing* pictures to their friends as for *taking* them.)

- You want to send a batch of pictures on a CD to someone.

Exporting by Dragging

It's amazingly easy to export photos from iPhoto: Just drag their thumbnails out of the photo viewing area and onto the desktop (or onto a folder, or into a window on the desktop), as shown in Figure 13-3. After a moment, you'll see their icons appear.

Figure 13-3:
This technique produces full-size JPEG graphics, exactly as they appear in iPhoto. Their names, however, are not particularly user-friendly. Instead of "Persimmon Close Up," as you named it in iPhoto, a picture might wind up on the desktop named 200205040035140.JPG or IMG_5197.JPG.

The drag-and-drop method has enormous virtue in its simplicity and speed. It does not, however, grant you much flexibility. It produces files in the original format only, at the original camera resolution, with the camera's own cryptic naming scheme.

Exporting by Dialog Box

To gain control over the dimensions, names, and file formats of the exported graphics, use the Export command. After selecting one picture, a group of pictures, or an album, you can invoke this command by choosing File→Export (Shift-⌘-E).

The Export Photos dialog box appears, as shown in Figure 13-4. Click the File Export tab, if necessary, and then make the following decisions:

File format

You can use the Format pop-up menu to specify the file format of the graphics that you're about to export. Here are your options:

- **Original.** iPhoto exports the images in whatever format they were in when you imported them. If the picture came from a digital camera, for example, it's probably JPEG.

- **JPG.** This abbreviation is shorthand for JPEG, which stands for Joint Photographic Experts Group (that's the group of geeks who came up with this format). The JPEG format is, of course, the most popular format for photos on the Internet (and in iPhoto), thanks to its high image quality and small file size.

- **TIFF.** These files (whose abbreviation is short for Tagged Image File Format) are something like JPEG without the "lossy" compression. That is, they maintain every bit of quality available in the original photograph, but usually take up much more disk space (or memory-card space) as a result. TIFF is a good choice if quality is more important than portability.

- **PNG.** This relatively new format (Portable Network Graphics) was designed to replace the GIF format on the Web. (The company that came up with the algorithms behind the GIF format exercised its legal muscle...long story.)

Whereas GIF graphics generally don't make good photos because they're limited to 256 colors, PNG is a good choice for photos (except the variation called *PNG-8*, which is just as limited as GIF). The resulting files are smaller than uncompressed

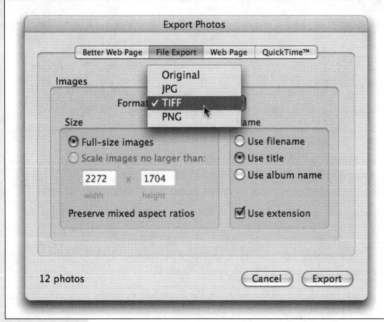

Figure 13-4:
The Export dialog box gives you control over the file format, names, and dimensions of the pictures you're about to send off from iPhoto. The number of photos you're about to export appears in the lower-left corner of the box.

You can even tell iPhoto to use whatever names you gave your pictures, instead of the original, incomprehensible file names bestowed by your camera. To do so, click "Use title."

TIFF images, yet exhibit even less compression-related quality loss than JPEGs. Not all graphics programs and Web browsers recognize this relatively new format, but the big ones—including iPhoto, GraphicConverter, Photoshop, and most recent browser versions—all do.

Named option

iPhoto maintains at least two names for each photo: its *original file name,* as it appears in the Finder, and its *iPhoto title,* the one you may have typed in while working in the program. Click either "Use filenames" or "Use titles" to specify what names iPhoto gives the icons of the graphics you're about to export. (When you export just *one* photo, you're offered the chance to name it whatever you like.)

Your third option is "Use album name." It tells iPhoto to name your exported photos according to their album name—and sequence within that album. If an exported photo is the fourth picture in the first row of an album titled Dry Creek, iPhoto will call the exported file "Dry Creek – 04.jpg." Because *you* determine the order within an album (by dragging), this is the only option that lets you control the numbering of the exported result.

Size options

Remember that although digital camera graphics files may not always have enough resolution for prints, they generally have far *too much* resolution for displaying on the screen.

As Chapter 9 makes clear, iPhoto offers to scale them down automatically whenever you email them or transfer them to the Web. If you turn on "Scale images no larger than," and then fill in some pixel dimensions in the boxes, you can oversee the same kind of shrinkage for your exported graphics. Points of reference: 1024 x 768 is exactly the right size to completely fill a standard 15-inch monitor, and 640 x 480 is a good size for emailing (it fills up about a quarter of the screen).

Tip: You can also use this option to de-megapixelize a bunch of photos. Suppose they're all 6-megapixel photos—more than you'll ever need. Export them at, say, 2272 x 1704 pixels (about four megapixels) to a folder on your desktop called "4 Megas" (or something). Delete the originals from your Photo Library, if you like, and then re-import the scaled-down versions by dragging that 4 Megas folder off the desktop and into the album list.

Plug-Ins and Add-Ons

On one thing, friends and foes of Apple can all agree: iPhoto is no Photoshop. iPhoto was deliberately designed to be simple and streamlined.

Yet Apple thoughtfully left the back door open. Other programmers are free to write add-ons and plug-ins—software modules that contribute additional features, lend new flexibility, and goose up the power of iPhoto.

And yet, with great power comes great complexity—in this case, power and complexity that Apple chose to omit. But at least this plug-in arrangement means that nobody can blame *Apple* for junking up iPhoto with extra features. After all, *you're* the one who installed them.

Some of the most important plug-ins and accessory programs are described in the relevant chapters of this book:

- **BetterHTMLExport** is designed to lend flexibility to the Web pages that iPhoto generates. (See page 209.)

- **Portraits & Prints** vastly expands iPhoto's printing features. It lets you create a multiple-photo layout on a single sheet of paper for printing. (See page 184.)

As the popularity of iPhoto grows, new add-ons and plug-ins will surely sprout up like roses in your macro lens. It's worthwhile to visit the Version Tracker Web site from time to time *(www.versiontracker.com/macosx)*. Search for *iPhoto*; you'll be surprised at the number of goodies just waiting for you to try. In the meantime, here's a sampling.

Pictures to Your Palm Organizer

You can't always carry around your Mac to show off the brilliance of your iPhoto collection. But if you have a Palm organizer or Palm–based cellphone—and among the digital intelligentsia, who doesn't?—you can carry around your photos on an electronic gizmo in your pocket. While ordinary citizens fumble with ratty, dog-eared photos in their wallets, you can smile smugly and whip out a tiny, shiny Palm that displays one perfect, bright colored photo after another.

The brains behind this operation is a little program called SplashPhoto, which you can download either from *www.missingmanuals.com* or from its own home page *(www.splashdata.com/splashphoto/index.htm)*. For $30, you get a little converter that lets you drag images directly out of iPhoto, ready to copy onto your Palm (or Handspring or Sony) the next time you HotSync.

Note: If your palmtop came with a desktop icon called Send to Handheld, you may not need SplashPhoto. Just drag your photos right out of iPhoto and onto the Send to Handheld icon. The next time you sync, your photos will arrive, neatly resized to fit the screen, on the palmtop. You can then view them with Palm's Photo application. (SplashPhoto offers many, many more options, however.)

Using SplashPhoto

Start by opening both iPhoto and SplashPhoto. Position the windows so you can see both simultaneously; then proceed as shown at top in Figure 13-5.

The real fun begins, though, after the photos are safely HotSynced onto your Palm. And once your colleagues and associates have picked their jaws up from off the floor, mention to them that you can beam both the SplashPhoto viewer and your pictures to them using the Palm's infrared transceiver. (This may be the only time complete strangers will ever ask for copies of your "wallet" photos.)

In fact, if you have a current Palm device running Palm OS 5 or later, you can send photos via Bluetooth or SMS, or as email attachments, right from your palmtop. Many of the new Palm handhelds, such as the Tungsten T3, have Bluetooth file-sharing built in, so that you can connect the Palm to your mobile phone and send text and pictures to other wireless devices, or directly to your Mac.

Figure 13-5:
Top: You can drag a photo from iPhoto (background) directly into Splash-Photo. Make a few adjustments in the Edit Photos dialog box (rotate, crop, zoom, or tweak brightness and contrast), and then click Done. Your photo is ready for uploading to your Palm organizer the next time you synchronize it.

Bottom: Following your first HotSync, you'll discover the SplashPhoto viewer program installed on your Palm. Visit your Application screen and tap its icon to begin looking at your pictures.

You can view the pictures either individually or as part of a palmtop slideshow, complete with transitions. The quality is amazing.

AppleScript Tricks

AppleScript, of course, is the famous Macintosh *scripting language*—a software robot that you can program to perform certain repetitive or tedious tasks for you.

iPhoto 4 is fully *scriptable*, meaning that AppleScript gurus can manipulate it by remote control with AppleScripts that they create.

But even if you're not an AppleScript programmer yourself, this is still good news, because you're perfectly welcome to exploit the ready-made, prewritten AppleScripts that other people come up with.

Preparing for AppleScript

Apple has paved the way for all kinds of AppleScript fun with its AppleScripts for iPhoto 4, which you can download from the "Missing CD" page of *www.missing manuals.com*. You'll probably find that after decompression, this download turns into a folder called Archive on your hard drive.

Now you need some way to *run* these scripts—to trigger them—and the best way is to install Mac OS X's ingenious Script menu. Here's how you go about it:

1. **Rename the Archive folder *iPhoto Scripts*, or something equally helpful.**

   This is the folder you downloaded.

2. **Open your Applications→AppleScript folder.**

   You've just unearthed a few tools that Apple provides for AppleScript fun.

3. **Double-click the icon called *Script Menu.menu*.**

   A new icon, shaped like a scroll, appears at the upper-right end of your menu bar (Figure 13-6). This, ladies and gentlemen, is the *Script menu*.

Tip: You can remove the Script menu icon by ⌘-dragging it away from the menu bar.

   If you open the Script menu, you'll see that it already contains a variety of interesting scripts, none of which have anything to do with iPhoto.

4. **From the Script menu, choose Open Scripts Folder.**

   A window opens; this is actually your Home→Library→Scripts folder.

5. **Drag the iPhoto Scripts folder (or whatever you named it in step 1) into the Scripts window.**

From now on, the iPhoto Scripts folder is listed at the bottom of the Scripts scroll menu, as shown in Figure 13-6. You can trigger any of the iPhoto scripts by choosing its name from the submenu.

The Scripts, One by One

Now that your downloaded scripts are easily accessible, here's what they're for.

Assign Keywords for Last Imports

This script is supposed to automate the process of assigning keywords to your last batch of imported images by presenting a Keyword dialog box, over and over again, for each photo in that batch. But it's much slower than just using the Keywords dialog box as described on page 129, and a bit buggy too. You're best off ignoring this one.

Delete Album and Contents

As you know from Chapter 5, deleting an album doesn't actually delete any photos from your collection—at least not usually.

When you run this script (by choosing its name from your Scripts→iPhoto scripts menu), however, you're presented with a dialog box listing all of your albums. Select the album you want to delete, and then click OK. After asking your permission, iPhoto moves both the album *and the photos inside it* to the iPhoto Trash.

Figure 13-6:
Apple's iPhoto scripts, along with Apple's other scripts, have a convenient home in the Script menu. (You open it by clicking the little scroll in the menu bar.) You can load up this submenu with iPhoto scripts of your own, too, by adding them to your Home→Library→Scripts folder.

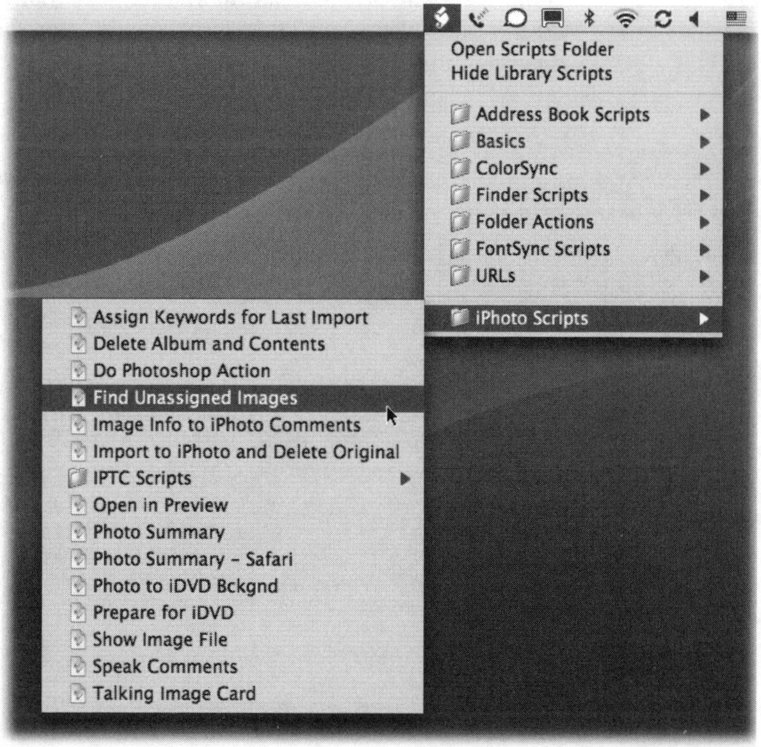

Once you choose File→Empty Trash, the album and the photos in it are *gone forever,* even from the master Photo Library. Be careful!

Do Photoshop Action

Do Photoshop Action is the mother of all iPhoto AppleScripts. It lets high-end graphics nerds run Photoshop *Actions* (also known as macros—that is, canned software robots that perform repetitive processing steps) on iPhoto pictures.

In the graphic-design world, Photoshop actions automate tedious tasks like opening each photo, scaling it to a certain size and resolution, changing it to grayscale instead of full color, and then exporting it in a different graphic format. If you're not quite that high-powered a graphics professional, you can still use Photoshop to color-balance your photos and adjust their contrast—tasks that Photoshop's AutoLevels command performs with better results than iPhoto's own Enhance tool.

If you have Photoshop CS, your software is ready to go right out of the box. You don't have to download anything.

But if you use Photoshop 7, you need to do the following before you can take advantage of this powerful script:

• Go to *www.adobe.com/support/downloads/detail.jsp?ftpID=1535* and download the file called Photoshop 7.0 Scripting plug-in. Run the downloaded installer by double-clicking it.

Figure 13-7:
When you click Set Prefs (top), the script asks you to type in the name of the action you want to apply (bottom). It also lets you specify a different action set (a collection of actions in Photoshop). But unless you've created your own, Default Actions is the set you want.

Type in the precise name of the action you want, and then click Set. In the next dialog box, click Continue.

Then the AppleScript asks you where you want each modified image saved. Choose a folder location for them, or click New Folder to create a new one.

Finally, click Choose. Photoshop opens each selected iPhoto image in Photoshop, executes the Action you've specified, and saves the picture into the folder you selected. Once it's finished, you can return to iPhoto for more work.

- Become familiar with actions in Photoshop. You can find the starter set by choosing Window→Actions. You have a dozen prefab actions to choose from, such as Custom RGB to Grayscale and Save As Photoshop PDF, and you can also "record" actions of your own.

- Note the name of the Action you want to use. The Do Photoshop Actions AppleScript will ask you what action you want it to apply, but you'll have to type the action's name *exactly* as it appears in Photoshop's Actions palette, including capitalization.

Now, in iPhoto, highlight a thumbnail (or several). From your Script menu, choose iPhoto Scripts→Do Photoshop Action, and then proceed as described in Figure 13-7. You've just harnessed the power of Photoshop's batch processing, right from within iPhoto.

Note: If you get an error message at the end of the process telling you that, "There is no such element," you've just run up against a quirk of the script. The script attempts to open the resulting file in Preview—but if your Photoshop action contains a Close command, the file closes, and there's nothing for Preview to open.

Glitches like this are a good argument for learning to open up a script in Script Editor and make minor edits—in this case, deleting the "Open in Preview" lines of the script.

Find Unassigned Images

This command rounds up all photos that you haven't put into any album and drops them into a new album called Unassigned. You might use this script when, for example, you're burning all of your photos onto various CDs by category, and you want to make sure you're not leaving any out.

As the message tells you, this might take some time to complete, especially if you have more than 1,000 photos or so. (AppleScript will inform you along the way that it's still working.) When it's done scanning your entire library, it also lets you know how many unassigned images it discovered.

Open in Preview

This script opens an iPhoto picture in Preview, Mac OS X's graphics viewing program.

You might, at first, wonder if perhaps Apple's AppleScript team inhaled a bit too much of that new-computer smell. Why would you want to open a photo in Preview, when it's already in iPhoto, the world's greatest graphics viewer?

Actually, Preview has a few tricks up its sleeve that iPhoto doesn't know, including its ability to export graphics in a huge variety of formats (see Figure 13-8).

To use this script, click a photo in iPhoto and then choose this command's name from the Script→iPhoto Scripts menu. The photo appears in Preview a moment later.

If you select more than one picture in iPhoto before running the script, the script offers you (via a small, misspelled dialog box) a choice: You can open the pictures either in individual windows or as a *collection* in Preview. Collections are much cooler and easier to manage; for example, once you've clicked a thumbnail in the thumbnails "drawer" (shown at right in Figure 13-8), you can move to the next or previous one by pressing the up or down arrow keys.

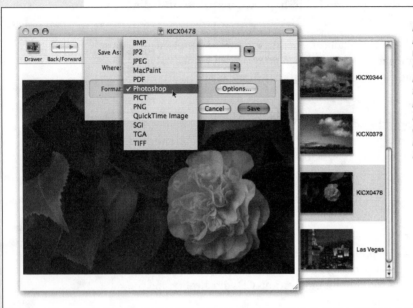

Figure 13-8:
In iPhoto, you're stuck with four export options: Original, JPG, TIFF, and PNG. But if you open that same image in Preview, choosing File→ Export offers you twelve conversion formats, including JPEG2000, PDF, and Photoshop.

Photo Summary

This handy little script builds tidy, ready-to-print catalog pages of your photos, as shown in Figure 13-9.

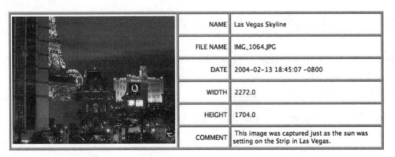

Figure 13-9:
Select the pictures you want in iPhoto and then choose this script's name from the Scripts→iPhoto Scripts submenu. You get a page in TextEdit that includes each photo's thumbnail, title, file name, width, and so on. Print or save.

Photo to iDVD Background

Once you've clicked a photo, you can use this script to turn it into the menu background for your current iDVD project. For best results, crop your picture first in iPhoto to 4 x 3 dimensions (see page 141), to make sure that your photo will neatly fit the TV when played on a DVD player.

Prepare for iDVD

This script is supposed to open each of the selected images in Adobe Photoshop, scale them to 640 x 480 pixels, superimpose each photo's Comment text, and then open the results in Preview as a catalog for review.

The idea is to help you prepare your photos for use in an iDVD slideshow (see Chapter 12).

Show Image File

This script is handy whenever you're looking at a photo in iPhoto and wish you could leap instantly to the Finder icon that represents it (deep inside your iPhoto Library folder), so that you can copy it to a disk, send it across a network, or whatever. It's one of the most useful Apple scripts by far.

Tip: Once you locate the picture, don't drag it out of its folder! Doing so will hopelessly confuse iPhoto. Instead, if you want to repurpose this photo, *Option*-drag it out of its window. That ritual makes a copy of the original file, leaving the original safe and sound in the iPhoto Library folder.

Speak Comments

Here's a wild one that can be truly handy when you want to treat visitors (or trade-show attendees) to a slideshow of your photographic work—when you're not around to narrate.

When you choose this script's name from the Script menu→iPhoto Scripts submenu, iPhoto presents each of the selected photos, one at a time, at full iPhoto-window size and adds *spoken narration* that's based on whatever you've typed into those photos' Comments boxes. iPhoto uses whatever voice you've chosen on the Speech panel of System Preferences. It's weird, wacky, and strangely satisfying.

Make Talking Image Card

This one is a lot like the previous script, except that instead of performing the spoken cyber-recital out loud, it saves the result as a QuickTime movie, ready for distributing or archiving. Never let it be said that the geeks at Apple don't know how to have a good time.

To run this script, click a photo, and then choose this script's name from the Script menu→iPhoto Scripts submenu. Just in case you're not in a Victoria mood, a dialog box now offers you the chance to change the voice of the narrator—and, while you're at it, the dimensions of your movie. Click Continue when you're ready.

Finally, another dialog box lets you name the movie and choose a folder location for saving it (Figure 13-10). Click OK. AppleScript builds the movie and opens it in QuickTime. Click the Play button to let the party begin.

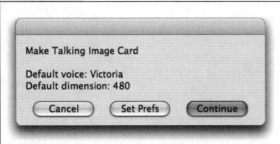

Figure 13-10:
You can go with the proposed voice and pixel dimension for your movie, or click Set Prefs to select your own.

Make Talking Image Card

Default voice: Victoria
Default dimension: 480

Cancel   Set Prefs   Continue

Editing AppleScripts

Using the menu bar to access and use your AppleScripts is terrific if you never need to make any adjustments to the scripts.

But part of the fun is fiddling with these scripts, peering into the lines of code that compose them and adjusting them to your own devious designs.

For example, the standard Photo Summary script opens your catalog page in TextEdit, but you can change it to open in Apple's Safari Web browser.

To do that, drag the Photo Summary script icon onto the icon of Script Editor, a little AppleScript-editing program in your Applications→AppleScript folder. The script opens as a page of computer code; just change the name of the program you want to open, as shown in Figure 13-11.

While you're at it, you could easily change the typeface or size in your catalog. Once again, open the script in Script Editor. Scroll down until you find this line:

```
<FONT FACE=\"Lucida Grande\" SIZE=\"1\">
```

Carefully replace the font name and size to suit your taste, like this:

```
<FONT FACE=\"Verdana\" SIZE=\"3\">
```

Note: Clearly, the size isn't represented in points, as you're probably used to. Instead, the numbers 1, 2, and 3 refer to the *relative* size system used by Web-page designers. They range from 1 (very small) to 7 (jumbo).

Now your catalog will display all the entries in Verdana type with a larger, more readable font size.

As you go, you can click Run within Script Editor to see the effects of your editing. When you're finished fiddling, use the File→Save As command, give your modified script a new, descriptive name (so that you don't overwrite the original script), and save the result onto the desktop. (From there, you'll probably want to move it into your Home→Library→Scripts→iPhoto Scripts folder.)

Transferring Cameraphone Pictures via Bluetooth

If you got all excited about the idea of taking pictures with a cameraphone back in Chapter 1, you've probably been wondering for about 250 pages how you're supposed to transfer them into iPhoto. You can't exactly plug in a USB cable (on most phones, anyway).

If you thought the owner's manual for your digital camera was cryptic, crack open the documentation that comes with your cellphone. Programming the custom functions on your whiz-bang handset makes operating the Mars rover look like a high-school science project. That's why most people never get beyond ordering pizzas and checking in with the kids on their cellphones—and why most pictures taken with a cameraphone stay in the cameraphone.

Figure 13-11:
If you change this line—

tell application "Text-Edit"

to this—

tell application "Safari"

—your catalog will open in Safari instead of TextEdit. Posting the result on the Web may be more trouble than it's worth (you'll have to locate the image source files, copy them, then adjust the HTML code accordingly), but it gives a good glimpse into the workings of AppleScript.

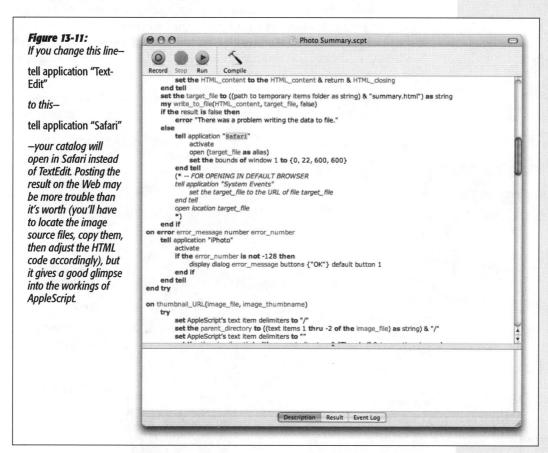

If both your cellphone and your Mac have Bluetooth transmitters, you're in luck. Bluetooth is a short-range, wireless cable-elimination technology. It can also be a pain-elimination technology for transferring cameraphone shots to your Mac.

Sending Cameraphone Photos to Your Mac

To transfer pictures that you snapped with your cell to your Mac, where you can save and work with them in iPhoto, you need three things:

- **Mac OS X 10.2.8 or newer (Panther preferred).** You can set up Bluetooth in its System Preferences panel, or let the Bluetooth Setup Assistant make configuration a snap (Figure 13-12).

- **Bluetooth on your Mac.** Many Mac models have Bluetooth transmitters built in, or offer Bluetooth as an added-cost option. If yours doesn't, you can join the fun by buying the D-Link Bluetooth Adapter, available from the Apple Store for less than $40. Just plug the adapter into a USB port; you're ready to play.

- **Cameraphone with Bluetooth.** You can see a sampling of Bluetooth-equipped cellphones on Apple's Devices page (*www.apple.com/isync/devices.html*). All of the major brands, such as Motorola, Nokia, and Sony Ericsson offer Bluetooth handsets. If your current phone doesn't have Bluetooth, most cell carriers let you upgrade to a newer phone for a small fee.

Once you're equipped, the first step is to *pair* the phone to your Mac—to introduce it. This is a clever security step that ensures that interlopers can't send you their own

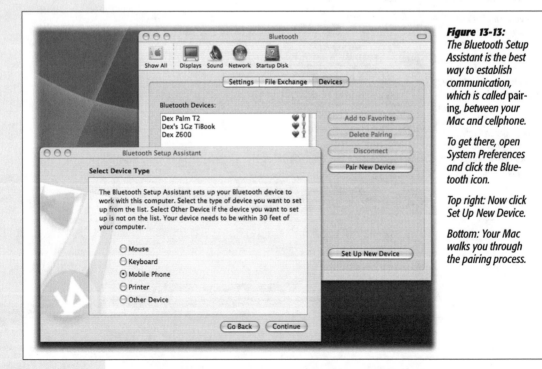

Figure 13-13:
The Bluetooth Setup Assistant is the best way to establish communication, which is called pairing, *between your Mac and cellphone.*

To get there, open System Preferences and click the Bluetooth icon.

Top right: Now click Set Up New Device.

Bottom: Your Mac walks you through the pairing process.

photos without your permission. Your Mac won't recognize their phones until you've paired them.

You use the Bluetooth Setup Assistant to achieve this union, shown in Figure 13-12.

Then, on your phone, find the picture that you want to add to iPhoto. Tap the Send button or menu command. You'll see the options your phone offers for transferring pictures, such as via Picture Message, Email, and Bluetooth. Select Bluetooth.

If you've paired this phone with more than one computer, the next screen asks which one gets the photos. Select your Mac and click Send. (If you have a Bluetooth Palm, there's more about sending files to your Palm on the next page.)

Note: The name of your Mac that appears in your phone list comes from the Sharing panel of System Preferences. If you don't like the current name describing your Mac, change it there, then pair your phone again using the Setup Assistant. Like magic, the new name for your Mac will appear in your phone's option list.

Figure 13-13:
Top: Once your phone begins to send the picture, a message appears on your Mac asking you to accept the file.

Bottom: After you accept, the actual transfer only takes seconds. The photos generally wind up sitting on your Mac's desktop.

Your phone now contacts your Mac. A request appears on your screen, as shown at top in Figure 13-13. Click Accept. The photo transfer begins, as shown at bottom in Figure 13-13.

Once the image is safely copied to your Mac desktop (it's also still on your phone where you can keep or delete it), you're only moments away from iPhoto bliss. Before you add the picture to your iPhoto library, you might want to create a special album just for cameraphone images (click the + button in the lower-left corner to create a new album).

Then drag the new photo file from the desktop to the iPhoto album, just as you can with any photo. You have successfully moved a picture from your phone to your Mac and stored it in iPhoto. Your pictures are no longer held hostage in your phone, and they now have the same rights and privileges that iPhoto provides to all digital images. You can publish them to your .Mac Web site, attach them to email, and add them to QuickTime movies.

Note: Of course, today's cameraphones take very low-resolution pictures. Chances are, the pictures you just added to iPhoto are 640 x 480 or smaller—so forget about using these as your Desktop wallpaper on a 17-inch iMac, or even making a photo-quality 5 x 7 print. It's not going to happen. Still, your phone shots are handy for sharing electronically via mail, Web, and QuickTime.

Sending Cameraphone Pictures to Your Palm Organizer

Your pix may be stunning on your phone's LCD screen, but they aren't big enough to fill the corners of your brand new Apple Cinema Display. Fortunately, they fit Palm organizer screens very nicely indeed. If iPhoto is your digital shoebox, then think of the Palm as a handy digital wallet.

Palm's Tungsten series (T, T2, and T3) have built-in Bluetooth, meaning they can talk to both your Mac and your phone. If your Palm doesn't have Bluetooth built in, but accepts SD expansion cards, you can equip it with a Palm Bluetooth Card. (Sony offers a Bluetooth Memory Stick for its Palm-based Clié palmtops.)

Moving pictures from the phone to the Palm is just as easy as it was on the Mac. Once again, you must first pair the two devices so they can send information back and forth. In Palm OS 5 (or later), this process is easy:

On the Palm's Applications screen, tap Prefs, then tap Bluetooth, which is in the Communication category. The four settings here should be:

- **Bluetooth:** On

- **Device Name:** Enter a name here that distinguishes your Palm from other Bluetooth devices, such as "Joe's Palm T2."

- **Discoverable:** Yes

- **Allow Wakeup:** Yes

Then tap the Trusted Devices button at the bottom of this preference pane. At the moment, the ensuing list is blank. Tap Add Device to make your Palm search for all Bluetooth devices within 30 feet, including your cameraphone (Figure 13-14). (You did turn on Bluetooth for your cameraphone, right?) On your Palm, highlight the name of your cameraphone once it appears (in other words, once the Palm has *discovered* the phone), and click OK.

Your Palm asks you to enter a *passkey*—in essence, a one-shot password that you'll never need again. Keep this simple and use only numbers—like *456*, for example. Click OK. Now your phone asks for the same number sequence—once again, a security step to prevent strangers from pairing to one of your gadgets without your knowledge. Do so and hit the Enter button. Your two devices are now paired in Bluetooth harmony and can talk to each other.

Palm OS 5 devices include a helpful application called Photos. When you send an image from your cameraphone to the Palm, you can use this program to view the picture. Although this little program pales in comparison to iPhoto, it does let you organize pictures by category, view them full screen on the Palm, beam them to other palmtops, and even send them to other gadgets via one of these three networking protocols:

- **Bluetooth.** The best way to send a picture if the other device has Bluetooth—like your Mac.

- **SMS.** Short Messaging Service, available on many modern mobile phones, lets you send brief text notes to other phones. You can attach pictures to SMS messages, too, but the results are hit-or-miss. Use SMS to say hello with text, not pictures.

- **Email.** Many Palm palmtops come with a built-in email program that can send and retrieve mail by using a cellphone as a glorified Internet antenna. (It connects to the phone either by Bluetooth or via a special cable.) You must have Internet service on your calling plan, which costs a few extra dollars a month. If you do, you can attach your pictures to email messages on your Palm and send them to friends and family all over the world.

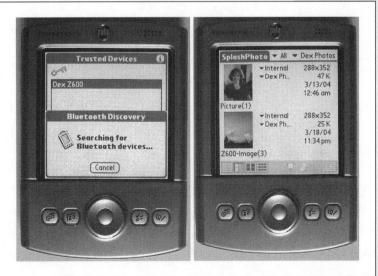

Figure 13-14:
Left: In the Trusted Devices pane, your Palm finds your cameraphone and helps you make the pairing.

Right: SplashPhoto displays your images in a variety of ways, including this handy thumbnails-plus-information view.

If you want more imaging options on your Palm than what its own Photos program can do, then take a look at SplashPhoto (page 292). SplashPhoto covers all the same functions as Photos, and adds a slideshow feature and many more ways to view your collection (Figure 13-14).

iPhoto File Management

W hen you don't have to buy film or pay for processing, photos have a way
of piling up very quickly. Apple says iPhoto can hold an unlimited number of photos and, technically, that's true (as long as you have enough
memory and hard drive space). But in fact, once you go much above 25,000 pictures,
iPhoto winds up gasping for RAM and acts as if you've slathered it with a thick coat
of molasses.

For some photo fans, this comes as a distressing bit of news. You downloaded the
software, entrusted your best work to it, even bought a book about it—and now you
learn it's going to cop out on you in another couple of years.

Fortunately, a little knowledge—and a handful of blank, recordable CDs or DVDs—
can keep you happily in iPhoto at reasonable speeds. The trick is learning how to manage iPhoto's library files—wisdom that will also serve you when you want to transfer
photos to another Mac or when it comes time to *backing up* your photo collection.

This chapter covers both iPhoto's behind-the-scenes filing system and what's involved
in backing it up: swapping photo libraries, burning them to CD, transferring them to
other machines, and merging them together.

About iPhoto Discs

iPhoto CDs are discs (either CDs or DVDs, actually) that you can create directly
from within iPhoto to archive your entire Photo Library—or any selected portion of
it—with just a few mouse clicks.

The beauty of iPhoto's Burn command is that it exports much more than just the
photos themselves to a disc; it also copies the thumbnails, titles, keywords, comments,

ratings, and all the other important data about your Photo Library. Once you've burned all of this valuable information to disc, you can do all sorts of useful things:

- Make a backup of your whole Photo Library for safekeeping.

- Transfer specific photos, albums or a whole Photo Library to another Mac without losing all your keywords, descriptions, ratings, and titles.

- Share discs with other iPhoto fans so that your friends or family can view your photo albums in their own copies of iPhoto.

- Offload photos to CD or DVD as your photo collection grows, to keep your current Photo Library at a trim, manageable size.

- Merge separate Photo Libraries (such as the one on your iBook and the one on your iMac) into a single master Photo Library.

Note: One thing an iPhoto CD is *not* good for is sharing your photos with somebody who doesn't have iPhoto! Page 311 has the details, but the bottom line is this: An iPhoto CD from iPhoto 4 is designed *exclusively* for transferring pictures into another copy of iPhoto 4. (iPhoto 4 can read iPhoto 2 discs, though.)

Burning an iPhoto CD or DVD

All you need to create an iPhoto CD is a Mac with a CD burner or DVD burner and a blank disc.

1. **In iPhoto's Organize mode, select the albums or photos that you want to include on the disc.**

   Click the Photo Library icon if you want to burn your whole photo collection. Make sure that no individual photos are selected. If you do, iPhoto assumes you want to burn *only* those selected photos to disc.

   To burn only a specific album or group of albums, select them in the Source list. Either way, the photo-viewing area should now be showing the photos you want to save onto a disc.

2. **Click the Burn icon at the bottom of the iPhoto window (Figure 14-1).**

   A dialog box appears, prompting you to insert a blank disc. Pop in the disc; the dialog box vanishes after a few moments.

3. **Check the size of your selection to make sure it will fit.**

   Take a look at the Info panel just below with Source list, as shown in Figure 14-2. If the set of photos you want to burn is smaller than 650 or 700 megabytes (for a CD) or about 4.3 gigabytes (for a DVD), you're good to go. You can burn the whole thing to a single disc.

   If your photo collection is larger than that, however, it's not going to fit. You'll have to split your backup operation across multiple discs. Select whatever number of photo albums or individual pictures you can that *will* fit on a single disc, using the

---

indicator icons shown in Figure 14-2 as your guide. (Also shown in the figure: The Disc Name box, where you can name the disc you're about to burn.)

For example, you might decide to copy the 2001 folder onto one disk, the 2002 folder onto another, and so on, using the built-in year "collections" in the Source list as your source material.

Figure 14-1:
The Burn button, which makes it possible to create CDs or DVDs directly from within iPhoto, has two faces. The "closed shutter" icon (top) is the usual state. When you click the button to set up the disc-burning process, the shutter opens to reveal the pulsating "burn" icon (bottom).

Figure 14-2:
Top left: Once you've clicked Burn and inserted a blank disc, the Info panel lets you know how close you are to filling the disc. The indicator icon updates itself as you select or deselect photos and albums to show you how much free space is available on the disc.

Top right: If your photos take up more space than is available on the disc, the little disc icon turns red and you see the Disc Full message shown here.

Bottom: Disregarding this warning won't get you very far; if you attempt to burn the disc anyway, iPhoto will stop you with yet another message.

After burning one disc, select the next set of photos, and burn another CD or DVD. Burn as many discs as needed to contain your entire collection of photos. If and when you ever need to restore your photos from the multiple discs, you'll be able to merge them back together into a single Photo Library using the technique described in "Merging Photo Libraries" later in this chapter.

4. Click the Burn icon again.

Before iPhoto fires up your Mac's disc-burning laser, it presents a confirmation dialog box, telling you exactly how many photos it's going to burn to disc. (If you've chosen specific photo albums for backup, the total number of albums is listed, too.) If you want to back out of the operation, click Cancel.

5. Click the Burn button.

First, iPhoto makes a disk image—a sort of pretend disk that serves as a temporary holding area for the photos that will be burned. (You may even see the icon for this imaginary disk pop up on your desktop during the process.) Next, iPhoto copies the photos from your iPhoto Library folder to the disk image.

Finally, the real burning begins. When the process is done, your Mac spits out the finished CD or DVD, ready to use, bearing whatever name you gave it.

Tip: You can safely bail out of the CD-creating process at any time by clicking the Cancel button in the Progress dialog box.

But don't click the Stop button once the Burning dialog box appears. At that point, your CD or DVD drive is already busy etching data onto the disc itself. Clicking Stop will indeed bring the burning to a screeching halt—but you'll end up with a partially burned, nonfunctioning disc.

What you get

The finished iPhoto disc contains not just your photos, but a clone of your iPhoto Library folder as well. In other words, all the thumbnails, keywords, comments, ratings, photo album information—even the unedited original versions of your photos that iPhoto keeps secretly tucked away—are all included on the disk. (See page 94 for a detailed rundown on the contents of the iPhoto Library folder.)

Figure 14-3:
Pop an iPhoto CD into your Mac and it appears right along with your albums in iPhoto. Click on the disc icon itself or one of the disc's album icons (as shown here) to display the photos it contains. In essence, iPhoto is giving you access to two different libraries at once—the active Photo Library on your Mac's hard drive and a second library on the CD.

If you want to view the contents of your finished CD in iPhoto, pop the disc back into the drive. (If iPhoto isn't running, your Mac opens it automatically.)

Moments later, the icon for the CD appears in the Source list of the iPhoto window. If you click the disc's icon, the photos it contains appear in the photo-viewing area, just as if they were stored in your Photo Library.

You can't make changes to them, of course—that's the thing about CDs and DVDs. But you can copy them into your own albums, and make changes to the copies.

When Not to Burn

The Burn command is convenient for creating quick backups, archiving portions of your Photo Library, or transferring photos to another Mac. But it's definitely not the best way to share your photos with Windows users, or even other Mac fans running Mac OS 9.

Think about it: Burning an iPhoto CD automatically organizes your photos into a series of numerically named subfolders inside an iPhoto Library folder, surrounded by scads of special data files like *.attr* files, *Library.cache,* and *Dir.data.* All of this makes perfect sense to iPhoto, but is essentially meaningless to anyone who doesn't use iPhoto. A Windows user, for example, would have to dig through folder after folder on your iPhoto CD to find and open your photos.

So if the destination of your CD or DVD *isn't* another iPhoto user, *don't* use the Burn command. Instead, export the photos using the File Export or Web Page options described in Chapter 9. The pictures won't have any ratings, comments, keywords, and so on, but they'll be organized in a way that will be much easier for non-iPhoto folk to navigate. (In fact, to create a particularly easy-to-navigate CD of photos, use the Web Page export technique described in the box on page 211.)

iPhoto Backups

Bad things can happen to digital photos. They can be accidentally deleted with a slip of your pinkie. They can become mysteriously corrupted and subsequently unopenable. They can get mangled by a crashed hard disk and be lost forever. Losing one-of-a-kind family photos can be extremely painful, and in some documented cases, even marriage threatening. So if you value your digital photos, you should back them up regularly, perhaps after each major batch of new photos joins your collection.

Backing Up to CD or DVD

The quickest and most convenient way to back up your Photo Library is to archive it onto a blank CD or DVD using iPhoto's Burn command, as described on the previous pages. (If you don't have a disc-burning drive, don't worry; the next section explains how to perform a complete iPhoto backup *without* burning a disc.)

If anything bad ever happens to your photo collection, you'll be able to restore your Photo Library from the backup discs, with all your thumbnails, keywords, comments, and other tidbits intact.

To restore your photo collection from such a backup, see "Merging Photo Libraries" later in this chapter.

Backing Up (No CD Burner)

Fortunately, even if you don't have a CD burner (and therefore can't use iPhoto's Burn command), backing up thousands of photos is a simple task for the iPhoto maven. After all, one of iPhoto's main jobs is to keep all your photos together in *one* place, one folder that's easy to copy to a backup disk of any kind.

That all-important folder is the *iPhoto Library* folder, which resides inside the Pictures folder of the Home folder that bears your name. If your user name (the short name you use to log into Mac OS X) is *corky*, the full path to your iPhoto Library folder from your main hard drive window drive is: Users→corky→Pictures→iPhoto Library.

As described in Chapter 4, the iPhoto Library folder contains not just your photos, but also a huge assortment of additional files, including:

- All the thumbnail images in the iPhoto window.
- The original, safety copies of photos you've edited in iPhoto.
- Various data files that keep track of keywords, comments, ratings, and photo albums you've created within iPhoto.

To prepare for a disaster, you should back up *all* of these components.

To perform a complete backup, copy the entire iPhoto Library folder to another location. Copying it to a different disk—to an iPod, say, or to the hard drive of another Mac via network—is the best solution. (Copying it to another folder on the *same* disk means you'll lose both the original iPhoto Library folder and its backup if, say, your hard drive crashes or your computer is hit by an asteroid.)

Note: Of course, you can also back up your photos by dragging their thumbnails out of the iPhoto window and into a folder or disk on your desktop, once you've dragged the iPhoto window to one side.

Unfortunately, this method doesn't preserve your keywords, comments, album organization, or any other information you've created in iPhoto. If something bad happens to your Photo Library, you'll have to import the raw photos again and reorganize them from scratch.

Managing Photo Libraries

iPhoto 4's best new feature may be its speed. It's enjoyable to work with as many as 25,000 photos in a single collection, give or take a few thousand, depending on your Mac model and how much memory it has.

But for some people, 25,000 pictures isn't a very distant threshold. As your collection of digital photos grows into the tens of thousands (and if you have a digital camera, this will happen sooner than you think), iPhoto eventually starts slowing down as it sifts through more and more data to find and display your pictures. At that point, scrolling the photos in the main Photo Library becomes an exercise in patience that would drive a Zen master crazy.

When your Photo Library becomes too large to manage comfortably, you can always do what people used to do in iPhoto 2, when the limit was only *2,000* pictures: Archive some of the photos to CD or DVD using the Burn command described earlier—and then *delete* the archived photos from your library to shrink it down in size. You might choose to archive older photos, or albums you rarely use.

Note: Remember, archiving photos to CD using the Burn command doesn't automatically remove them from iPhoto; you have to do that part yourself. If you don't, your Photo Library won't get any smaller. Just make sure that the CD you've burned works properly before deleting your original photos from iPhoto.

---

iPhoto Disk Images

The one disadvantage of that offload-to-disc technique is that it takes a big hunk of your photo collection *offline,* so that you can no longer get to it easily. If you suddenly need a set of photos that you've already archived, you have to hunt down the right disc before you can see the photos. That could be a problem if you happen to be on the road in New York and need the photos you left on a CD in San Francisco.

Here's a brilliant solution to that CD-management problem: Turn your iPhoto CDs into *disk image files* on your hard drive.

Open Disk Utility (which sits in your Applications→Utilities folder). Insert the iPhoto CD or DVD you've burned; in the left pane of the Disk Utility window, click the disc's icon. (Click the CD or DVD icon bearing a plain-English name, like "iPhoto Library." It's usually the last one listed. Don't click the icon bearing your CD burner's name, like PIONEER DVR-103.)

Then choose Images→New→Image From [disk name], or click the New Image button in the toolbar at the top of the window. In the Convert Image dialog box, you can type a name for the disk image you're about to create. (You can even password-protect it by choosing AES-128 from the Encryption pop-up menu.) Choose a location for the disk image, like your Desktop, and then click Save.

You've just created a disk image file, whose name ends with .dmg. It's a "virtual CD" that you can keep on your hard drive at all times. When you want to view its contents in iPhoto, double-click the .dmg icon. You'll see its contents appear in the form of a CD icon in the iPhoto album list, just as though you'd inserted the original iPhoto disc.

You can spin off numerous chunks of your iPhoto collection this way, and "mount" as many of them simultaneously as you like—a spectacular way to manage tens of thousands of photos, chunk by chunk, without having to deal with a clumsy collection of CDs.

Multiple iPhoto Libraries

Here's another way to keep your Photo Library from becoming impossibly bloated without transferring part of it to a CD: Start a new one, right there on your hard drive.

Here's what splitting your photo collection into smaller libraries gains you:

- iPhoto itself is *much* faster, especially during scrolling, because there are fewer photos in it.

- You can keep different types of collections or projects separate. You might want to maintain a Home library for personal use, for example, and a Work library for images that pertain to your business.

Creating new libraries

Unfortunately, iPhoto provides no built-in tools for retiring one Photo Library and starting a fresh one. You must fool it into creating a new one by using the following trick:

1. **Quit iPhoto.**

   Return to the Finder.

2. **Move the whole iPhoto Library folder out of your Home→Pictures folder to a different location, or just give it a new name.**

   The idea is simply to *hide* this folder from iPhoto. You can drag it to a new folder on your hard drive, rename it something like Old iPhoto Library, or even stash it in a new folder called Old Libraries *inside* your Pictures folder.

   The point is to move the *whole* iPhoto Library folder. Messing around with the files and folders inside the iPhoto Library folder can cause problems.

3. **Open iPhoto again.**

   When iPhoto starts up, it notices that its library is missing, and tells you so, in no uncertain terms (Figure 14-4).

Figure 14-4:
If you hide the iPhoto Library from iPhoto, the program invites you either to find it or to create a new one. If your goal is to begin a fresh, smaller library for the new year, for example, click Create Library.

4. **Click Create Library. In the following dialog box, type a name for the new library** (like *New iPhoto Library*) **and click Save.**

This is a new twist in iPhoto 4, an acknowledgment by Apple that people actually use this iPhoto Library-switching routine. You're offered not only the chance to create a new library, but even the opportunities to name it anything you like and choose a location for it that's not your regularly scheduled Pictures folder.

When iPhoto finishes opening, all remnants of your old Photo Library are gone. You're left with a blank window, ready to import fresh photos.

Using this technique, you can spawn as many new Photo Libraries as you need. You can archive the old libraries on CD or DVD, move them to another Mac, or just keep them somewhere on your hard drive so that you can swap any one of them back in whenever you need it, as shown in Figure 14-5.

As for *how* you swap them back in you have two options: a manual way, and an automatic way.

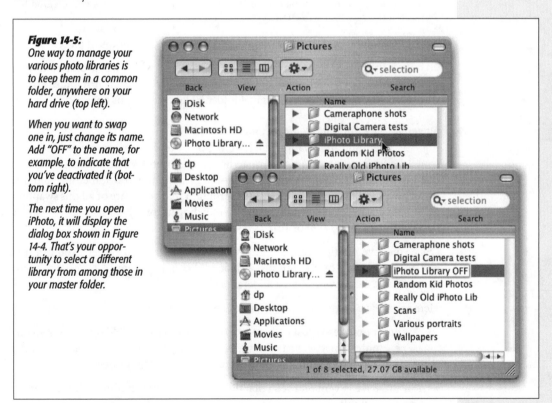

Figure 14-5:
One way to manage your various photo libraries is to keep them in a common folder, anywhere on your hard drive (top left).

When you want to swap one in, just change its name. Add "OFF" to the name, for example, to indicate that you've deactivated it (bottom right).

The next time you open iPhoto, it will display the dialog box shown in Figure 14-4. That's your opportunity to select a different library from among those in your master folder.

Swapping libraries (manual method)

The photos and albums from your old Photo Library aren't really gone, of course. They're still safely stored in the *old* iPhoto Library folder. You can resurrect them at any time by following these two steps:

1. **Quit iPhoto. Change the current iPhoto Library's name to something else.**

   A single letter's difference is plenty. You could just add an asterisk (*) to the end of its name, or you could add a suffix that reminds you of its meaning, like OFF or INACTIVE.

Tip: Dragging the folder into a different folder works, too. The point is to confuse iPhoto, to ensure that it can't find the same folder in the same place.

---

2. **Open iPhoto again. When the dialog box shown in Figure 14-4 appears, click Find Library. Choose the new library folder that you want to open.**

   This would presumably be one of the creatively named libraries you created following the steps on page 314–315.

When iPhoto finishes reopening, you'll find the new set of photos in place.

To reverse the procedure, change the new folder's name, which will prompt iPhoto to ask yet again where your library folder is. (Also take *OFF* off of the *first* folder's name, if you like, or put it back in its original folder.) The cycle begins anew.

Swapping libraries (automatic method)

If all this renaming and swapping of iPhoto Library folders strikes you as a little tiresome, confusing, and even risky, you're not alone. Brian Webster, a self-proclaimed computer nerd, thought the same thing—but *he* decided to do something about it. He wrote iPhoto Library Manager, a free program that takes care of all this swapping and moving for you. Waste no time in downloading it from the "Missing CD" page at *www.missingmanuals.com* or Brian's own site at *http://homepage.mac.com/bwebster*.

Once you have multiple iPhoto Library folders (as described earlier), you can turn any one of them on or off with just a click, as shown in Figure 14-6. You don't have to move or rename your library folders.

Here are a few pointers for using iPhoto Library Manager:

- The program doesn't just activate *existing* iPhoto Library folders; it can also create new folders for you. Just click the New Library button in the toolbar, choose a location and name for the library, and click OK (see Figure 14-6).

- You still have to quit and relaunch iPhoto for a change in libraries to take effect. Conveniently, iPhoto Library Manager includes Quit iPhoto and Relaunch iPhoto buttons in its toolbar.

Tip: You can also switch libraries using the pop-up menu from iPhoto Library Manager's Dock icon.

**Managing Photo
Libraries**

- iPhoto Library Manager is fully AppleScriptable. If you're handy with writing Apple-Script scripts, you can write one that swaps your various libraries automatically with a double-click.

- You still might want to investigate iPhoto Library Manager even if you have no intention of using multiple Library folders, thanks to another great feature. iPhoto Library Manager lets several account holders on a single Mac share one Photo Library.

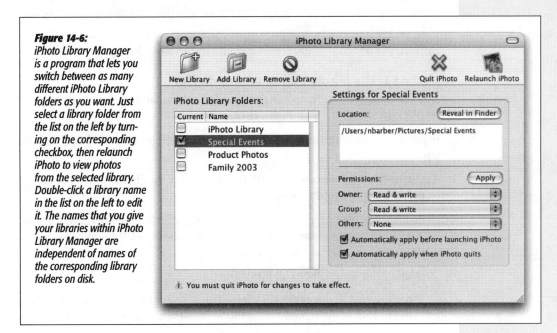

Figure 14-6:
iPhoto Library Manager is a program that lets you switch between as many different iPhoto Library folders as you want. Just select a library folder from the list on the left by turning on the corresponding checkbox, then relaunch iPhoto to view photos from the selected library. Double-click a library name in the list on the left to edit it. The names that you give your libraries within iPhoto Library Manager are independent of names of the corresponding library folders on disk.

Merging Photo Libraries

You've just arrived home from your photo safari of deepest Kenya. You're jet-lagged and dusty, but your iBook is bursting at the seams with fresh photo meat. You can't wait to transfer the new pictures into your main Photo Library—you know, the one on your Power Macintosh G5 with 2 gigs of RAM and a 35-inch Apple Imax Display.

Or, less dramatically, suppose you've just upgraded to iPhoto 4. You're thrilled that you can now fit 25,000 pictures into a single library—but under iPhoto 2, you had to create six different iPhoto Library folders containing about 2,000 pictures each.

In both cases, you have the same problem: How are you supposed to merge the libraries into a single, unified one?

How Not to Do It

You certainly can combine the *photos* of two Macs' Photo Libraries—just export them from one (File→Export) and then import them into the other (File→Import). As a result, however, you lose all of your album organization, comments, and keywords.

Your next instinct might be: "Hey, I know! I'll just drag the iPhoto Library folder from computer #1 into the iPhoto window of computer #2!"

Big mistake. You'll end up importing not only the photos, but also the tiny thumbnail versions of each photo (which are stored separately in the iPhoto Library folder) *and* the original versions of any photos that you edited. You'll wind up with duplicates or triplicates of every photo in the viewing area, in one enormous, unmanageable, uncategorized, sloshing library.

No, merging iPhoto libraries is slightly more complicated than that.

Method 1: Use iPhoto CDs as Intermediaries

One way to merge two Photo Libraries is to burn the second one onto an iPhoto CD or DVD, as described earlier in this chapter.

Begin with the smaller library. (In the Kenya safari example, you'd begin with the laptop.)

1. **Open iPhoto and burn a CD or DVD containing all the photos you want to merge into the larger Photo Library.**

   Follow exactly the same disc-creation steps outlined in the steps beginning on page 308. If you want to preserve any albums you've created, select the albums, not just the photos themselves, when you burn the discs.

2. **Quit iPhoto. Swap iPhoto Library folders.**

   If you're trying to merge the libraries of two different Macs, skip this instruction. Instead, move to the second Mac at this point—the one that will serve as the final resting place for the photos you exported.

   If you're merging two libraries on the same Mac, swap the iPhoto Library folders either manually or using iPhoto Library Manager, as described earlier in this chapter. In any case, the master, larger photo collection should now be before you in iPhoto.

3. **Insert the iPhoto CD you just created.**

   iPhoto opens (if it's not already running) and the iPhoto CD icon appears in the Source list of the iPhoto window, as shown in Figure 14-7. Albums on the disc appear underneath the CD icon.

4. **Select one album, or several, on the iPhoto CD.**

You can select multiple albums just as you would lists of files in the Finder: Shift-click to select several consecutive albums, ⌘-click to select nonconsecutive albums, and so on.

When you select the albums, the thumbnails of the corresponding photos stored on the CD appear in the photo-viewing area.

5. **Drag the selected albums (using any one of them as a handle) to a blank spot at the bottom of the Source list, below all the other albums (see Figure 14-7)—or onto the Photo Library icon at the very top.**

You can't drag them onto an existing album, and you can't drag the entire disc icon.

In any case, this is the big moment when the "merge" actually happens. iPhoto switches into Import mode and copies the selected albums from the iPhoto CD into your main Photo Library. Any keywords, comments, ratings, and titles that were applied to the photos on the CD are imported too.

When it's all over, you won't find any new albums. You will, however, find that your Photo Library now contains the merged pictures. (Click the Last Roll icon to see them.)

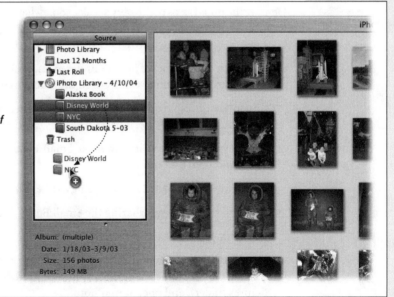

Figure 14-7:
To merge photo libraries, drag and drop albums from an iPhoto CD onto a blank spot in the Source list, or onto the Photo Library icon at the very top.

In this example, the contents of photo albums named Disney World and NYC, which are stored on the iPhoto CD, are being merged into the main Photo Library.

Using this technique, you can combine the photos stored on any number of CDs into a single library, without losing a single comment, keyword, album, or original photo.

Method 2: Share the Library with Yourself

Burning iPhoto CDs is a great way to merge two or more iPhoto Libraries, because it leaves you with backup discs. And in its way, it's a lot simpler than what you're about to read.

Still, you use up a lot of blanks this way, and you spend a lot of time waiting for discs to burn.

If the photo libraries you want to merge are all on the same Mac—in separate accounts, for example, or just in different places—there's another method that doesn't involve burning iPhoto CDs. Instead, it involves using the photo sharing feature described on page 218. (It also works only in Panther, Mac OS X 10.3, or later.)

If one of the photo libraries is already in some other account holder's copy of iPhoto, great. With Fast User Switching turn on (see step 1 below), share the appropriate albums in the other person's account, exactly as described on page 218. Then in your account, just drag the shared albums onto your Photo Library or a blank spot in the album list to copy them in, essentially as shown in Figure 14-7.

If all of the library folders belong to you, however, merging through sharing is slightly hairier. You'll need two free pieces of software: ShareAlike and iPhoto Library Manager, both available on the "Missing CD" page of *www.missingmanuals.com.*

Here are the broad steps of this very sneaky, somewhat advanced procedure. For clarity, let's say that you want to merge a library called Small Batch into a bigger one called Big Library, both of which are currently in your Pictures folder.

1. **On the Accounts panel of System Preferences, click Login Options. Turn on "Enable fast user switching." Click OK in the confirmation box.**

   This operation also requires at least one account in addition to your own. Take this opportunity to create one, if necessary. Let's call that other account Casey.

2. **Using iPhoto Library Manager, make Small Batch your working iPhoto library folder, and then quit iPhoto.**

   See Figure 14-6 for details on choosing a different library folder.

3. **Open ShareAlike. Begin sharing the Small Batch library.**

   Now both you and Casey can work with the same library.

4. **Switch into Casey's account. Using iPhoto Library Manager, choose Small Batch as Casey's library folder (it's probably in your hard drive's Users→[Your Name]→ Pictures folder), and open it in iPhoto.**

   You should now see the photos from Small Batch in Casey's copy of iPhoto.

5. **In Casey's copy of iPhoto, share the albums you'll want to merge.**

   See page 218 for details on photo sharing.

6. **Switch back to your own account. Using iPhoto Library Manager, open up the Big Library in iPhoto.**

Now you're looking at the main photo collection—but there, in the Source list, you'll see an icon for Casey's shared photos. (If not, choose iPhoto→Preferences, click Sharing, and turn on "Look for shared photos." Close the Preferences window.)

Click the flippy triangle to reveal Casey's albums.

7. **Drag Casey's albums into a blank spot in your own Source list.**

   You've just copied the albums from the Small Batch library into your own Big Library. Put another way, you've just merged two iPhoto libraries without having to burn any discs!

   (And they said it couldn't be done…)

8. **Switch back into Casey's account and quit iPhoto. If you like, use iPhoto Library Manager to re-choose Casey's original library folder. Return to your account; in ShareAlike, click Stop Sharing, click Fix Permissions, and quit the program.**

   Once you've confirmed that the photos have safely arrived in your main library, you can throw away the Small Batch folder.

Beyond iPhoto

Depending on how massive your collection of digital photos grows and how you use it, you may find yourself wanting more file-management power than iPhoto can offer. Maybe you wish you could organize 50,000 or 100,000 photos in a single catalog, without having to swap photo libraries or load archive CDs. Maybe you'd like to search for photos based on something other than just titles, keywords, and

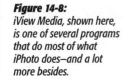

Figure 14-8:
iView Media, shown here, is one of several programs that do most of what iPhoto does—and a lot more besides.

For example, it can "watch" certain folders on your Mac, so that when new graphics arrive, iView catalogs them automatically.

And its photo limit is 128,000 pictures.

comments—perhaps by file type, creation date, or the camera model used to shoot them. Maybe you have a small network, and you'd like a system that lets a whole workgroup share a library of photos simultaneously.

To enjoy such features, you'll have to move beyond iPhoto into the world of *digital asset management,* which means spending a little money. Programs like Extensis Portfolio ($200, *www.extensis.com*), Canto Cumulus ($100, *www.canto.com*), and iView MediaPro ($160, *www.iview-multimedia.com*) are terrific programs for someone who wants to take the next step up (Figure 14-8). (All three companies offer free trial versions on their Web sites.)

Here are a few of the stunts these more advanced programs can do that iPhoto can't:

- Create custom fields to store any other kind of information you want about your files—dates, prices, Web addresses, and so on.

- Track graphics files stored in any location on a network, not just in a specific folder.

- Catalog not just photos, but other file types, too: QuarkXPress and InDesign documents, QuickTime movies, sound files, PowerPoint slides, and so on.

- Share a catalog of images with dozens of other people simultaneously over a network.

- Rename an entire group of images en masse.

- Customize the fonts, colors, and borders of the thumbnail view.

- Create catalogs that can be read on both Mac and Windows.

- Display previews of "offline" photo files that aren't actually on the Mac at the moment (they're on CDs or DVDs on your shelf, for example).

- Handle tens of thousands of photos in a single catalog.

Some of the features in this list were obviously developed with professional users in mind, like graphic designers and studio photographers. But this kind of program is worth considering if your photo collection—and your passion for digital photography—one day outgrows iPhoto.

Part Five: Appendixes

5

Troubleshooting

1 Photo isn't just a Mac OS X program—it's a *Cocoa* Mac OS X program, meaning that it was written exclusively for Mac OS X. As a result, it should, in theory, be one of the most rock-solid programs under the sun.

Still, iPhoto does have its vulnerabilities. Many of these shortcomings stem from the fact that iPhoto works under the supervision of a lot of cooks, since it must interact with plug-ins, connect to printers, talk to Web servers, and cope with an array of file corruptions.

If trouble strikes, keep hands and feet inside the tram at all times—and consult the following collection of problems, solutions, questions, and answers.

Importing

Getting photos into iPhoto is supposed to be one of the most effortless parts of the process. Remember, Steve Jobs promised that iPhoto would forever banish the "chain of pain" from digital photography. And yet…

iPhoto doesn't recognize my camera.

iPhoto generally "sees" any recent camera model, even if it's not listed on Apple's Device Compatibility page (*www.apple.com/iphoto/compatibility*). If you click the Import mode button and see "No camera is connected" in the lower-left corner of the screen, even though the camera most assuredly *is* connected, try these steps in order:

- Make sure you're turning on the camera only *after* connecting its USB cable to the Mac.

- Turn the camera off, then on again, while it's plugged in.

• If iPhoto absolutely won't notice its digital companion, use a memory-card reader as described on page 87.

iPhoto crashes when I try to import.

This problem is most likely to crop up when you're bringing pictures in from your hard drive or another disk. Here are the possibilities:

• The culprit is usually a single corrupted file. Try a test: Import only half the photos in the batch. If nothing bad happens, split the remaining photos in half again and import *them*. Keep going until you've isolated the offending file.

• Consider the graphics program you're using to save the files. It's conceivable that its version of JPEG or TIFF doesn't jibe perfectly with iPhoto's. (This scenario is most likely to occur right after you've upgraded either your graphics program or iPhoto itself.)

To test this possibility, open a handful of images in a different editing program, save them, and then try the import again. If they work, then you might have a temporary compatibility problem. Check the editing program's Web site for update and troubleshooting information.

• If you're attempting to import hundreds of photos at once, break the import into batches. You'll have fewer problems with a couple of medium-sized imports instead of a single big one.

• Some JPEGs that were originally saved in Mac OS 9 won't import into iPhoto. Try opening and resaving these images in a native Mac OS X editor such as Photoshop. Speaking of Photoshop, it has an excellent batching tool that you can use to automatically process mountains of images while you go grab some lunch.

Finally, a reminder, just in case you think iPhoto is acting up: iPhoto doesn't import *movies* from digital cameras. It also doesn't import proprietary formats like RAW and CAM. For those tasks, see the box on page 86.

iPhoto won't import images from my video camera.

Most modern digital camcorders can store your still images on a memory card instead of DV tape. If you're having a hard time importing these stills into iPhoto with a direct camera connection, try these tips:

• Take out the tape cassette before connecting the camcorder to your Mac.

• Try copying the files directly from the memory card to your hard drive with a memory-card reader or a PC Card adapter. Once the images are on your hard drive, you should be able to import them into iPhoto.

What if I don't want iPhoto to import all the pictures from my camera?

You can't tell iPhoto not to import them all—but you can use Image Capture. A sort of grandfather to iPhoto, this Mac OS X program comes on every Mac. Although it doesn't perform even a hundredth of the feats that iPhoto can, it does offer one feature iPhoto lacks—*selective* importing.

First, however, you must tell iPhoto not to open automatically when you plug in your camera. You want Image Capture to do your importing, instead. To make this change, see Figure A-1. From now on, Image Capture, not iPhoto, will open whenever you plug in your camera.

Once the pictures are on your hard drive, copy them into iPhoto simply by dragging them (or the folder they're in) into the photo-viewing area.

Figure A-1:
Top: First, make sure that Image Capture, not iPhoto, intercepts and downloads the photos when you connect your digital camera. To do so, open Image Capture, then choose Image Capture→Preferences.

From the Camera Preferences pop-up menu, choose Image Capture. You could even choose another program to intervene when your camera is plugged in (by choosing Other).

Middle: This is the main Image Capture window that now appears when you plug in your camera. To download only some of the photos, click Download Some.

Bottom: This "slide sorter" window is where you can choose the individual pictures you want to download. Or, use the buttons at the top to rotate or delete selected shots from the camera. In slide sorter view, Shift-click or ⌘-click the thumbnails of the pictures you want. In list view, Shift-click or ⌘-click as though they're Finder list-view files.

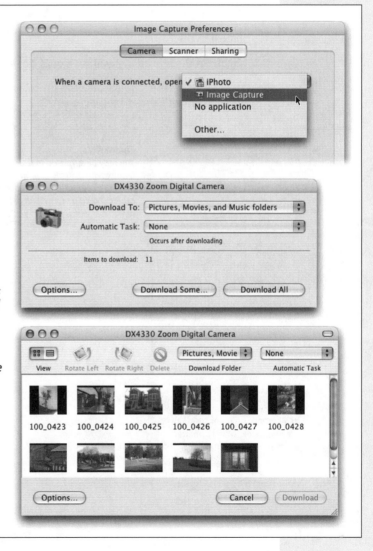

Exporting

Clearly, "Easy come, easy go" doesn't always apply to photos.

After I upgraded iPhoto to the latest version, my Export button became disabled.
This problem is usually caused by outdated *plug-ins*. If you have any older plug-ins, such as an outdated version of the Toast Titanium export plug-in, disable it and then relaunch iPhoto to see whether that solves the problem.

Here's how to turn your plug-ins on or off:

1. **Quit iPhoto.**

   Return to the Finder.

2. **Highlight the iPhoto application icon. Choose File→Get Info.**

   You may have seen the Get Info box for other files in your day, but you probably haven't seen a *Plugins* panel (Figure A-2).

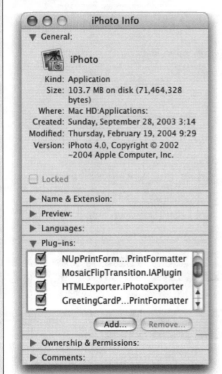

Figure A-2:
You may be surprised to discover that a number of iPhoto's "built-in" features are actually plug-ins written by Apple's programmers. Most of them are responsible for familiar printing and exporting options. Any others should be turned off in times of troubleshooting. (If you can't remember which plug-ins you've installed yourself, reinstall iPhoto.)

3. **Click the triangle to expand the Plugins panel.**

   A complete list of the plug-ins you currently have loaded appears with a checkbox next to each item.

4. **Turn off the non-Apple plug-ins that you suspect might be causing the problem.**

Now open iPhoto and test the export function. If the technology gods are smiling, the function should work now. All that's left is to figure out which *one* of the plug-ins was causing your headaches.

To find out, quit iPhoto. Open its Get Info window again. Reinstate your plug-ins one by one, using the on/off switches depicted in Figure A-2, until you find the offending software.

Once you locate the culprit, highlight its name and then click Remove. (You may also want to check the Web site of the offending plug-in for an updated version.)

Tip: Here's another, somewhat more interesting way to remove a plug-in. Control-click the iPhoto icon; from the shortcut menu, choose Show Package Contents. In the resulting window, open the Contents→PlugIns folder, where each plug-in is represented by an easily removable icon.

I get the message, "An unexpected error has occurred" when I try to export a HomePage photo album.

You've probably named one of your photos with an Option-key character (™, ®, ©, é, ç, ñ, è, ü, î, or whatever) or a *double-byte* character (a Japanese or Chinese character, for example). These are no-nos on the Internet, so iPhoto won't let you export them.

There's no solution except to rename the offending photos.

But you're not out of the woods yet. If you change the title of a photo *in iPhoto,* remember that you haven't changed the original file name of the JPEG file buried deep within your Library folder.

After you've changed your picture titles, therefore, you should export them to a folder on your desktop, delete the originals from iPhoto, and then reimport the set you exported. Doing so makes sure that iPhoto adopts their new, authorized names, both internally and externally. They should now give you no further trouble.

Printing

How many things can go wrong when you print? Let us count the ways.

I can't print more than one photo per page. It seems like a waste to use a whole sheet of paper for one 4 x 6 print.

Check the following:

- Have you, in fact, selected more than one photo to print?

- Choose File→Page Setup. Make sure the paper size is US Letter (or whatever paper you've loaded). Click OK.

- Choose File→Print. From the Presets pop-up menu, choose Standard; from the Style pop-up menu, choose N-Up; then choose a number from the "Photos per page" pop-up menu. (Make sure "One photo per page" is turned off.) You'll now see all of your selected images side by side in the preview pane. They're ready to print.

Editing

There's not much that can go wrong here, but when it does, it *really* goes wrong.

iPhoto crashes when I double-click a thumbnail to edit it.

You probably changed a photo file's name in the Finder—in the iPhoto Library folder, behind the program's back. iPhoto hates this! Only grief can follow.

Sometimes, too, a corrupted picture file will also make iPhoto crash when you try to edit it. Use the script described on page 299 to locate the scrambled file in the Finder. Open the file in another graphics program, use its File→Save As command to replace the corrupted picture file, and then try again in iPhoto.

iPhoto won't let me use an external graphics program when I double-click a thumbnail.

Choose File→Preferences. Make sure that the Other button is selected and that a graphics program's name appears next to it. (If not, click Other, then click Set, and then choose the program you want to use.)

Also make sure that your external editing program still *exists*. You might have upgraded to a newer version of that program, one whose file name is slightly different from the version you originally specified in iPhoto.

My picture doesn't fit right on 4 x 6, 5 x 7, or 8 x 10 inch paper.

Most digital cameras produce photos in a 4:3 width-to-height ratio. Unfortunately, those dimensions don't fit squarely into any of the standard print sizes.

The solution: Crop the photos first, using the appropriate print size in the Constrain pop-up menu (see page 141).

I've messed up a photo while editing it, and now it's ruined!

Highlight the file's thumbnail and then choose File→Revert to Original. iPhoto restores your photo to its original state, drawing on a backup it has secretly kept.

General Questions

Finally, here's a handful of general—although perfectly terrifying—troubles.

iPhoto's wigging out.

If the program "unexpectedly quits," well, that's life. It happens. This is Mac OS X, though, so you can generally open the program right back up again and pick up where you left off.

If the flakiness is becoming really severe, try logging out (choose ♠→Log Out) and logging back in again.

Man, this program's slow!

Installing more memory is by far the best solution to this problem. iPhoto loves RAM like Madonna loves attention.

For an immediate (and less expensive) fix, keep your Photo Library a reasonable size and collapse your film rolls (page 104).

I can't change an album's name.

Double-click its name, and then type in the new label.

When I try to choose a soundtrack for a slide show, my iTunes music collection doesn't show up!

First, try opening iTunes before opening iPhoto. That way, iPhoto will be sure to "see" the open iTunes library.

If that doesn't solve the problem, you might have to recreate one of your iTunes preference files, like this:

First, quit all of your iLife programs. Open your Home→Music→iTunes folder. Drag the file called iTunes Music Library.xml file to your desktop.

Now open iTunes and create a new playlist by choosing File→New Playlist. (Doing so triggers iTunes to build a new .xml file, which is what you want.) Quit iTunes.

When you return to iPhoto, your iTunes library should show up just fine.

iPhoto crashes when I try to open it.

This "unexpectedly quit" business can arise when each of several Mac OS X 10.2 account holders upgrade from an older version of iPhoto.

Fixing the problem is easy enough: Just upgrade to iPhoto 4.0.1 or later. (Either click the Software Update icon in System Preferences to find the updater ready to install, or visit *www.apple.com/downloads/macosx/apple/iphoto.html.*)

I can't export a picture.

If exporting a photo gives you a "not enough disk space" message, but you know that you do, in fact, have space, it's probably because, as Apple's help files cheerfully point out, "iPhoto 4 may incorrectly think a photo's file size is several billion megabytes."

Installing iPhoto 4.0.1 or later, described above, solves the problem.

I can't delete a photo!

You may be trying to delete a photo right out of a smart album. That's a no-no.

There's only one workaround: Find the same photo in the Photo Library, the Last Roll icon, or the Last Months icon—and delete it from there.

My QuickTime slideshows don't show the right transitions between slides.

That's normal, actually. All you get in QuickTime Player are standard cross-dissolves between photos. The fancy cube effect, wipe effect, and so on are just for use within iPhoto.

I get an error message when I try to share my albums on a network.

Ah, yes—the old, "Other users will not be able to access your shared photos because port 8770 is being blocked by your firewall software" message.

Evidently, you've turned on the Mac OS X firewall feature, which is designed to insulate your Mac from no-goodnicks on the Internet. Trouble is, it's also blocking innocent activity like sharing your photos.

You can turn the firewall off, if you like (open System Preferences, click Sharing, click the Firewall tab, and click Stop). That will certainly solve the problem.

If you want the firewall on in general, though, you may prefer to simply poke a hole in the firewall just big enough—and only on the proper channel—for iPhoto's photo sharing feature to work.

To try this slightly more involved workaround, see Figure A-2.

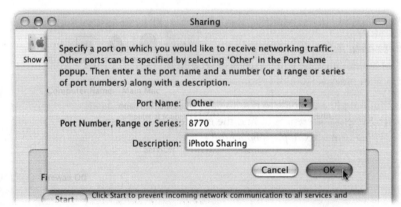

Figure A-2:
To allow photo sharing to pass through your firewall, open System Preferences, click Sharing, click the Firewall tab, and click New. From the Port Name pop-up menu, choose Other, as shown here; type 8770 into the middle box; and type a description, if you like. Click OK to complete the deed.

When I edit a photo, it appears blocky, and takes a minute to become sharp.

That's an iPhoto speed trick, and it's normal for high-megapixel images. When you're just paging through pictures, the low-resolution, blocky version is usually enough for you to get the visual idea without having to wait for iPhoto to display the full high-res version. When you finally pause, iPhoto will rebuild its display of that photo at the highest resolution your window will allow.

I've got the opposite problem. The photo appears sharp, and then gets blurry after a moment.

You're probably witnessing the same effect described above—but you're just describing it differently. That is, the "blurry" version of the photo is iPhoto's approximation of it; remember, your monitor simply isn't big enough to show the entire photo at full size (that is, showing every pixel). So iPhoto, in effect, averages pixels in order to come up with a smaller version.

Some people report being able to kick iPhoto into displaying a sharper image just by clicking inside it, or by paging to the next photo and then back again.

iPhoto is freezing up when rebuilding thumbnails.

iPhoto 4.0.1 updater is designed to make iPhoto convert every thumbnail image into a newer, better format that takes less time to display on the screen. Unfortunately, the thumbnail converter chokes when it encounters graphics that aren't JPEG images, even though iPhoto itself is perfectly compatible with them. The upgrader stalls when it attempts to build a new thumbnail image for, say, a Photoshop document.

Here's how you solve the problem.

1. **Start iPhoto. When the program announces that it wants to convert your thumbnails, click Upgrade Later.**

   Now, at least, you can get into your collection.

2. **Create a smart album (page 127) whose criteria read, "Title" "does not contain" ".jpg."**

   The idea is to ferret out all pictures that aren't JPEG files. Once you've confirmed that they're all rounded up in your smart album, continue:

3. **Export the smart album's photos to a new folder on your hard drive.**

   See page 288 for instructions on exporting. The point is to get these pictures out of iPhoto.

4. **Delete all of the non-JPEG images.**

   As noted earlier in this appendix, you can't delete them straight from the smart album; you have to delete them from the photo library itself. Be sure to empty the iPhoto Trash once you're done.

5. **Quit iPhoto. Reopen it and this time, permit the program to update its thumbnails.**

6. **Finally, reimport the non-JPEG photos that you had exported to a folder.**

iPhoto is doing something bizarre.

Maybe it's trying to import phantom photos. Maybe it's stuck at the "Loading photos..." screen forever. Maybe the photos just don't look right. There's a long list, in fact, of rare but mystifying glitches that can arise.

Fortunately, setting things aright is fairly easy if you know what to do. Follow these steps, in order; after each one, check to see if the problem is gone.

- **Rebuild the photo library.** Quit iPhoto. Press the Shift, Option, and ⌘ keys as you reopen it.

  iPhoto asks you if you're sure you want to "rebuild your Photo Library," and warns that you might lose some data. What it's referring to here is corrupted data—photo files that are slightly damaged, for example. Since these are probably what's causing iPhoto to misbehave, you probably don't mind losing them. Click Yes.

  In the next dialog box, iPhoto asks you to save the freshly rebuilt iPhoto Library folder somewhere. You can name it "Rescued Library" or whatever you like, and save it into your Pictures folder or wherever you like.

  Once you click Save, iPhoto works its way through each album and each photo, inspecting it for damage, repairing it if possible, and finally presenting you with your new, cleaned-up library.

- **Repair your file permissions.** An amazing number of mysterious glitches—not just in iPhoto—arise because file *permissions* have become muddled. Permissions is a complex subject, and refers to a complex mesh of interconnected Unix settings on every file in Mac OS X.

  When something just doesn't seem to be working right, therefore, open your Applications→Utilities folder and open Disk Utility. Click your hard drive's name in the left-side list; click the First Aid tab; click Repair Disk Permissions; and then read an article while the Mac checks out your disk. If the program finds anything amiss, you'll see Unix shorthand messages that tell you what it fixed.

Tip: Most Mac mavens, in fact, believe in running this Repair Permissions routine after running *any kind of installer*, just to nip nascent problems in the bud. That includes both installers of new programs and of Apple's own updates.

- **Throw away the iPhoto preferences file.** Here we are in the age of Mac OS X, and we're still throwing away preference files?

  Absolutely. A corrupted preference file can still bewilder the program that depends on it.

  Before you go on a dumpfest, however, take this simple test. Log in using a *different account* (perhaps a dummy account that you create just for testing purposes). Run iPhoto. Is the problem gone? If so, then the glitch exists only when *you* are logged in—which means it's a problem with *your* copy of the program's preferences.

Return to your own account. Open your Home→Library→Preferences folder, where you'll find neatly labeled preference files for all of the programs you use. In this case, trash the file called com.apple.iPhoto.plist.

The next time you run iPhoto, it will build itself a brand-new preference file that, if you're lucky, lacks whatever corruption was causing your problems.

iPhoto 4, Menu by Menu

S ome people use iPhoto for years without pulling down a single menu. But unless you explore its menu commands, you're likely to miss some of the options and controls that make it a surprisingly powerful little photo manager. Especially since some commands, like Export, appear *only* in menus.

Here's a menu-by-menu look at iPhoto's commands.

iPhoto Menu

This first menu, Mac OS X's Application menu, takes on the name of whatever program happens to be running in the foreground. In iPhoto's case, that would be iPhoto.

About iPhoto

This command opens the "About" box containing the requisite Apple copyright, trademark, and version information. In iPhoto's About box, you'll also find some fascinating details about the recordings of the two J. S. Bach tunes—*Minuet in G* and *Jesu, Joy of Man's Desiring*—that are included as sample soundtracks for use with iPhoto's Slideshow feature. (Here, at last, you can learn that you've been listening to the guitar playing of Leo Kottke and Harvey Reid.)

There's really only one good reason to open the About iPhoto window: It's the easiest way to find out exactly which version of iPhoto you have.

iPhoto Hot Tips

Opens a page on Apple's Web site that lists tricks like keyboard shortcuts and a brief overview of iPhoto 4's newest features, like batch processing (page 114) and smart albums (page 127).

Preferences

Opens the Preferences window (Figure B-1), which has three panels to choose from:

General

- Tell iPhoto how many months to show in the Last ___ Months album and how many rolls to show in the Last ___ Rolls album, as discussed in Chapter 5.

- Have iPhoto display the total photo count, in parentheses, next to each album in the Source list.

- Choose how you want iPhoto to open photos when you double-click them. You have three choices: Open the photo for editing in the main iPhoto window, open the photo in a *separate* window, or open it using another program (which you choose by clicking the Set button).

- Change the setting of iPhoto's Rotate button so that it spins selected photos counter-clockwise instead of clockwise.

- Choose the email program that you want iPhoto to use when emailing pictures as attachments using the Mail Photo feature.

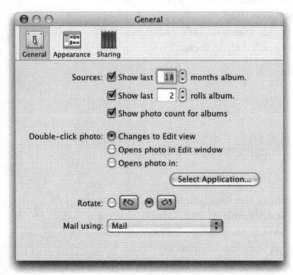

Figure B-1:
You'll probably be visiting iPhoto's Preferences window fairly regularly, so remember the keyboard shortcut that takes you here: ⌘-comma. You need to open Preferences every time you want to turn Photo Sharing on or off, for example.

Appearance

- Add a drop shadow or thin black outline frame to your thumbnails in the photo-viewing area.

- Change the background of the photo-viewing area from white to black—or any shade of gray.

- Align thumbnails to a grid in the iPhoto window (page 135).
- Put the most recently imported photos at the top of the iPhoto window instead of the bottom, when sorted by date (or the most recent film rolls at the top when sorted by film roll).
- Choose a size (small or large) for the album titles in the Source list.

Sharing

Set up iPhoto for sharing your iPhoto Library via Mac OS X's Rendezvous feature, as described on page 218.

Shop for iPhoto Products

This isn't so much a command as it is a marketing ploy. It opens your Web browser and opens a page on Apple's Web site that offers to sell you digital cameras, tripods, printers, and other accessories.

Provide iPhoto Feedback

This command takes you to a Web form on Apple's site where you can register complaints, make suggestions, or gush enthusiastically about iPhoto.

Register iPhoto

This is a link to yet another Apple Web page. Registering iPhoto simply means giving Apple your contact information. There's no penalty for not registering, by the way. Apple just wants to know more about who you are, so that it can offer you exciting new waves of junk mail.

Hide iPhoto, Hide Others, Show All

These aren't iPhoto's commands—they're Mac OS X's.

In any case, they determine which of the various programs running on your Mac are *visible* onscreen at any given moment. The Hide Others command is probably the most popular of these three. It zaps away the windows of all other programs—including the Finder—so that the iPhoto window is the only one you see.

Tip: If you know this golden Mac OS X trick, you may never need to use the Hide Others command: To switch into iPhoto from another program, hold down the Option and ⌘ keys when clicking the iPhoto icon in the Dock. Doing so simultaneously brings iPhoto to the front *and* hides all other programs you have running, producing an uncluttered, distraction-free view of iPhoto.

Quit iPhoto

This command closes iPhoto, no questions asked. You're not even asked to save changes, because as you've probably noticed, iPhoto doesn't even *have* a Save command. Like Filemaker Pro, 4D, and other database programs, iPhoto—itself a glorified database—continually saves changes as you add, delete, or edit photos.

File Menu

Most of the commands in the File menu involve moving photo files into or out of iPhoto. This is also where you go to get information about specific photos and do all your printing.

New Album

Creates a new photo album in the Source list, and prompts you to name it. Shortcuts: pressing ⌘-N or clicking the + button in the main iPhoto window.

New Album From Selection

This new iPhoto 4 command provides an alternate way to create an album. Simply select some photos in the iPhoto window, then choose this command.

New Smart Album

Opens a dialog box where you can set up criteria for a smart album, as described on page 127. (Also new in iPhoto 4.)

Edit Smart Album

Lets you edit the criteria for an existing smart album. Select the album before choosing this command. When you click OK, iPhoto updates the smart album.

New Film Roll From Selection

Creates a new film roll (page 101) from selected photos. Great for dividing a huge import into more manageable chunks.

Close Window

Closes the frontmost window *if* it happens to be a photo that you've opened into its own window for editing. (Neither Close Window nor ⌘-W closes the main iPhoto window. Only clicking the red Close button does that, and it quits the program to boot.)

Import

Use this command to add photos to your iPhoto library from your hard disk, a CD, or some other disk. Choose Import, select the file or folder you want to add, then click the Import button in the Import Photos dialog box.

You *don't* use this command when you're bringing in photos from a camera, card reader, or Kodak PhotoCD. In that case, put iPhoto in Import mode, connect your camera or insert the memory card, and then click the Import *button* on the bottom pane of the iPhoto window. Keyboard shortcut: Shift-⌘-I.

Export

Opens the Export Images window. Its panels offer the following three different ways of copying photos:

- **File Export.** Makes fresh copies of your photos in the file format and size you specify. You can export photos in their existing file format or convert them to JPEG, TIFF, or PNG format. You also can set a maximum size for the photos, so that iPhoto scales down larger photos on the fly as it exports them.

- **Web Page.** Publishes selected photos as a series of HTML pages that you can post on a Web site. The finished product includes an index page with clickable thumbnails that open individual pages containing each photo. (See Chapter 9 for step-by-step instructions on using this pane to set image sizes and format the HTML pages.)

- **QuickTime.** Turns a series of photos into a self-running slideshow, saved as a QuickTime movie that you can post on the Internet, send to friends, or burn to a CD. You can set the size of the movie, pick a background color, and add music (the sound file currently selected in Music section of iPhoto→Preferences) before exporting. You'll find more about going from iPhoto to QuickTime in Chapter 11.

You can save yourself a trip to the Export menu by using the keyboard shortcut Shift-⌘-E. (You may find additional tabs in the Export dialog box if you've installed iPhoto plug-in software.)

Empty Trash

Purges the contents of the iPhoto Trash, permanently deleting any photos and albums in it. There's no turning back once you choose Empty Trash: Your photos are gone, and there's no Undo command. Think before you empty.

Page Setup

Opens the standard Page Setup dialog box for your printer, where you can select the paper size, orientation, and scaling of your print job.

Print

Opens iPhoto's Print dialog box, where you can print contact sheets, greeting cards, full-page photos, or groups of photos in standard sizes like 4 x 6 or 5 x 7. See Chapter 8 for details.

Edit Menu

As you would expect, the commands in the Edit menu let you edit various parts of your photo library, such as keywords, photo titles, and the sort order. The standard Cut, Copy, and Paste commands operate on selected text and photos as normal.

Undo

Where would this world be without Undo? In iPhoto, you even have a *multiple* Undo; using this command (and its keyboard equivalent, ⌘-Z), you can reverse your last series of actions in iPhoto, backing out of your bad decisions with no harm done (Figure B-2). How nice to know that if you go too heavy on the contrast, delete an important photo, or crop out your grandmother's earlobe, there's a quick and easy way out.

Note, however, that the Undo command tracks your changes in each window independently. For example, suppose you're in the main iPhoto window. You enter Edit mode, where you crop a photo and rotate it.

Now you double-click the photo so that it opens in its own window. Here, you fix some red-eye and adjust the contrast.

As long as you remain in the new window, you can undo the contrast and red-eye adjustments—but if you return to the main window, you'll find that the Undo command will take back only your *original* actions—the cropping and rotating.

So while iPhoto can handle multiple levels of undo, keep in mind that each window maintains its own private stash of Undoes.

Figure B-2:
Just about any action you perform in iPhoto can be reversed with the Undo command. The menu command itself always spells out exactly what it's going to undo—Undo Add Photo to Album, Undo Cropping, and so on—so that you know which action you're backing out of. The one un-undoable action to keep in mind is emptying the iPhoto Trash. Once that's done, your trashed photos are gone.

Redo

Redo (Shift-⌘-Z) lets you undo what you just undid. In other words, it reapplies the action you just reversed using the Undo command.

Cut, Copy, Paste

These commands work exactly the way they do in your word processor when you're editing photo titles, comments, keywords, or any other text fields. In addition, they have a few special functions when they're used in certain parts of iPhoto.

- In a photo album (not the main Photo Library), you can select photos and use Cut to remove them from the album. (This doesn't delete them from the Photo Library, only from that particular album.) To move the photos to a different album, click the album's name, or click one of its photos, and then choose Paste.

- You can assign photos from the main Photo Library to a specific album using the Copy and Paste commands. Select a file, choose Copy, click the destination photo album, and finally choose Paste.

- Cut, Copy, and Paste are all inactive when you're in Editing mode (Chapter 6).

Select All

This command (⌘-A) behaves in three different ways, depending on when you use it in iPhoto.

- It selects all thumbnails visible in the viewing area—either those in the selected album or the whole Photo Library.

- In Edit mode, with a photo opened in the main iPhoto window, the Select All command extends the cropping rectangle to the very edges of the photo.

- When you're editing photo titles, comments, keywords, or any other text fields, the Select All command selects all of the text in the field you're editing.

Deselect All

As you would expect, this command is the opposite of Select All. The only practical way to use this command is to employ its handy keyboard shortcut, Shift-⌘-A, to quickly deselect a group of photos without having to click the mouse.

Note: The Set Title To command that, in iPhoto 2, let you apply new titles to a whole batch of photos at once, has disappeared from the Edit menu. iPhoto 4's batch processing feature has made it obsolete. See page 114.

Font

Opens the standard Mac OS X Font Panel, which is of little use except when using iPhoto's book-designing feature (Chapter 10). You can't change the font used to display titles, comments, or keywords.

If you *are* formatting a Photo Book, choose Edit→Fonts→Show Fonts (or press ⌘-T) to open the panel and make your selections.

Spelling

Use the Spelling commands to check for misspelled words within iPhoto. It's primarily useful when you're typing in the captions and photo names for Photo Books that you plan to order, as described in Chapter 10. Even then, you may find this feature a bit cumbersome (page 242).

Photos Menu

New in iPhoto 4, this menu contains commands that come in handy when you're working with one or more photos. Most of the time, you need to select the photos, using any of the methods described on page 106, before choosing from this menu.

Show Info

This command (or ⌘-I) opens the Photo Info window. Click the Photo tab in the Photo Info window to see information about a selected photo, such as its creation date and the camera model used to create it. Switch to the Exposure panel for details about the specific camera settings that were used to take the picture. (iPhoto gathers all this information by reading *EXIF* tags—snippets of data invisibly embedded in the photo files created by most of today's digital cameras.)

You can open the Photo Info window even when no photos are selected, but it won't have any info filled in. The data pops into the window as soon as you select a photo.

Tip: Once the Photo Info window is open, you can leave it open. As you click different photos, the information in the window changes instantly to reflect your selection.

Show Keywords

Opens the Keywords window, where you can edit and apply keywords and perform searches for photos based on them. See Chapter 5 for a complete discussion on working with keywords.

Rotate

You can use the two Rotate commands in the submenu—Counter Clockwise or Clockwise—to rotate selected photos in 90-degree increments, switching them from landscape to portrait orientation as needed.

However, the Rotate menu command is by far the *least* convenient way to rotate your photos. Here are some alternatives:

- Click the Rotate button in the main iPhoto window, just under the Info pane.

- Option-click the Rotate button to reverse the direction of the rotation. (You specify the "main" rotation direction by choosing iPhoto→Preferences.)

- Press ⌘-R to rotate selected photos counter-clockwise, or Shift-⌘-R to rotate them clockwise.

- Control-click a photo or a thumbnail; choose Rotate from the shortcut menu.

Batch Change

Opens a dialog box where you can apply a new title, date, or comment to any number of selected photos. See page 114 for full detail.

Duplicate

Just as in the Finder, this command creates a duplicate of whichever photo is selected and adds it to the Photo Library. And just as in the Finder, the keyboard shortcut is ⌘-D. If you select multiple photos, they'll all be duplicated.

If an album is selected (and no photos are), this command duplicates the album itself. The copy appears at the bottom of the Source list, named Album-1 (or whatever number it's up to).

My Rating

Lets you apply a rating of one through five stars to selected photos. See page 118 for the full story on this new iPhoto 4 feature, which is a cousin to the ratings feature in iTunes.

Remove from Album

Deletes selected photo(s) from the current album. This command doesn't delete any photos from your iPhoto Library, or even move them to the iPhoto Trash. It just takes them out of the album. (That's why you only see this command, in place of Move to Trash, when you're working in an album.)

Move to Trash

Moves selected photos to iPhoto's private Trash, a holding bin for files you plan to permanently delete from your Photo Library. Instead of choosing this command, you can just drag thumbnails onto the Trash icon in the Source list; Control-click selected photos and choose Move to Trash from the shortcut menu; or press ⌘-Delete. (They're not actually deleted until you choose Empty Trash.)

Revert to Original

The Revert to Original command restores edited photos to the condition they were in when you first imported them into iPhoto, reversing all the cropping, rotating, brightening, or anything else you've done (although it leaves titles, comments, and keywords undisturbed). This command is active only if you've edited the selected photo at least once.

If the Revert to Original command is dimmed out, one of these conditions is probably true:

- You don't have a photo selected.

- The photo you've selected hasn't been edited, so there's nothing to revert to.

- You edited the photo outside of iPhoto in an unauthorized way (by dragging the thumbnail to the Photoshop icon in the Dock, for example). iPhoto never has the chance to make a backup of the original version, which it needs to revert the file.

    On the other hand, it's totally OK to edit photos outside of iPhoto—thereby activating the Revert to Original feature—if you do it by *double-clicking* the photo's thumbnail rather than dragging it, or by Control-clicking it and choosing "Edit in external editor" from the shortcut menu. Page 154 has all the details.

Restore to Photo Library

The Move to Trash command morphs into this command when you're viewing the contents of iPhoto's Trash and have at least one thumbnail selected. It moves the selected photos out of the Trash and back into your Photo Library. The shortcut is the same as the one for Move to Trash—⌘-Delete.

View Menu

This menu lets you change the order of your photos in the main viewing area, as well the kind of information you want displayed along with each picture (Figure B-3).

Titles, Keywords, Film Rolls

Select any of these commands to display titles, keywords, or film roll info in the main photo-viewing area. Titles and keywords always appear beneath each thumbnail.

You can turn each of these three commands on or off, in any combination, by repeatedly selecting it or by using the corresponding keyboard shortcuts: Shift-⌘-T for Titles, Shift-⌘-K for Keywords, and Shift-⌘-F for Film Rolls. A checkmark next to a command shows that it is currently turned on.

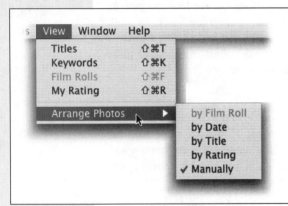

Figure B-3:
The View menu lets you customize how iPhoto displays and sorts thumbnails. The option to view photos by Film Roll option is dimmed out (as shown here) if you're currently viewing an album instead of your whole Photo Library.

Arrange Photos

Determines how iPhoto sorts the photos in the viewing area. You have four options:

- **by Film Roll.** Sorts the photos chronologically according to when each batch was first imported into iPhoto.

- **by Date.** Arranges the photos chronologically based on the creation dates of each file.

- **by Title.** Uses the titles to sort photos alphabetically.

- **Manually.** Lets you drag your photos into any order you like. (This choice is dimmed unless you're in an album. In the main Photo Library, you must use one of the first two options.)

Window Menu

The Window menu is filled with all the standard Mac OS X window-manipulating commands.

Zoom

Zooms any iPhoto window to fill your entire screen (although it's nice enough to avoid covering up your Dock). Choosing this command is the same as clicking the green Zoom button in the upper-left corner of any iPhoto window.

If you choose the Zoom Window command (or click the Zoom button) again, the window shrinks back to its original proportions.

Minimize

Collapses the frontmost iPhoto window into the Dock, in standard Mac OS X fashion. It's just as though you pressed ⌘-M or clicked the yellow Minimize button in the upper-left corner of any window.

Show/Hide Toolbar

This command is active only when you've opened a photo into its own window. Choose Show Toolbar to display the iPhoto editing tools across the top of the window and Hide Toolbar to get rid of them. (Clicking the small white glob of toothpaste gel in the upper-right corner of the window does the same thing.)

Customize Toolbar

Produces a customization panel that drops down from the toolbar, loaded with 20 different icons that you can drag to the toolbar to tailor it to your editing needs (page 150). After you've added and removed the icons you want, click the Done button to roll the customization panel back up into the toolbar. See Chapter 6 for much more about using and customizing the editing toolbar.

Bring All to Front

Every now and then, the windows of two different Mac OS X programs get shuffled together, so that one iPhoto window is sandwiched between, say, two Internet Explorer windows. This command brings all your iPhoto windows to the front so they're not being blocked by any other program's windows. (Clicking iPhoto's icon on the Dock does the same thing.)

Help Menu

You know all too well that iPhoto comes with no user manual; that's why you're reading this book! What official Apple documentation you do get appears in this menu. (Hint: It ain't much.)

iPhoto Help

This command opens Apple's Help Viewer program.

The assistance available through iPhoto Help is pretty limited. The articles are extremely brief and the explanations tend to skim the surface. Furthermore, many help screens are stored on Apple's Web site, meaning that you need an Internet connection to see them. But at least you've got a searchable reference at your disposal if you forget how to do something (or lose this book).

Books and Prints Customer Service

Fires up your Web browser and opens Apple's main iPhoto support page. You may be asked to enter your Apple ID and password. (This is usually your email address plus the password you created when you registered iPhoto or another Apple product.)

Keyboard Shortcuts

This is really just another link into the iPhoto Help system, but a particularly valuable one. It takes you to a table showing more than 50 keyboard shortcuts in iPhoto. This is one help page that's worth printing out.

Where to Go From Here

Your Mac, your trusty digital camera, and this book are all you need to *begin* enjoying the art and science of modern photography. But as your skills increase and your interests broaden, you may want to explore new techniques, add equipment, and learn from people who've become just as obsessed as you. Here's a tasty menu of online resources to help you along the way.

iPhoto and the Web

- **Apple's iPhoto site** features the latest product information, QuickTime tutorials, FAQ (Frequently Asked Question) lists, and camera and printer compatibility charts. There's even a feedback form that goes directly to Apple. In fact, each piece of feedback is read personally by Steve Jobs. (Just a little joke there.) *www.apple. com/iphoto*

- **Apple's iPhoto support page** contains answers to the most common questions, and links to discussion forums where other iPhoto users share knowledge and lend helping hands. *www.info.apple.com/support/iphoto*

- **VersionTracker** is a massive database that tracks, and provides links to, all of the latest software for Mac OS X, including the cool iPhoto add-ons described in this book. *www.versiontracker.com*

- **The Mac DevCenter** features the latest iPhoto techniques for power users and programmers. *www.macdevcenter.com*

Digital Photo Equipment on the Web

- **Imaging-Resource** offers equipment reviews, price comparisons, and forums all dedicated to putting the right digital camera in your hands. *www.imaging-resource. com*

- **Digital Photography Review** is similar: It offers news, reviews, buying guides, photo galleries, and forums. It's a must-visit site for the digicam nut. *www.dpreview. com*

- **Digital Camera Resource** is just what it says: a comprehensive resource page comparing the latest in digital cameras. *www.dcresource.com*

- **Photo.net** offers industry news, galleries, shopping, travel, critique, and community sharing. *www.photo.net*

Show Your Pictures

- **Fotki.com** is a thriving online community of photo fans who share their work online. Chime in with your shots, or just check out what everyone else is shooting. *www.fotki.com*

Online Instruction

- **ShortCourses.com** offers short courses in digital photography techniques and how to use current equipment. *www.shortcourses.com*

Online Printing

- **Shutterfly** is an alternative to iPhoto's built-in photo-ordering system. It's Mac OS X–friendly and highly reviewed (at least by *Macworld*). *www.shutterfly.com*

- **PhotoAccess** is another Mac OS X–friendly photo printing site that's also received high marks for quality. *www.photoaccess.com*

Pocket Guide

Digital Photography Pocket Guide by Derrick Story is a handy, on-the-go digital-photo reference that fits nicely in your camera bag or back pocket.

Index

Fokti.com

Colophon

This book was written and edited in Microsoft Word X on various Macs.

The screenshots were captured with Ambrosia Software's Snapz Pro X *(www. ambrosiasw.com)*. Adobe Photoshop CS and Macromedia Freehand MX *(www.adobe. com)* were called in as required for touching them up.

The book was designed and laid out in Adobe InDesign 3.0 on a PowerBook G3, Power Mac G4, and Power Mac G5. The fonts used include Formata (as the sans-serif family) and Minion (as the serif body face). To provide the and ⌘ symbols, custom fonts were created using Macromedia Fontographer.

The book was then generated as an Adobe Acrobat PDF file for proofreading, indexing, and final transmission to the printing plant.

Related Titles Available from O'Reilly

Missing Manuals

AppleWorks 6: The Missing Manual

Dreamweaver MX 2004: The Missing Manual

GarageBand: The Missing Manual

Google: The Missing Manual

iLife '04: The Missing Manual

iMovie 3 and iDVD: The Missing Manual

iPhoto2: The Missing Manual

iPod & iTunes: The Missing Manual, *2nd Edition*

Mac OS X: The Missing Manual, *Panther Edition*

Office X for Macintosh: The Missing Manual

Windows 2000 Pro: The Missing Manual

Windows XP Pro: The Missing Manual

Windows XP Home Edition: The Missing Manual

POGUE PRESS™
O'REILLY®

Our books are available at most retail and online bookstores.
To order direct: 1-800-998-9938 • *order@oreilly.com* • *www.oreilly.com*
Online editions of most O'Reilly titles are available by subscription at *safari.oreilly.com*

Keep in touch with O'Reilly

1. Download examples from our books

To find example files for a book, go to:
www.oreilly.com/catalog
select the book, and follow the "Examples" link.

2. Register your O'Reilly books

Register your book at *register.oreilly.com*

Why register your books?
Once you've registered your O'Reilly books you can:

- Win O'Reilly books, T-shirts or discount coupons in our monthly drawing.
- Get special offers available only to registered O'Reilly customers.
- Get catalogs announcing new books (US and UK only).
- Get email notification of new editions of the O'Reilly books you own.

3. Join our email lists

Sign up to get topic-specific email announcements of new books and conferences, special offers, and O'Reilly Network technology newsletters at:

elists.oreilly.com

It's easy to customize your free elists subscription so you'll get exactly the O'Reilly news you want.

4. Get the latest news, tips, and tools

www.oreilly.com

- "Top 100 Sites on the Web"—PC Magazine
- CIO Magazine's Web Business 50 Awards

Our web site contains a library of comprehensive product information (including book excerpts and tables of contents), downloadable software, background articles, interviews with technology leaders, links to relevant sites, book cover art, and more.

5. Work for O'Reilly

Check out our web site for current employment opportunities:

jobs.oreilly.com

6. Contact us

O'Reilly & Associates
1005 Gravenstein Hwy North
Sebastopol, CA 95472 USA

TEL: 707-827-7000 or 800-998-9938
(6am to 5pm PST)

FAX: 707-829-0104

order@oreilly.com
For answers to problems regarding your order or our products. To place a book order online, visit:
www.oreilly.com/order_new

catalog@oreilly.com
To request a copy of our latest catalog.

booktech@oreilly.com
For book content technical questions or corrections.

corporate@oreilly.com
For educational, library, government, and corporate sales.

proposals@oreilly.com
To submit new book proposals to our editors and product managers.

international@oreilly.com
For information about our international distributors or translation queries. For a list of our distributors outside of North America check out:
international.oreilly.com/distributors.html

adoption@oreilly.com
For information about academic use of O'Reilly books, visit:
academic.oreilly.com

POGUE PRESS™
O'REILLY®

Our books are available at most retail and online bookstores.
To order direct: 1-800-998-9938 • *order@oreilly.com* • *www.oreilly.com*
Online editions of most O'Reilly titles are available by subscription at *safari.oreilly.com*